REPUBLICAN CUBA

COLECCION CUBA Y SUS JUECES

From the Same Author: Historia de la Química Industrial
Total Quality and Productivity Management
Performance Management
Strategic Planning Management Development
Process Improvement Teams
Quality Strategies
Gestión de Futuro
Once Upon a Time (co-author)
Contramaestre
Baraguá
Poetas y Memorias de Cuba
Jimaguayú
Freedom Embattled (co-author)
Republican Cuba
Colonial Cuba
Exiled Cuba
Three Days in March
Raíces Cubanas
Album de Cuba
Un Festín de Palabras
Madame Secretary
Damn the Revolution
Rescatando a Martí

EDICIONES UNIVERSAL, Miami, Florida, 2017

The **REPUBLIC OF CUBA** by *Angelo Zanelli* (1879-1942);
49 Tons Bronze covered with 22 Carat Gold Leaf;
15 meters tall (49ft), sculpted in 1929.
At the Main Hall, under the Cupola of the
National Capitol, under the Dome.

RAÚL EDUARDO CHAO

REPUBLICAN CUBA

An Illustrated History of the Years from 1902 to 1959

Copyright © 2017 by Raul Eduardo Chao

(First Edition by Dupont Circle Editions, 2011 / 978-0-9791777-8-1)

Second Edition by:

EDICIONES UNIVERSAL
P.O. Box 450353 (Shenandoah Station)
Miami, FL 33245-0353. USA
Tel: (305) 642-3234 Fax: (305) 642-7978
e-mail: ediciones@ediciones.com
http://www.ediciones.com
SINCE 1965

Library of Congress Catalog Card No.: 2017937609
ISBN-10: 1-59388-279-283-1
ISBN-13: 978-1-59388-283-9

Diseño de la cubierta: Luis García Fresquet

Front Cover:
Statue of the *Republic of Cuba* on the National Capitol
by Angelo Zanelli (1879-1942)
at the main Capitol Hall, under the Cupola.

Back Cover:
The Viñales Valley in Pinar del Río, Cuba.

All rights reserved Under International and Pan American Copyright Conventions.
No part of this publication may be reproduced, stored or introduced
into a retrieval system, or transmitted, in any form, or by any
means, without the prior written permission of both the
copyright owner and the above
publisher of this book.
The scanning, uploading, selling and/or distribution of this book,
by any means, including the Internet, without the permission
of the publisher is illegal and punishable by law.

To Tomás Raúl

and to all Cubans
and their children,
and all future generations of
their descendants... in particular
to those who wish to know the
reasons for the devotion
to Cuba by the generation
of exiles that left their country in their years of
adolescence and dreams.

Index

Prologue 13

Introduction 14

I. The Road to Independence
The years before 1902 — 18

II. Cuba at the Time of Independence
The Inheritance from Spain — 71

III. Learning Self-Government
The Years 1902 to 1909 — 101

IV. The War Veterans in Charge
The Years 1909 to 1921 — 156

V. An Interlude with a Civilian President
The Years 1921 to 1925 — 209

VI. A Veteran again in the Presidency
The Years 1925 to 1929 — 231

VII. Times of Revolution and Violence
The Years 1929 to 1933 — 252

VIII. Failed Attempts to Reform
The Years 1933 to 1940 — 268

IX. Once More on the Road to Democracy
The Years 1941 to 1944 — 316

X. The Republic back on its Feet
The Years 1944 to 1948 — 332

XI. The Consolidation of Democracy
The Years 1948 to 1952 — 354

XII.	**A Relapse into Illegitimacy** The Years 1952 to 1958	374
XIII.	**The End of the Republic** The Fateful Year 1959	423
	Epilogue	447

Appendices

A Chronology of the Hispano-Cuban-American War of 1898	454
A Quick Chronology of USA-Cuba Relations (1898-1959)	456
Presidents of Cuba during its Colonial and Republican times.	462
Main Characters of the Republic of Cuba	467
Authors Index	490

Prologue

THIS BOOK IS a fair history of the fifty years of existence of the Republic of Cuba. Time and traitorous ambitions have blurred the significance of May 20, 1902, but on that day Cuba became an independent republic in real, irreversible and unalterable ways; that would be the start of our narrative.

Evidently Cuba was not prepared to sail on its own. Years of obedience and subjection to Spain had prevented Cuba from forming a politically independent cadre of national leaders; there was no experience in managing an economy, in negotiating contracts, setting up and controlling budgets, protecting the national resources or even in running a political party. As a result, the Republic, much to the dismay of honorable men, was plagued by rampart government corruption, nepotism, bickering about the role of the United States in Cuban matters and Cubans' inability to work or think together

For many years Cuba depended on the United States for most of its needs. The State Department and the American banks controlled commerce, vetted the politicians, acted as arbiters in internal disputes, managed the flow of cash into the treasury and dictated the national foreign policy. The economic life of Cuba depended on the ups and downs of the American economic system. The political viability of Cuban political leaders depended on the blessings of American statesmen.

The intention of this book is to review events, champions, heroes and anti-heroes during the fifty years of Republican Cuba. This is not a book intended for scholars. It is not easy to describe and analyze 50 years of Republican life in Cuba in one book and we do not intend to do so. It is a book meant for those who wish to explore the paradox of Cuba: a land blessed by nature, flush with generous and good human talent, inadvertedly fallen prey to ambitious and unscrupulous men who did not stop at separating families, killing their brothers and sisters while exploiting Cuba's bounty for their private use.

Introduction

> «*History makes men wise; poetry makes them witty, philosophy makes them deep and logic makes them able to contend.*»
> Sir Francis Bacon, English Philosopher(1561-1626).

AT THE *PALACIO de los Capitanes Generales* in Havana, on January 1st 1899, Spanish General Adolfo Jiménez Castellanos, on behalf of the Spanish government, transferred the executive powers over the island of Cuba to General John R. Brooke, the new American governor of the island. There were no representatives of the Cuban Independence Army or any Cuban civilians linked to the recent war of 1895-1888.

A few weeks later, on February 1st, in the town of Remedios, Robert P. Porter, a special envoy of US President McKinley, met with General Máximo Gómez and Cuban diplomat Gonzalo de Quesada to reiterate that the US had no interest in the annexation of Cuba and that President McKinley was ready to provide the necessary funds to furlough the standing Cuban Independence Army. Porter specifically informed Gómez and Quesada that his comments were a courtesy that President McKinley was extending to them on a personal —not on an official— basis.

The following week, on February 9th, General Brooke, in one of his first decisions as the top civilian authority in the island, decided on his own the order of the funeral procession accompanying the body of General Calixto García to its final resting place. García had died while on a mission to Washington, D.C. to discuss US-Cuba pending business issues. Misinformed or unaware of the tense relationship of the Cuban veterans with the US government, Brooke unwillingly hurt the sensitivities of the Cuban Army and Cuba's General Assembly by setting himself and his staff at the head of the procession. Both the representatives of the Cuban Army and the members of the General Assembly retired in protest for the seemingly reduced role they had been assigned in the cortege.

On March 4th, a poet, literary critic and political activist, Diego Vicente Tejera (1848-1903), founded the first Cuban Socialist Party in the island. The event went unnoticed, failed to attract followers and the party was dissolved by the autumn of 1899. Tejera, a journalist, poet and literary critic, was famous among his friends for his always inconclusive plans and dreams. He had quit his studies to be a priest at Santiago de Cuba's San Basilio Magno Seminary; at age 16 he had attempted to enlist as a soldier in the Spanish Army but was rejected. At school he had started —and never finished— the careers of law, medicine and philosophy. He had joined Betances in Puerto Rico during the failed pro-independence *Grito de Lares* and had to leave the island surreptitiously. Miguel de Aldama, in 1876, had rejected his offer to join the Cuban Independence rebels in the Cuban War of 1868-1878. He finally quit politics after a new attempt to found a left-leaning group, the *Partido Popular*, failed to gain followers.   By and large, Cubans —then and many years later— paid very little attention to the siren songs of the revolutionary left.

Before the end of the month (March 9th and March 13th) both Máximo Gómez and Gonzalo de Quesada were relieved from their positions as Chief of the Army and Special Commissioner of Cuba to the US. The reason: their unauthorized meeting with Robert P. Porter in Remedios.

These seemingly unrelated events were foretelling of events to happen in Cuba over the next fifty years of republican life:

Cubans were rationally thankful but not emotionally keen about the US intervention in Cuban affairs. In one way or another they were inwardly pro-American and liked the American political values and its way of life; outwardly they resented the geopolitical implications of the US proximity.

The US failed to grasp the finer points of dealing with overconfident Cuban leaders. These leaders expected to be recognized on an equal footing and were unquestionably excessively upbeat about their capabilities to administer the island.

Cubans had inherited from Spain the habit of pronouncements and revolutions; they systematically ignored the art and discipline of democratic participation and hierarchical decision making, as well as the mindset necessary to reach consensus. Whenever they disagreed with the choices of their peers or their superiors, they would defy compliance and set their tent apart. In the worst of cases they would chose the path of violence in order to satisfy their wishes or their pretenses.

In the end, there were fifteen different presidents in fifty seven years of republican life in Cuba. Many of the presidents had good and honest intentions when they persistently yearned or accidentally accepted to lead the republic; yet they all retired with a considerably enlarged personal patrimony.

The United States, so often called ‚*the occupying power*,` never intervened militarily on its own in spite of a Platt Amendment that openly and legally authorized it. Throughout history, different groups of Cubans resorted to and asked for the presence of the American troops in order to tilt the balance on the side of their interests. On balance, there were revolu- tions, armed conflicts, conspirators and deadly gangs in almost every presidency; some of them were tolerated by leaders in high positions.

There were also, it is more than fair to say, hundreds of dedicated Cubans persistently trying to improve the country and contribute to a safe, democratic, civilized and humane environment where children would thrive, workers would receive adequate compensation and living standards, and seniors would retire with peace and security to enjoy their just rewards in their final years. Those Cubans vastly overwhelmed in numbers the wicked ones but did not have the resolve or the means to stop their misdeeds. In a country as small as Cuba, everyone knew who were the righteous and who were the wicked; the first ones will always be remembered with gratitude and admiration by all honest Cubans and their descendants, who will eternally feel proud of their silent deeds and their character.

The unholy, vile and evil Cubans who destroyed the republic in 1959 will also be remembered by many future generations. They ended the best dreams, the most generous gifts and talents bestowed on the republic by generations of good men and women, and reduced the island into the most insalubrious and unwholesome of nightmares. Their infamy will never be forgotten.

Havana in 1900, a view from the South Side.

I

The Road to Independence
The years before 1902.

> «There is always a struggle between father and son;
> while one aims at power, the other aims at independence.»
> SAMUEL JOHNSON, English poet and writer (1709-1784).

THE ROAD TO INDEPENDENCE in Cuba started midway into the XIX century, after Cuba had been an important source of wealth for Spain for over 350 years. Spain's affluence at the expense of Cuba had been fueled by a slave economy; the royal coffers in the Metropolis grew to extraordinary levels in the 1800s due to the seemingly boundless exports of sugar and tobacco. The colonial authorities had numerous conflicts and disagreements with the *criollos* and Cuba-based landowners in general, yet the *always faithful island of Cuba* remained loyal and resisted the temptations that assaulted all other Spanish colonies in the New World: to replicate the revolutions in Haiti and the US and be independent.

Things changed after the mid nineteenth century, however. After several slave rebellions were stirred up by the inhumane conditions in the sugar plantations, the Cuban landowners began their own struggle for freedom and the right to choose their own destiny. From that point on it was inevitable that Cuba would achieve its independence. The Spaniards nevertheless attached themselves so fiercely to Cuba that it brought unnecessary grief, unhappiness, insecurity, death and ruin for both Cuba and Spain.

The way in which Cuba achieved its independence and the legacy of Spain in independent Cuba were very different that the corresponding experiences in continental America. At the time of independence —for good or for bad— Cuba did not have an indigenous population with an ancient culture or a flourishing pre-Hispanic past that could be claimed as the root of its national identity. Its population was entirely made of black African or white European stock. *Indigenism* could not be made to be part of its ethos, like it was to be for Emiliano Zapata and other leaders of the Mexican Revolution or for Peru's Haya de la Torre's *Indo-Americanists*. The glories of ancient African Kingdoms were never recalled or mentioned for two centuries of colonial domination. They were after all as much newcomers in Cuba as the intrepid Spaniards. Hence Cuba had no choice but to resort to a single source in its cultural roots. By default it had to be Spain —and it exclusively became *la Madre Patria* (the mother country).

It was from Spain that Cuba acquired its entrepreneurial spirit, its casual disregard for democracy, its stubbornness, its *Cabeza Dura*, its shrewdness and its lack of respect for hierarchies. Being an island persistently threatened by pretenders, Cuba never had a legacy of ancestral nationalism to rely on. Cubans responded to the abuses and exploitation of Spaniards —their only mistreaters— with the same character tools they had inherited from Spain: determination, obstinacy, sacrifice and martyrdom if needed be.

Félix Varela (1787-1853), Miguel de Aldama (1821-1888), Francisco Vicente Aguilera (1821-1877), José Antonio Saco (1797-1879), Luz y Caballero (1800-1862), Domingo del Monte (1804-1853), Rafael María de Mendive (1821-1886) and José Martí (1853-1895), among many others, had no problem choosing exile instead of submission when the time of self- immolation came about. Several millions of other Cubans would do the same after half a century of republican life.

It is interesting to know that the crucial drive for Cuban independence in 1895 came about mostly from Oriente property owners, Havana intellectuals and obsessed exiles. All three re sented the economic and political exploitation of Cuba that — after years of neglect and abandonment— came about very late, when Spain had already lost all of her continental possessions. Here was another cultural trait Cubans inherited from the Spaniards: reluctance to forgive past affronts.

Such was the legacy of Spain in Cuba. There were no great institutions to be continued, perhaps with the exception of the *Sociedad Económica de Amigos del País*. There was not a tradition of good government and respect for the law. There was not even a symbolic ritual of respect for the island's patrimony: Colonial Spain had plundered the island's resources and the accumulated stores of wealth. There were no examples of voluntarism except those of the criminal *Cuerpo de Voluntarios* who had wrongfully terrorized everyone supporting the right to free speech and free assembly.

There were some valuable buildings, too big to be transported to the peninsula as they did with the historical archives, many artworks and the questionable remains of Cristobal Colón. There were churches, theaters and a Cathedral but very few roads and paved streets. There were harbors and bridges, but most of them had been built to smooth the way for the tobacco and sugar monopolies, to expedite the traffic of Spanish goods to Cuban ports and to enable the commerce laws that the metropolis had imposed on Cuba.

Were the Cubans resentful of the 400 years of submission to Spain? Decidedly not. They were happy to see the ending of the political control of Spain and in spite of the rebuff and snub of Madrid to recognize the *Mambises* as one of the victorious armies, they were welcomed to stay in Cuba —as visitors or citizens. Many of them did stay. They found no backlash, contempt or disdain. Inspired by the romance of Cuba, many new Spaniards began to pour into the island in large numbers after the end of the *Hispano-Cuban-American War*. They were welcomed without reluctance, slight or cold shoulders. Perhaps after suffering so much fractiousness during the wars, the Cubans —contrary to what the Spaniards had taught them— had learned to forgive and forget.

The history of Republican Cuba, after hundreds of patriots died in the course of three wars of independence, was irrevocably marked by an event that occurred on January 28, 1853. On that day Leonor Pérez Cabrera gave birth in Havana to a son that was destined to unite the minds and wills of many Cubans to secure the independence of their native soil.

José Martí (1853-1895), poet, writer, journalist, extraordinary orator, was first incarcerated at age 16 for his work on behalf of the independence of Cuba. The photo at left shows him in chains in 1869; at the center, with his best friend Fermín Valdés Domínguez and Panchito Gómez Toro, a future patriot; at right, Martí with Máximo Gómez, a true military genius.

 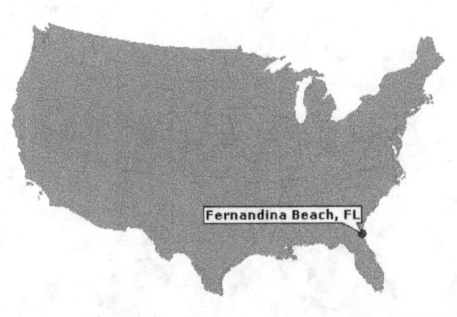

The independence of Cuba came about by the resolve and persistance of many Cuban patriots that never gave up on their quest for the sovereignty of their land.

In early 1895, after years of organizing, Martí launched a failed three-pronged invasion of Cuba out of **Fernandina Beach** in Florida. Months later, with his support, patriots in Cuba took arms on February 24, starting the **Hispano-Cuban War**; Martí promptly entered the island with General Máximo Gómez, hero of the War of 1868.

From 1895 to 1898 the Cubans were very successful in their war against colonial Spain. The two high reliefs shown above are from the base of a monumental statue to **General Serafín Sánchez** by Thelvia Marín Mederos in Sancti Spíritus, Cuba. By 1898 the Cuban Army controlled the entire countryside of Cuba.

The photo shows soldiers and officers of the **Cuban *Mambí* Army of Independence** in the Independence War of 1895. Unlike the War of 1868, in 1895-1989 the Cuban Army was active all across the island.

The **Three Friends**, one of many expeditionary ships that brought Cuban exiles and weapons to fight for the independence of Cuba during the **Hispano-Cuban War of Independence**.

Every Spanish General in the **Hispano-Cuban War** of 1895 was defeated at one time or another by the Cuban Generals of the *Mambi* Army. **Antonio Maceo** defeated General Martínez Campos at *Peralejo* on July 12, 1895; **Calixto García** defeated Spanish General Segura on August 30, 1897 and took the town of *Las Tunas*; **Máximo Gómez** defeated General Weyler at the battle of *La Reforma*, in May 1897, among many other battles.

The control of territory by the Cuban Army was so tight and absolute that from 1895 to 1898 the only way to correspond within the island was to use the services of the **Postal System** of the Cuban Independence Army.

On this humble building in *Montecristi*, a town in the northwest of the Dominican Republic, on March 25, 1895, José Martí and Máximo Gómez signed the **Manifesto of Montecristi**, setting the terms and ideals of the Cuban War of Independence.

A view of the Cuban Independence Army, probably after the victorious **Battle of Peralejo** (July 13, 1895, near the town of Manzanillo). Under the leadership of **General Antonio Maceo**, the army of Arsenio Martínez Campos, the top General in the Spanish Army, was humbled by the superior tactical maneuvers of his nemesis from the first Cuban Independence War in 1868.

Unfortunately two early deaths took place during the first two years of combats in the 1895 War of Cuban Independence. On May 19, 1895 **José Martí** was shot in battle and died in *Dos Rios*, the place where the Contramaestre River joins the Cauto, in western Oriente province (photo at left). On December 7, 1896, **General Antonio Maceo**, after a succession of important battles across the island, died at an ambush in San Pedro, Punta Brava (drawing at right), close to the town of *Santiago de las Vegas* in the province of Havana.

A group of expedicionaries abord a ship bound for Cuba in 1896. The arrow on the right shows **Panchito Gómez Toro**, son of Máximo Gómez, who would die trying to recover the body of Gen Antonio Maceo after his fatal encounter with Spanish troops in San Pedro, Punta Brava, on December 7, 1896. In front of him, Gen **Juan Rius Rivera**, the general that replaced Maceo when he was shot dead. He would be Secretary of the Treasury during the Republic. The arrow on the left shows Col **José Ramón Villalón Sánchez** (1864-1938) future member of the Cuban Senate and Secretary of Public Works.

After his defeat by Antonio Maceo and the extension of the war to western Cuba, General Martínez Campos was replaced early in 1896 by the infamous General **Valeriano Weyler (1838-1930)**, the dreadful inventor of the *Concentration Camps*. Thousands of Cubans from the countryside died of starvation in the camps organized by this villainous man.
Photo at left: some of the victims of Weyler executed without trials.

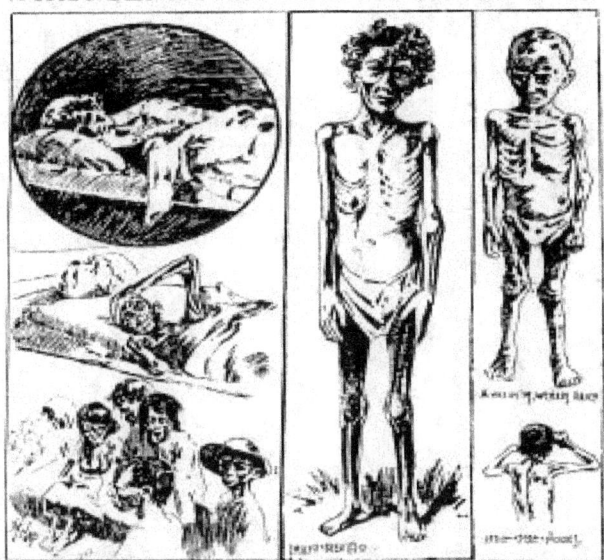

A drawing from a report by **US Senator Redfield Proctor** of Vermont on the floor of the US Senate on March 17, 1898, after a visit to Cuba. It severely denounced the concentration camps established by Weyler in the island. Testimonies like this had an impact on public opinion in the US, favoring more and more the need to intervene and pacify the island of Cuba.

Ever since 1895 a growing interest developed in the US about events in Cuba. The idea of annexing the island first came up during the times of Thomas Jefferson. By the time Cuba was fighting for its independence at the end of the XIX century, Americans had become obsessed with the political future of Cuba. In the photo, crowds in NY waiting to buy *The New York Journal*.

In 1898 **Henry Moore Teller (1830-1914)** was the *US Secretary of Interior*; he authored the *Teller Amendment*, approved by the US Congress, which disclaimed any US intention of taking control of the island of Cuba.

On the far right of the photo above is **Theodore Roosevelt (1858-1919)**; in 1898 he was *US Assistant Secretary of State*; to his left is Col. **Leonard Wood (1860-1927)**, the leader of the Rough Riders; to the left of Wood is Mayor General **Joseph Wheeler (1836-1906)**, a former Confederate General in the American Civil War. All three played an important role in what would be called the ***Hispano-Cuban-American War***.

The entrance of the US in what was until then a **War of Independence** fought by the *Cubans* against *Spain*, was soon seen by cartoonists in the US as a fight between the US and Spain.

On February 15, 1898, the *USS Maine,* on a courtesy visit, exploded in Havana. On April 25, **President McKinley (1843-1901)** obtained a declaration of War by the US against Spain. McKinley would be assassinated in 1901, before he could finish his presidential term in the US.

The **USS Maine**, sailing into Havana Bay a few days before the fatal explosion on February 15, 1898.

Public opinion in the US was instantly and immensely influenced by the papers of the *yellow press*, the *New York Journal* of William Randolph Hearst and *The World* of Joseph Pulitzer. After the sinking of the *Maine*, the stage was set for the US to intervene in the **Hispano-Cuban War of Independence** and turn it into the **Hispano-Cuban-American War**.

The **USS Maine Board of Inquire** or Sampson Commission at their final meet- ing, March 21, 1898. They found the Maine had been blown up by a mine but decided there was not enough evidence to accuse any particular individual.

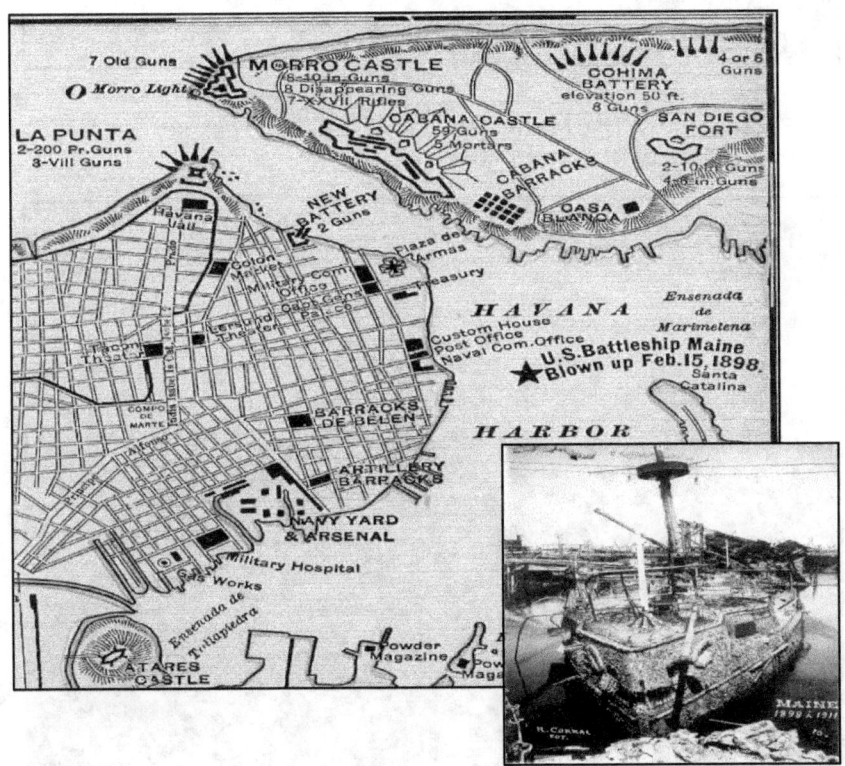

Map at Left: The exact location of the *USS Maine* (in front of the Havana Customs Office, south of the San Francisco Plaza), at the time of the fatal explosion on February 15, 1898. *Photo at Right*: the vessel when it was resurfaced from the bottom of the bay.

Photo above: The **Maine wreck** when it was carried out by two tug boats to be buried at sea.

The port at **Tampa** in 1898. US Soldiers and military equipment was being loaded for transport to Cuba.

Theodore Roosevelt (1858-1919), US Assistant Secretary of the Navy in 1898, was ecstatic about the prospect of war in Cuba and was determined to fight in it and personally revenge the fate of the *USS Maine*. He was 40 years old and had six children to support. He received an army commission, purchased an outfit at *Brooks Brothers* in NY and departed for training at San Antonio, Texas. He was made second in command of the *First US Volunteer Cavalry* under the leadership of Leonard Wood. The unit was baptized as the *Rough Riders*.

The world renown photo of **Brig. General William Ludlow (1843-1901)** meeting with **General Calixto García (1839-1898)** in Cuba, carrying a message from Pres. McKinley asking for the help of the Cuban Army during the landing of the US Military contingents in Cuba in 1898. The meeting was the basis of Elbert Hubbard's article ***A Message to García*** in February 1899.

A strategy session during the **Hispano-Cuban-American War**. *From left to right*: Generals Demetrio Castillo Duany, William Shafter, Joe Wheeler, Kent, Nelson Miles and Calixto García.

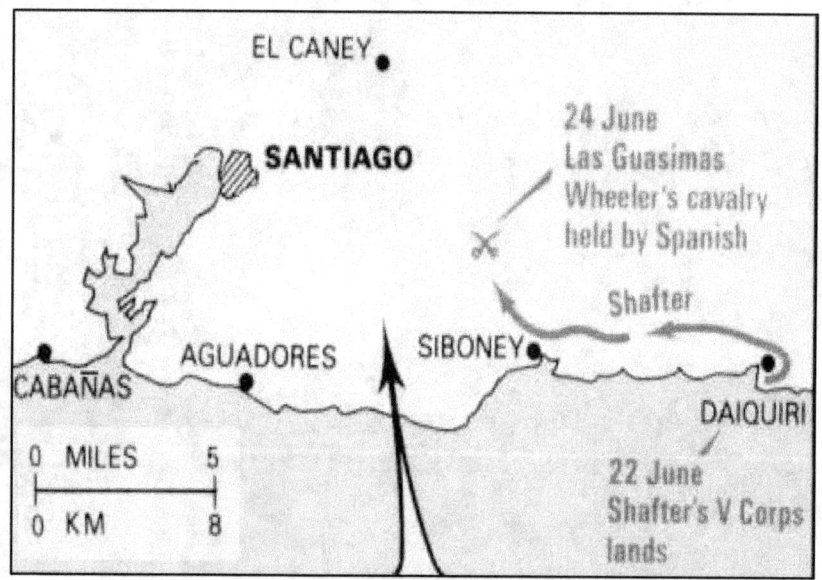

By most impartial accounts, the first encounter of the US troops with the Spanish Army on Cuba's soil was lost by the US troops at **Las Guásimas**, east of Santiago de Cuba. On June 24, 1898. Spanish General Antero Rubin prevailed over US Mayor General Joe Wheeler.

On top: the town of **El Caney**, as seen from the *El Viso Fort*. *On the bottom*: Theodore Roosevelt (center) and Leonard Wood (right), the actual commandant of the *Rough Riders,* on their advance towards **San Juan Hill**.

The battle of *El Caney* was on July 1, 1898. The Spanish were equipped with smokeless high-velocity 7 mm *Mauser* rifles. The Americans had black powder single-shot Springfield rifles.

In *San Juan Hill* (the following day) the Spanish Army was mostly fresh conscripts; in the American Army most of the fighting was done by Black troops. Both battles ended with hand-to-hand combat. In both battles, the victorious US Army came on top thanks to the *Gattling* guns, the first use of these machine guns by the US. The battles of *El Caney* and *San Juan Hill* proved to be of little value for the Americans. They diluted the strength of the US forces at a cost of delays and many casualties.

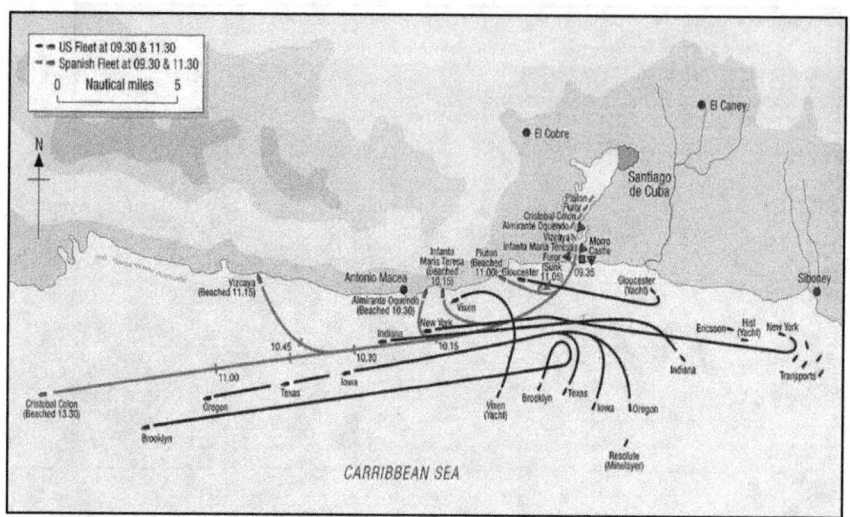

A very different outcome occurred at the **Naval Battle of Santiago de Cuba** late in July 1898, when Rear Admiral William T. Sampson and Commodore Winfield Scott Schley (with four battleships, one armored cruiser and two auxiliary cruisers) destroyed the Spanish Fleet (consisting of four armored cruisers and two destroyers) under Admiral Pascual Cervera. The US Navy thus turned into victory a war that the US Army was losing on land.

At **Santiago de Cuba** Spain lost 474 dead or wounded men; the US had one casualty and 10 wounded. The entire leadership of the Spanish Navy was taken prisoner and incarcerated in Annapolis, Maryland. The photo shows *Admiral Cervera* with his officers.

The way the Spanish press looked at the insurgents in Cuba.

Above, during the **War of 1868**, the members of the **Government of Cuba in Arms:** *from left to right*, Eduardo Agramonte (Interior); Cristobal Mendoza (Foreign Relations); Carlos Manuel de Céspedes (President); Francisco Vicente Aguilera (War Minister); and Eligio Aguirre (Treasury).

On the right, the Spanish press could only see black men among the insurgents in the **War of 1895**.

A drawing showing Spanish General José Toral **surrendering the City of Santiago de Cuba** on July 16, 1898 to US Major Generals Joseph Wheeler and H. W. Lawton. It was the first time a Navy had won a battle for the Army.

On October 24, 1898, the Government of Cuba in Arms, concerned about the decisions to be taken once the war was finished, organized a meeting in Santa Cruz del Sur, Camagüey, which concluded its deliberations at a house in *Calzada del Cerro*, Havana. Hence its name **La Asamblea del Cerro** (*see photo above*). It decided to send a high level commission to Washington presided by Calixto García to, among other things, discuss the issue of licensing the *Cuban Independence Army*.

In this photo John Jay signs the ratification of the **Treaty of Paris** ending the *Hispano-Cuban-American War* of 1898. US agreed to pay Spain $ 20 Million for Puerto Rico, Guam and the Philippines, and to nurse the Cubans into full independence. Spain renounced all claims against any future Cuban government.

The Spanish troops began to abandon the territory of the future **Republic of Cuba** with a deadline of December 31, 1898.

On December 11, 1898, General **Calixto García**, on a five man mission to Washington, DC to arrange for the licensing of the Cuban Army, died from pneumonia; he was 59 years old and was temporarily interned at *Arlington National Cemetery*. *On the photo, above, left to right*: **José Miguel Gómez**, future President of Cuba; **José Ramón Villalón**, future Minister of Public Works, **Calixto García**, **José Antonio González Llanuza**, future Minister of Education and Justice and **Manuel Sanguily**, future Minister of the Interior.

The US troops completed the temporary occupation of the island of Cuba by June of 1899.

Calixto Garcia Iñiguez (1839-1898), was a general in the three wars of independence in Cuba and one of the most brilliant military strategists in the history of Latin America. He was a descendant of *Iñigo Arista*, a Basque King mentioned in *La Chanson de Roland* (the Song of Roland), the oldest surviving work in French literature —dating from the XII century. In 1873, during the Cuban War of 1868-1878, he was about to be captured by the Spaniards; to avoid be taken prisoner, he attempted suicide and left a 0.45 bullet exit mark in his forehead, for which he was famous.

In 1898, during the *Spanish American War*, he was the lead man in the strategic decisions of US General Shafter for the disembarkment of US troops and the *Battle of Santiago*. Once the wars were over, at age 59, he went on a diplomatic mission to Washington to negotiate a US loan to Cuba, and died of pneumonia while staying at the *Hotel Raleigh*. He was temporarily buried at Arlington Cemetery.

Photos: *at top*, as a young man; *at center* at the start of the 1895 War; *below*, the Washington Commission received by Cuban ambassador Gonzalo de Quesada in Washington.

In December of 1898 Tomás Estrada Palma closed **Patria**, the newspaper founded by José Martí, and dissolved the **Partido Revolucionario Cubano**, also founded by Martí, alleging that their purpose was to secure the independence of Cuba, which was already a reality. Estrada Palma, a patriotic and very pro-American man, did not realize that by both actions he was leaving Cuba without an institutional voice on future events.

Once the Spanish Army surrendered, **John Rutter Brooke (1838-1926)** was appointed military governor and head of the US Army in Cuba. He was 60 years old and had distinguished himself in the battles of *Manasas* and *Gettysburg* during the American Civil War. At his death in 1926 he was the next to last survivor of the Generals of the Civil War and was laid to rest with honors at Arlington.

Joseph Benson Foraker (1846-1917) was born in Ohio, served with Sherman on the march through Georgia and graduated with honors on the first class of Cornell University. He was elected US Senator in 1896. He was the Senate sponsor of an amendment to the Army Bill which prohibited any military government in Cuba to authorize commercial contracts with US citizens. The *Foraker Amendment* effectively prevented, according to Wood

«*the looting of Cuba by unscrupulous US persons signing the most infamous of schemes with people in the island.*»

On the building shown in the photo on top the Representatives of the Constitutional Convention that had first met in Santa Cruz del Sur, Camagüey, met again in the celebrated **Asamblea del Cerro** after moving to Havana.

Máximo Gómez supported the concept of accepting the offer by President McKinley of a gift of $3 Million to pay the salaries owed to the soldiers of the Cuban Army. He pointed out that the new Government of Cuba should not be saddled with large loans. The Assembly members preferred a loan from an American banker for $20 Million, paying 5% semi-annual interest. They argued that a loan of this magnitude would solidly establish the credit of the government of Cuba. Because of this disagreement, the Assembly fired Gómez as commander of the Army. In the middle photo, the friends of Máximo Gómez demonstrate their support for Gómez in front of his house at the *Quinta los Molinos*.

On March 11, 1899, General Enrique Collazo wrote in *La Lucha*: «*Gómez without the Assembly has no real authority. The Assembly without Gómez has no life and we will be left orphans.*» On April 7 Gómez was reinstated by a majority of the Cuban generals and he subsequently renewed with the US Military Governor General Brooke the negotiations for the payments to the Cuban army.

The cartoon below shows how the Spanish press interpreted the disagreements between Máximo Gómez and the Assembly.

Within a few days of the installation of Brooke's government in Cuba the dockyard workers of Cárdenas (below) went on strike; they were followed by those of Havana, the street workers in Matanzas and the masons in Havana. Brooks mandate ended on Dec 31, 1899, when **Gen. Leonard Wood** was appointed Governor of the island. The city of Cárdenas was the first in Cuba to fly the Cuban flag (1850); to have a sugar refinery (1851); to erect a monument to Colón (1862); to install an electrical plant (1889); to be bombarded in the *Hispano-Cuban-American War* (1898); and to organize a strike against the government of Wood (1899).

Photo below: the celebrated *Espigón de* Cárdenas (land reclaimed from the bay).

By 1899 there was already a strong ideological movement in Cuba with deep anti-American tendencies and a strong advocacy for the ―emancipation‖ of the proletarian classes. One of its leaders was **Enrique Creci** (photo at right), one of a trio of anarchists called Enrique (the others were Enrique Roig de San Martín and Enrique Messonier). On November 19, 1899, Creci was given a mass funeral in Havana after his death in the War of 1895. It has been alleged that two secret members of the anarchist movement were **Salvador Cisneros Betancourt**, twice President of Cuba in Arms (1873-1875 and 1895-1897) and **Juan Gualberto Gómez**, one of Martí's closest friends. No such affiliations were ever proved. On the side, the universally used anarchist logo.

Major General **Leonard Wood** was the personal physician to presidents Cleveland and McKinley until 1898. That year he organized the *Rough Riders* to participate in the *Hispano-Cuban-American War* of 1898. He led the *Riders* to famous victories at Kettle Hill and San Juan Hill (both in reality were trivial victories as less than 200 American soldiers fought two dozen Spanish opponents) and on Jan 1, 1900 he was appointed military governor of Cuba. As such he organized Cuba's first municipal elections on June 16, 1900 (won easily by the *Cuban National Party*, mostly the independence supporters) and the first Cuban Constitutional Convention of November 1901. See profile of Leonard Wood on the following page.

The American occupation from 1898 to 1902, although distressful and frustrating from the political standpoint, was immensely beneficial from the educational, health, physical and economic points of view. The painting reproduced here (at left) shows the US Department of Health efforts to eradicate **Yellow Fever** in Cuba. It was unfortunately one instance in which credit was not properly due to a Cuban involved in the effort: **Carlos J. Findlay (1833-1915),** a Cuban-born epidemiologist, with research credentials from Havana, Paris and Philadelphia. He theorized as early as 1881 that the carrier of yellow fever was the mosquito *Aedes Aegypti*.

Major General **Leonard Wood (1860-1927)** was a man of transcendental importance in the history of Cuba, yet his work in Republican Cuba has not been the subject of much study throughout the years.

He was a **Harvard educated physician** and for his work during the US Indian Wars (he played a part in the capture of Geronimo in 1886) he was awarded the Congressional Medal of Honor. Afterwards he was White House Physician to President Grover Cleveland and became a good friend of Theodore Roosevelt, who was his second-in-command during the *Spanish-Cuban-American War* (Wood was the top commander of the *Rough Riders*). Following the war, he served as Military Governor of Santiago de Cuba and later of the entire island until 1902.

Wood **traveled extensively through Cuba** between 1898 and 1902 and quickly realized that eastern Cuba had been the battleground of three wars of independence because it was **inaccessible** to investment, political control, and development. He also concluded that no revolution could have been possible in Cuba if some means of easy access, such a railroad, had existed between east and west. In his words «*nothing will so rapidly tend to the revival of commerce and general business as the facility for quick passage from one end of the island to the other. All political turbu- lence will be quieted thereby and prevented in the future. The en- tire country will open to commerce, lands now practically of no value and unproductive will be worked, the seaport towns will be- come active, and commerce between the island and other coun- tries could bring wealth to this island...*»

Photo above: Leonardo Wood with President Roosevelt in 1906 and on the cover of *Time Magazine* in 1926.

Wood envisioned Cuba not as a colony but as a new American state; he favored annexation, although he knew that after the **Joint Resolution of 1898** (*the people of the island of Cuba are and of right ought to be free and independent*), the **Teller Amendment** (*the US disavows any disposition or intention to exercise sovereignty, jurisdiction, or control over Cuba*) and the **Foraker Amendment** (*the US Military Government shall not grant any concessions to U.S. companies*), the annexation of Cuba would have never be allowed by the US Congress.

Granting that annexation was not possible, Wood believed that the best for Cuba and the US was to establish intimate ties. «*Cuban prosperity and stability requires political, economic, and social programs that will reconstruct the Cuban economy and society. It could be achieved with the help of U.S. investors who are looking to use their excess capital overseas,*» he expressed to President Theodore Roosevelt. One way or another he also realized that it was impossible to pursue his goals without a massive American investment in Cuba's infrastructure.

Leonard Wood's ideas for the future of Cuba were crystallized by **The Cuba Company** (stock certificate below), an enterprise incorporated in New Jersey in 1900. Its Certificate of Incorporation stated that «*its purpose is the construction and operation of railroads, including a central railroad line traversing the island, telegraphs, and all other forms of transportation and communication in Cuba, as well as engaging in manufacture, mine, agriculture and real estate.*» The main investor was one of the wealthiest and most powerful men in North America: **Sir William Cornelius Van Horne (1843-1915)**, former president and chairman of the *Canadian Pacific Railroad*. He limited stock ownership in the US to wealthy, well-connected men (like Levi Morton, president of *Morton Trust Company*, E. Harriman, of the *Union Pacific Railroad*, William Day, *U.S. Secretary of State*), and promoted many Cubans into the newly created ranks of middle managers: engineers, accountants, corporate lawyers and executives, to ensure success.

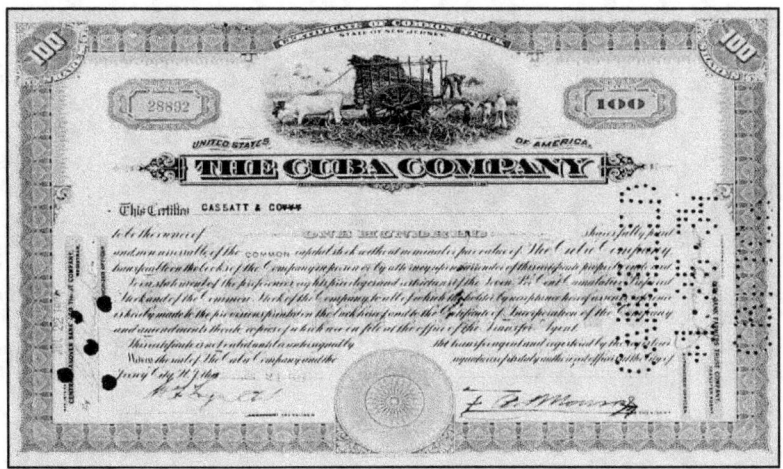

In addition, Wood appointed to military government posts Cubans who were U.S. educated and would benefit from close connections with America. The beneficial effects of Wood's efforts to develop Cuba and prevent additional revolts and war after its independence, were best expressed by Senator George Frisbie Hoar, grandson of Roger Sherman, a signer of the US Constitution and a Harvard alumnus, during a speech in May 1902 in the US Senate: « *This has been the most honorable single war in all history... A war in which there did not enter the slightest thought or desire of foreign conquest, or of national gain, or advantage ...*»

When Leonard Wood left Cuba he was promoted to Brigadier General in 1902, served as commander of the Philippines Division of the US Army in 1903, became Army Chief of Staff in 1910, developed the program known as *Reserve Officer Training Corps (ROTC)* in American Universities and was an unsuccessful candidate for the Republican presidential nomination in the election of 1920 (the nomination went to Warren Harding). He died of a brain tumor at age 67 and is buried at Arlington Cemetery. Interestingly, his brain is preserved at the *Yale University School of Medicine* as part of an historic collection of brains of exceptional Americans.

Long after Wood left Cuba, **The Cuba Company** continued to influence the development and expansion of the Cuban economy; it grew to be the largest corporation in Cuba, operating railroads, sugar plantations and mills, hotels, and steamships in Cuba, providing jobs for 110,000 workers and managers. All its properties were confiscated in 1959.

Photos above: Sir William Cornelius Van Horne; original stock certificate of *The Cuba Company* owned by Van Horne.

On top, a sketch of McKinley's assassination on September 6, 1901. At right the official Roosevelt presidential photo. Upon the death of President McKinley, shot by a fanatic Polish anarchist called Leon Czolgosz while at the *Pan American Exposition* in Buffalo, NY, on September 1901, **Theodore Roosevelt (1858-1919)** was sworn in as the 26th President of the US. He was the champion of the *Panama Canal* and instrumental in ending the Russo-Japanese war, for which he received the *Nobel Peace Prize*.

On several occasions he expressed that the US had three basic reasons for its interest in Cuba, none of which had to do with land expansion, annexation or imperialism: *First*, they needed political stability in a land so close to theirs; *Second*, they needed to rehabilitate Cuba's economic picture to attract and sustain investments from American entrepreneurs; *Third*, they needed a progressive Cuba within the sphere of political influence of the US.

One of the most solid supporters of Cuban Independence in the US was William P. Frye, Maine's Attorney General, a close friend of Theodore Roosevelt and an admirer of Walt Whitman and José Martí. Once the war was over, he encouraged his son **Alexis Everett Frye (1859-1936)**, a Harvard graduate, to volunteer to teach in Cuba.

Alexis was appointed *Superintendent of Public Schools* in Cuba from 1898 to 1902. He enlisted the best minds in Cuba to create a national system of schools to provide education for all children. During his tenure the number of schools in Cuba rose from **312** in 1898 to **3,628** by 1901.

The system was more progressive that anything similar in the US. Schools were desegregated; male and female teachers received the same salary for the same work and background. Using contributions he sought in Maine and Massachusetts, he sent **1,700 Cuban teachers** to *Harvard* in the summer of 1899.

He married a Cuban lady in 1901 and, at his expense, printed **200,000 copies of the *Cuban National Anthem*** (text and music) for distribution to all children and teachers in Cuba. This last step got him into an argument with the US Department of State and he left Cuba with his wife in the winter of 1902.

Fry died back in Maine in 1936. Until the 1950s many public schools in Cuba had pictures of Frye in their walls. His books in Spanish on *Geography*, *Education* and *History* were used throughout Latin America for years.

Thanks to Frye, schools were founded (top photo), and teachers were sent to top schools in the US to get trained (bottom photo, part of the 1700 teachers sent to summer school at Harvard in 1899)

Cubans had an initial enthusiasm for the involvement of the US in the *Hispanic-Cuban War of Independence*; quickly, however, they became suspicious of the intentions of the US. History showed, however, that most of the US efforts after the end of the *Hispano-Cuban-American War* were directed to **rebuilding Cuba** rather than exploiting it. Once the *Spanish Evacuation Commission* finished its work (*top photo*), hospitals, asylums, public parks and all sort of nation-building works were carried out by the US. The photo at the bottom shows crowds in Havana looking as the Spaniards abandon their positions in Cuba.

Cuban roads were essential for the economic development of the island and many were paved (top left) in the first two years. To guide in the social and physical work an **Interim Cabinet** was first appointed by Brooke with some of the best and most capable professionals in the island (above right). The Cabinet included **Domingo Méndez Capote, José González Lanuza, Pablo Desvernine** y **Adolfo Sáenz**. By the end of 1900 most Cubans knew that —*it was not the best of worlds but it was known that eventually the North Americans planned to leave,*‖ in the words of Manuel Sanguily.

Under the government of Leonard Wood, a **Constitutional Assembly** was elected in 1901 to write the *Law of the Land* in Cuba (*photo above*).

Both Generals, **John R. Brooke** and **Leonard Wood**, were old soldiers with lots of experience. Both believed that Cuba, much like the US south had been after the Civil War, was a territory that had to be —*disciplined from sin.*‖ Both were assertive but fair-minded men and governed Cuba honestly and impartially. Both were sure that after a brief period of independence it was most likely that Cubans would voluntarily ask to be admitted in the Union. Roosevelt himself had given orders to Secretary of State Hay to «*handle the Cuban leaders with a proper mixture of firmness, courtesy, recognition and patience.*»

In the photos above the first and the last Cabinets of General Leonard Wood. The first included **Wood**, **Diego Tamayo** (Interior), **Enrique José Varona** (Treasury), **Hernández Barreiro** (Education), **Luis Estévez** (Justice), **José R. Villalón** (Public Works) and **Juan Rius Rivera** (Agriculture).

The last Cabinet included **Wood**, Diego **Tamayo**, **José Varela Jado**, **Perfecto Lacoste**, **Leopoldo Cancio**, **Enrique José Varona** and **José R. Villalón**.

Upon taking over the position of Governor of Cuba on December 20, 1899, Wood wrote to McKinley: «*One of my greatest challenges is the great mass of public opinion that remains inert. After a century of political inactivity it is difficult to get them out of their pessimism, the old ruts and the traditional grooves.*»

One of the key architects of Cuba's independence was **Gonzalo de Quesada (1868-1915)**, a friend of Martí and a graduate from *Columbia University* in NY. After a very active participation in the expeditions and financing of the war, he became Special Commissioner of Cuba to the US in 1900. In his words «*Americans have been fair with Cuba even if they first approached the participation in the war with an air of superiority. The idealism of Jefferson was too big a load for them to ignore.*»

The photo at left is that of **Orville H. Platt (1827-1905)**, US Senator from Connecticut. He was considered a strong conservative in the Senate in 1900, having voted against the Sherman Anti-Trust Law, the Eight-Hour Labor Law and the Anti-Injunction Bill. He served five six year terms in the US Senate. As Chairman of the *Committee on Cuban Relations* he had an Amendment to the Cuban Constitution (written by US Secretary of War Elihu Root) passed in the US Senate and added to the Cuban Constitution of 1901.

The photo at right is **Sir William Cornelius Van Horne (1843-1915)**, former Chairman of the *Canadian Pacific Railway*. In 1900 he registered *The Cuba Company* in New Jersey, a firm dedicated to the construction of the Central Railroad in Cuba; it was a project that no one had been able to make a reality since 1850. He became twice a millionaire, acquiring sugar lands and many other properties: it was the first (nominally) Cuban international company. See page 47.

Photo above: Americans of extraordinary influence in the destiny of Cuba as a Nation: **Cabot Lodge**, Republican Senate Leader in 1898, good friend of Cuba; **Randolph Hearst**, made the Cuban War of Independence known the world over; **Theodore Roosevelt**, *Rough Rider* in Santiago, 25th US President (1901-1909), always very friendly to Cuba; **Elihu Root**, US Secretary of War in 1899, worked hard to turn Cuba to the Cubans; **John Hay**, Secretary of State for McKinley and Roosevelt, defended Cuban interests at the US-Spain Treaty of Paris on December 1898.

Diego Vicente Tejera (1848-1903), in the photo above, was a celebrated literary figure, a friend of Martí, a founder of the *Partido Socialista Cubano* on February 10, 1899, and the *Partido Popular* in November 1900. In both instances his political ideas, mostly *proto-socialist*, were of little influence in the dawn of the republic. Over the years Marxists and left-leaning activists in Cuba have tried to present him as a precursor of Marxism in Cuba, which he was not. Almost from the start of the Cuban Republic, beginning with Tejera, a dense cloud of sophistic arguments and doctrinaire nonsense has attempted to kidnap the thinking of the founders of the Cuban Republic and present them as Anti- Americans advocating socialist or Marxist ideals.

Horatio S. Rubens (1869-1941) was a New York lawyer, friend of Gonzalo de Quesada and José Martí, lawyer for the Junta in NY and a supporter of the *Partido Revolucionario Cubano* during the 1895 war. He was also the author of the popular book *Liberty*, shown above. In 1899 he was shown a letter from President McKinley to Gen. Leonard Wood in which the policy of the US with regard to Cuba was clear and explicit:

«*Get the people of Cuba ready for a republican form of government. I leave the details of procedure to you. Give them a good school system, try to strengthen out the courts, put them on their feet the best you can. We want to do all we can for them and to get out of the island as soon as we can successfully turn the government to them.*»

Rubens was also a very eccentric man. He moved to Cuba and became a prosperous lawyer, particularly for many American capitalists (such as John D. Rockefeller). He enticed many of them to invest in Cuba. In the bay of Mariel he began to build a palace for himself in 1918 and never finished it. After giving up this property —due the amount of his time it was requiring— it was used as the main building of the *Mariel Naval Academy*. His Mariel house is shown above as he left it, almost finished, in 1920.

On the next page, photos of Cuban survivors from the Wars of Independence who had an extraordinary influence in the early days of Cuba as a Republic:

Top Row:

Gonzalo de Quesada (1868-1915), From Habana, friend of Martí, recruiter for expeditions, fundraiser, advocate in the US Congress, book writer, diplomat. Cuban Ambassador to the US; died while serving as Cuban Ambassador to Germany.

Juan Gualberto Gómez (1854-1933), From Matanzas, son of slaves, friend of Martí, educated in France, rose to the rank of General in the War of 1895, vigorously opposed the Platt Ammendment in the *1901 Constitutional Assembly*;

Salvador Cisneros Betancourt (1828-1914), From Camagüey, ex Marqués de Santa Lucía, president of the Cuban Republic in Arms from 1873 to 1875 and from 1895 to 1897, forcefully protested the *Pacto del Zanjón*;

Middle Row:

Major General Emilio Núñez (1855-1922), From Las Villas, graduate of the University of Pennsylvania, friend of Martí, Commander of the Department of Expeditions in the War of 1895, Cuban V.P. (from 1917 to 1921) and Secretary of Agriculture in 1913;

General Domingo Méndez Capote (1863-1934), former Chief of Staff of Máximo Gómez (1897), VP of the Cuban Republic in Arms (1898), president of the *1901 Cuban Constitutional Assembly*, VP of Estrada Palma in his second term; he was instrumental in the success of the revolt against Machado in 1933.

Maj. General Máximo Gómez (1836-1905), fought in the Ten Year War (1868-1878) and was recruited by Martí for the War of 1895. In the last war was General in Chief of all the Cuban Armies.

Bottom row:

General Bartolomé Masó (1830-1907), his first political involvement was to protest the execution of Narciso López in 1851. Loyal friend of Céspedes and Aguilera in the War of 1868. He was at Baraguá with Maceo, and at *Bayate* (see page 455) at the start of the War of 1895. Died very poor after declining to be a candidate or the VP of Cuba. (see page 131)

Major General Calixto García (1839-1898), leader of the Ten Year Cuban War of Independence (1868-1878); main strategist of the Hispano-Cuban-American War of 1898.

Manuel Sanguily Garritt (1849-1925), a pupil of Don José de la Luz Caballero, brother of Julio Sanguily, a War hero in the first Cuban War of Independence (1868-1878). He became a lawyer in Madrid and edited the *Revista Cubana* of Enrique José Varona. Senator for Matanzas, Senate President, Secretary of State, one of Cuba's greatest intellectuals.

Original building of the **Teatro Irijoa** (Dragones between Prado and Zulueta Streets) in 1884, later rebaptized as **Teatro Martí** in 1901. People referred to it as *El Coliseo de las Cien Puertas*. It had 3 floors of seats and six rows of boxes.

On January 30, 1901, the finished draft of the *1901 Cuban Constitution* was approved there. On February 11 it was adopted. On February 27 the US Senate, and on March 1 the US House, passed the *Platt Amendment*. A series of disturbances and riots exploded all around Cuba to protest the amendment. On March 2, 1901, more than 15,000 persons marched in Havana with Juan Gualberto Gómez and Salvador Cisneros Betancourt (their photos above) on the front row.

Juan Gualberto and **Salvador Cisneros**, because of their strong opposition to the *Platt Amendment*, were portrayed as anarchists by the anti-American Marxists in Cuba in the early 1900s; they never wrote anything that would have justified that assertion. Anarchism at the time was mostly concentrated in Cataluña, Mexico and Perú. It would have been very easy for them to approach the leaders of the movement seeking support, which they never did.

On March 21, 1900, the Newspaper **La Discusión** published a cartoon entitled *Asalto y Robo*, in which Uncle San was threatening Cuba with a weapon called *Enmienda Platt*. Many other cartoons followed. A year later, March 20, 1901, Secretary of War Elihu Root declared that «*The Platt Amendment is final... if the Cuban Constitutional Convention refuses to accept it, it will only injure its country.*»

On March 21, in **La Discusión**, Manuel Sanguily finally said «*Independence with some restrictions is preferable to a continuance of military rule, which will happen if we reject the Platt Amendment.*»

To many political commentators in the US, Cuba had to be satisfied with «*a piece of the pie of independence,*» something that was not even offered to **Puerto Rico** or the **Philippines**.

There were positive and negative cartoons in the press in Cuba in 1901, just like there were different opinions when it came to the inevitability of the **Platt Amendment** as an appendix to the approved 1901 Cuban Constitution. On April 6, a vote to *accept* the Amendment was defeated 24 to 2. On April 12 a vote *not to accept* the Amendment was carried 18 to 10. On April 25 a commission of delegates met with McKinley and Elihu Root in Washington. Root presented the Amendment as simply «*an extension of the Monroe Doctrine.*» On May 28, finally, the Cuban Constitutional Convention accepted the *Platt Amendment*, with Article I of the *Treaty of Paris* (stating Cuba would not be a protectorate) added on, by a vote of 15 to 14.

The cartoons above show the burdens of the US with the new territories (babysitting on top; teaching at center, while Máximo Gómez is reading on the left side of the cartoon and two other Cubans are fighting each other), and the burdens of the Cuban people (*below left*) as they had to swallow the bitter pill of the *Platt Amendment*.

Elihu Root rejected the addition of any wording to an Amendment that had already been approved by the US Congress and insisted that the text of the Platt Amendment had to be approved *verbatim*. The **Cuban Constitutional Convention** met again on June 12 and finally approved the text *verbatim*. Nine of the eleven opponents were from the Oriente, Camagüey and Santa Clara provinces. One from Havana and one from Matanzas completed the eleven. On June 27 Orville Platt commented that «*Cubans had been acting like children.*» The path was now free for the Republic to exercise its sovereignty, even if it was somewhat compromised.

The good intentions of the US were shown in the cartoon above. Public opinion in the US was firmly committed to the principles of the **Teller Amendment**, which stated that the US had no intention to conquer Cuba. Objectively, in the opinion of most unbiased scholars, the intervention of the US in Cuban affairs during the period 1899 to 1902 would be beneficial in the long run.

As wars go, the **Hispano-Cuban-American War of 1898** was neither very cruel nor very long. During the Civil War (1861-1865) the US suffered 625,000 dead and wounded; during the War of Independence (1775-1783) it was 50,000; during World War I (1917-1918), 320,000; during World War II (1941-1945), 1,076,000. The *Hispano-Cuban-American War* (June-July 1898) resulted in only 4,068 dead and wounded from all sides.

Yet the War had considerable historical consequences. It **turned the US into a world power**, taking Europeans by surprise. It made US pride soar as it provided proof that Northern and Southern American soldiers could fight side-by-side against a common enemy. On the political front it made Roosevelt the most important US figure of his time.

The cartoons *above* show Uncle Sam showing the British and the Germans a line in the sand (the *Monroe Doctrine*, i.e., European powers were not welcome in the American continent); *on the left*, Uncle Sam is flirting and entertaining Cuba; finally, *on the bottom right*, Teddy Roosevelt reaching for the highest seat in the US.

A popular illustration in 1899 showed the war in Cuba to be the catalyst for a reconciliation between North and South after the US Civil War.

Above, a graphical representation of a widespread perception of Americans after the **1898 Hispano-Cuban-American War**. In the US, Americans saw themselves as a generous people that mobilized for war against Spain on behalf of Cuban independence. They felt they had succeeded where Cubans by themselves had failed, as the Cuban troops only reached an impasse with the Spaniards. The US took full credit and did not share any with the Cubans, who had fought relentlessly for three years and, in the least of cases, had exhausted the Spanish army and brought it to the brink of defeat.

Cubans were thus expected to be forever grateful. This editorial cartoon from *Puck* on Sept 7, 1898 had the legend «*Taking Cuba from Spain was easy. Preserving it from overzealous Cuban patriots is another matter.*» A counter-narrative in Cuba, exploited by socialists and ultra-leftists, created the black legend that the US had always intended to rob Cuba of its rightful desire to be free and independent.

Anti-Americanism has been defined as a relentless critical impulse against American traditions and values as well as the social, economic, and political institutions of the US. In 1900 Cuba, anti-Americanism had to flourish for several reasons:

1- Since the 18th century it had been a fashionable ideology in Europe to argue that creatures and minds in the new continent **were feeble** and incapable of full development.

2- For many years Europeans (including Talleyrand, Voltaire, Dickens and others) **criticized Americans for lacking taste, grace and civility**. The basis for this was an idealized image of European refinement that lasted well into the 20th century.

3- The **expansion of the US in the 19th century** into territories of Mexico and Texas resulted in a vehement opposition to the US throughout all countries in Latin America.

4- With the advent of the economic power developed by the US, the **jealousy** of its commercial rival countries had resulted into a strong anti-American prejudice.

Anti-Americanism (continuation)

5- **After Spain was defeated** by the US, it joined the chorus accusing the US of being a degraded and hypocritical democracy, a travesty and a failure.

6- The projection of the US political, strategic and ideological power across the planet seriously **inconvenienced other nations** that had the hope but not the capability of wielding the cultural, economic and military influence that the US so naturally exercised. Those nations soon found support in movements, such as *Anarchism*, *Socialism*, *Fascism*, *Marxism; these* movements became permanent critics of the very existence of the US. Finally,

7- The perceived **racist and xenophobic attitudes** of white Anglo-Saxon Americans toward the Spanish speaking peoples multiplied the always latent resentment of Cubans against their neighbors to the North

Three early influential figures in the anarchist movement in Cuba at the time of the inauguration of the republic. *From left to right:*

Cuban born **Paul Lafargue (1842-1919),** a Marxist socialist journalist, political activist and Karl Marx son-in-law. He lived in France most of his life and fled to Spain after the *Paris Commune* in 1871. There he met many of the Cubans who founded the Marxist and Anarchist parties in Cuba. His father-in-law, Karl Marx, detested him and on one occasion wrote to Engels that «*if Paul is a Marxist, I (Marx) will renounce to Marxism.*»

Enrique Roig de San Martín (1843-1889), born in Havana, disciple of Proudhon, was the most influential and charismatic anarchist in Cuban history. In 1887 he founded the newspaper *El Productor*, a paper that quickly became required reading for active leftist anti-American revolutionaries in Cuba.

Pierre Joseph Proudhon (1809-1865) was a French politician, journalist, philosopher and Member of Parliament. He was the first person to call himself *anarchist*, although he was also a confessed socialist. He favored a society without authority or property. He was also a fuming atheist and on one occasion said «*What capital does to labor, and the State to liberty, the Church does to the spirit.*» He wrote little about Marx or Marxism, because in his time Marx was a relatively unknown thinker; it was after Proudhon's death that Marxism became an important societal ideology.

The way the **Spanish Press** saw the conflict in Cuba during the War of Independence in 1898.

The way the **Spanish Press** saw the conflict in Cuba during the War of Independence in 1898.

II

Cuba at the Time of Independence:
The inheritance from Spain.

> «The legacy of nations is the memory of great patriots and the inheritance of great examples.».
> BENJAMIN DISRAELI, British Prime Minister (1804-1881)

DURING THE 400 YEARS of possession of Cuba, Colonial Spain never made any significant effort to encourage a democratic system of government. Moreover, it never set in motion even a minimal attempt to create a reasonable educational system. She believed that Spanish-born bureaucrats, traders, conscripts and civil officials would extract whatever richness was available in Cuba and that the trusted personnel from the Catholic Church would take care of any educational needs of the Cubans.

Early after the discovery of the New World, in the continental colonies, the conquistadores and the indigenous people fought large scale competitions for the rights to gold and silver. In the precious-metals poor but sugar-and-tobacco-rich territory of Cuba, the Spanish crown was contented to exploit the geographic location and the fertility of the lands. Spaniards fought all types of encounters with the British and the French, simply to preserve the control of political and commercial structures in the island of Cuba, with no real interest in developing any civic or cultural institutions.

Interest in Cuba, however, did not materialize overnight, as it happened in Mexico, Perú, Guatemala, Colombia and other promising gold-rich areas.

During the first century of Spanish Cuba, the crown established the *encomiendas*, i.e., grants of land to Spaniard immigrants whose only obligation was to pay tribute to Madrid and to be responsible for the Christianization and assimilation into the Spanish culture of the people assigned to them. It was sort of a New World neo-feudalism. It never received in Spain the attention it probably deserved. Spain —more or less— ignored Cuba for two hundred years and the island developed as an agricultural society by itself, almost in isolation.

In spite of this, late in the XVIII century and after the French and American Revolutions, the Spanish crown found itself with one of the most magnificent colonial empires. It controlled nearly one half —the most productive half— of the North American continent, the whole of the Isthmus of Darien (today's Panama), the better part of South America and all the continent's adjoining islands.

When Bonaparte invaded Spain and imprisoned Fernando VII in the early 1800s, however, the colonies in America took advantage of the Spanish moment of weakness and declared their independence, leaving the Bourbon crown with only the possessions of Cuba and Puerto Rico. In most of America the rule of Spain was replaced by the rule of the *caudillos*; in Cuba no attempt to gain the hearts and souls of the population seemed necessary to Madrid, even though it was one the last territories left to the Metropolis.

Had Spain learned the lessons of the American Revolution before the age of Bonaparte, she could have been an imperial power for several more centuries. She stubbornly continued, however, to see the American continental territories and islands as opportunities for rapacious enrichment. She never visualized that her predatory greed would cause the loss of all its continental territories within the course of one generation. Even more, had she reflected on her fate after losing the mainland territories, she would have reasoned that, as in the continent, all could also be lost in Cuba.

What the entire world knew, Spain continued to ignore. The independence of Cuba was inevitable; within three more generations, the Spanish flag would no longer have a place to wave anywhere else in the New World.

This chapter simply presents the only tangible evidence that Spain left behind; aside from some powerful intangibles —the language, some metaphysical beliefs and the character and personal traits of the Cubans— the only indications that there was a Spanish presence in the island have been, since 1899, the buildings that were added to physical Cuba. Some people believe that the physical legacy was a worthy albeit nostalgic inheritance. It was certainly more that what Spain had found when it first entered the territory. But it was far less that what the Spanish empire could have provided for one of its richest provinces.

Panoramic view of Havana in 1902

The three sources of power in colonial Cuba were the **Government**, represented by the Captain General and the many bureaucrats across the island, the **Church**, always very present through a multitude of bishops, schools, temples and monastic orders, and the **Civil Society**, comprised by white men and women, and their slaves, if any, led by land proprietors, businessmen and agricultural magnates. When it came to visibility, however, the Church had a most decided advantage because of the many places of worship and shrines built with the contributions of the faithful.

Photos above top to bottom: La Fuerza Castle, the old Church of San Francisco de Paula and the Plaza del Vapor, all in Havana.

Only one of the churches from before the XVII century reached the arrival of the Republic in 1902. The **Iglesia del Espíritu Santo** (Church of the Holy Spirit) survived at Cuba Street between Acosta and Jesús María Streets, in what was then called the neighborhood of *Campeche* or *Belén*. It had been founded in 1632 and renovated numerous times over the years. In 1936 its floor gave way under the weight of a parishioner and the burial chamber of Bishop *Gerónimo Valdés (1646-1729)* was found; a move that many worshipers interpreted as a blessing of the ancient Bishop to the initiatives of the 1933 revolution. In 1953, due to another floor collapse, an ancient *catacumba* (catacomb) was discovered with many funeral crypts.

Cuba Street was the most religious street in Old Havana. Aside from *Espíritu Santo* it also had the churches of *San Francisco el Nuevo*, la *Merced* and the *Convent of Santa Clara*. *Espíritu Santo* also has the oldest organ in Cuba, dating from *1868*.

Photos: *Top left*, the church of the *Espíritu Santo* in Havana in 1900; *Top right*, an early 1700s painting of the church. *Bottom*, the sepulcher of Bishop Valdés (found inside this church); he was the founder of the orphanage of Havana in 1687.

During the XIX century, side by side with the Church, the strongest driving force for education in Cuba was the *Sociedad de Amigos del País, founded in 1793; it was* an institution closely linked to educators such as **Don Francisco de Arango y Parreño** (1765-1837), secular priests like **Félix Varela** (1788-1853) and **José Agustín Caballero** (1762-1835), and such eminent intellectuals as **Don José Antonio Saco** (1797-1879) and **Don José de la Luz y Caballero** (1800-1862).

To most of these educators it became clear that the challenges to education were beyond their control: low enrolments, low school attendance, uneven distribution of schools and teachers, poor school hygiene, lack of materials, high teacher turnover, student and teacher absenteeism, too many students in lower grades and excessive drop-outs.

Drawings, from left to right: educators **Don Francisco de Arango y Parreño**, the old seal of the *Economic Society* and **Pbro. Félix Varela**.

For years to come —until probably the end of the Republic in 1959— one of the many battlegrounds of education in Cuba was the notion that private and religious schools were not completely in tune with the promotion of **national values**, although they were certainly superior in their discipline and quality of teaching than public schools. The champions of public education erroneously argued that private schools, fostered class differences and developed a low level of patriotism among the privileged classes. The extraordinary patriotic deeds of private school alumni from the 1920s to the 1959 proved beyond a doubt the fallacy of these arguments.

Photos and Drawings, from left to right, top to bottom: educators **Pbro. José Agustín Caballero**, his nephew **Don José de la Luz y Caballero**, the new seal of the *Economic Society* and **Don José Antonio Saco**.

Up until 1898 the education of children in Cuba rested upon the shoulders of the Church. Spain, at the time of independence, left the country with an illiteracy rate of 65%. Cuba developed a strong educational system between 1898 and 1902 and in the early years of the Republic, mostly with the help of the US and the extraordinary concerns for education by Cuba's first president **Tomás Estrada Palma** and other Cuban pioneering educators. Education, however, was only reached by children living in large cities. On the countryside there was a low literacy rate compared to the cities.

Once the intervention of the US took place (1898-1902) the government of **Leonard Wood** launched a program to introduce educational practices and democratic political beliefs to Cuban youngsters, teachers and their families. Their declared purpose was to accelerate the withdrawal of the US army forces by leaving behind a self sustaining cadre of administrators and a community of informed citizens with knowledge and skills to...

«... *carry on the economy principles that would guarantee the growth of the new Republic.*»

Cubans at the time were concerned that the Americans were planning to —*Americanize*‖ education to facilitate an eventual annexation. Americans, on the other hand, were fearful that, as it was happening in many Latin American societies...

«... *the people could turn into an impulsive populace easily led by hotheaded orators.*»

(Both quotes from President Roosevelt).

Photos: Presidents McKinley and Roosevelt after the war in Cuba in 1898, and a Cuban stamp honoring Teddy Roosevelt.

In spite of their misapprehensions, Cubans showed great enthusiasm for the American contribution to the educational system of the island. They had great faith in the power of education to succeed in life, both personally and for the nation as a whole. Towns built their own schools; benefactors provided the capital to construct facilities; many organizations and trade unions established, funded and financed their own special schools.

A young man in his twenties, **Ramiro Guerra Sánchez (1880-1970)**, one of the teachers sent by General Leonard Wood to *Harvard University* for training, led the march for universal education with the dictum «*not to stress education is the worst crime which can be committed against the nation.*» Guerra was responsible for preparing teachers for the young republic. In 1912 he graduated as a doctor of education from the University of Havana and directed the *Escuela Normal de Maestros* (Cuban Teacher's School) between 1912 and 1913. He was later general superintendent of schools in Cuba.

Photos above: Young and old *Ramiro Guerra* and one of his most notable books on Cuban History.

Scenes from the times when the Republic of Cuba was founded in 1902

Carlos III Avenue, looking towards the *El Principe Fort* in Havana.

O'Reilly Street in Havana.

The Terrace at the *Teatro Martí*. The theater was inaugurated in 1884 as *Teatro Irijoa;* in 1900 it was rebaptized as *Teatro Martí*. The sessions of the *1901 Cuban Constitutional Assembly* were held there.

Monte Street in Havana.

Calzada del Cerro in Havana, where the rich families spent their summers in sumptuous residences.

The **Teatro Tacón** in Havana. It became part of the *Centro Gallego* in 1911. In 1900 its famous chandelier (a gift of the Aldama family) fell to the ground and broke in thousands of pieces.

Parque Central in Havana, with the statue of *Queen Isabel II*. On the right the *Hotel Inglaterra*.

Polyteama Theaters, (the large and the small one) both in the upper floor of what later became the *Manzana de Gómez*.

Loma de la Pirotecnia; years later it was the site where the main campus of the *University of Havana* was built.

The famous gingerbread clubhouse of the **Vedado Tennis Club**, born with the century in 1900.

El Templete, to the right, the place where the City of Havana was founded and the first mass celebrated.

Havana Jail, built in the XVII century. José Martí and the medical students shot in 1871, as well as Fermín Valdés Domínguez, were prisoners there. In 1865 the 2nd floor was turned into a hospital.

Spanish soldiers remove cannon balls from the patio of the **Cabaña Fortress** to send them to Cadiz, Spain.

The luxurious and comfortable interior of the **Tacón Theater**. The theater was later enclosed inside the Centro Gallego and called **Teatro Nacional.**

Paseo del Prado; a view from the statue of *La India* towards the bay.

The Harbor at Nueva Gerona, **Isle of Pines**. A boat unloading charcoal, the only fuel used in the island in 1900.

Imposing buildings at the Main Street in **Pinar del Rio**, part of the *Imperial Road* built by the Spaniards to move troops easily.

The **Cathedral of Matanzas**. Founded in 1693.

A business street in **Matanzas**. A picture taken in 1899, before the revival of business at the end of the War of 1898.

The **Cathedral of Cárdenas**, very different from almost all other churches in Cuba. An armed policeman in the front.

The entrance to the **City Park at Cienfuegos**. The pedestals with the lions were ordered by Isabel II.

Railway Station and Quartermaster's Office in Cárdenas. The *Arch of Victory* was in celebration of the liberation of Cuba.

A bridge over the **Velasco River** in Santa Clara. The *Imperial Road* passed over this bridge. It honors Luis de Velasco, defender of *El Morro* against the British in 1762. He has a monument in Westminster Abbey.

The **Governors Palace** in Santa Clara.

The **Plaza and Cathedral** in Cienfuegos, formerly called *Fernandina de Sagua*; it is the city in the Caribbean with the most neoclassical structures.

The **Tomás Terry Theater** in Cienfuegos. It was built in 1889. Terry was a wealthy Englishman who fell in love with the City.

The **Central Plaza** in **Puerto Principe** (Camagüey).

El Morro Castle at the entrance of Santiago Harbor. The fort stood so high that ca- nons could not be pointed down towards the immediate waters to target vessels trying to enter the bay.

A **street in Santiago** showing the pavement sloping to the garbage drain in the center. Residents would throw refuse and waste in the streets; it would run downhill, producing disease and smelling awfully.

A street in **Holguín**. One of the main tasks during the American occupation of 1898 was to provide **underground drainage** in most large Cuban cities. Crowds came daily to witness the progress of these works and enthusiastically praised the American assistance in improving the quality of life.

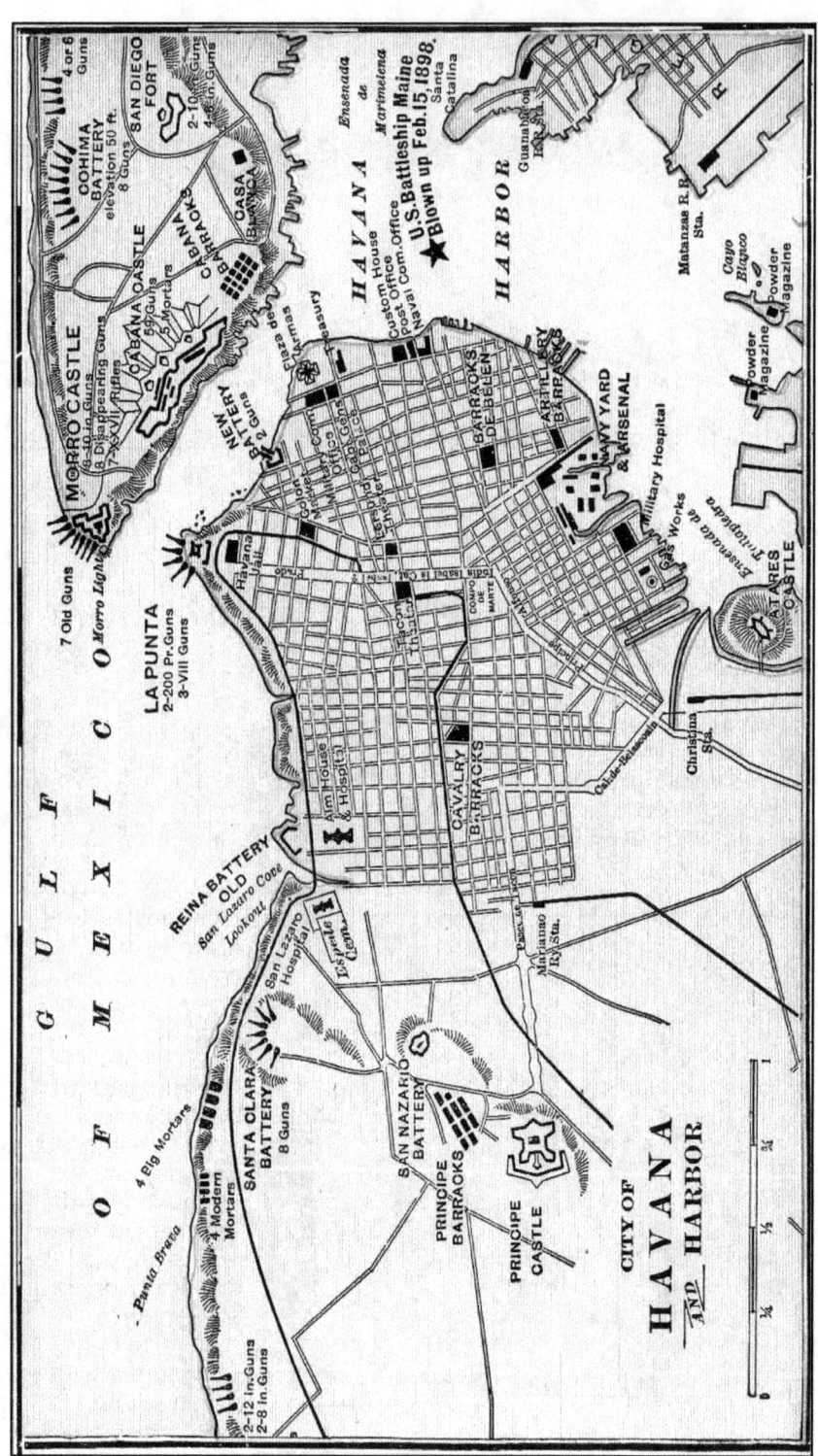

From 1791 (the Haiti Revolution) to 1898 (the Cuban War of Independence) the sugar industry experimented an explosive growth in Cuba. **Central Tuinicú**, in Sancti Spíritus, was one of the most emblematic examples of this unprecedented growth.

The **Tuinicú** was acquired in 1891 by the Rionda family, also proprietors of the *Eli*, *Manatí*, *Francisco*, *Céspedes* and *La Vega* sugar mills. Most *Ingenios Azucareros* were originally built with Zinc and Wood but in good times, as they became *Centrales Azucareros*, owners incorporated steel and masonry, as well as modern equipment, in their constructions.

In 1926 the Riondas build paper and alcohol manufacturing facilities next to the *Central*, as well as a soda bottling plant to make use of the bagasse and the residual sugar and molasses. Those investments were followed by the construction of warehouses, animal feed production plants, port loading facilities and a private railroad system. At the time of its peak in 1958 the **Tuinicú** compound employed close to 700 employees.

Interestingly, it was at **Central Tuinicú** in 1923 that Frank Jones, a **Tuinicú** engineer, set up in his office the *first radio transmission* ever done in Cuba; the station was 6KW, 372 meters. It transmitted Cuban music across the Americas. In 1928 he also received in his office the *first TV signal* ever detected in Cuba, from a GE experimental TV Station in Schenectady, NY.

At right, the office of **Frank Jones** at Central Tuinicú in the 1920s.

The Theater always had a loyal following in Cuba since the XVI century when a play called —*Los Buenos en el Cielo y los Malos en el Suelo*— (The good ones to Heaven and the bad ones to Hell) opened in Havana on June 24, 1598. It was shown on a barge anchored by the *La Fuerza Castle* before there was a single auditorium in Havana.

The first two theaters of importance had to wait until 1775 (**El Coliseo** at Luz and Oficios Streets) and 1829 (**El Gran Diorama** at Industria, San José, San Rafael and Amistad Streets). They were both destroyed by the 1846 hurricane.

Luckily, in 1838, Francisco Marty, a Catalonian, opened the **Teatro Tacón**; at the time it had 2000 seats, and was considered one of the best three theaters in the world.

In 1865 José Nin y Pons opened the **Teatro Villanueva** in the city block limited by Zulueta, Colón, Morro and Refugio Streets, near the fort of *La Punta*. It was the scene of the events of January 22, 1869, causing the prison term of José Martí when he was 16 years old.

Photos: above, Teatro Tacón; *below* Teatro Alhambra.

Years later, in 1870, the **Teatro Albisu** was opened in Obispo, Monserrate and Zulueta Streets. One other Catalonian, Joaquín Payret, opened in 1877 the **Teatro Payret**, a fierce rival to the Tacón, situated practically in front of it. In 1884 Ricardo Irijoa, a Basque, opened the **Teatro Irijoa** at the corner of Dragones and Zulueta. It had an immense lobby and 100 doors to the outside.

Finally the **Alhambra Theater**, at the corner of Consulado and Virtudes Streets, became one of the classical theaters at the start of the Republic of Cuba; it fell to the ground in 1934 for lack of maintenance.

During the Republic, three other grand theaters were opened in Havana: the **Auditorium**, at Calzada and D Streets, the **Blanquita**, at the entrance of Miramar and the **National Theater** in the Plaza Cívica in 1952.

Photos above: Albisu, Irijoa, Payret, and Alhambra Theaters.

Old and New Cuban Theaters, from top to bottom: **Campoamor**, **Fausto**, **Principal de la Comedia**, in Havana; **Principal** in Camagüey; **Sauto** in Matanzas; **Blanquita** and **Nacional de la Plaza Cívica** in Havana; **Tomás Tierry** in Cienfuegos.

Just before the end of the Spanish domination and during the first years of the Republic, the most prestigious addresses in Havana were those in the neighborhood of **El Vedado**. Most people of means abandoned the congested and noisy Old Havana and began to buy lots and build for themselves beautiful and comfortable mansions. Some of the high officers of the *Cuban Independence Army* followed them as they received their pending salaries.

The best area of *El Vedado* was around the *University of Havana* and people began to call it the *Apache Zone*. From 9th Street to the coast and from the University grounds to the sea, all lots were sold in a few years. The government paved 17th Street and *Havana Electric* extended their power lines to allow trams to reach the *Almendares River*. The rich left the *Paseo del Prado* and the *Cerro* area; after *El Vedado* began to be crowded in the 1920s, the rich invested in construction lots across the *Almendares River* leaving behind the old aristocrats on the city side of the river.

At the time of Cuban independence one of the most interesting places in Havana was the **Queen's Battery** (also called the *San Lázaro Battery*), a defensive fort finished in 1861. It was a monumental circular plaza with a *parapet*, looking out to sea with 44 cannons that crossed their fire with the *Battery of Santa Clara* and the *Castillo de la Punta*. The fort had accommodations for a garrison of 250 men. It was demolished in the early twentieth century, leaving the place abandoned and full of debris. During the American occupation in 1898, the *Malecón* or retaining wall built around the bay ended at the **Cove of San Lázaro**, a place where pirates used to land in the 1500s and where horses and mules for the buses and carts of Havana were bathed in the 1800s. At the *Cove of San Lázaro*, the area east of the Queen's Battery was paved and a park was built for the statue of General **Antonio Maceo**.

On the photos above: views of the *Queen's Battery* and the Cove of *San Lázaro*, including a view of the *Casa de la Beneficencia* (old *Havana Foundling Home*, in a circle) followed by a photo of the dismantling of the *Queen's Battery* in the 1890s.

On May 21, 1902, one day after the inauguration of the Republic of Cuba, its new President, **Tomás Estrada Palma**, visited the *University of Havana* and met with the *Claustro*. Such was the importance that Estrada granted to education in the young Republic. Higher education in Cuba was in a precarious situation in 1898. High School students accounted for 0.1% of the total population. Only 0.5% of Cuban-born citizens had a college degree.

The University had its origins in the old *Universidad Literaria y Real*, which in turn inherited the organization and principles of the *Real y Pontificia Universidad de San Gerónimo*, founded on January 5, 1728, at the convent of *San Juan de Letrán* (also known as *Convento de Santo Domingo*) by the Dominican fathers and staffed by -illustrious foreigners,‖ according to the terminology of the times.

The *Real y Pontificia* was located at the block limited by the *San Ignacio, O'Reilly, Mercaderes* and *Obispo* Streets; it had been secularized in 1842. Early in the 1900s it was moved to the *Colina de Aróstegui* —a military powder and chemical factory— in the west of Havana, which soon became known as the *Colina Universitaria*.

Photos above: a maquette of the old building of the *University of Havana* in 1842, before it became a ruin —out of neglect— (photo at right) in 1902, after the war of independence.

In 1902 the University of Havana was still tied intellectually to the old scholasticism: learning by rote memory, with lack of research, excessive emphasis in rhetoric and theoretical argumentation. The government of General Wood ran a study of faculty backgrounds and appointments, admission standards, physical facilities, curricula and budgets; together with Cuban graduates from American Universities, Wood financed a subtle but effective transformation in teaching philosophy and didactic methods. He supported the Study Plans created by **José Antonio González Lanuza (1865-1917)** and **Enrique José Varona (1849-1933)**, as well as the creation of schools of engineering, architecture, chemistry and mechanics.

Among his more visible changes were the banning of political activities, the requirement of coat and ties as normal attire for students, and the replacement of textbooks by Fray Luis de Granada (1504-1588), Isidoro de Sevilla (560-636), and like authors, for books by Montessori (1870-1952), Kierkegaard (1813-1855), William James (1842-1910), and John Dewey (1859-1952).

Photos above: Enrique José Varona and José Antonio González Lanusa, followed by both, as seen by Massaguer.

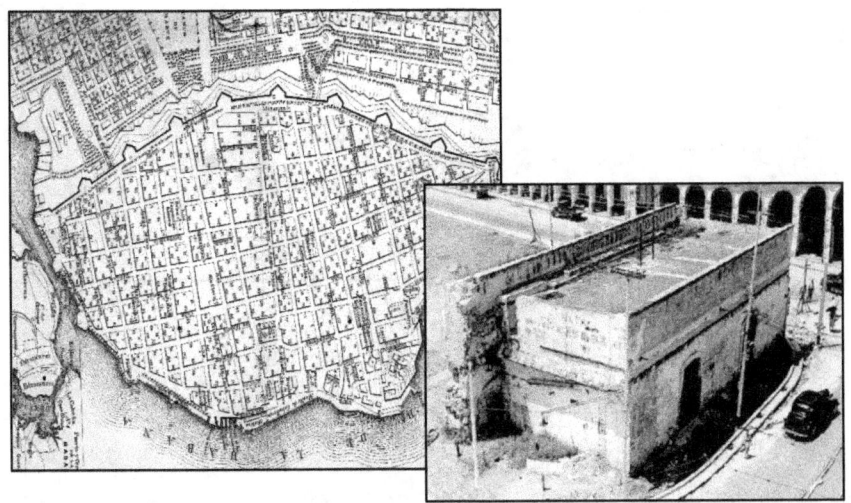

By the time Cuba gained its independence only a long stretch of the wall that protected the city of Havana from land-side attacks was left standing. Havana was one of the cities that the Spaniards protected against pirates and buccaneers just like San Juan, Santo Domingo, Cartagena, and other cities. In Havana the sea-side protection was offered by the fortresses of *El Morro*, *La Punta* and *La Fuerza*.

The wall in Havana was first planned in 1558, after the attack of the pirate *Jacques de Sores*; it was approved by the crown in 1656; was started in 1674; and was not finished until 1740. In 1863, when the city had grown well beyond the confines of the wall, a royal decree ordered its dismantling; the wall had been planned during 180 years yet was in service for only 120. The wall was never challenged, escalated or even tested by anyone; when Havana was taken by the British in 1762 the successful invaders attacked through an undefended hill where years later the fortress of *La Cabaña* was built.

The wall originally ran though what are now Egido, Monserrate and Zulueta Streets. Initially it had only two entrances at *La Punta* fortress and at Muralla Street. Two cannon shots, at 4:30 am and 9:00 pm announced the opening and closing of its gates. In 1898 long segments of the wall were interrupting the traffic through Havana and the government of Leonard Wood accelerated the work of removing the wall to allow vehicles to enter and leave the city. A final disposition of the wall came several years after 1902.

Photos: a plan of Havana showing the wall; detail of one of the gates at Monserrate Street; one of the sections left in 1902.

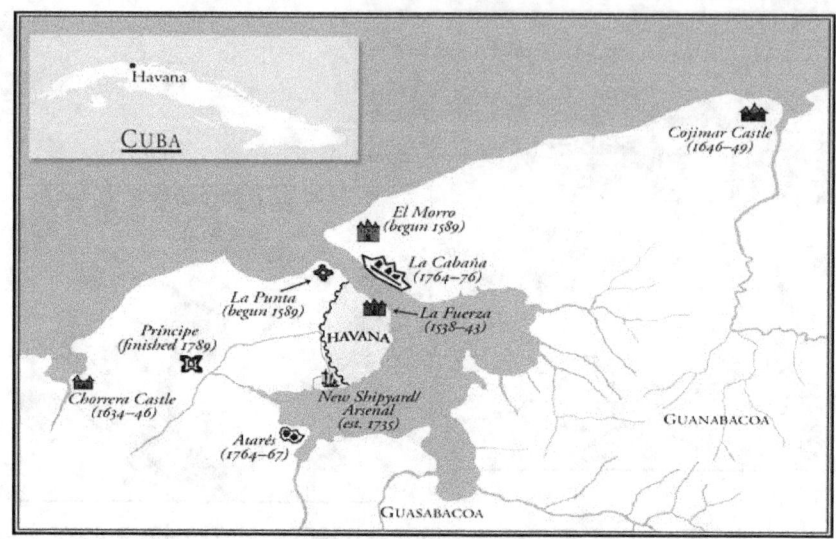

Photos: **Gates on Havana's big Wall**. *Top right*: *Puerta del Arsenal*, inaugurated in 1775, to which Felipe Poey dedicated a poem. *Top left*: *Puerta de Tierra*, the very first gate built, originally called *Puerta de la Muralla* for its location on Muralla Street. *Bottom*, the *Puerta de Monserrate*, built by Governor Tacón in front of the theater that carries his name. This gate remained open every night until the activities at the theater were finished, usually past midnight.

III

Learning Self-Government:
The Years 1902 to 1908

> «The best principle of any republic is to secure to all its citizens a perfect equality of rights.»
> THOMAS JEFFERSON, third US President (1762-1826).

THE FIRST ELECTIONS in independent Cuba left a lot to be desired. Two parties were formed, the *Nationalista* and the *Republicano*; they supported for president the man who had filled the position of Martí after his death in Dos Ríos: Tomás Estrada Palma. A third party, the *Unión Democrática*, supported Bartolomé Masó, an illustrious *Mambí* general. Two political tendencies began to shape up: Masó's liberalism and Estrada's conservatism. The educator —Estrada Palma— easily prevailed over Masó, the warrior-leader, who saw himself forced by circumstances to withdraw from the contest. Leaving abruptly an election became in 1902 a legitimate and normal choice for politicians to react to unfavorable conditions. It was a detestable repudiation of the most important democratic exercise of any self-governing nation: the right to vote. In years to come if would contribute to the weakening and the eventual demise of the republic.

On a letter to General Juan Ríus Rivera, dated September 7, 1901, Estrada Palma had advanced his priorities as President of Cuba:

First, to settle the debt that the Republic had with the Cuban Independence Army; second, to formalize the relations and secure possible commercial treaties between Cuba and the US, as well as to clarify the terms of the Platt Amendment and the rentals of Cuban territories to the Americans; third, to create an efficient management structure, to identify the real needs and administer the growth of the young Republic.

Cuba's great first President fulfilled all his promises.

Before the end of 1902 he reached an agreement with Roosevelt about a Reciprocity Treaty with the US. It was signed in May 1903.

During his first year in office he secured a $35 million loan —at 5% interest— with Speyer and Company, the reputed international bankers with operations in Manhattan since 1837. He became friends with James Speyer; the story was told that only Estrada Palma could fully understand his heavy German accent.

With the help of Luis Estévez Romero, his VP, Estrada — with no governance expertise other than his military and academic experiences— began the task of organizing from scratch a rational, prudent and frugal government structure and administration.

Very soon he was attacked as too paternalistic and too reluctant to discard his teacher-like style of relating to his ministers. Learning a lesson, for instance, from José Antonio Saco, who had once written that «*there is no city, village or corner of the island of Cuba into which this all consuming cancer* [gambling] *has not spread,*» Estrada vetoed a Lottery Law passed by Congress. This reinforced the notion that he was not only paternalistic but also authoritarian.

The truth was more serious than that. Estrada Palma, a remarkable and generous gentleman, was also a stubborn man not immune to adulation. He was flattered into believing that he was indispensable, that he deserved a second term and that the Republic needed four more years of his protective and benevolent rule.

The mid-term elections of February 1904 were indisputably fraudulent. Most of Estrada's opposition leaders were wiped out of municipal and provincial positions. The stage was set for his re-election two years later.

Until then, Estrada had stayed above the fray as a non- partisan president. He became a member of the *Partido Mo- derado* and accepted to be a candidate for re-election in 1906. The *Republicanos* dropped their support and, in an alliance with the *Nationalistas*, backed the candidacy of General José Miguel Gómez. Even General Máximo Gómez, who had traveled to New York to persuade him to run for president in 1901, was now opposing him and calling his re-election «*un azote para la República*» (a scourge to the Republic).

Estrada ran for a second term with Domingo Méndez Capote as his VP and won. Chaos sprouted everywhere. Enrique Villuendas, a Masó follower, was assassinated in a hotel in the city of Cienfuegos. *Republicanos* and *Nationalistas*, for the second time and for the second election in the history of the Republic, withdrew from the elections in 1906 and retracted the candidacy of José Miguel Gómez.

Within days General Faustino (Pino) Guerra, who had served with Antonio Maceo and became a congressman from Pinar del Rio in 1902, and who would later be Commander in Chief of the Army under President José Miguel Gómez, rebelled in his province. After a series of spectacular victories over a disorganized *Guardia Rural* supporting Estrada, his movement blossomed into a 15,000 men army and became a national insurrection.

Estrada had to resign and appeal to Roosevelt to intervene in Cuba —under the terms of the Platt Amendment— to pacify the island.

Roosevelt, who did not want to intervene in Cuba, sent William Taft, his War Secretary and future US president, to try to reconcile the Cubans. He had to take over the reins of the nation when the Cuban Congress refused to appoint a caretaker president. On September 29, 1906, a second US intervention started. On the morning of October 12, 1906 Charles E. Magoon, the governor of Panama's Canal Zone, was appointed governor of Cuba. He created an organization called the *Comisión Consultiva*, presided by Brigadier Enoch Crowder, to review the works of the Cuban Congress and develop additional laws and regulations for the young Republic. It was the first indication that Cubans were not quite ready to govern themselves and had not yet learned how to live in peace.

The US intervention lasted until January 29, 1909, when General José Miguel Gómez —elected on September 12 of 1908— took possession as the second president of Cuba. He was supported by followers of Alfredo Zayas (the *Zayistas*) and his own (the *Miguelistas*).

Teddy Roosevelt's Big Stick Policy

According to Gonzalo de Quesada, in 1905 the estimated daily attendance in public and private schools in Cuba was 231,869 students, which was 95% of the school census. The Estrada Palma government dedicated $3.7 million (more than 20% of its budget) to public instruction. The number of students at the *University of Havana* was 540. At *Artes y Oficios*, the trade school, 467 students were enrolled. At *San Alejandro*, the School of Arts, 543 students were registered, of which 209 were girls. By 1905 all the important and large schools were those that had been opened by Catholic teaching orders like the *Escolapios* and the *Jesuitas*.

Photo on top: **Escuelas Pías** de Guanabacoa; *Photo below: Colegio de* **Belén**, Habana.

Among the most important private schools were also **La Salle** in Havana and **El *Siglo*** in Matanzas; ***Champagnat*** and ***El Sagrado Corazón*** in Cienfuegos. Prior to 1902 there were only two public High Schools, Havana and Matanzas. Within five years there were four more, at Santa Clara, Camagüey, Santiago de Cuba and Pinar del Rio. By 1905 the total number of private schools had risen to 720 throughout the island. Cuba proudly boasted that it was the only nation on earth which had more teachers than soldiers.

*Photo on top the **Maristas** of Cienfuegos; On the bottom photo the Colegio de **La Salle** in Havana.*

One of the best known secular schools before the Republic was *Colegio San Cristobal,* also known as *Colegio Carraguao*, the school directed by **José de la Luz** in 1833. Luz y Caballero also founded and directed the *Colegio El Salvador* after 1848. *San Cristobal*, originally in the neighborhood of *Carraguao* (later called *Villanueva*), in *El Cerro*, moved to 257 Teniente Rey Street in 1850 and once again to 797 Calzada del Cerro in 1853, when the number of students reached 400.

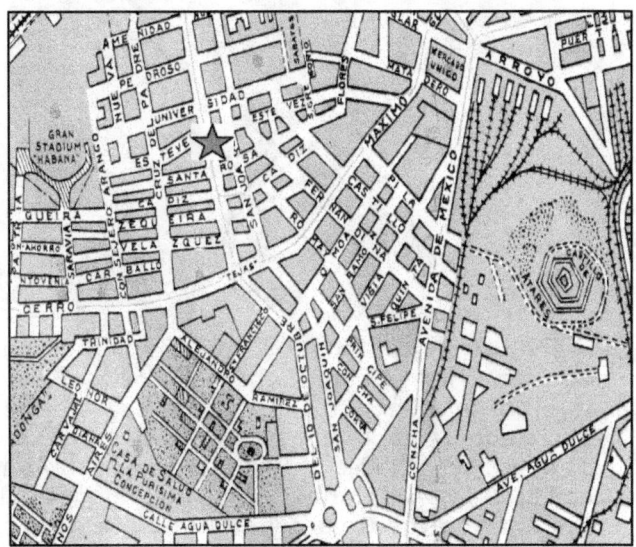

Photos: top, a drawing of the *Colegio San Cristobal o Carraguao,* at Infanta and Estévez Streets, in Havana, showing behind it the *Atarés Castle*; *at the bottom*, a map showing the Carraguao neighborhood in El Cerro and the location of the Colegio *San Cristobal*.

In early 1848 José de la Luz y Caballero founded and became director of the **Colegio El Salvador**. A large number of the heroes of 1868, those who Máximo Gomez called «*the men of 68,*» were related to either the *Colegio Carraguao* or *El Salvador*, whether as students or as teachers.

The list of students at *Carraguao* and *El Salvador*, is full of important names in Cuban history: **Francisco Vicente Aguilera**, founder of the independence wars; **Pedro (Perucho) Figueredo**, author of National Anthem; **Luis Ayestarán**, a member of the House of Representatives in Arms, shot on September 24, 1870; **Manuel Sanguily**, famous Cuban intellectual; **Ignacio Agramonte** and **Antonio Zambrana** both members of the Guáimaro Constitutional Assembly; **Enrique Piña**, former student and teacher in *El Salvador* and **Juan Clemente Zenea**, renowned Cuban poet, to name a few.

Photos: two views of the Colegio *El Salvador* at 257 Teniente Rey Street in Havana, as it was at the time of Luz y Caballero and in current times.

Since the early days of independence, the prospects of a Republic offering sensible guarantees and protection for capital investments incentivized many foreigners, Americans, Spaniards and Europeans in general, to launch commercial and industrial ventures in the young Republic of Cuba.

Banks, commercial establishments and all sorts of businesses were attracted to Havana and pretty soon their presence changed the outline of the city. Their visions were amply rewarded during the first decades of the XX century when the island enjoyed an impressive capital bonanza due to the high prices of Cuban sugar in the world market; the period was known as the time of the *vacas gordas* (fat cows).

The civil architecture of the city underwent a frantic construction renaissance. An example of these opportunities and results was the firm of **Casteleiro y Vizoso**, whose 1905 edifice at *Oficios*, *Lamparilla* and *Baratillo* Streets, across from the *Plaza de San Francisco*, set up the tone for other beautiful buildings in the commercial area near the port of Havana. It encompassed almost 2,000 square meters of warehouse facilities in three floors, with ceilings reaching almost four meters and easy access to the many conveyances transferring merchandise to and from the port of Havana.

The building of the **Lonja del Comercio** (the Mercantile Exchange) was also built across the *Plaza de San Francisco* in 1909. Its dome was crowned with a sculpture of Mercury, the roman god of commerce. It was a faithful copy of the Mercury of Juan de Bologna (1529-1608) at the Medici Palace in Florence. The Lonja had a total usable surface area of 12 million square meters.

Photos above: Cuban buildings at the time of Cuban independence or shortly thereafter (in or around 1902 to 1920), as well as some of their architectural details.

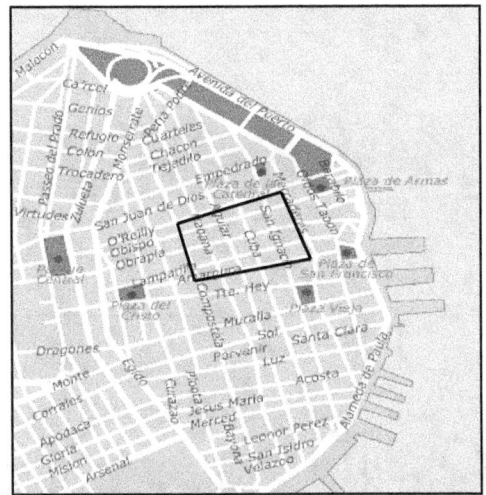

During the first years of the Republic, following a pattern well established during colonial times, a **Banking District** continued to develop in Havana; it comprised the areas between *O'Reilly*, *Amargura*, *Mercaderes* and *Compostela* Streets.

One of its important banking institutions was the **Banco Mendoza** at a building inaugurated in 1916 at 305 Obispo Street. Its business was concentrated in real estate, sugar futures and crop financing. Four solid columns made of Cuban granite from *Jaimanitas* were symbolic of the bank strength. Inside it had lots of marble, fine crystal and precious woods.

At 456 Aguilar Street near Lamparilla and Amargura, the Gelats family had opened their **Banco Gelats** in 1876. It was in the business of industrial commerce, shipping, personal banking, savings and investments. Years later, in 1910, it moved to 81 and 83 Aguiar Street. The new building was made of steel and stone, with marble floors, magnificent steel safes and abundant *boiserie*.

Photos above: *at the top*, a map of Old Havana showing the Banking District and the façade of *Banco Gelats*; *at the bottom*, the *Trust Company of Cuba* and the *Banco Mendoza*.

At Obrapía 257, in a remodeled drugstore, the **Royal Bank of Canada** (Santiago branch at bottom right) opened its Cuban operations in 1899. A new building was constructed in 1904 by *Purdy & Henderson*. This New York firm, with Havana offices since 1901, later built the Centros *Gallego* and *Asturiano*, the *National Capitol*, the *Plaza* and the *National* hotels and other important buildings in Havana. The Royal Bank introduced in Havana the concept of an entrance with a built-in renaissance-inspired *Arc of Triumph*.

At 225 O'Reilly, corner of Cuba Street, the **Bank of Nova Scotia** (bottom left) opened its doors in 1906. Within a few years it had seven branches across the island. Over 60% of its business was in the sugar sector. Its clients included Julio Lobo, General Motors, the Mestre brothers and the Aspuro family. By 1914 they had built a sumptuous building, instantly recognized for its terracotta façade. The architectural solution of its corner entrance soon became an inspiration for other grandiose buildings in Havana.

Other important financial institutions during the first years of the Republic were the **Havana Stock Exchange** (top left); the **Cuban National Bank** (top right); and the **Banco Nuñez** (the Camagüey branch at middle left), to mention only a few.

The history of the first presidential period in Republican Cuba began with a trip aboard the **Steamship Niagara**. This ship is shown in the *photo on top*, maneuvering at the entrance of the port of Havana; the *photo on the left* shows its second class promenade.

José Martí traveled several times in the *Niagara*. In 1901 Máximo Gómez was a passenger on a trip Havana-New York, to entice Tomás Estrada Palma to run for president of Cuba. **Manuel Márquez Sterling** and **Cosme de la Torriente** were with him. Máximo Gómez carried with him a letter signed by several prominent Cubans endorsing the candidature of **Estrada Palma** for president of Cuba. Among the signers were Generals José Miguel Gómez, Domingo Méndez Capote, Juan Rius Rivera, Pedro Betancourt and Diego Tamayo.

The prestigious **Estrada Palma Institute**, north of West Point in New York, was founded by Don Tomás as an exile after the Cuban War of Independence of 1868. Estrada Palma lived in Central Valley, New York, for over twenty years. The estate comprised twenty-five acres, superbly situated at the foot of the *Ramapo Mountains*. The school was a large four-story, modern building occupied by the *Estrada Palma Institute*. In front of the house there as a row of weeping-willow trees, and nearby a pretty pond, on which skaters had fun every winter. When Estrada entered the Ten Years' War, he had called his slaves and told them to go free. When Máximo Gómez came calling, Estrada Palma felt honored to answer the call of his native land.

In the photo above, the cell in the fortress of *El Morro* where **Tomás Estrada Palma (1835-1908)** was held prisoner of Spain in 1877. He had been selected president of the government of Cuba in Arms in 1876. After the death of Martí he was designated as his successor.

Alfredo Zayas (1861-1934), secretary of the 1901 Constitutional Convention, poet, co-editor of *Cuba Literaria*, and future president of Cuba in 1921, wrote a widely distributed manifesto with Domingo Méndez Capote, Máximo Gómez, Manuel Sanguily, Gonzalo de Quesada and others, urging the election of Estrada Palma. The only prominent non-signer was Juan Gualberto Gómez.

Cubans were jubilant for the inauguration of the republic. Several **Arcos del Triunfo** were built across the island. On the photos below: *on top*, an arch at the Central Park, next to the *Tacón Theater*, close to the statue of Isabel II, which was still there (between the flags on the left). *Below*: an arch in Santiago de Cuba at Santo Tomás Street. There was a great deal of expectation, however, not knowing if Estrada would accept the nomination or not.

On October 28, 1901, General Wood, who had fulfilled very well his mandate to nurse the young Cuban republic into life, made a serious error. He wrote to US President Roosevelt that **Bartolomé Masó (1830-1907)**, who opposed the *Platt Amendment*, was the «*favorite candidate of the radical and discontent element in Cuba.*» Wood proceeded to choose Estrada supporters to the *Electoral Commission*. Believing the elections would be rigged, Masó formally withdrew his candidacy.

The **1901 elections** finally took place. «*The vote was large but the conservative elements took little interest, and therefore they had very light representation in Congress,*» according to General Wood. Estrada received 158,970 votes out of 213,116 voters (335,700 persons had been qualified to vote.) For the Senate 24 seats were contested; 63 for the Chamber of Deputies, aside from 89 provincial positions and 6 governorships. According to the norms of the times Blacks, Women and Citizens with less than $250 worth of assets were excluded. In the US there was an extraordinary interest in the process and its outcome. Most Americans favored Tomás Estrada Palma.

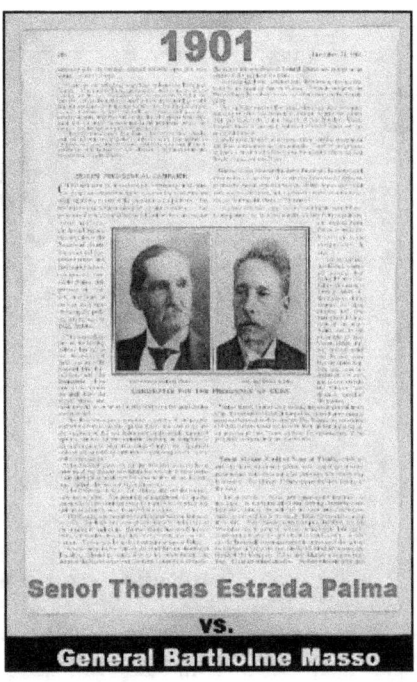

Photo above: A week before the ceremony of assuming the presidency in Cuba, a triumphal cavalry was organized from Bayamo, Oriente to Havana, in which close to 100 veterans participated, escorting the new president to the capital.

General Wood and **Tomas Estrada Palma** on 20 May, 1902, the day of the transfer of power from the USA to Cuba. On the left the Cubans, among them Generals *Emilio Núñez* and *Salvador Cisneros Betancourt* as well as *Gonzalo de Quesada*. On the right, officials from the American embassy staff.

There is no doubt that **Tomas Estrada Palma**, with his talent, his political wisdom, patriotism, courage, uprightness, modesty and his faith in God, was able to patiently win the favor of the US for the liberty of Cuba. The multitudes adored him.

On top, Máximo Gómez raising the Cuban flag on the roof of the presidential palace with Gen Wood. *On the center*, Gen. Wood turns over the **business** of Cuba to Estrada Palma.

On the right, Gen. Wood leaves the same day the port of Havana.

It has never been easy to place yourself at the time of the US intervention in Cuba and understand the motives and feelings regarding Cuba within the American society. The prevailing emotions in the US were affective, respectful and admiring, in spite of the negative propaganda that some tried to attribute to the intentions of the US government. On the cartoon at the top, the **Marquis of Lafayette** and **George Washington** recriminate Miss USA for not stopping the abuse of Cuba by the Spaniards. On the cartoon in the left Cuba is portrayed as a baby that needs the care and support of the US. The poster below shows great admiration for the gallantry and valor of the Cuban troops.

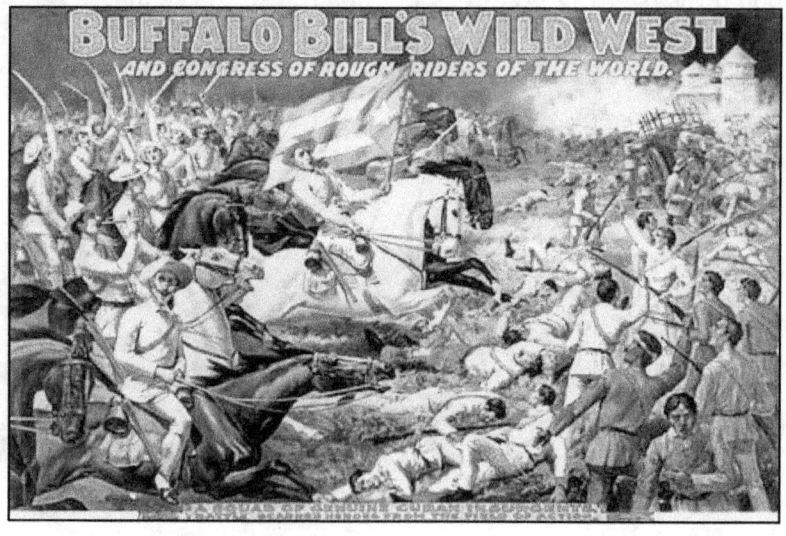

Two photos taken a few minutes apart. On top, the American flag is lowered at the *Spanish Palace of the Captain General*, now turned into the *Cuban Presidential Palace*, May 20, 1902. On the bottom, the Cuban flag is raised on the same mast. The ceremony took place in front of thousands of cheering Cubans.

On the left, the newly elected Cuban Senate during its first session.

On May 20, 1902 **Tomás Estrada Palma** took over a viable and working country. The treasury had enough funds. There were no debts, to Spain or anybody else. Not every- thing was sweet, however. There were lots of unemployed demanding jobs and govern- ment support at a time when sugar prices were depressed. Cubans had not yet mastered the art of political discourse. Political parties were weak and inconsistent. The *Nationalist* became the *Liberals*. The *Con- servatives* became the *Mode- rates*. Party labels and political principles were meaningless. The senior veteran generals were *de facto* political leaders. They enjoyed a world of intrigue fighting for leadership. An existing cultured class of intelle- ctuals were handicapped by their non-military past.

No one had a realistic plan on how to deal effectively against the **Platt Amendment**: tolerate it, reject it unconditionally, fight it, try to modify it, get used to it...?

The initial **Cabinet of Tomás Estrada Palma.**

Left to right in the photo: **Carlos de Zaldo y Beurmann**, Secretary of State and Justice; **Diego Tamayo**, Secretary of the Interior; **José M. García Montes**, Secretary of the Treasury; **Eduardo Yero Badién**, Secretary of Education; **Manuel Luciano Díaz**, Secretary of Public Works; **Emilio Terry**, Secretary of Agriculture. Missing, the Minister of Cuba in Washington, **Gonzalo de Quesada.** At the extreme right **Don Tomás Estrada Palma**.

Most, if not all of the cabinet members in the government of **Tomas Estrada Palma** shared with him his friendliness and positive disposition towards the US. It became a point of contention with many Cubans who had resented the entrance of the US into the Hispano-Cuban War of 1895. On occasion of a 10 of October celebration Estrada Palma had written:

«*I have not been shy to confess that a political dependency that will bring us the blessings of a sovereign republic is better than an independent republic discredited and ruined by the harmful action of periodic civil wars.*»

On the final report addressed to the US President and the US Congress by **Leonard Wood as Military Governor of Cuba**, the following final decisions were highlighted:
1) A project for paving and installing sewers in the city of Havana has been adjudicated and is underway.
2) A project for bringing water from San Juan canyon to supply the city of Santiago, and a project for installing sewers in the city have been paid for and are underway.
3) The projects for protecting the ports of Havana, Matanzas, Cienfuegos and Santiago and thereafter all other ports against epidemic diseases has been completed.

Above photos: sanitation of streets, road construction and harbor dredging in Cuba during the American occupation (1898-1902) under Leonard Wood as Military Governor.

When the time came in 1902 to sign the US-Cuban commerce treaty that had been left pending since the Platt amendment was accepted, two formidable speakers presented opposing points of view in the Cuban legislature. **Antonio Sánchez de Bustamante** (on the left) supported the treaty while **Manuel Sanguily** (right) opposed it saying: «*They ask for big concessions but give us much smaller ones in return.*» The Treaty was agreed on 11 March 1903.

Photos, left to right, top to bottom:
The first meeting of the *1901 Cuban Constitutional Assembly*; Máximo Gómez receiving Tomás Estrada Palma in Havana; **Domingo Méndez Capote**, as VP the first president of the Cuban Senate in 1902; **Pelayo García**, first president of the Cuban House of Representatives in 1902.

All together, Cubans were of two minds during the occupation of their country from 1898 to 1902.

On one hand many Cubans recognized the **headstart** that the government of the US was providing to bring the island into the twentieth century. Spain had not done much in Cuba that was not to her specific benefit and the island suffered from lack of hygiene, communications, roads and transportation, good ports, irrigation and many other necessities, except in those places where it did benefit the Spanish proprietors.

On the other hand **the finale** of the Spanish American War had been a story of wounded pride. In spite of having fought a war for three years and having controlled 90% of the Cuban territory, the US Army made heroes of Teddy Roosevelt, Wheeler, Shafter, Hobson and Sampson, and did not even allow the Cuban Army to take the vanquished arms from the hands of the Spanish.

In 1902, not many Cubans believed that the US would ever withdraw from Cuba; yet they did, on time and in full. The photo on the right shows the **American forces leaving Havana**. The US papers applauded the move: «*Money and time well spent,*» declared the *Buffalo News*. Within a few months after the inauguration of the Republic of Cuba, the government of Tomás Estrada Palma began to recruit youngsters to form a professional Cuban Army.

The Government of Estrada Palma began to rule effectively with administrative principles similar to those of the United States. On Nov 3, 1902 it submitted to the recently elected Cuban Congress an initial budget of less than $15 Million. On Nov 24, the first discontents declared a strike and Estrada had to call the **Guardia Rural** (*photo on top*) to help police maintain order. It resulted in the first political fatalities of Republican Cuba.

On February 17th, 1903 Estrada Palma and Roosevelt signed a Treaty that stipulated that Cuba would perpetually lease **Guantánamo Bay** to the US. Other requests of the US for bases in Bahía Honda, Cienfuegos and Nipe were discounted but the Treaty did not resolve the issue of the status of **Isla de Pinos**, which was left uncertain in the Platt Amendment.

The photo on top shows the removal of the statue of Isabel II from its pedestal in the Central Park of Havana in 1903. A debate followed about whose statue should be there: **Carlos Manuel de Céspedes** or **José Martí** (*see middle photo*). José Martí won. Years later President Zayas had no doubt that his statue should be at the gardens of the new Presidential Palace. The photo at the bottom shows the statue that Zayas erected for himself in 1925 at the end of his presidential period. Zayas, not having time to pose, allegedly ordered a ready-made, off-the-shelf statue to which his name was simply attached.

The **Reciprocity Treaty of 1903** (*top illustration*) drew the Cuban economy closer to that of the US. Cuban sugar received a 20 percent tariff reduction in the United States. It was also the compensation designed to pacify the Cubans for accepting the *Platt Amendment*. It gave Cuba a favored position in the American market and made her the world's greatest sugar producer. American capital was invested in Cuba and Cuba became the richest of the Caribbean states. On the other hand, the public payroll, municipal, provincial, and na-tional, expanded to an estimated 20,000 public employees, with some 8,000 in the city of Havana. *Above*: two cartoons from **Puck**, the humor magazine of colorful cartoons and political satire (1871-1918), showing the opposition of American sugar producers to the 20% tariff reduction received by Cuba in 1903.

Two powerful symbols of the independence of Cuba. The postage stamps and the seat of government.

Photos above: the postal transition. Stamps from Spain in 1898, from the US in 1899 and from the Republic of Cuba in 1902.

In the lower photo, the Cuban flag in the **first Presidential Palace**, the old *Palacio del Gobernador General Español* at the *Plaza de Armas*, Tacón Street, from Obispo to O'Reilly. It served as the Presidential Palace until 1920.

In February 1903 a coalition party was organized in Cuba, the ―*Partido Liberal Nacional*‖ under the leadership of **Alfredo Zayas (1861-1934)**, a future president of Cuba in 1921; a non- combatant who spent the war of 1895 in the prisons of Ceuta. The *Liberal Party* was a coalition of the *Partido Nacional Cubano* of Zayas, the *Partido Republicano Independiente* of Juan Gualberto Gómez, the *Partido Nacional de Liberales de Camagüey* of Lope Recio, the *Republicanos Independientes de Las Villas* of José Juis Robau, the *Nacionales Libres* of José B. Alemán, the *Republicanos Liberales de Vueltabajo* of Luis Pérez and the *Republicanos Casti- llistas* of Demetrio Castillo Duany. This profusion of political parties barely 10 months after Independence is evidence of the passion for politics Cubans had, a fact that would become much worse over the years.

Fernando Figueredo Socares (1846-1929) (*photo above*) was probably the most experienced administrator in Cuba during the first years of the republic. He had served in the House of Representatives in Florida, and as Mayor of West Tampa. In Cuba he was Postmaster, Controller and Treasurer.

On one occasion he remarked: «... *we lack the tradetion and knowledge of governing ourselves. Our people have a low level of basic education and most have been improverished by the war. We are trapped between prosperous Americans who know the value of our land and seasoned Spaniards that control our commerce. For many Cubans the only way to shine is to be in politics, hence our destructive internal wars.*»

Bartolomé Masó Márquez (1830-1907) (*photo below*) was a logical presidential candidate for the new Republic of Cuba but was bypassed by historical circumstances in favor of Estrada Palma. He had been a close friend of Carlos Manuel de Céspedes; was present at la *Demajagua* en 1968, at *Baraguá* in 1878 and at *Baire* (better called *Bayate*) in 1895, the three most important events in Cuban history.

He was elected VP at *Jimaguayú* and President at *La Yaya*, the two Constitutional Assemblies during his lifetime. When he withdrew his presidential candidacy in 1902 he retired sad and poor (the only Cuban independence general that never received his pension) to *La Jagüita*, near Manzanillo, his only property, the farm where he initiated the war of independence of 1895.

He died on June 14, 1907, during the US second occupation; when the time came to dress his cadaver his friends realized his only pair of shoes had holes in the soles. His widow Panchita (Francisca Rosales) objected to the idea of borrowing a pair from a friend.

Don Tomás Estrada Palma is generally exempted by critics and historians from the corruption that was prevalent in Cuba since the first days of the republic. The institution most prone to easy malfeasance was without doubt the **lottery**. It was suppressed by the US from 1898 to the advent of the republic and then vetoed by Estrada Palma in 1904, when it was part of a bill introduced in Congress by Senator Morúa Delgado. In 1909 it was resurrected during the government of José Miguel Gómez. In the *photo on top*, children from the *Casa de la Beneficencia* prepare for the Christmas lottery draw in 1910.

The **Lottery** was part of the Cuban tradition since late in the 18th century, when it was introduced by the Spaniards. It had a close association with *Saint Ildefonso School for Orphans.* It Cuba it was first introduced in 1811 as a hobby of the upper classes. The worst part of the lottery was that it was the basis for *the Charada China* (the numbers game, see drawing at right), an addi- tional source of corruption by unscrupulous politicians that sold protection to professional gamblers. Most people in Cuba during 1903 knew that 36 stood for **pipe**, 10 for **fish**, 34 for **monkey**, 17 for **moon**, and so on.

The Vice President under Tomás Estrada Palma, at the suggestion and with the support of Máximo Gómez, was Dr. **Luis Estévez Romero (1850-1909)**, husband of Marta Abreu the celebrated Santa Clara philanthropist. With his wife, Esteban contributed large portions of their fortune to the Cuban Independence cause. They lived mostly in Paris although they also kept a residence in the *Paseo del Prado* in Havana. When Estrada Palma decided to run for re-election Estévez resigned and returned to Paris. In 1909 Marta fell sick and died after an appendix operation. Not able to bear the sadness of his loneliness, Luis Estévez committed suicide 33 days later.

The *Partido Republicano Conservador* took the name of *Partido Moderado* on August 1905 under the leadership of **Domingo Méndez Capote (1863-1934)** (*on the left*). Its political base was the civilians in the independence movement, former soldiers (mostly Blacks) and peasants. The *Partido Nacional Liberal* (a fusion of disaffected *Republicans* and *National Liberals*) selected **José Miguel Gómez** and **Alfredo Zayas** (no longer hostile to each other) as its leaders. Class and racial tensions exacerbated the differences between the two political parties. Domingo Méndez Capote was elected president of the *1901 Cuban Constitutional Convention*.

In April of 1905 President Tomas Estrada Palma presented a progress report of his accomplishments to the people of Cuba:

Hundreds of workers had been employed building roads, light-houses, docks, telegraph lines, hospitals, schools and other infrastructure needs of the republic.

After paying all debts and accounts, the **Treasury** had a balance of $10,764,000.

The veterans had received their **past salaries**, even though it required a secured loan from the US, backed by the import taxes and dock receipts in general.

The 1903-1904 **sugar crops** had reached a record at 1,200,000 tons.

Estrada Palma also informed about the failures of the government in its first three years:

The **electoral law had failed** to prevent frauds, abuses and injustices.

The **judicial branch** was not as independent from influence as it needed to be.

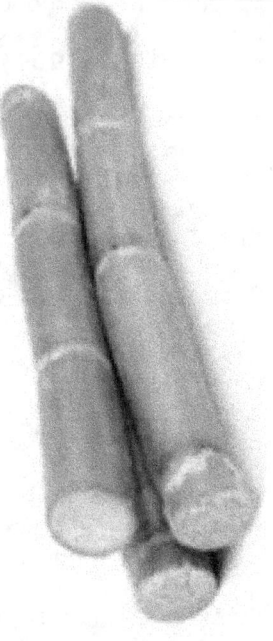

The first elections under the republic took place in February 28, 1904. They were characterized as «*a farce represented with less shame than in colonial times,*» by Emilio Terry, Secretary of Agriculture. **Juan Gualberto Gómez (1854-1933)** (left), of the *National Liberal Party*, recused himself for having received more votes than electors. The *Conservative Republican Party* claimed victory almost everywhere. When the new Congress opened in April, the *Liberals* protested by not showing up. Four out of sixty three new congressmen and one of twelve senators were Black.

The story goes that Estrada Palma, who knew himself to be old, tired and not particularly pleased with his administrative duties, was willing to stand again as presidential candidate because he was afraid that José Miguel Gómez and Alfredo Zayas would squander the surplus funds that he had accumulated in the treasury with so much effort.

In March of 1904 his Secretary of the Interior, **General Freyre de Andrade (1863-1916)**, —*photo at right*— a leading *Moderate*, began a rigorous program of cleaning the public rolls of any employee not a *Moderate* sympathizer. Freyre had arrived in Cuba in the expedition of the *Dauntless* in October 1896 and had served under Máximo Gómez. He was later member the *Santa Cruz Convention* and the *Asamblea del Cerro*. His credentials were impeccable yet he had to resort to policemen and *Guardias Rurales* to fulfill Estrada Palma's orders since the Cuban Army was not yet ready for such a task.

Photos above: the Cuban House of Representatives in 1906 and a patriotic march celebrating Cuba's independence in 1905.

On June 17, 1905, **General Máximo Gómez (1836-1905)** died in Havana. Two months earlier he had traveled to Oriente to visit one of his surviving children. He had lost *Panchito Gómez Toro* trying to save the cadaver of General Antonio Maceo in 1896; four of his children had died of starvation and misery while in exile. As he started his trip to eastern Cuba he was mobbed by a crowd of sympathizers at the *Villanueva* railroad station (where the *National Capitol* was later built). At every stop thereafter hundreds of former combatants wanted to shake his hand. His right hand began to swell after so many friends had squeezed it and he suffered an infection that developed into a septicemia. He was taken to Havana immediately and along the way two surgeries were performed. He never recovered.

The *photo above* shows him at his house in the *Quinta los Molinos*, a few months before his death. The lady with white hair is **Bernarda Toro**, his wife, whom he always called *Manana*. He volunteered in 1902 to go to New York and talk Tomás Estrada Palma into running for President. Máximo Gómez, who was born in the Dominican Republic, would have won for himself the presidency of Cuba unopposed; he died very frustrated at the progress of a Republic very different from the one the men who fought had envisioned.

The history of Máximo Gómez is a living example of a man who gave his entire life for justice and fairness to his fellow men. In *República Dominicana*, his native country, he was appointed *Captain of the Spanish Army* for his extraordinary contribution in 1855 to the fight against the Haitian invasion to his country.

By 1865 he had settled down in Cuba with his family and shortly thereafter he applied to be discharged from the Spanish Army. Four days after the beginning of the First Cuban War of Independence, he joined the insurgent forces. For his military knowledge he was appointed sergeant and given the mission of training inexperienced soldiers. On October 18, Carlos Manuel de Céspedes, the leader of the movement, appointed him Mayor General.

In the war of 1895 he led the Cuban Army to extraordinary victories over the Spaniards and ever since he has been considered a military genius.

The beautiful lady on the left is **Bernarda del Toro Pelegrín (1852-1911)**, Máximo Gómez' wife. When she married Gómez she was 17; he was 34. Witnesses were *Fernando Figueredo Socarrás* and *Salvador Cisneros, Marqués de Santa Lucía*. When Gómez died in 1905 she was offered a life-long pension by President Tomas Estrada Palma, which she declined, asking that it be given to the poor in Cuba.

DIARIO DE LA MARINA
Junio 18 de 1905.

EL GENERAL MAXIMO GOMEZ

El Secretario de Gobernacion y el Jefe de la Guardia Rural estuvieron ayer, a las cuatro de la tarde, en la residencia del general Maximo Gomez para enterarse del estado del caudillo el cual les manifestaron era sumamente grave.

El senor Freire de Andrade, dado el estado gravisimo de peligro inminente en que se encontraba el general, se puso de acuerdo con la familia para que pudiera pasar a visitarlo el Presidente de la Republica.

De regreso a Palacio el senor Freire de Andrade, volvio a salir en carruaje nuevamente para la morada del caudillo, acompañando al Jefe de Estado que iba con su ayudante de guardia, el capitan Poey.

A las seis y diez minutos de la tarde dejo de existir el caudillo de las dos guerras separatistas.

Que Dios lo haya acogido en su seno y de a su familia la resignacion necesaria para sufrir tan rudo golpe.

MAXIMO GOMEZ DIES, PALMA AT HIS SIDE

$100,000 Voted by Cuba Received Few Hours Before.

MAN MOST FEARED BY SPAIN

Domingan-Born Commander in Chief of Cuba's Patriot Army Once Served Under the Spanish Flag.

HAVANA, June 17.—Gen. Maximo Gomez died at 6 o'clock this evening at his temporary home in the suburb Vedado. "El Caudillo," (Chieftain) as he was called by his countrymen, passed away in the presence not only of his family, but also of his old-time friend, Estrado Palma, President of the Republic, whose tears freely mingled with those of the sorrowing relatives.

Gen. Gomez leaves a widow, five sons, and one daughter. Only to-day the Secretary of the Treasury delivered to one of the sons a check for $100,000, which had been voted unanimously by Congress for the General's benefit and approved by President Palma. This was in addition to the $50,000 previously voted by Congress.

Two newspaper accounts of the death of Máximo Gómez in Havana on June 17th 1905.

On top: from the *Diario de la Marina* in Havana.

On the center: from the *New York Times*, the first two paragraphs of a full column on the day of the event.

On the bottom: Funeral cortege of General Máximo Gómez, going through Reina Street in Havana.

Col. Enrique Villuendas (1874-1905), right arm of Gen José Miguel Gómez during the war, a member of the *Asamblea de Santa Cruz*, delegate for Santa Clara to the *1901 Constitutional Convention*, elected member of *Congress* in 1902, and a firm opponent to the reelection of Estrada Palma, was killed at a brawl at a hotel in Cienfuegos on September 22, 1905.

A few days before, he had written a letter to Máximo Gómez expressing fear for his life. By the time the letter got to Havana, Máximo Gómez had died of natural causes.

Villuendas, one of the most promising young members of the House of Representatives, was one of the first victims of political violence in Cuba. He had been, with Alfredo Zayas, one of the secretaries of the *1901 Constitutional Convention*. In fact, he was the youngest of the 31 constituents in 1901.

Six other persons were killed with Villuendas, and 25 were wounded. One of the dead was Miguel A. Illance, the Chief of Police of Cienfuegos. The next day the *Liberales* called off all their candidates to the elections of December of 1905. As in 1901, Estrada Palma was again elected without opposition.

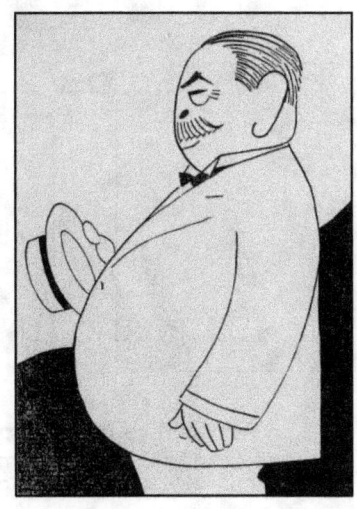

A key part of the election process was to first elect the **Registration Boards**. Held on September 1905, these elections were marred by widespread fraud. *Moderates* (the party of Estrada Palma) padded the rolls with fictitious names. Over 425,000 electors were registered, probably 150,000 too many. Like Masó had done in the elections of 1901, **José Miguel Gómez** (cartoon by Massaguer on the right), an opposition candidate for the 1905 elections, declared that he would abstain from participation in the elections.

Above: the **Liberal Party leadership** in 1905. Left to Right: José Miguel Gómez, Alfredo Zayas, Juan Gualberto Gómez. Juan Guiteras, Martín Morúa Delgado.

Above: the **Moderate Party leadership** in 1905. Left to Right: Tomás Estrada Palma, Emilio Nuñez, Domingo Méndez Capote, Manuel Sanguily, Juan Rius Rivera.

Practically **all the members of the local election boards were from the *Moderate Party*.** The president controlled the police, the rural guards, the municipal Mayors. The Government ousted opposition officials in twenty one municipalities. The officials who were removed had been elected by popular vote during the first intervention and their summary dismissal by the Estrada Palma government aroused intense opposition among the common people since it was the responsibility of local boards to supervise the voter registration and count the ballots in the December general elections. Estrada did not participate in those purges but his followers did, all across the country.

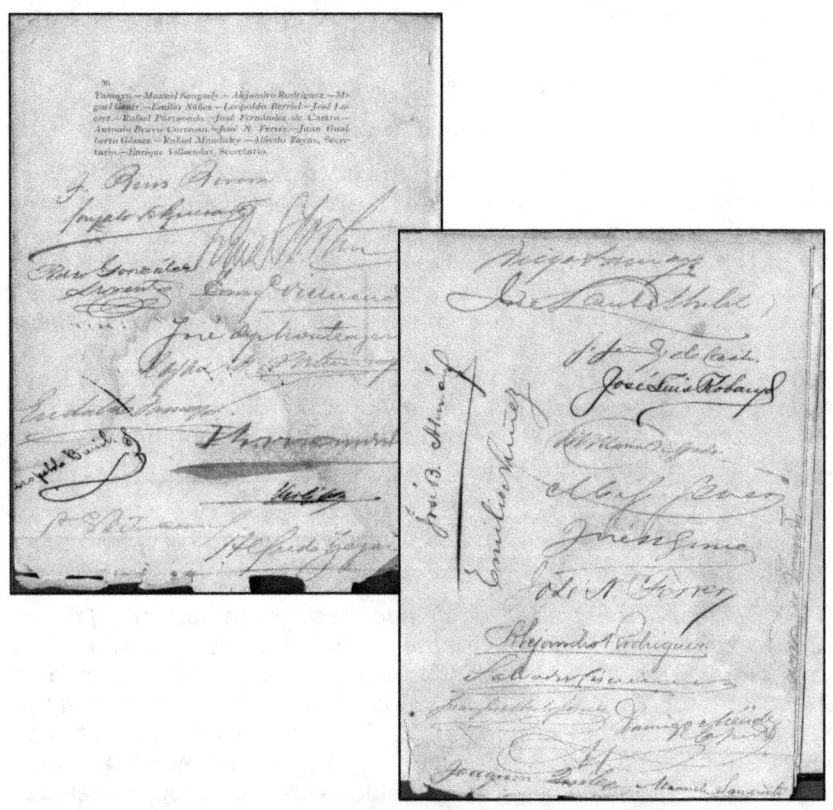

The decision by **Tomás Estrada Palma** to seek re-election in 1906 was absolutely legal and in compliance with the *Cuban Constitution of 1901*. The Cuban Constitution had been inspired by the US Constitution; it was customary in the US for a president to seek reelection. In spite of this, even members of the *Asamblea Constituyente* and Máximo Gómez opposed his re-election.

Above, the two pages with the signatures of the 31 members of the *Constituyente of 1901*. For more details see the covers of this book. (Collection of Olga and Raúl Chao)

On September 27, 1905, **José Miguel Gómez** resigned as chief of the *Partido Liberal*. On October 4, fearing assassination, he went into exile in New York. By mid-October he called for the intervention of the US in Cuba. He received the support of the newspapers *Diario de la Marina* and *El Mundo*. By the end of October the *Partido Liberal* withdrew from the elections. At the end of November there were armed rebellions and resistance in *Alquizar* (Havana) and *San Juan y Martínez* (Pinar del Rio). On December 2, *Liberals* did not show up to vote and Estrada Palma won by a discredited landslide. Not a single liberal was elected to any position anywhere. On February 24, 1906 a group of rebels attacked *Guanabacoa* in Havana.

A summary of events in the year 1905 showed that it had been witness to a series of important events in Cuba.

On February 1 Estrada Palma had decided to join the *Partido Moderado*. Domingo Méndez Capote a few days later renounced to the Senate Presidency. At the end of March Luis Estevez resigned as VP and left for Paris. In mid May José Miguel Gómez and Alfredo Zayas announced they would be the Partido Liberal candidates to the presidency and the vice-presidency. In mid June Máximo Gómez died and in September Enrique Villuendas was murdered in Cienfuegos. By mid-September José Miguel Gómez and Alfredo Zayas retired their nominations and Gómez formally requested the US Army to intervene in Cuba. Finally on December 1, the elections took place and Estrada Palma was elected to a second term, once more without opposition. It was nevertheless one of the worse years in terms of growth of the young Cuban republic.

Photo above: Inauguration of the monument to José Miguel Gómez (a cartoon by Massaguer in the upper corner) in the Avenue of the Presidents in Havana (G Street), on May 16, 1936.

When in April 1906 the Cuban Congress met to certify the 1905 elections, the deputies from the *Liberal Party* walked out to a man. Estrada Palma and Méndez Capote were nevertheless proclaimed as President and Vice-President of the Republic.

The liberals immediately started to plot a revolt that became known as *La Guerrita de Agosto*. Liberal leaders **Faustino (Pino) Guerra Puente, Ernesto Asbert** and **Loynaz del Castillo** began to organize their partisans while Estrada Palma ordered all liberal politicians to be arrested. To the 20,000 men the liberals placed in the countryside, Estrada Palma could only oppose 2,000 Rural Guards, mostly old and poorly armed war veterans. Pino Guerra, soon to be known as ―The Hero of 1906,‖ was one of several Cuban *politicos* that got used to rely on US interventions to secure his national goals; it was a frequent and unfortunate cop-out devised by politically immature men that had otherwise served the young Cuban republic with dignity and decor.

Years later Pino Guerra became the president of the *Liberal party* and, once more, asked the US to supervise the elections of 1920 when Zayas, as a Conservative, defeated José Miguel Gómez. Men like Guerra never paid attention to the 1897 declaration of Máximo Gómez, for whom advocacy of US intervention was tantamount to treason.

Photos, left to right: Faustino (Pino) Guerra Puente, Ernesto Asbert and Enrique Loynaz del Castillo.

When the *Guerrita de Agosto* broke out on August 1906, **Enrique Loynaz del Castillo (1871-1963)** and **Quintín Bandera (1833-1906)** —*photos at right*— were the military men with the highest rank among the rebels. Bandera had fought in the *Ten Year War* with Antonio Maceo and in 1895 under Calixto García and Máximo Gómez. He was one of the first fatalities, assassinated in the town of Bauta, Havana. The uprising had revived hopes among Blacks (overrepresented in the Cuban Army) that their time for a rightful share in Cuba's government had arrived. The rebellion was never a popular movement yet it placed 20,000 men in the countryside to face less than two thousand Rural Guards.

Photo at left: the burial of **Quintín Bandera**. He was placed in a common horse cart and was accompanied by an undistinguished formation of rural guards.

In July of 1898, at the time of the Spanish surrender, the most famous black Cuban officer had been **Quintín Bandera**. He had participated in anti-Spanish conspiracies since 1850 and had fought in the three Cuban Wars of Independence. Yet at that moment of glory in 1898 he had to watch the end of the war from the sidelines. In 1897, before the US intervention, Bandera had been court- martialed (allegedly for disobedience, insubordination, sedition and immorality), stripped of his command and told to leave the army until further notice. He was denied full payment and suitable employment in the government. He even had to work as a garbage collector to make a living. By 1906 he had been, restored to his rank; at the very beginning of the *Guerrita de Agosto*, however, he was ambushed and killed. He was, unlike other rebel soldiers, black or white, repeatedly accused as a thief and a laggard. It was unlike- ly that he was discriminated against, given the successful history of other black generals.

General **José Monteagudo** had revolted in Santa Clara in August 1906; **Juan Gualberto Gómez** had done it in Oriente. On September 8 Estrada Palma accepted the mediation of **Gen Mario García Menocal** (all three on the right), as head of a commission of veterans, to negotiate a compromise between Liberals and Moderates. His services failed since Estrada insisted that the rebels first depose their arms. That same day Estrada Palma talked to Frank Steinhart, the US Consul, requesting that two US war ships and 2 to 3 thousand men be sent to Havana.

The **crisis continued** after the failed attempts of Menocal to mediate. Faustino (Pino) Guerra took *San Juan y Martínez*; Campos Marquetti got close to *Guanabacoa*; Enrique Loynaz del Castillo was victorious in *Wajay* against the government forces. Loynaz tried with the telegram shown below to get Estrada Palma to resign to the presidency and bring peace to Cuba.

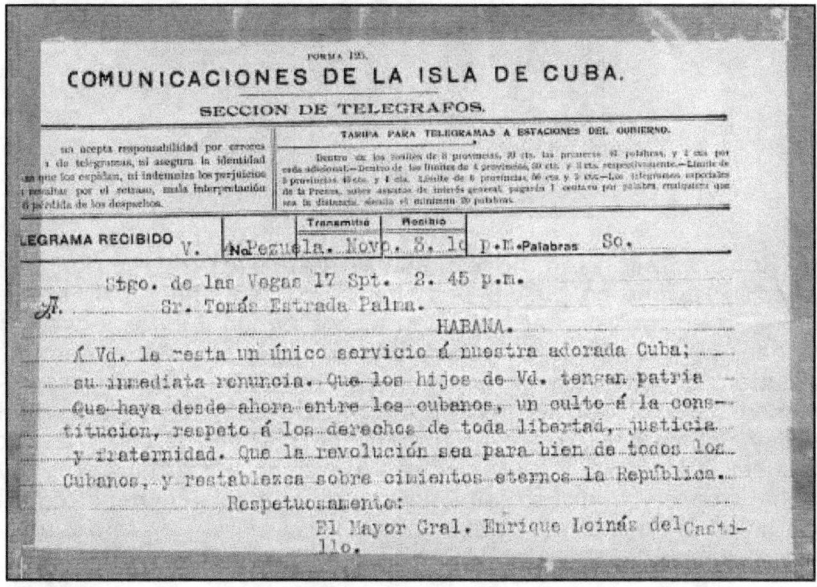

A few days later, at the request of Estrada Palma, the Consul General of the US sent a telegram to Washington asking President Roosevelt for two warships to preserve order, one for Cienfuegos and one for Havana. It also announced that President Estrada could not protect life and property and would ask Congress for a forcible intervention as contemplated in the **Platt Amendment**. The battleships *Denver* and *Marietta* soon arrived in Havana. President Roosevelt, trying to avert intervention, sent two emissaries to Havana: Secretary of War **William H. Taft (1857-1930)** and Assistant Secretary of State **Robert Bacon (1860-1919)**.

Robert Bacon (on the left) and **William Taft** (on the right) arrived in Havana on the *SS Des Moines* on September 19. Estrada Palma tried to resign at a session of the *Cuban Congress* on September 28 but finding that there was no quorum resigned through a letter to Taft. Méndez Capote and the entire cabinet also resigned. Taft took possession as *Interim Governor* of Cuba on Saturday September 29 and ordered 7,600 marines to come ashore and set up camp at 27 posts across the island. He received the national treasury from Estrada Palma, who immediately departed for his home in Bayamo, Oriente.

Photo of the *Joint Session* of the Cuban Congress on September 28, 1906, when Tomás Estrada Palma failed to present his resignation as well as those of Méndez Capote and his entire Cabinet.

The session was presided by **Dr. Ricardo Dolz**, *photo at left*, a former autonomist, prestigious lawyer and politician, who had been elected Senate President at the same time Fernando Freyre de Andrade had become President of the House. Representative Alfredo Betancourt y Manduley, a former captain of the Cuban Army during the war of 1895, proposed to reject the letters of resignation, at which point the session was interrupted while the supporters of Estrada Palma met at the private home of Dolz. The *Moderates*, not able to convince Estrada Palma to withdraw his resignation, decided 20 to 15 votes not to return to the *Joint Session*. The Legislative and the Executive branches of the Cuban government were thus given a devastating deathblow.

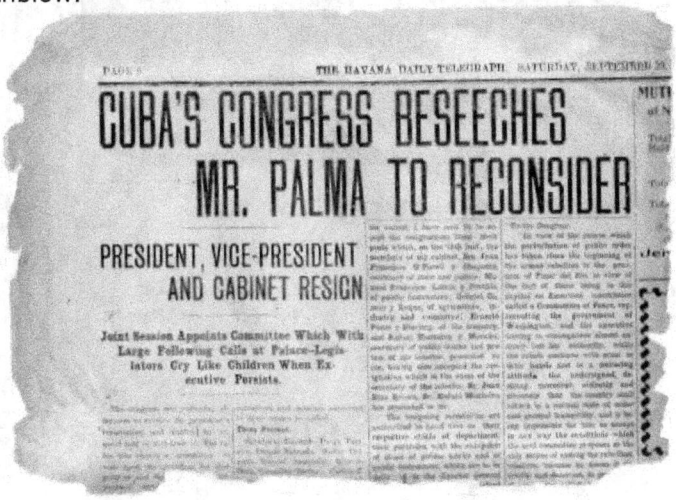

The English press in Havana on September 29, 1906, reports about Estrada Palma's irrevocable resignation.

On October 13, 1906 **Charles Edward Magoon (1878-1920)**, a former Governor of the *Panama Canal Zone*, was appointed *Governor of Cuba* by Taft. He immediately declared void the election of 1905 and took over the legislative powers for himself until an *Advisory Law Commission* was appointed (nine Cubans, three Americans). All department chiefs were confirmed in their positions and the Cuban flag was ordered to be flown in all public buildings. In spite of a black legend, there are no proofs that Magoon profited from his position as Governor of Cuba.

Magoon believed in the economic principles of a school (later called *Keynesian*) that stipulated that any downturn in business could be alleviated by an increase in government spending. He undertook a vast public works program which resulted in a decrease of the Cuban treasury from $20 million surplus to $11 million deficit during his years as Governor, 1906-1909.

MR. PALMA BEGGED FOR INTERVENTION

Official Correspondence Made Public Shows That He Asked It on September 8.

PRESIDENT HELD OFF

Mr. Roosevelt Explained Gravity of Sending Troops and Asked Effort to Quell Rebels.

GOVERNMENT WAS IN PANIC

Consul General Steinhardt Besieged by Cuban Officials—Palma Decided to Resign on September 13.

TAFT WILL NOT NAME A CABINET

Tells Cubans He Will Leave Filling of Posts to His Successor as Governor.

DAMAGE CLAIMS PUT IN

Question of Compensation for Losses Caused by Rebels Held in Abeyance.

RAPIDLY GIVING UP ARMS

Eleven Hundred Rebels in Cienfuegos Surrender Rifles, and Situation Everywhere Is Quiet.

Several historical distortions became erroneously accepted as fact when the US Army took possession of Cuba during the US intervention of 1906.

First was the myth that the US had sent its Army into Cuba, **abusing the dictates of the Platt Amendment** they had forced into the Cuban Constitution of 1901. The reality was that upon receiving the petition for intervention from Estrada Palma, Roosevelt had immediately proclaimed (on a letter to Gonzalo de Quesada) that «*the USA has been compelled to intervene in Cuba. Our only purpose is to create the necessary conditions for a peaceful election. Our intervention in Cuban affairs will only come if Cuba herself shows that it lacks the self restraint necessary to secure peace.*» (see a paper clip on the previous page.) In fact, sending Taft and Bacon to Cuba was Roosevelt's effort to avoid intervention.

The ***second*** myth was the accusation that Estrada had been an agent of the US or had favored annexation to the US all along. This ignores the fact that Mario García Menocal, Alfredo Zayas and most Cuban businessmen **favored a US intervention** and were unanimous in their perception that the situation in Cuba was beyond the capacity of the Cuban government or the army to solve peacefully

Photo above: Estrada Palma's modest last resting place in Santiago de Cuba on the day of his burial.

The **third** myth was the notion that Estrada Palma had been dishonest and ineffective as President. The fact was that Estrada Palma's possessions when he retired were just what he had inherited from his parents, except for a small farm he had acquired in his youth, at the time he married his wife Genoveva. Such record of honesty and modesty was in total contrast with those of all other presidents that succeeded him in Cuba until the end of the republic.

If **Charles Magoon** can be accused of something is that he allowed and even encouraged administrative corruption and waste of resources in order to appease the bad temper of those exalted by the uprising of August 1906 and the frustrated reelection fiasco. He cannot be blamed as the man responsible for the administrative dishonesty that years later drowned and suffocated the republic. On the positive side, he encouraged the formation of a new *Conservative Party* to replace the discredited *Moderates* of Estrada Palma and modified the electoral laws (and others dating from colonial times) to guarantee future honest elections.

One of the great contributions of Charles Magoon was to set up the **Advisory Law Commission** in Cuba to assist in the promulgations of laws compatible with the 1901 Constitution at a time when most laws were rollovers from Spanish times. To that effect he incorporated dozens of Cuban notables and experts. *Above top*: **Enrique José Varona**, **Rafael Montoro** and **Ramiro Guerra**. *On the bottom*: **Alfredo Zayas** and **Juan Gualberto Gómez**.

A photograph signed by the twelve members of the **Advisory Law Commission** in 1907. *From left to right*: Francisco Carrera Justiz, Blanton Winship, Alfredo Zayas, Erasmo Regüeiferos, Juan Gualberto Gómez, General Enoch H. Crowder, Otto Schoenrich, Rafael Montoro, Manuel M.Coronado, Miguel F.Viondi, Juan de Dios García Kohly, Felipe González Sarrain. The dedicatory above reads «For the Honorable The Secretary of War William H. Taft, with compliments of the Advisory Commission. Havana January 11, 1907.»

The members of the **1907 Crowder Advisory Law Commission** were a *Who is Who in Cuba*.

Francisco Carrera Justiz (university professor of government, political independent), **Blanton Winship** (former US Judge Advocate who had served in the Philippines), **Alfredo Zayas** (1906 Liberal Presidential candidate), **Erasmo Regüeiferos** (Zayista liberal and lawyer), **Juan Gualberto Gómez** (an important Afro-Cuban leader, editor of the Zayista newspaper *El Liberal*), **General Enoch H. Crowder**, presiding, **Otto Schoenrich** (former US Judge in Puerto Rico), **Rafael Montoro** (conservative, former Cuban Minister to England and Germany), **Manuel M.Coronado** (a conservative party leader, owner and editor of *La Discusión*), **Miguel F.Viondi** (*Miguelista* liberal and lawyer), **Juan de Dios García Kohly** (conservative member of the Cuban House of Representatives), **Felipe González Sarraín** (Zayista liberal member of the Cuban House of Representatives).

Cuban Black veterans had kept silent for several years in spite of being practically excluded from public positions. On September 1907, however, they abandoned any hope of redress and, following Black **General Evaristo Estenoz** (*photo on the right below*) they founded the *Independent Party of Color*, non-violently challenging the liberals, who needed their support badly. The second leader in command was **Colonel Pedro Ivonet**, *shown below at left*. The party headquarters were at Amargura 63, Havana. In 1910 an amendment to the electoral law (no parties were to be based on race) made the party illegal. In 1912 they took arms during the government of José Miguel Gómez. Juan Gualberto Gómez is seated, extreme right in the photo above but was not part of the revolt. See page 170.

On May 8, 1907 **Magoon** ordered the taking of a Census in Cuba. It was evident that the election was to be fought on personalities and not ideology.

By the spring of 1908 there were three parties: The *Liberal Miguelistas* (for José Miguel Gómez), the *Liberal Zayaistas* (for Alfredo Zayas) and the *Conservatives* (for Mario García Menocal).

The census results were: **Population**: 2,000,000. **Birth Rate**: 19.8 per thousand (an astronomical figure). Magoon informed Roosevelt that «*the Cuban Army is capable of maintaining order and defeat any insurrection, hence the intervention should be finished.*»

A report by Magoon to the US Congress stated:

«*The bill after the resignation of the Estrada Palma government has been at least $10 million. Had Estrada completed his term (1906-1910) he would have retired more or less at the time our intervention will come to an end.*»

Above: Caricature of Uncle Sam enjoying the occupation; letter from Magoon to Gómez, 1908.

Four scenes from the times of **the second US intervention (1906-1909)**. *Top photo*: *la Cabaña* fortress. In order to minimize their visible presence in Cuba the American troops bivouacked at *Camp Columbia*, west of Havana, instead of the more comfortable *La Cabaña*. *Center*: the paper *La Discusión* continued to hammer on the unresolved issue of the status of *Isla de Pinos*; at right, the American troops retiring from Havana. *Bottom*: Magoon facing *Liborio* (the Cuban people). On his desk, a picture of a Spaniard, signifying his ―*preference*‖ for former Spanish functionaries to occupy government jobs. On his hand he is holding a toad. To *dream of toads*, in the lore of the times, was to engage in unfortunate and miserable adventures.

IV

The War Veterans in Charge:
The Years 1909 to 1921

> «Public virtue cannot exist in a nation without private virtue, which is the only foundation for a republic.»
> JOHN ADAMS, Second US President (1735-1826)

FROM JANUARY 28, 1909 to May 20, 1921, Republican Cuba was under the leadership of two Generals from the War of Independence: José Miguel Gómez (1909-1913) and Aurelio Mario García Menocal (1913-1921).

The inauguration of José Miguel Gómez was a joyful event. Gómez was a very popular General, had been a first-rate governor of Las Villas province and, after the second US intervention, was the man that renewed the normalcy of Cuba being governed by Cubans. Also, history would tell that he was the man who inaugurated the age of *caudillismo* in Cuba, government by a strong man. He was a typical rural chieftain, open, hearty, funny, unassuming, tolerant, accessible and strong.

He found the public treasury at the border of insolvency due to the financial recklessness of Magoon, the US governor during the intervention. He inherited a short term national debt amounting to $12 Million, with only $3 million in the coffers. He had no choice but to ask for the first installment ($5.5 million) of a new *empréstito* (sovereign loan) of $16.5 million that had been authorized by a decree from Governor Magoon. As soon as he obtained these funds, Gómez signed contracts for «*paving and sewering the Cities of Havana and Cienfuegos and began to make arrangements to carry off surface water from the lower to the higher parts of Havana and to excavate a tunnel under the Cabaña fortress to pump sewage to an outlet in deep waters east of El Morro,»* as reported by the *New York Times* on August 23, 1909.

The largest public work undertaken by Gómez, however, was the *Ley del Dragado*, a project to dredge several ports in Cuba. A contract was extended to the *Cuba Ports Company* in February of 1911. *Cuba Ports* in turn emitted bonds and subcontracted the work with many smaller companies. The transactions were so complicated that they left a lot of room for corruption. The government set up a docking tax over every ship entering the port of Havana to pay *Cuba Ports*, as well as a tax on imported coal. Lots of politicians received the benefit of all that lose money, giving rise to the popular saying that «*tiburón se baña pero salpica,*» (the shark —Gómez— takes a bath but gets everybody wet).

By far, the most disrupting incident in the Gómez presidency was the racist insurrection of the *Partido Independiente de Color*, under the leadership of Evaristo Estenoz and Pedro Ivonet. It was repressed by Gómez with unwarranted violence, causing the death of probably 6,000 men. Gómez had to personally talk to US President Taft to prevent the marines to disembark in Cuba to prevent genocide.

On the positive side José Miguel Gómez passed the *Arteaga Law*, making it illegal to pay workers with vouchers or tokens; started a *Cuban National Army*; created the *Academy of History* and the *Academy of Arts and Sciences*; reorganized the *Judicial Branch* and started *telephone service* in the island. His liberal party symbol of the *Rooster and the Plow* attracted the masses like a magnet.

Many of his followers pressured Gómez to seek a re-election in 1912 but he was smart enough to learn the lesson of Estrada Palma. The Liberal Party split into the *Zayistas* (supporting Alfredo Zayas as candidate in 1912) and the defectors, who joined the Conservative Party and formed the *Conjunción Patriótica Nacional*, choosing General Mario García Menocal as a candidate for president under the motto ‚Honesty, Peace and Jobs.' José Miguel Gómez, to his credit, presided over a clean election and Mario García Menocal was elected as president, with Enrique José Varona as his VP. They took possession on May 20, 1913.

Menocal had also been a General during the Independence War of 1895. He fought under Calixto García and distinguished himself in the fall of the town of Las Tunas, where Cubans used heavy artillery for the first time. Menocal was the *aristocratic president* as much as Gómez had been the *down-to-earth president*. His first decree was to abolish Gomez' *Ley del Dragado*. He also secured funds for his government plans by enacting an additional ‚sovereign loan' or *empréstito* for $10 million.

One of Menocal's most important achievements was to create the Cuban currency. Until then, the Spanish, French and US coins and bills circulated in Cuba. Under the leadership of Menocal's Minister of the Treasury, Leopoldo Cancio, the Cuba gold-backed currency —no bills, only coins— with the motto *patria y libertad*, was born in 1917.

The second most important achievement of Menocal was the successful rejection of the joint claim of France, Germany and the UK for damages sustained during the Cuban War of Independence. Under the leadership of Cosme de la Torriente the courts decided that it was questionable whether they had authority to review the consequences of military operations. Much like the claims of US Naval Officers and Seamen arising from the destruction of the *USS Maine* on February 15, 1898 in the harbor of Havana, the courts reasoned that, had they had the authority, the losses were probably «*justifiable under the rules and usages of war.*»

In 1916 Menocal decided to seek re-election. Liberals united under the support of José Miguel Gómez for the candidacy Zayas-Mendieta for president and VP. Menocal presented his candidature as Menocal-Núñez for president and VP.

The stubborn and conceited clique loyal to Menocal did not hesitate to cause problems. They attempted to improve their chances at the polls by altering the results in their favor in what was called the *cambiazo* (big change); it led to numerous legal claims that culminated in the revolt of the *Chambelona*. Gómez and other chiefs took over Oriente and Camagüey provinces.

The US declared that no insurgent government would be recognized; that declaration settled the situation. After the American declaration, the rebels were imprisoned by the same armed forces that had supported them. Gómez and his lieutenants Alfredo Zayas and Enrique Loynaz del Castillo surrendered in the town of Caicaje, in the Las Villas province, on March 9, 1917. They went down in history as the rebels of the ,*Little War of 1917*.` It was said that the US had covertly provided military support to Menocal from the Guantánamo Naval Base.

Menocal was re-elected and held a census that showed a total population of 2,889,004 people, an increase of over 80 percent in less than 20 years.

In a way, Menocal's government was blessed with the catastrophe of WWI. The war brought with it skyrocketing prices of sugar and a *Dance of the Millions* in Cuba. With the average production cost of three cents a pound, sugar was sold by the Menocal government for over 22 cents; fresh exports reached almost one billion dollars in 1920. Cuba, in 1920, was probably the richest country in the world on a *per capita* basis.

The bubble burst later that same year when overproduction in Cuba found no buyers for sugar even at about four cents a pound. Cuban settlers and landowners lost their properties as they were unable to repay the loans granted during the boom. Cuban banks, suffering a severe liquidity crisis and lacking the capital to face the losses of so many sugar companies —with few exceptions— had to declare themselves bankrupt and finish their operations. Most Cuban banks disappeared overnight; having served 70% of the Cuban economy in 1918 they reduced their participation to 6.5% in 1921.

Menocal called for new elections in 1920. The Liberals were divided once more after some insisted that Gómez should again be the candidate. Alfredo Zayas broke ranks and founded the *Partido Popular*; it soon became known as the *Par- tido de los Cuatro Gatos*. Zayas, a shrewd man, founded the *Liga Nacional* with the *Partido Conservador* and won the elections. It is fair to add that during his presidency Menocal created several valuable institutions in Cuba. He founded the first Cuban public *Normales Nacionales* (Teacher Schools) in Havana,

Las Villas and Oriente provinces. Prior to that, the only school for teachers in Cuba had been the *Escuela Normal de Maestros de Cuba,* founded by the Padres Escolapios in Guanabacoa, on November 19, 1857. Menocal also founded the *Preventorio Martí* for destitute and abandoned children in Cojimar and the *Calixto García Hospital* in Havana.

In spite of violence and fraud during the 1920 elections, Menocal dutifully yielded the presidency of Cuba to Alfredo Zayas on May 20, 1921. This interrupted briefly the succession of military veterans turned presidents and produced the first non-military presidency in Cuba.

Two great apolitical Cubans:
Manuel Sanguily and
Enrique José Varona

A cartoon in 1909 shows Cuban politicians running after stealing everything in sight, even the clothes of the Republic, while the founding fathers come out of their resting places: Céspedes, Maceo, Máximo Gómez and José Martí.

When the second American intervention ended, Cuba was somewhat different than what it was in 1906. The population had grown significantly, partly because the immigration of over 200,000 Spaniards —mostly from Galicia and Asturias. Havana had grown by 60,000 inhabitants; the suburb of *El Vedado* had been integrated into the city; taxis were now on the streets, as well as *guaguas* (buses); there were *serenos* like in Madrid (night watchmen), *vitrolas* (phonographs) and numerous *tiendas* for ladies (dress shops).

Not everything had been updated, however. Land was difficult to buy because the property records were not clear; people in the countryside lived in *bohios* (palm huts); the squatters abounded, something that had defied the best intentions of Magoon.

Lots of prime property were in the hands of foreigners —mostly Americans and Spanish. Almost 25% of Cuba's residents had been born in Spain and no one knew where their loyalties resided. The chief newspaper was *El Diario de la Marina*, owned and run by an outstanding and honest businessman, **Nicolás Rivero (1849-1919)**, a Spaniard whose journalistic merit was generally dictated by his loyalty to Cuba, his new country, and its best interests.

The American presence was notable, almost 7,000 permanent residents, mostly land-owners, investors and skilled technicians. Most of them thought Cuba's future would be eventually to join the US. The social center for Americans was the *American Club*, or the *Hotel Miramar*, at *Prado Avenue*.

Photos above, left: **Hotel Miramar**, Havana, 1923. *Right*: the **American Club** in Havana.

Photo above: the *New York Tribune* on the day the American occupation ended. It brought pictures of **José Miguel Gómez**, the new President and his wife América Arias, as well as exterior and interior photos of the presidential palace. On the bottom of the page, photos of the four Gómez children, including (*bottom right*) a photo of Miguel Mariano Gómez, future President of Cuba.

In 1909, **most taxes in Cuba were paid by foreigners**, either by their commercial businesses or by their industries. 85% of the government income came from duties on imported goods, mostly manufactured in the US. During that year 170 sugar mills were grinding; 34% of these belonged to Americans, 35% to Spaniards and 31% to Cubans. Many houses, industrial buildings, factories, mills and lands in Cuba were mortgaged —they had to be to get the republic started— and those mortgages were in the hands of American banks.

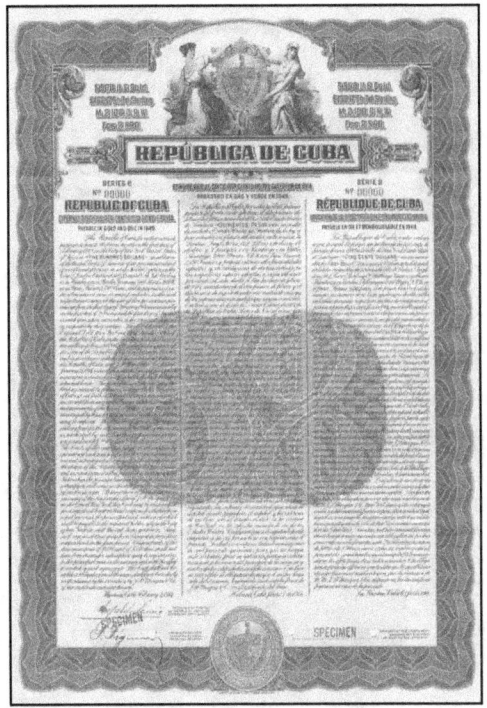

Photos above, top to bottom: a Cuban Republican Bond in 1917, signed by Leopoldo Cancio and Fernando Figueredo Socarrás; Nicolás Rivero, director of the *Diario de la Marina*; a sugar mill in 1910.

A main irritant in Cuban-American relations was **the status of *Isla de Pinos***. Hundreds of Americans had settled there — 25% of its population— and had brought prosperity to the island. Land prices had gone up substantially —roughly 175% by some accounts. Yet Cubans insisted the island was theirs by virtue of its proximity and historical roots. American politicians kept comparing *Isla de Pinos* to *Vieques* and *Puerto Rico*, which were considered legitimate conquests from Spain during the *Hispano-Cuban-American War*. In 1907 the US Supreme Court had decided that **the island belonged to Cuba**, yet it would not be until 1925 that the US Senate recognized that ruling. Few Americans stayed in the island under the Cuban flag.

Photos above: two views of the landscape of the island; Americans living in *Isla de Pinos* in 1922.

On November 14, 1908 **José Miguel Gómez** was elected President of Cuba and **Alfredo Zayas** became his VP. **Magoon**'s last decree was to assign a lifetime pension to Gevoveva Estrada of $5,000 per year, and $50 per month for each of Estrada Palma's children. **Tomás Estrada Palma** had died on Nov 4, 1908. On the left one of **Gómez** ads; on the right, Cubans paid homage to its first president.

The cabinet of **José Miguel Gómez** was composed of members of the *Liberal Party*. It included: **Marcelino Diaz de Villegas**, Secretary of the Treasury; **Luis Octavio Divine**, Secretary of Justice; **Matías Duque**, Secretary of Health; **Nicolas Alberdi**, Interior Minister; **Benito Lagueruela**, Minister of Public Works; **Calixto García Vélez**, Secretary of State (son of Calixto García Iñiguez); **Ortelio Foyo**, Secretary of Agriculture and the writer **Ramón Meza**, Secretary of Public Instruction.

In 1908 the garment workers, the skilled tobacco workers and all port and maritime workers went on strike asking to be **paid in dollars** and not in Spanish pesetas since their products and services were paid by customers using US currency.

The phenomenon of a **multitude of small parties** did not abate. In 1908 the citizens in Cuba, aside from the *Liberal Miguelista*, the *Liberal Zayaista* and the *Conservative Party*, could vote for the *Partido Legión Municipal*, the *Coalición Independiente*, the *Partido Obrero Socialista*, the *Independientes Baracoanos o* la *Agrupación Independiente de Color*.

In the national elections of November 14, 1908, the *Liberals* elected, not only Gómez and Zayas (who had joined forces, Gómez for president, Zayas for VP) but also all twenty-four senators, and fifty-one representatives (losing only thirty-two), on a vote of 201,199 to 130,256. The losers were Mario García Menocal and his Vice-Presidential candidate Rafael Montoro.

Photos: Tobacco workers in 1908 and a cartoon published by *El Diario de la Marina* in 1909, entitled **Los Partidos Acosan al Pueblo** (the Parties harrass the people).

For many Cubans, young and old, living in Cuba during the years of **José Miguel Gómez** marked the best times of their lives.

El Vedado was the center of social life in Havana. The city had become very friendly to businesses and youngsters. Tourists began to pour in by the hundreds. Everyone had time for a *siesta*. Women were gaining in status and importance. Obispo Street was crowded with shoppers every afternoon. International actors were entertaining in half a dozen good theaters in Havana, some priced very reasonably. Dancing was popular at very many attractive clubs catering to all income levels. *Art nouveau* and *Art Gaudí* were becoming the standards for Cuban middle and high class architecture. Ranch houses coexisted with bohios in the countryside and both used *mosquiteros* to keep away the bothersome insects. Yellow fever had been eradicated. It seemed that even *guajiros* were happy.

Food habits were slowly changing from the Spanish *potages* to American *bistés*. Many Cubans skipped breakfast. Ladies began to sport thinner and thinner silhouettes. People with money were acquiring small farms outside the big cities and *Santiago de las Vegas* became an important weekend destination for *habaneros*. Many Cubans noticed that there were fewer and fewer vagrants in the streets. Not having an ambition to succeed became embarrassing. Capital was in the hands of the Americans and the Spaniards were the proprietors of almost everything in sight, but the Cubans were pleased they were once again the masters of their own destiny.

No country in the Caribbean was happier and had a nicer president than Cuba. For several years nobody paid any attention to politicians. Following a line that the Spaniards were using in 1812 to support the liberal *Cádiz Constitution* everybody was saying... ¡Qué viva la Pepa! (Long live *Pepa*! —i.e., the Cádiz Constitution).

Photo above: José Miguel Gómez and his wife America Arias as they left the Chapel of los *Escolapios de Guanabacoa* in 1909.

Above, a US caricature that simply said:
Can he play alone?

On January 29, 1909 **The Havana Post**, an English language newspaper published in Havana since the days of the first **US intervention**, declared in its editorial: «*The work of Magoon has been far-reaching and all embracing. Even considering the cost of the intervention, it has nourished two blades of grass in Cuba where but one had grown before.*»

Commenting on the fact that **José Miguez Gómez** was notorious for his loose hand with government funds, but that he shared his boot with his friends, Cubans began to refer to him as «el *Tiburón se Baña pero Salpica*» (the shark splashes while it bathes.)

On March 4, 1909, **William Howard Taft (1857-1930)** became the 27th President of the US. He inaugurated a new approach for the application of the Platt Amendment. From then on instead of *intervention* the new US policy would be *interference* in the government of Cuba.

El chino de la charada

1 — CABALLO
2 — MARIPOSA
3 — MARINERO
4 — GATO BOCA
5 — MONJA
6 — JICOTEA
7 — CARACOL
8 — MUERTO
9 — ELEFANTE
10 — PESCADO GRANDE
11 — GALLO
12 — RAMERA
13 — PAVO REAL
14 — GATO TIGRE
15 — PERRO
16 — TORO
17 — LUNA
18 — PESCADO CHICO
19 — LOMBRIZ
20 — GATO FINO
21 — MAJÁ
22 — SAPO
23 — VAPOR
24 — PALOMA
25 — PIEDRA FINA
26 — ANGUILA
27 — AVISPA
28 — CHIVO
29 — RATÓN
30 — CAMARÓN
31 — VENADO
32 — COCHINO
33 — TIÑOSA
34 — MONO
35 — ARAÑA
36 — CACHIMBA

One of the first acts of José Miguel Gómez as President was to reinstate the **Cuban lottery**; it had existed since 1812 but had been discontinued by Brooke and Wood during the US intervention and by Estrada Palma later on. The lottery was the means to appease the runaway political and economic ambitions of his followers. The *Renta de la Lotería* produced the lottery tickets and organized the lottery drawings. The *Colecturías* handled the cash receipts, set up the retail commissions and distributed the tickets. Both institutions were sources of corruption in Cuba. The illegal cash flow they produced rewarded the loyal followers of the President in charge and bought the silence of his opponents. *Diagram on top:* the *Charada China* (a numbers game), an illegal lottery piggyback that also produced an abundance of illegal cash.

During the government of José Miguel Gómez (28 January 1909 to 20 May 1913) the racial situation in Cuba came to the forefront. **Generoso Campos Marquetti** (*photo at right*), a Black member of the Liberal Party, wrote a newspaper article saying «*Blacks have found jobs as porters, coachmen, servants and for manual positions in the post office and customs but when an important visitor shows up there are no Blacks in the festivities or among the escorts.*» It looked as if peace had changed the perspective on Blacks. 86,000 Blacks had died in the Wars of Independence and yet, when the Cuban Armies were demobilized, the only institution where Blacks had registered important advances disappeared and with them the ranks, political positions and their *modus vivendi*.

By 1910, the *Independent Party of Color*, founded in 1907, counted among its members 12 Black Generals and 30 Black Colonels from the War of 1895. Nevertheless it found its political development blocked by the February 1910 **Morúa Law**, which banned political parties based on race or religion. **Gen Evaristo Estenoz** reacted with alarming belligerence threatening to organize armed resistance to provoke a new American intervention that would topple the Gómez government.

Above: A photo taken in Costa Rica in 1892. Senate President Martín Morúa is sitting first on the left. Standing, left to right: Antonio Collazo, Flor Crombet, Antonio Maceo, Agustín Cebreco and José Barrenqui. Left to Morúa are Rojas, Castelló, Peña and José Rogelio Castillo, who had a remarkable likeness to José Martí.

Race relations in Cuba during the first years of Republican life were difficult to analyze. Many families, particularly in the upper classes, had at least some mulatto blood due to the inevitable relations between slave owners and slave women. Whites were predominantly in the **professions** (doctors, lawyers, architects, managers, teachers) and Blacks in the **crafts and trades** (dressmakers, construction workers, soldiers, policemen, tailors, musicians, barbers, ebanists, domestic servants). Long freed blacks had more access to classical white jobs than recently freed blacks.

Criollo families, to a certain extent, inherited the apprehension and anxiety experienced by their ascendants after the slave revolts in Haiti. They were also heirs to a certain prejudice against blacks by those ancestors who knew of the suffering of their forefathers at the hand of the Black *mambises* during the three wars of independence. Because of these factors, **Blacks and White seldom mixed** socially after the inauguration of the Republic, except possibly during the popular sport of *cock-fighting*.

During the US occupation the authorities banned all public religious ceremonies. Catholics workshipped inside their churches. Blacks, having no such established refuges, began to bring their religion to the same sanctuaries; syncretism was popularized and reinforced among both Blacks and Whites, to the dismay of newly arrived Spaniards and the hierarchy of the Catholic Church.

By and large, however, racial prejudice was not strong in Cuba. In fact, after the flood of new Spanish immigrants in the first years of the Republic, the racial intolerance increased, much to the surprise of families of Spanish origins that had been in Cuba for several generations.

Above: two photos of Black and White *mambises* fighting together in the 1895 Cuban War of Independence.

On February 11, 1910, **Martín Morúa Delgado**, Cuban Senate President, added an appendix to Article 17 of the Cuban Electoral Law that stated: «*No group formed exclusively by individuals of one race or color, or by individuals in a class by reason of birth, wealth or professional title, shall be considered in any case a political party or an independent group.*» It was passed by an ample majority on both chambers of the legislature. The only objection was presented by **Salvador Cisneros Betancourt** who stated for the record: «*Yo digo al señor Morúa y llamo la atención, que lo mejor es no menear ese caldo.*» (I dare say to Mr. Morúa, hoping this will come to his attention... it's best not to stir this soup.) Morúa died on April 28, 1910, barely ten weeks after his famous law went into effect.

Both of these statements were related to the founding of the *Partido Independiente de Color* on August 7, 1907 by **Evaristo Estenoz Corominas (187?-1912)**, a former assistant to General Quintín Bandera; **Pedro Ivonet Dofourt (1860-1912)**, former General of the 1895 War of Independence, and a group of Blacks that had served in the Mambí army. The party's intention was to advocate for Black Cubans' equal participation in government and equal rights as citizens.

From 1910 to 1912 **Evaristo Estenoz** and **Pedro Ivonnet** were made prisoners, judged and found innocent of insubordination several times. In May 1912 they led an uprising that involved most of Cuba, particularly the Oriente province. Many newspapers were calling it the **Race War** or **La Guerrita de los Negros**, terms that white Cubans had dreaded for a century. Havana was overwhelmed by panic. The Cuban Army did a search and destroy operation on the Independents of Color, killing over 6,000 men and effectively disbanding the party. Both Estenoz (June 27, 1912) and Ivonet (July 16, 1912) were killed during the war; both under suspicious circumstances.

Evidently Evaristo Estenoz had quickly lost control of the situation. When the US Marines went ashore in Guantanamo on June 2. the Cuban Army, feeling liberated from having to protect civilians and property, took to the fields with vengeance; there were indiscriminate killings and widespread abuses and lynchings of Black rebels. By midsummer the leaders of the insurrection were dead and their followers (upwards of 6,000) killed or disbanded. Estenoz died on June 27, near *Alto Songo*, Oriente. The circumstances of the death of Ivonet were never known.

Photos above: a cartoon showing Blacks facing a Cuban soldier; the front page of *La Política Cómica*, a 1912 newspaper in Havana; and the autopsy of Pedro Ivonnet, who was probably assassinated near *El Caney* on July 16.

Other events captured the attention of the Cubans once the **Race War** was over. On February 1913, the Cuban ambassador to Mexico, **Manuel Márquez Sterling**, with the support of President José Miguel Gómez, tried in vain to save the life of President **Francisco I. Madero** and his Vice President **José Pino Suárez**, both prisoners in the National Palace during the initial days of the Mexican Revolution. This noble and humane act, undertaken by Márquez Sterling in his personal capacity, constituted one of the most generous deeds in the convulsive history of Latin America.

Cuba's Minister of State, Manuel Sanguily, had informed Washington of Cuba's reluctance to acknowledge the government of General Victoriano Huerta. Brasil, Chile and Argentina followed the example of Cuba within a few days. Madero's parents, friends of Márquez Sterling, had secured refuge in the Japanese legation in Mexico City and begged Márquez Sterling to intercede for the lives of both of their sons, Francisco, the President and Gustavo, a Member of Congress; they extended their appeal to the life of Ma- dero's Vice President, José Pino Suarez.

Madero had assumed the presidency of Mexico 15 months before, after leading the movement that ended the three decades of dictatorship of General **Porfirio Díaz**. At the time, the diplomatic corps was largely hostile or indifferent to Madero. President José Miguel Gómez placed a Cuban Naval ship in Veracruz, the *Cuba*, ready to transport Madero, his brothers and Pino Suárez to Cuba.

Unknown to Madero, Victoriano Huerta had conspired with Félix Díaz, a nephew of Porfirio, to siege *la Ciudadela*, a flea market in Mexico City where many citizens loyal to Madero had taken refuge; it became known as *La Decena Trágica* (the ten tragic days).

After Márquez was told on February 19 that the life of Madero was not in peril and that he would depart that very same night towards Veracruz, Marquez Sterling received from Madero a photo inscribed «*To my fine friend Manuel Marquez Sterling, a proof of my esteem and gratitude.*» That same night Madero and Pino were murdered.

Photos above: Francisco Madero, President of Mexico, Manuel Márquez Sterling, Cuban Ambassador and Porfirio Díaz, Mexico's President at the time the Mexican Revolution exploded.

In 1911 the sculptor Domenico Boni was selected to design and execute the monument to General Antonio Maceo at the place where the *Queen's Battery* had been located during Spanish colonial times.

The monument was done in granite with all its sculptures in bronze. An equestrian statue crowns a tall column, with four key moments in the life of General Maceo remembered in *bas-reliefs* on all four sides: the battles of Cacaragícara, *La Indiana, Mangos de Megía*, and the *Protest of Baraguá*,

On the base of the monument there is a *bas-relief* of Mariana Grajales, Maceo's mother. On the four angles of the base there are allegorical figures representing *Action*, *Thought*, *Justice* and *Law*. Maceo is facing the city (not facing the sea as would correspond to a monument to honor a foreigner, as is the case for the Máximo Gómez statue), with his horse standing on its two hind legs (since Maceo was killed in action, according to equestrian statuary protocol). The monument was inaugurated in 1916.

Photos: The monuments, its equestrian figure, the *bas-relief* of Maceo's mother blessing her son; sculptural details.

The greatest success of the government of **José Miguel Gómez (1858-1921)** was its defense of Cuban sovereignty, as was shown during the *Race War* of 1912 when he forcefully complained about US troops coming ashore. He respected the many excesses of the opposition press, as well as all expressions of the people's freedoms. For the first time in Cuba he opened public positions for his political rivals the conservatives, and met with his opponents both in the *Veteran Crisis* and the *Race War*.

He was not careful with corruption and had the unfortunate idea of restarting the dreadful **lottery**. He was also accused of looking away after several acts of political violence were perpetrated by the leaders of the Army and the Rural Guard.

By and large, nevertheless, Cubans had a great opinion of José Miguel Gómez, particularly when he refused to run for reelection and retired quietly after his term.

He died on June 13, 1921, at a room in the *Plaza Hotel* in New York.

One of the most extraordinary characters during the presidency of José Miguel Gómez was **José López Rodríguez**, aka **Pote (1862-1921).** *See picture above left*. He immigrated to Cuba from Spain in 1880 and in time married **Ana Luisa Serrano**, a widow who owned *La Moderna Poesía*, the best bookstore in Havana. He became a serious *independentista* and during the 1910's he financed the career of José Miguel Gómez. Eventually he got the right to print all Cuban stamps and lottery tickets. He got control of the *Banco Nacional de Cuba* and all its 87 branches. The market slump of 1920 broke him and he ended taking his life in his luxurious mansion of *El Vedado*.

During the government of José Miguel Gómez, **Enrique José Piñeyro y Barry (1839-1911)** died in Paris. He was a professional Cuban critic, lawyer, journalist, professor and noted Latinist, second only to Domingo del Monte, founder of literary criticism in Cuba. He was a disciple of José de la Luz y Caballero at the *Colegio San Salvador*. At sixteen he translated a text by Victor Hugo and published it in *Brisas de Cuba* in 1856. In 1863 he obtained a Bachelor of Jurisprudence at the *University of Havana*. Shortly thereafter he was vice-director of the *Colegio El Salvador*. When the War of 1868 broke out Piñeyro went to the United States to join the separatists. In this, his first exile, he acted as secretary of Morales Lemus at the legation of Cuba and directed the magazines *La Revolution* and *New World*.

Just like José Martí had done, Enrique Piñeyro played the dual role of intellectual and man of action in favor of Cuban independence. In between wars he wrote a biography of *General San Martín* (1870), as well as *Men and Glory of America*. During the War of 1895 he travelled through South America collecting funds for the war in Cuba. He was sentenced to death *in absentia* by the colonial government in Cuba. Thanks to his ample culture and high spirits, his greatest interest and contribution to his country was the dissemination of knowledge and understanding of Cuba in Europe. He died in Paris at age 71 and is buried at the *Père Lachaise* Cemetery.

Photos: Enrique Piñeyro and his monument at *Père Lachaise* Cemetery in Paris.

The four great educators of the first years of republican life in Cuba were **Enrique José Varona (1849-1933)**, **Arturo Montori (1878-1941)**, **Ramiro Guerra (1880-1970)** and **María Luisa Dolz (1854- 1928)**.

In 1914, **Enrique José Varona** became Cuba's VP and immediately a climate of raised expectations for educational reforms invaded all schools in the island. Varona launched a plan to reform the curriculum by emphasizing the need to stimulate children's imagination, decrease the emphasis on rote memorization, raise the study of nature and natural history, and promote pride in one's self, home and country.

Prior to Varona, in spite of efforts by Estrada Palma and José Miguel Gómez, the educational system still had many shortcomings: education funds were drawn off for alternate purposes, new schools were not being built, existing schools were overcrowded, few books and teaching resources were available, and many school had an unhealthful environment: no playgrounds, no running water, no bathroom facilities. Others were located too close to distracting factories, bars or in bad neigh- borhoods. In many instances teachers had to pay for materials, look out after children in their free time, provide food to their pupils out of their own pockets and close windows to prevent noise to interrupt the lessons.

Photos above: **Enrique José Varona** and **Maria Luisa Dolz**.

Varona, with **Arturo Montori**, and **Ramiro Guerra**, both directors of the *Escuela Normal de Maestros de la Habana*, made great progress getting the government to open schools and provide them with resources. By 1925 the number of schools in Cuba had increased by 110% compared to the number of schools that existed in 1909. Besides offering a traditional curriculum of arts and sciences, the new schools' ultimate goal was to provide an environment in which students learned to be both good and illustrated men and women and good citizens.

María Luisa Dolz in the late 1800s was the «*first woman to link educational reform with nationalism and feminism,*» believing education of women was key to righting social injustices. Her school (*Colegio Isabel la Católica*), reserved for girls, was an institution com- mitted to the study of scientific disciplines that would prepare her students to assume professional careers outside the home.

Arturo Montori was an educator, literary critic, and the Chair of Spanish and Cuban Literature in Havana's *Normal School for Teachers*, of which he came to be the principal. He was a precursor of the so-called —*New School*‖ and developer of lay teaching. He wrote textbooks, some in collaboration with Ramiro Guerra; he directed the *Cuba Pedagógica Journal* (Pedagogical Cuba) as well as the *Revista Bimestre Cubana* (Cuban Bimonthly Journal).

Photos above: Young Ramiro Guerra; the students of the *Colegio Cubano Arturo Montori* on a gala to commemorate Martí's birthday in 1936.

The 1912 elections were very peaceful. José Miguel Gómez attempted to retain control of his party against the claims of his Liberal rival, Alfredo Zayas but when Zayas won the resulting power struggle for the soul of the *Liberal Party*, the very popular Gómez proclaimed his support for Mario García Menocal, the *Con- servative Party* candidate. The alliance Gómez-Menocal became known as the **Conjunción Pa- triótica**. Menocal, with Enrique José Varona as Vice, easily defeated Zayas, whose party was hopelessly split. Menocal received 194,504 votes; Alfredo Zayas 180,640. A few days later Joseph Woodrow Wilson was elected President of the US. *Photo at left*: The official Menocal presidential portrait.

Photo above: On May 20, 1913, after a twenty one gun salute fired by the batteries of the fortress of *La Cabana*, Menocal assumed the government of the nation; it was the first time the handover was done from a Cuban to a Cuban. Moments later Menocal and Gómez went to the palace balcony that faces the *Plaza de Armas* and greeted the audience gathered there. The troops presented arms and the band played the National Anthem.

A new **Havana Railroad Central Station** was inaugurated on November 30, 1912, at the old track of land of the *Havana Arsenal*, limited by Egido, Desamparados, Factoría and Esperanza Streets. The trains of *Ferrocarriles Unidos*, *Havana Central* and *Ferrocarril del Oeste* began to use the Station. The old *Estación de Villanueva* was to be demolished for a future construction of a *National Capitol*. The old *Estación de Cristina* was to be closed. The inauguration closed a scandalous financial maneuver —exchange of land at the abandoned *Arsenal* for prime land where the *Villanueva Station* was located— in which lots of politicians made enormous and illegal profits.

Menocal instantly became the darling of the American press, the US presidency and the US Department of State. He was handsome, a graduate of *Cornell*, spoke accent-free English, had charisma and was friendly to the US. The conservatives began to fire hundreds of public employees loyal to the *Liberal Party*. Menocal responded to the critics by pardoning hundreds of prisoners jailed during the *Race War*, which was a very popular decision.

Mario García Menocal was 46 when he was elected to the presidency of Cuba. He had managed the *Central Chaparra* in *Las Tunas* (property of the *Cuban American Sugar Company*); under his leadership it had produced 70,000 tons of sugar, comparable to the total crop by all Cuban mills in the 1850s; yet the yield of the *Chaparra* was less than 8% (weight of sugar per weight of came milled), one of the lowest in Cuba. It was said that when Menocal became president he already had $1 million in the bank but, when he retired, he had $40.

Photos above: Central Chaparra in 1909; what is left of *Central Chaparra* in 2010. Shown also is a token used by the *Central Chaparra* (like all other sugar mills) as currency to pay wages, redimable only at the stores of the company.

Menocal was a veteran, an engineer, a manager and a businessman. That was all the people in Cuba wanted to know to elect him as president; he was the man Cubans desperately needed.

He started his first term with very popular and reasonable decisions: repudiated the contract that José Miguel Gómez had signed with the **Cuban Ports Company**; established compulsory workmen compensation insurance; launched an effective monetary policy that placed the dollar on a par to the Cuban peso; encouraged high quality immigration of professionals and technicians.

Two other measures, however, were harmful to the Cuban economy since they were traditional sources of corruption: the reestablishment of the lottery and requests for the additional *empréstitos* (sovereign loans) from **J.P. Morgan**.

Drawing, clockwise from top left: J.P. Morgan and his Cuban businesses; *Cuban Ports Company* and *Cuban American Sugar Company* bonds.

During Menocal's presidency the Secretary of Treasury, **Dr. Leopoldo Cancio Luna (1851-1927)**, prepared Cuba for the minting of its own currency. It became law on September of 1915, bringing a lot of new prosperity to Cuba. He had been a student at the *El Salvador School* of **José de la Luz y Caballero**, graduated from the *University of Havana* and was elected to the Madrid Cortes in 1879. He served under **John R. Brooke** and **Leonard Wood**, and with **Emilio Nuñez** was one of the founders of the *Conservative Party*.

Three magnificent buildings were finished in Havana during the presidency of *Mario García Menocal*: the **Palacio del Centro Gallego**, finished in 1914 at a cost of $3 million (*top left*); the **Palacio del Centro Asturiano**, finished in 1920 at a cost of $2.5 million (*top right*); and the **Palacio Presidencial**, finished in 1920 at a cost of $3.7 million (*at the bottom*).

In January 1916 Mario García Menocal announced his candidature for a second term. **Enrique Loynaz del Castillo** sent him a telegram like the one he had sent to Estrada Palma (see page 145), advising that it was not fair to «*seek power from the seat of power*.» Menocal did not pay attention. Menocal ran as President with Emilio Nuñez as VP. On the Liberal side Alfredo Zayas became the presidential candidate with Carlos Mendieta for VP. In the 1932 photo at right Enrique with his daughter Dulce María in the patio of their residence at 19 and E Street in *El Vedado*.

The political stability of Cuba during the presidency of *Menocal* depended on the world price of sugar more than in any other period of Cuban history. In **November 1918** sugar sold for 7.28 ₡ a pound; in **March 1920** for 13.54 ₡ a pound; in **April 1920** for 19.56 ₡ a pound; in **May 1920** for 22.51 ₡ a pound; in **June 1920** for 20.31 ₡ a pound; in **July 1920** for 18.56 ₡ a pound; in **September 1920** for 10.78 ₡ a pound; in **October 1920** for 9 ₡ a pound; in **December 1920** for 3.70 ₡ a pound. The times when the sugar was on the upswing became known as the —*Danza de los Millones*‖ .

The 1916 elections were passionate, violent and corrupt. Money flew excessively from both parties. Even the press took sides: For the Liberals (the party of Zayas), el **Heraldo de Cuba**, **La Nación** and **El Triunfo**. For the *Conservatives* (the party of Menocal) were **El Día**, **El Comercio**, **La Discusión** y el **Diario de la Marina**. (its building is shown at right). There were meetings every day. The official songs were la **Conga**, for the *Conservatives* and la **Chambelona** for the *Liberals*. The government of Menocal intercepted and changed many ballots and people called it the -*cambiazo*. Menocal was then re-elected to a second term.

On 12 February of 1917 General **José Miguel Gómez** and many of his liberal followers took up arms in several provinces. The affair was known as the *Cuartelazo de Febrero* or the **Chambelona Uprising** because of the popular liberal song in vogue at the time. US President Wilson made it clear that no revolutionary government would be recognized by the US government. American troops landed in Santiago, Manzanillo, Nuevitas and other locations. On March 7, in a town of Santa Clara called *Caicaje*, Gómez was surrounded by the official army and surrendered; 30 days later there were no rebels in the countryside. *On the right*, a 1936 stamp honoring José Miguel Gómez.

The re-election of a president, once more, became the cause for a civil war in Cuba. Unlike the 1906 rebellion, this time most of the rebels were veterans of the War of 1895. In Havana the rebels tried to take **Camp Columbia** (*photos above and below in 1916*) the military camp that the Americans had set up in 1898 in *Los Quemados* in Marianao, near Havana. The camp had been the central headquarters of Major General **Fitzhugh Lee (1835-1905)**, nephew of Confederate General Robert E. Lee and governor of Havana during 1899 to 1902.

In the midst of the liberal rebellion of 1917 **Dr. Alfredo Zayas** was returning by train to Havana from Santa Clara. When the conductor advised him of the uprising in Camagüey he asked for the train to stop at a non-scheduled place called *Palatino*, near Havana, and took refuge at *Las Delicias*, the home of **Rosalía Abreu (1862-1930)**, sister of Marta Abreu, the great benefactor of Santa Clara. Rosalía was famous for her extraordinary collection of monkeys and her devotion to the anthropological study of their behavior. When she died her collection was acquired by the *Carnegie Institution*. Her photo is at right.

The disfunctionality of political parties in Cuba became evident when in 1920 a *Liberal* (Alfredo Zayas) became the *Conservative* Party candidate and a *Conservative* (Miguel Arango) became the *Liberal Party* VP candidate. In many ways the 1920 elections were **a battle for control of the Cuban sugar industry**.

The *Cuban-American Sugar Company* (property of the *House of Morgan* and *Havemeyer Sugar*), and General Crowder favored Menocal and his candidate Alfredo Zayas, i.e., the *Conservative- Popular alliance*. The *Cuba Cane Corporation* favored the Gómez- Arango Liberal candidacy since the VP candidate was part owner of *Cuba Cane*, an affiliate of the powerful *Czarnikow-Rionda Group*.

«*The sugar industry depended on slavery for its prosperity and when the slavery ended the sugar barons were unable to save it,*» commented Herminio Portell Vilá in 1923, adding « *Sugar has been Cuba's great blessing and curse all at once.*»

During the last years of the 19th century there was a dramatic transformation of the Cuban sugar industry. An intermediate class of planters emerged as slavery ended; it was often referred to as the **colonos**. They basically contracted to plant, cultivate, harvest and then deliver the cut cane to the mills, or **Centrales**, which eventually became huge complexes. The **Zafra** months of November to April, the dry season, featured full employment for cane laborers; it was followed by the **tiempo muerto**, the rainy season of May through October, when there was nothing to do on the cane fields. This was the sad reality of sugar industry in Cuba at the turn of the century.

HARVESTING SUGAR-CANE IN CUBA.

To make matters worse, the independence war seriously damaged the sugar industry. The fields were blighted; the pastures, barren; and the sugar cane mostly burned. The rich sugar provinces of Havana and Matanzas were cultivating less than one-half of the area in 1899 than they had before the war; from 1,400,000 total acres under cultivation in 1895, only some 900,000 acres returned to production when Cuba became independent.

In Pinar del Río, out of 70 sugar mills before the war only 7 survived. In Las Villas, 332 sugar mills had been reduced to 73. Altogether, of the 1,100 sugar mills registered in Cuba in 1894, only 207 were ready to start the harvest in 1898. Cuban farmers had to sell their lands to foreign investors, who found land prices to their liking.

Sketch above: Harvesting sugar in Cuba in 1895.

In 1901, for instance, *United Fruit* was able to purchase 200,000 acres of land in Oriente at $1 per acre. The *Cuban American Sugar Company* paid a similar price for 70,000 acres of land for the *Chaparra Sugar Mill* it established in Oriente Province. *Milton Hershey* also purchased land at those prices to build a sugar factory that would supply his Pennsylvania-based chocolate empire.

To compound things, many of these companies were given special dispensations to import *braceros* (workers) that would earn less than Cuban workers. So was the case with *United Fruit Company* in 1912; most of these immigrant workers would return to their countries after the *zafra*, but many stayed; with their low wages they displaced Cuban workers across the entire island. Only with the abrogation of the *Platt Amendment* in 1934, Americans began a steady withdrawal from Cuba's sugar industry, and the industry returned to Cuban hands once more, as a modest number of wealthy Cubans bought the American properties.

Photos: Braceros cutting sugar cane in Oriente; vignette from a sugar stock certificate showing two women sitting on both sides of a sugar cane plant.

Menocal's motto during his campaign was —**Honradez, Paz y Trabajo**. He fulfilled his promises during his first period but after his reelection in 1918 (which coincided with the convulsion of WWI), he unquestionably failed on all his promises. By then his inner circle was composed mostly of his social friends, some war companions and old enemies of Estrada Palma's *Moderate Party*. They were not the best and most capable administrators he could find. The war produced the *Danza de los Millones*, a period of high sugar prices that was not properly controlled. After February 1917 he had to contend with very low sugar prices and the presence of US General Crowder looking over his shoulders in the style of a third intervention.

Among the best legislation passed during the government of Mario García Menocal were: the **Divorce Law**, a great effort for a conservative party; the **Electoral Law**, also known as the Crowder Electoral Code; the educational laws creating the **Schools for teachers** (*Normales del Maestro*); the **Law of National Defense**, which created for the first time a Cuban Currency; the **Commercial Tax Laws**; the **Law of Mortgage Moratorium**, which prevented an economic collapse, and the so called **Torriente Laws** that regulated the banking crisis; the **Workers Safety Act** and the **Retirement Laws** for the Postal, Educational, Civil Service Employees, Police, Army, Veterans and Judicial Workers.

Before 1857 the Spanish currency circulated in Cuba. In 1857, banknotes denominated **pesos** were specifically printed by Spain for use in Cuba, pegged to the US dollar at par. After the independence, on October 29, 1914, Menocal signed the law that authorized the creation of **Cuban gold coinage**, of which the $10 piece on the left is an example. They were designed by Charles E. Barber, the same man who was designing American coins at the US Mint in Philadelphia.

Photos above: *on top*, Menocal meeting with his Cabinet. Some of his ministers were **Aurelio Hevia** (Interior), **Ramiro Guerra** (Education), **Enrique Nuñez** (Sanidad y Beneficencia), **José Ramón Villalón** (Obras Públicas), **Luis Azcarate** (Justicia) and **Leopoldo Cancio** (Hacienda).

On the Bottom, years later, in 1923, some of the same Menocal followers met in exile in Miami during the government of Alfredo Zayas.

When **the price of sugar skyrocketed**, as world politicians felt the inevitability of World War I, several candidates decided to challenge Menocal for a second term: Alfredo Zayas, José Miguel Gómez, the Generals Emilio Nuñez, Pino Guerra, Gerardo Machado, Ernesto Asbert and Colonel Carlos Mendieta. Even though Machado, Gómez, Asbert and Mendieta rallied around Alfredo Zayas, Menocal won in the midst of questionable practices and numerous armed incidents. Three conservative election supervisors were shot and wounded; the man Asbert had supported for mayor of Güines from the *Liberal Party* shot and killed his *Conservative Party* rival.

The US **immediately recognized Menocal**, the old *Cornell University* alumnus. Apparently, for the second time (Wood had blindly supported the Conservatives) the Liberals were denied an election. For the second time also, several Cuban *políticos* asked for a US intervention: this time they were Orestes Ferrara, Raimundo Cabrera, José Miguel Gómez, Alfredo Zayas, Ernesto Asbert and Gerardo Machado. The US ignored the request. On May 8, Menocal and Emilio Nuñez were officially declared the new president and VP.

Cuban politicians who asked for US intervention in 1917:
Top row, from left to right: **Orestes Ferrara, Raimundo Cabrera, José Miguel Gómez**; *Bottom row, left to right*: **Alfredo Zayas, Ernesto Asbert, Gerardo Machado.**

The Presidential Palace in Havana —constructed under Menocal's presidency— was the creation of two notable architects: **Rodolfo Mauri**, Cuban, and **Jean Beleau**, Belgian. They were also responsible for the *Centro Gallego*. The palace, at number 1, Refugio Street, is a four floor building made of white stone from *Isla de Pinos*, with a lantern on top in yellow and blue, covered with 18 carat laminations. The palace replaced the old Palace of the Captain Generals as the seat of the executive branch of government. The driving force for the construction of this palace was Mariana Seba, Menocal's wife, who convinced her husband to acquire for the national government a building that was originally intended for the provincial government of Havana.

Menocal inaugurated the building in 1920. *Tiffany* from New York was in charge of the interior building details, as well as the accesories, such as an exquisite porcelain dinnerware, Limoges, that showed Cuba's coat of arms in each piece. The ceiling of its largest hall was decorated with a painting by **Armando García Menocal,** the president's uncle, entitled —*The Triumph of the Republic*.‖ Other artists participating were Mariano Miguel, Antonio Rodriguez, Enrique García Cabrera, Juan Emilio Hernández and Leopoldo Romañach.

Photos above: the Palace under construction in 1916, during the presidency of Mario García Menocal, and as it looked once finished; the ceiling in the Main Hall, *The Triumph of the Republic*.

An event in February 1917, during the presidency of Menocal (1913-1921), would have enormous consequences in Cuban history. Popular demonstrations in Russia, provoked by the hardship of World War I, forced Tsar Nicholas II to abdicate. **Vladimir Ilyich Lenin (1870-1924)**, the Russian revolutionary, author, lawyer, economic theorist and political philosopher, was living in exile in Zürich at the time; upon knowing the news, he immediately returned to Russia, arriving in Petrograd to the sounds of the *Marsellaise* intoned by a large crowd of workers bearing red flags.

By October all power had been transferred to the *Soviets* (as the Russian political organizations) relatively peacefully and by December *Chekas* (C*HREZVY- CHAYNAYA* K*OMISSIYA,* Extraordinary Commissions) were created by a decree issued by Lenin to defend the Russian Revolution.

The *Chekas* carried out Lenin's campaigns to «*suppress and liquidate the enemies of the people.*» They made possible some strategic penetrations of the top levels of government, with decisive campaigns to influence journalists, businessmen, students and peasants.

Photos: Lenin in Moscow on May 5, 1920, and in a portrait of the times.

Over the years Lenin felt that with a structure of *Soviets*, political parties were unnecessary. History betrayed him. One week after he died, Stalin used his majority in the *Central Committee of the Communist Party* to go after Trotsky, under an article adopted at the *Tenth Bolshevik Congress*. It was there that Russian-style totalitarianism was born, a historical aberration that shook the twentieth century and would eventually submerge Cuba in chaos.

For years on end, Cuban governments decried and disregarded the evidence of infiltration, espionage, and influence by Communist spy services, even as millions of Soviet citizens, «*enemies of the people,*» went to their deaths for «*crimes against the Soviet state.*» The tradition of anti-Americanism and knee-jerk hatred of the US in Cuba, first started by Spain during the Wars of Independence in the late 1800s, was reinforced by the Soviet's agents of influence: from the 1920s into the 1950s Cuban intellectuals, teachers, artists and poli- ticians became rabid anti-Americans. It eventually resulted in the events that ended the Republic.

Photos above, Lenin and Stalin. *Below, left to right.* Cuban Communist leaders from the 1920s to the 1950s: **Blas Roca, Juan Marinello, Lázaro Peña** and **Julio Antonio Mella**.

Communism made its first appearance in Cuba in the 19th century. In 1822, **George Weerth** was born in Germany; he met Marx in person and after landing in jail for his subversive ideas, escaped to Cuba in 1872. In one of his works he stated «*The turning point of America towards Communism will start in Cuba.*» He spent his years in Cuba teaching, lecturing and writing poetry.

One of his students was a Cuban youngster born in Santiago de Cuba in 1842 named **Pablo Lafargue**. Under the influence of Weerth he went to Paris to study, met Karl Marx in person, became his secretary and ended up marrying Laura Marx, Karl's daughter.

Lafargue became a Frenchman once he got used to life in Paris. For a long while his only ties to Cuba were his correspondence with two Cuban poets: **Carlos Baliño** and **Diego Vicente Tejera**. Both participated in the Cu- ban struggles for independence and there is evidence that both got to know José Martí in New York.

Carlos Baliño, born in 1848, was an ardent defender of the Russian Revolution in 1905 and the October Revolution in 1918. He was a close friend of Mella.

Diego Vicente Tejera was the founder of the *Cuban Socialist Party* in 1899 and the *People's Party* in 1900. He was a member of the 1901 Constitutional Assembly.

Fabio Grobart, following orders from the *Comintern* in the 1920s, settled in Cuba and became a founding member of the *Cuban Communist Party*. Presumably he was the man who recruited Fidel Castro in 1948.

Enrique Roig was an anarcho-syndicalist that became Cuba's great defender of Marx. He tried to dissuade workers to fight for Cuban independence and give priority to the independence of the working classes.

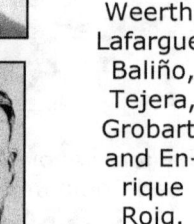

Photos top to bottom, left to right:

Weerth, Lafargue, Baliño, Tejera, Grobart, and Enrique Roig.

Edwin James Meeker (1853-1936) was a skilled US illustrator that provided detailed drawings for books and newspapers before photography became a common medium. Meeker's visited Cuba during the government of Menocal and made a beautiful drawing of Menocal's birthplace that was published in *Scribner's* and *Harper's Weekly* magazines.

Photo above: the Meeker drawing of Menocal's place of birth in Jaguey Grande, Matanzas, as published in *Harper's Weekly*.

During most of his two terms in the presidency Menocal attracted very important men to serve in his Cabinets. **Rafael Montoro** was Secretary of the Presidency. The Secretaries of Government were first **Aurelio Hevia** and later **Charles Hernández-Montalvo** The Secretaries of State were first **Cosme de la Torriente-Peraza** and later **Desvernine-Galdos**. **Leopol- do Cancio** was Secretary of the Treasure. **José Ramón Villalón** was Secretary of Public Works. **Nuñez Rodri**guez the Secretary of Agriculture and **Enrique Nuñez** the Secretary of Health. The Secretary of War was **José Martí Zayas-Bazán**. Other Secreta- ries were: **Ezequiel Garcia-Enseñat** in Education, **Arróstegui- Castillo, Núñez-Villavicencio,** and **Méndez Capote**.

Photo on the right: the **brothers Menocal** during the 1895 War; Mario García Menocal is dressed in black.

From the times of the frugal management of Estrada Palma, to those of spendthrift Menocal, Cuba financed bank loans with the *Speyers*, partners of the Rothschilds. **Sir Edgar Speyer (1862-1932)**, Chairman of **Speyer Brothers**, friend of musicians Elgar, Strauss and Debussy, sponsor of *Scott's Antartic Expedition*, financier of the *London Under-ground,* was the main lender to the government of Estrada Palma. **Speyer & Company** were the bankers of Mexico before the Revolution, had financed the construction of railroads in South America and the Philippines and when the Republic of Cuba was born they made the first $35,000,000 loan to establish credit for the young country.

The **JP Morgan Bank**, however, was the financial mainstay during the Menocal administration, from 1912 until 1925. **Chase Bank National Bank** of Rockefeller, in full partnership with JP Morgan, was the preferred lending bank in Cuba after 1925.

Photos below, left to right: Caricatures of Sir Edgar Speyer, John Rockefeller and J.P. Morgan during the late 1910s.

As president of Cuba Menocal was often referred to as «*the British Lord that became a tropical politico.*» He was born in Bolondrón, Matanzas, graduated from *Cornell* and became a railroad man until he joined the War of 1895, fighting under Calixto García. After the war he was Chief of Police of Havana, finally joining the **Cuban American Sugar Company** as administrator of the *Delicias* and the *Chaparra* sugar mills. He was a Masó rather than an Estrada Palma man.

Bonds of the Cuban Sovereign Debt.

Some **Cuban Políticos** during the presidency of
Mario García Menocal.

On top from left to right: Liberals **Fernando Ortiz (1881-1969)**, ethnologist, member of the House of Representatives from 1917 to 1922; **José Manuel Cortina (1880-1970)**, Cuba's foremost orator and diplomat, Senator, delegate to the *League of Nations*, Foreign Minister; **Orestes Ferrara (1876-1972)**, member of the staff of Máximo Gómez during the war, diplomat, writer, member of the Senate in Cuba, Ambassador to the US, Secretary of State, liberal delegate to the 1940 Constitutional Assembly and **Cosme de la Torriente (1872-1956)**, Colonel in the 1895 War, president of the *League of Nations* from 1923 to 1924, *French Legion of Honor* recipient.

Bottom from left to right, Conservatives **Carlos Manuel de Céspedes Quesada (1871-1939)**, son of Carlos Manuel de Céspedes, graduate from the *Institute Stanislas* in Paris, president of Cuba in 1933, Ambassador to the US and Spain, legislator, Foreign Minister, *French Legion of Honor* recipient; **Alfredo Zayas (1861-1934)**, lawyer, poet, Mayor of Havana, secretary of the *1901 Constitutional Convention*, legislator, VP in 1908 and President of Cuba from 1921 to 1925; **Miguel Coyula (1888-1948)**, commander in the War of 1895, journalist, president of the House of Representatives in 1917, founding president of the *Inter- American Press Association*; **Rafael Montoro (1852-1933)**, law- yer, literary critic, historian, Secretary of State, founder of the *Cu- ban Academy of Arts*, member of the *Spanish Royal Academy*.

Orestes Ferrara was an extraordinary man whose life expanded almost a century of accomplishments. He was born in Naples, the son of an Italian patriot who had fought with Garibaldi during the unification of Italy. He fell in love with the cause of Cuban independence, contacted Tomás Estrada Palma in New York and Emeterio Betances in Paris and **joined the War of 1895 in Cuba** (abord the *Dauntless*) in 1897.

His first encounter with the war was in Calixto García's siege of *Las Tunas*. He was chosen as a delegate to the *Yaya Constitutional Assembly* in 1897. At the end of the war he began to work with José Miguel Gómez while continuing his studies at the *University of Naples*, where he obtained a doctorate in Jurisprudence. He was appointed governor of Santa Clara by Leonard Wood and was elected to Congress in 1911, after serving as Cuban ambassador to the US in 1912.

In 1914 he founded the newspaper *El Heraldo de Cuba*. During the presidency of Menocal he immigrated to New York, returning to Cuba to serve under the presidency of Machado. In 1926 he was appointed **ambassador to Brasil** and in 1927 **ambassador to Washington**. In 1928 he built in Havana a celebrated mansion, *la Dolce Dimora*, in the style of ancient Florentine renaissance palaces. At the fall of Machado in 1933 he escaped with his hydroplane (50 gun impacts were later found) under heavy fire from the revolutionaries. Back in Cuba in 1937 he became **leader of the Liberal Party** and was elected to the *1940 Constitutional Assembly*. He went into exile when his car was attacked as he approached the Capitol and he suffered some wounds. He lived his last days in *Costa do Sol*, Portugal, at the *Meurice Hotel* in Paris and at his home in Rome. He died in Rome after writing several scholarly books about Machiavelli, the Borgia popes and Alexander VI.

Photos above: Ferrara during the Cuban War of Independence (standing up in front of the flag); in his diplomatic days, on the left; and his last photo, on the right.

At the end of World War I, the controls on sugar prices were suddenly abandoned, and a wild speculation produced what came to be called the «*dance of the millions*.» As the government of Menocal was coming to a close in 1920, however, the sugar market collapsed. Europe was recovering from the war and in the second part of the year sugar prices dropped from more than 17 cents a pound to less than 4 cents. Cuba, because of the war, had been producing record crops and 1920 had not been an exception. All of a sudden there were no takers for Cuban sugar. Because the way payments and credit had been arranged, workers and *colonos* were minimally affected; sugar mill owners, however, were devastated.

On October 10, 1920, Menocal had to call a **moratorium on bank payments** in order to allow the sugar barons to organize their debts. Banks began to feel the crisis. *Banco Mercantil, Banco Español* and *Banco Internacional* were at the brink of going under. The *Banco Nacional de Cuba* (formerly North American Trust Company) fell on the hands of **José López Rodríguez**, the ubiquitous —*Pote*.‖ Menocal, too busy helping the election of Alfredo Zayas (who had defected from the *Liberales* to join the *Conservadores*) against the Liberal candidate, ex-president José Miguel Gómez, declared he was **too busy to save the banks** from their own mistakes (lending too much money to the sugar lords when they should have known that the high sugar prices would not continue after the end of the war).

Photos: The *Banco Nacional de Cuba*, the bank safe, José López Rodríguez (Pote) and a Bank stock certificate.

As things stood, Menocal got Zayas (his former rival) elected and then took care of asking J.P.Morgan for a loan to stabilize the banking situation. The US did not intervene in spite of knowing that Gómez' VP candidate was **Miguel Arango**, president of *Cuba Cane Sugar Corporation*, an American subsidiary of *Czarnikow-Rionda*. On November 7 —once again— **José Miguel Gómez asked for new elections under US supervision**. Some districts indeed had new elections; Zayas kept his advantage and was pronounced the new president. The banks collapsed all over the island. The first one to do so was the *Banco Nacional de Cuba*, showing $1 million in assets and $70 in liabilities. *Pote* was found the next day hanging from the balcony of his apartment. It was never established if he had been murdered or had taken his own life. By the time Alfredo Zayas took power, the warehouses in Cuba were filled to the brim with the sweet crystals that no one wanted to buy.

The situation in the early 1920s became more confusing when General Sugar (almost entirely owned by the National City Bank) announced it was no longer shipping sugar using the national railroads but would build its own private network. It would have been a death blow to the *Cuban Northern Railroad*, owned by **Colonel José Tarafa**. In successive years Tarafa would skillfully save his interests by merging with *Cuba Railway*, *Nuevitas*, *Guantánamo* and *Western Railroad Companies* and formed *Ferrocarriles Consolidados de Cuba*. His success was due in great part to the help of an old hand at Cuban finances, **Horatio Rubens**, the man who had been a valuable allied of José Martí and Gonzalo de Quesada during the War of Independence.

Photos above: A stock certifícate of *Ferrocarriles Consolidados de Cuba* signed by Horatio Rubens; Colonel José Tarafa; a stock certifícate of *Cuba Cane Sugar Corporation*.

The story of Cuban railroads is intimately linked to the beginnings of the Republic of Cuba. On December 8, 1902, the first train running from Las Villas to Oriente (573 kilometers) was inaugurated. It was a product of the perseverance and capital infusion of **Sir William van Horne (1843-1915)**, a successful Canadian entrepreneur that had fallen in love with Cuba. It was also a tribute to **Gaspar Betancourt Cisneros (1803-1866)**, founder of the Puerto Príncipe-Nuevitas railroad, a pioneering sugar railroader. In his time, Betancourt Cisneros had to overcome the objections of Miguel Tacón (1775-1855), Spain's Governor General who allegedly had a financial interest in a competing company from the peninsula.

The story goes that the railroad *Havana-Bejucal* was the first railroad in Cuba; it was opened in 1837. *El Lugareño*, as Betancourt Cisneros was known, **opened his railroad in Camagüey in 1836**, a year earlier, hence he has the honor of being the pioneer of railroads in the entire Spanish empire, including the peninsula.

Camagüey, on that moment, became the «*centro ferroviario de Cuba,*» in the words of van Horne. Seventy years later, in 1907, The *Cuba Railroad Company* was founded; by 1911 almost 300 kilometers were added to link Camagüey with Nipe, Antilla, Manzanillo and San Luis. By 1923 it reached Santa Cruz del Sur; Cuban trains were conquering steep mountains and rich sugar lands in the valleys.

Ferrocarriles del Norte, the work of another railroad pioneer, **Colonel José Tarafa**, had been founded in 1918, linking equally fertile sugar lands: Chambas, Moron, Nuevitas. It became an inevitability that *The Cuba Railroad Company*, *Ferrocarril Camagüey-Nuevitas* and *Ferrocarriles del Norte de Cuba*, would join forces in 1924 to form *Ferrocarriles Consolidados de Cuba*. The new railroad later absorbed the *Ferrocarril Espirituano* and the *Ferrocarril Guantánamo-Occidente*. No country south of Rio Grande could rival Cuba in its railroad network during the first quarter of the 20th century.

Photos left to right: Sir William van Horne; Gaspar Betancourt Cisneros; Cuban sugar railroad in the 1920s; railroad lines used for public transportation in Cienfuegos, 1920.

For many years during the early days of the Republic, two of the men that dominated public life were implacable enemies: **José Miguel Gómez** and **Alfredo Zayas**. It was known that Menocal, for instance, had been elected president as a consequence of this unrelenting hostility. José Miguel mobilized the army on Election Day, claiming that a veteran (Menocal) was more deserving to be president than a non-veteran (Zayas). Once elected, the first Menocal period of was a disaster: budgets and corruption went wild without the citizens receiving any perceptible benefit. When Menocal announced his intention to be re-elected, as in 1912 against Zayas, most people were reminded of Estrada Palma and the possibility of insurrections and riots that would justify another US intervention.

Photos above: Menocal and his family; a 1916 cartoon showing a painting of *La Chambelona*, the name of the 1916 rebellion. *La Chambelona* had been a well know prostitute from the town of Chambas, in Las Villas. The song was as old as the colonial days and went like this: *Desde que se fue Chinchilla / y ha venido Polavieja / yo no como mantequilla / ni tampoco ropa vieja / ¡Aé, aé, aé la Chambelona.*

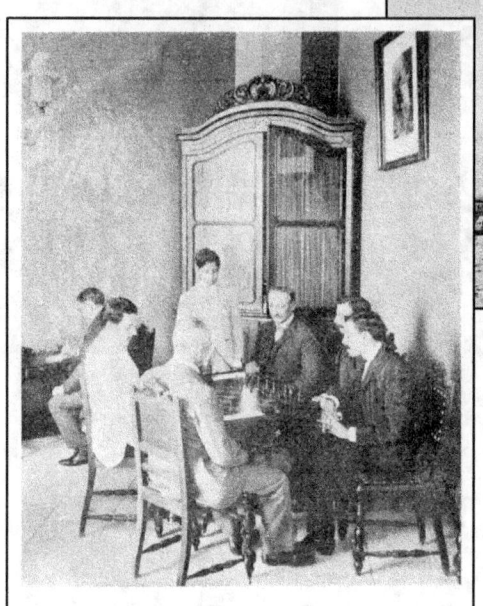

Miembros del Club de Ajedréz de la Habana, Sres. M. Márquez Sterling, Antonio Fiol, Enrique y Juan Corzo, José A. Blanco y niño José Raúl Capablanca, que jugaron el Cable-Match con el Manhattan Chess Club, de New York, en 1903.

Menocal, Cuba's most illustrious *Cornell* engineering graduate, received the tacit approval of Washington; his followers began to claim that his re-election was the only warrantee of «*good government.*» Expediency prevailed over good sense and Menocal was re-elected in 1916. The liberals appealed to the *Junta Central Electoral* and the *Cuban Supreme Court* with only partial success. Some elections were repeated in certain areas but the results did not change the outcome of the original vote. It was said that *Valeriano Weyler* and *Cristobal Colón* were found years later as registered voters in the 1916 election. What made that election irreversible was the strong pronouncement of Washington: the US would not recognize any government resulting from an armed conflict. When José Miguel Gómez learned of that decision, he explicitly asked for a third military intervention. The army, the intellectuals, the students and the population in general rejected that appeal. **Manuel Márquez Sterling**, although strongly condemning the 1916 election for its entrapments and corruption, felt that «*a corrupt president is preferable to another interference by the US.*» Evidence of that possible misfortune was the presence of the US cruiser *Minnesota* in the harbor of Havana.

Photos Above: The US Cruiser *Minnesota* entering the Havana harbor; Manuel Márquez Sterling, a notable chess player, at the *Club de Ajedrez de La Havana* (Havana Chess Club) in 1903. The young boy next to Márquez Sterling is **José Raúl Capablanca** at age 15.

In April of 1921, **Emanuel Lasker (1868-1941)** and **José Raúl Capablanca (1888-1942)** competed for the World Chess Championship in Havana. The Cuban Grandmaster had been playing Chess since age 4 (*photo below*). In Havana, in 1921, he dethroned Lasker after the Russian Grand Master had been defending his title for 27 consecutive years. Capablanca's photo made the cover of *Time;* he was a genius, a *bon vivant*, and a weaver of intricate movements; he got better at chess by practice rather than by complex theoretical studies.

The story is told that at age 4 Capablanca called to the attention of his father an illegal move he had made; after that warning, he beat his father twice on that day. Capablanca registered at *Columbia University* in 1905 to study Chemical Engineering but dropped out when he became the best player in the *Manhattan Chess Club* at age 18. In 1913 Menocal gave him the position of Cuban Ambassador at large so that he could dedicate himself to Chess. The following year he established a record, playing 602 games in 27 cities and winning 580 of them. In 1921 he played 103 opponents simultaneously in Cleveland and won 102 games, tying one. He became the most sought after player in the world. On March 7, 1942, while watching a tournament at the *Manhattan Chess Club*, he collapsed with a cerebral hemorrhage provoked by hypertension. He died and was buried in Havana.

Manuel García Ponce (1851-1895), aka *El Rey de los Campos de Cuba*, became a popular hero in 1921 when *Santos y Artigas* presented a film in Cuba honoring the man. The film was based on a book by **Alvaro de la Iglesia Santos (1859-1940)**, a writer who achieved great notoriety in Cuba for his books relating Cuban anecdotes and traditions. The producer of the film was **Enrique Díaz Quesada (1883-1923)**, one of the pioneers of silent films in Cuba. The film —*El Rey de los Campos de Cuba*,‖ was gone forever when all of Diaz Quesada's productions were lost on a fire a little after his death.

Manuel García had been born in Alacranes, Matanzas, in February of 1851. He **proclaimed himself to be pro-independence** and provided assistance to Cuban patriots in Cuba and in Cayo Hueso. He soon became Cuba's *Robin Hood*, stealing from the rich hacendados and using the funds to buy weapons for the war of independence in the late 1870s. He allegedly worked with Francisco Vicente Aguilera receiving Aguilera's expeditions in Cuba.

In 1885 he escaped from Cuba —he had been found guilty of fighting with and killing a town mayor— and worked in the tobacco factories in Cayo Hueso. A year later he returned to Cuba and took to the mountains, escaping numerous ambushes by the Spanish Army. In 1895 **he offered Martí a donation of $8,000** that Martí rejected in a message he sent him through Juan Gualberto Gómez. Martí tried without success to turn Manuel García into an honest man but the call of the *manigua* was too strong and the man continued to be a *Robin Hood* all his life. He was finally killed —legend goes he was assassinated by a Spanish soldier— in Ceiba Mocha, Matanzas, on February 23, 1895. Manuel García's life was celebrated once more on a film directed by Jean Angelo in 1940.

Photos above: Manuel García, the *Santos y Artigas Theater* in Sagua la Grande in 1921 and Enrique Díaz Quesada.

V

An Interlude with a Civilian President
The Years 1921 to 1925

> «That government is best which governs the least,
> because its people discipline themselves.»
> HENRY DAVID THOREAU, American Philosopher (1817-1862)

ALFREDO ZAYAS ALFONSO was a journalist, a poet and a biographer of José de la Luz y Caballero with a conspiratorial past. He had been editor of *La Habana Literaria* with Enrique Hernández Miyares in 1891, had been affiliated to the *Autonomist Party* before joining the *Partido Revolucionario Cubano* of José Martí; later, in 1896, he became —under the pseudonym of Manuel Vivar— the party representative in Havana. His brother, Juan Bruno Zayas, had been killed in action in the 1895 Cuban War of Independence. Alfredo was detained in Havana after the death of his brother and sent to the *Cárcel Modelo* in Madrid. After he left the prison, as a fluent English speaker, he was invaluable to the war in Cuba. He was a *1901 Constitutional Assembly* member and secretary, and in 1906 he became a member of the *Comisión Consultiva* organized by Enoch Crowder to review and define the laws in Cuba. He was more than qualified to be president of Cuba although he did not have the rank of General and had not served in the War of Independence, as seemed to be a prime requirement at the time. In the elections of 1920 his Partido Popular carried him to the presidency, which he assumed on May 20, 1921.

His leadership style appeared more rational and less intuitive from day one. He appointed what he called *el Gabinete de la Honradez*, (the honesty cabinet) stressing that his government would be honest and transparent. Some of the best personalities of the island served in the Cabinet: Nestor Carbonell, Manuel Sanguily, Enrique José Varona, Generoso Campos and Juan Guiteras, to mention a few.

Zayas opposed the intentions of Enoch Crowder —by then formally promoted to US Ambassador— to have a say in his appointments to the Cabinet. He became a champion of civil liberties at a time when Cubans were singing «*Tumba la caña y anda ligero que ahí viene el mayoral (Menocal) sonando el cuero.*» (Cut the cane and run 'cause the overseer —Menocal— is coming whipping his flog). He did not abuse his privileges even when judge Augusto Saladrigas Lunar in 1922 falsely intimated that Zayas had been involved in the disappearance of hundreds of thousands of Liberty Bonds deposited in the National Treasury.

Zayas inherited an empty treasury, a ruined sugar industry and an epidemic of bankrupt Cuban banks. He promptly secured a $50 million *empréstito* or sovereign loan from J.P. Morgan, as many of his predecessors had done. He was a laid-back man and his ministers probably took advantage of that, as it most certainly happened with the government purchase of the old and dilapidated *Convento Santa Clara* for $2,350,000, twice what its previous owners, the *Compañía Urbanizadora Santa Clara, S.A.*, had paid a few months before. This incident, which is related elsewhere in this book, gave rise to the *Protesta de los Trece* when Rubén Martínez Villena and a group of students interrupted Erasmo Regueiferos, Zayas' Secretary of Justice, as he was speaking during an homage to the Uruguayan writer Paulina Luisi in the *Cuban Academy of Sciences*.

In his zest for honesty and responsibility, or as a reaction to the venality of his administration, Zayas earned the opposition of the war veterans who organized as the *Movimiento de Vetera-*

nos y Patriotas. Once more they took to the mountains, this time led by Colonel Federico Laredo Bru. Instead of sending the troops, Zayas went looking for them in the town of Cienfuegos and persuaded the leaders to return to their homes.

In the midst of students rebelling to acquire similar rights than faculty in the world of university education, workers demanding higher wages in spite of serious economic constraints and veterans dissatisfied with the first non-veteran president, Zayas was able to advance some of the most progressive legislation in the short history of the Republic:

He negotiated the return of Cuban sovereignty over the Isle of Pines (111 square kilometers) which had been occupied by the US since 1898 (the Hay-Quesada Treaty of 1925);

The *Federación de Estudiantes Universitarios* (FEU) was recognized as a legitimate organization in spite that, in the mind of many conservative Cubans, its very existence was intimidating and fraught with danger;

The interference of politicians in the functioning of the National Lottery was reined in with a *Lottery Reform Law* that secured a hands-off operation; the unwieldy and uneconomical expansions of hundreds of railroad operations —many of them at the edge of insolvency— was brought to order with the *Ley Tarafa*; it limited the number of railroad terminals and ports through which sugar could be exported, hence preventing the innumerable outlets that were making possible export tax evasions; finally, it supported laws that would guarantee the expropriation of land to facilitate the path of electrical service in Cuba.

Not all was impeccably clean during the government of Zayas. His enemies —many of them with reason— accused him of «*outrageous prevarication,*» offering as examples a long list of frauds and deceptions: the purchase of land in *el Vedado* to extend *Havana's Malecón*; the scandals with the funds to dredge the port of Cárdenas; the popularization of *botellas* or sinecures —non-existing employees in the payrolls; the luck of Zayas' wife and first lady, María de la Asunción Jaén y Planas, when she won the lottery's first price while Zayas' son was assistant director of the Lottery, among others.

When the time came to organize the elections of 1924, however, Zayas absolutely refused to seek re-election. His party presented as candidates General Gerardo Machado y Morales for President and Colonel Carlos de la Rosa for VP. The opposition advanced the candidatures of Menocal and Méndez Capote for President and VP. Gerardo Machado won the elections, probably one of the most honest and transparent since the beginning of the Republic. Cuba was back to the leadership of war veterans from the war of independence, an unfortunate choice that would later bring about a lot of grief.

It was during the government of Alfredo Zayas that the Communists began to make inroads in Cuba's political life.

When Alfredo Zayas became a presidential candidate, everybody thought the year 1921 would mark the sunset for the generation of *políticos* who were military leaders during the 1895 Cuban War of Independence. After all, **Alfredo Zayas** was a civilian intellectual and poet, not a military man. He had been deported for his sympathies but had never been in the battlefield. As president of the republic his destiny was to be in constant conflict with Enoch Crowder. He had to fight this battle almost by himself. **Máximo Gómez** had died ten years early; so had **Calixto García**. On June 13 **José Miguel Gómez** died of pneumonia in New York. **Mario García Menocal** had taken his family to Europe and was also out of the political scene.

Photos above: *on top*, the funeral procession of Calixto García (through Prado Avenue; *below*, the finished monument to José Miguel Gómez at the top of G Street, with his impressive 10 ft tall statue of the President.

Alfredo Zayas Alfonso (1861-1934) arrived to the presidency in 1921, during the period of economic crisis that followed the *—Danza de los Millones.*‖ He was supported by President Menocal, who had been his adversary in the elections of 1916. Zayas quit the *Liberal Party* — which was tightly controlled by former president José Miguel Gómez, and had started the *Partido Popular*, forging an alliance with Menocal and his *Partido Conservador*. The *Partido Popular* was so small that people soon began to call it the *Partido de los Cuatro Gatos*. At the core of all parties in Cuba, personalities more than ideology were the decisive feature. *On the right:* a caricature of Zayas by Massaguer.

Photo above: The first Cabinet of **Alfredo Zayas Alfonso**. Sitting with Zayas are Mario Martínez Lufriú, Erasmo Regüeiferos, Freyre, Montoro, José Manuel Cortina, Guiteras, Collantes y Pancho Zayas.

In 1921, a few years after the end of World War I, the precipitous collapse of sugar prices caused chaos in the Cuban econo- my. Sugar magnates had taken loans to expand production during the war and banks were now calling in those loans. The *Banco Nacional* collapsed. Worse yet, the US raised the tariff on sugar by one cent. The *First National Bank of New York* took over several bankrupt sugar mills. The US, no longer *intervening* but rather *interfering*, sent **Enoch Crowder** to administer a $50 million US emergency loan to the Cuban government. It was said that he ruled Cuba from his headquarters in the *Hotel Sevilla*, without ever leaving the premises.

Photo at the top: the Banco Nacional de Cuba in 1921.

Major General **Enoch Herbert Crowder (1859-1932)**, (*photo on the left*), was appointed in 1920 as President Woodrow Wilson's personal representative in Cuba to settle the dispute over elections. Soon he became the first US Ambassador to Cuba, a post he held until 1927. He had been in the island from 1906 to 1909, when he served as Secretary of State and Justice on the staff of provisional governor Charles E. Magoon. He supervised the election of 1908, and contributed significantly to drafting of a body of organic law as Chairman of the **Advisory Law Commission**.

He is known to have said once that...

«*President Zayas is unethical, egotistical, power-hungry and resentful of his subordinate position to me.*»

His nomination as *Rector Honoris Causa* of the University of Havana would, late in 1921, resulted in numerous complaints from the students, particularly **Julio Antonio Mella**.

Alfredo Zayas governed mostly by decree, in a typical Menocal fashion. With the help of his nemesis Crowder he had secured loans to rescue the Cuban finances in exchange for far- reaching reforms practically dic- tated by Crowder. Zayas had his best success when **Cosme de la Torriente (1872-1956)**, his Minister in Washington, secured the ratification of the *Hay-Quesada Accord*, recognizing the territory of *Isla de Pinos* as Cuban. During Zayas term, by and large, the US tolerated corruption in Cuba as the means to political stability. Tax evasion, lottery fraud, illegal gambling, presidential pardons, usurpation of state lands, and bribes to government officials became the order of the day.

Not having a strong loyal party to support him, Zayas began to secure the loyalty of politicos and voters by distributing *colecturías* and *botellas* —sinecures, paid political appointments that did not require people to show up for work. The University students protested vigorously against corruption in government and absentee professors in the University. Zayas responded by **granting autonomy to the University**, i.e., a guarantee of non-intervention from the state.

Photo at the top: Alfredo Zayas at his desk. *On the left*: Cosme de la Torriente as a young man and as a senior. *On the right*: Gonzalo de Quesada as a young man and as a senior.

The **University of Havana** began to be important in Cuba's political life during the government of Zayas. The University had been for almost 200 years at a huge building bound by Obispo, O'Reilly, San Ignacio and Oficios Streets in Havana. With the republic it moved to its present site in San Lázaro and L Streets, in the old *Colina de Aróstegui* (Aróstegui's Hill), the site of a chemical plant (explosives) owned by the head of the *Tobacco Cartel*.

Between 1906 and 1911 the auditorium or *Aula Magna* was built by the architect Emilio Heredia, with six large frescoes by notable Cuban painter **Armando Menocal** (President Menocal's uncle) representing the *Law, Letters, Liberal Arts, Thought, Fine Arts, and the Sciences*.

In 1927, during the first term of Gerardo Machado, a monumental staircase replaced the much more modest steps that were used to climb to its major facilities.

Photos above, top row: The new staircase built by Machado at the entrance to the University in 1927. The old entrance access steps, built in 1901. *Bottom row*: the interior of the Auditorium with the Menocal frescoes and the exterior of the building.

Zayas had ample patriotic credentials. He had been in 1896 the delegate of Martí's party in Havana, for which he was deported to the *Cárcel Modelo* in Madrid. His brother, Juan Bruno Zayas, had been a war hero. As president, nevertheless, he had to suffer the fastidious interference of Enoch Crowder, a representative from US president Harding with strong supervisory pretentions. When on June 19, 1922 Zayas appointed the **Gabinete de la Honradez**, with the best and cleanest politicos in Cuba, he was accused of having followed Crowder's orders. *Enoch Crowder* is portrayed on the cartoon at left giving orders to *President Zayas* while *Liborio* (the Cuban people) is being left out of the loop.

In December of 1922, during an almost forgotten event in the history of Cuba, **José Arce (1881-1968)**, president of the *University of Buenos Aires*, lectured at the *University of Havana* about the participation (or **co-gobierno**, in the lore of the time) of the students of Argentinean Universities in the governance of their institutions, particularly after the so called *Reforma de Córdoba*. Dr. Arce was in Cuba for the *VI Latin-American Clinical Congress*. The students at the University of Havana had already opposed the attempt to invest Enoch Crowder with a **Doctorate Honoris Causa**.

After the visit by Arce (shown in the photo below at right with Albert Einstein), the students formed the *Directorio de la Federación de Estudiantes;* its first leader was a young man born in Havana known as **Nicanor McFarland**, an alumnus of *Chandler College* in Marianao, a top American school, and the *Escuelas Pías de Guanabacoa*, the best Catholic school in Cuba, from which he had been expelled. Nicanor was later known as **Julio Antonio Mella.**

The student's program for the universities of the future, as proposed by the reformists of the 1920s, was: «*autonomy, open access, no registration fees of any kind, total academic freedom and freedom of research; an institution of science and critical thinking, with a decisive participation of students in its institutional government and with a social mission that should address the problems and needs of the people and no others.*» These principles, originating in Argentina in 1918, were adopted by the students in Mexico in 1921; **Cuba in 1923**; Colombia in 1924 and Perú in 1926; they were probably the basis for the **US and European stu- dent revolts of the 1960s.**

Photos above: scenes from the students' revolts in Cordoba, Argentina; José Arce, President of the University of Buenos Aires.

On January 11, 1923, the students at the University of Havana went on strike, emulating those of the Universities in Argentina. They specifically wanted the firing of Dr. Rafael G. Menocal del Cueto as professor of Clinical Surgery. The Chancellor of the University **Don Carlos de la Torre y Huerta (1858- 1950)** and the newly formed *Federación Estudiantil Universitaria (FEU)* appealed to President Zayas to grant autonomy to the University, as well as define as a joint responsibility the evaluation of the faculty. The president formed a *Comisión Mixta* (six faculty and six students) to resolve the crisis. The Chancellor disagreed with the new dynamics of decisions in the University and requested a leave of absence, which he made permanent.

On October 15, 1923, the *First National Student Congress* took place in Havana (*photo at left*; Mella is the tallest person at the center). Julio Antonio Mella, the new president of the FEU presided. Three agreements were approved: the **Declaration of Rights and Duties of the Students**; the creation of the **José Martí Popular University** and the organization of a **Confederation of Cuban Students**.

In the meantime, all through the 1920s, a large group of **Ashkenazy Jews** from Central and Eastern Europe began to emigrate to Cuba from Poland, Russia, Lithuania and Germany; Cubans began to call them **Polacos**. They brought considerable knowhow, patience, acumen and business assertiveness to Cuba. Many of them began to intermarry in Cuba and felt like Cubans. They dis- placed the Spaniards in many fields of commerce and retail.

An event with unforeseen consequences took place in Cuba in 1923. The nuns of the **Convento de Santa Clara** (*photos center*), comprising four city blocks limited by Cuba, Sol, Habana and Luz Streets, decided to sell the *Convento* because it was no longer in a quiet and silent countryside environment.

The sale became a scandalous affair when its price to the government was set at four times its value. This produced a severe remonstration called the *Protesta de los Trece* when, at a meeting of the *Academy of Science* honoring *Paulina Luissi*, the Uruguayan writer, several university students, under the leadership of **Rubén Martínez Villena (1899-1934)**, publicly accused the government of corruption. The Secretary of Justice *Erasmo Regüeifeiros* was present; the students walked out of the meeting *en masse*.

Photo at the bottom: location of the *Convento de Santa Clara*.

The 13 students who walked out of the meeting at the **Academy of Sciences** on March 18, 1923, included (*see photo of the façade and the aula magna above*):

Juan Marinello, Rubén Martínez Villena, José Z. Tallet, Calixto Masó, Alberto Lamar Schweyer, José R. García Pedrosa, José M. Acosta, Luis Gómez Wangüemert, José A. Fernández de Castro, Felix Lizaso, Jorge Mañach, Primitivo Cordero and **Francisco Ichaso.**

They were all important young intellectuals that would play important roles in Cuban history. The first two, **Marinello** and **Martínez Villena** and possibly **Tallet**, were known radical leftists and active communists.

After 1923 this group of young intellectuals became famous as the men of the **Protesta de los Trece** (see page 222), met daily at noon at the banquet room of the *Hotel Inglaterra* in Central Park, shown in the pictures below. In the afternoon the *tertulias* were at the library of a school affiliated with the *Sociedad Económica de Amigos del País,* situated at Amargura and Compostela streets, whose director was Rubén Martínez Villena's father. As they became more and more active and moved to the university grounds, president Alfredo Zayas kept the police forces at bay and commented to his friends «*Déjenlos, que ya me extrañarán.*» (let them be, soon they will miss me.)

On November 1923 Mella started the **Universidad Popular José Martí (UPJM)**, a free lance academic institution with revolutionary goals. All sorts of intellectuals joined as professors. They began to proselytize presenting the ideas of declared Marxists like **Pablo Lafargue**, as well as Socialists like **Diego Vicente Tejera** and Communists like **Carlos Baliño**. Its founding led to the birth of the *Cuban Communist Party*. In the photo above left, **Victor Raúl Haya de la Torre (1895-1979)**, founder of the APRA movement in Perú and (*at right*) Haya with **Julio Antonio Mella** during the *founding of the UPJM* on November 3, 1923.

The impact of the Russian Revolution in Cuba was initially negligible and more emotional than political. The first large impact in the working classes was made by **Alfredo López Rojas (1894-1926)**, (*photo above*) an anarchist typographer, friend and cellmate of Julio Antonio Mella in 1925, who had supported the October Revolution. López organized in early 1925 the *Confederación Nacional Obrera de Cuba* (*CNOC*, an alliance of 75 unions), an outgrowth of his *Federación Obrera de La Habana* (*FOH*, aligning 21 unions), which he had founded in 1922. These movements were **Anarcho-Syndicalist** and **Reformist** in nature rather than Marxist or Communist. At the end of August, López organized the *Confederación Nacional Obrera (CNO)*, this time bringing together 128 worker's organizations, again with anarchist indoctrination. On July 10, 1926, López was seen for the last time walking along Gloria Street towards the Railroad Station. Rumor had it that he was slain by the Communists, who needed to get him out of the way.

On January 12, 1924, a group of young intellectuals formed the *Grupo Minorista*, which lasted until 1929. Many, but not all of the protagonists of the *Protesta de los Trece* were involved: **Juan Marinello, Rubén Martínez Villena, José Z. Tallet, José M. Acosta, Jorge Mañach, Eduardo Abela, Alejo Carpentier, Félix Lizaso, Conrado Massaguer, Mariano Brull, Emilio Roig de Leuchsenring** and **Amadeo Roldán.**

The members of the *Protesta de los Trece* had first reorganized as the *Falange de Acción Cubana*, a literary-political action group; they began to work together with the *Veteranos y Patriotas*, an organization committed to programmatic armed action.

1924 and 1925 were years of strikes, reversals, political affiliations and reconsiderations, as well as a generalization of thievery, pilfering and waste all across the Cuban government.

1924 opened with railroads in Camagüey on strike; residents of the Isle of Pines (95% US born and raised) asked the US Congress for the annexation of their territory to the mainland; **Carlos García Vélez (1867-1963)**, son of General Calixto García and Cuban ambassador to England, criticized the level of corruption in Cuba and was recalled and replaced (*photo on the left*).

Manuel Sanguily, brother of Julio, died on January 21, 1925; the **Hay-Quesada treaty** was ratified by the US Senate, recognizing *Isla de Pinos* as Cuban territory; **Cosme de la Torriente** resigned as Ambassador to Washington; **Julio Antonio Mella** was detained and charged with having explosives; he went for 30 days into a hunger strike.

In the last months of the government of Zayas, 1925, the **Cuban Communist Party** was initially organized by **Julio Antonio Mella (1903-1929)**, by now the top student leader at the *University of Havana*, **Carlos Baliño (1848-1926)**, an old founder in 1906 of the *Partido Socialista de Cuba*, the first Cuban Marxist organization, and **Fabio Grobart (1905-1994)**, aka Antonio Blanco, Abraham Simjovith, Yunger Semjovich, Otto Madler, Serguei Skalovich, José Michelón, Alberto Blanco and El Polaquito. Grobart was a Jewish tailor who had immigrated to Cuba to organize the *Cuban Communist Party* following orders from the *Comintern*.

Above, left to right, Mella, Baliño and Grobart.

The formal founding of the **Communist party** took place on August 16, 1925, at a meeting of the *First National Congress of Communist Organizations* on Calzada # 81, Havana. There was no doubt that Moscow-trained members of the Third International (*Comintern*) had played a significant role in ideological and organizational matters. In the late 1920s, within 5 years of its founding, the party —fully espousing the Stalinist line— had control of the Cuban labor unions and began to infiltrate union movements through- out Latin America. From the day it was founded the party was affiliated with Lenin's *Third International* organization. *Photo above*: Martínez Villena addresses the members at the founding meeting.

In the elections of 1924 President Alfredo **Zayas was hoping to run for re- election** but his hopes vaporized when the *Conservatives* (his party in 1920) selected ex-President Mario García Menocal as its candidate. Without hesitation Zayas threw his support to General Gerardo Machado, the *Liberal* party candidate. On November 1, 1924 the elections took place in an atmosphere of peace, tranquility and trust.

Gerardo Machado Morales (1861-1939) and **Carlos de la Rosa Hernández (1874-1933)** (*photos on the right*) seriously defeated Menocal and Méndez Capote everywhere except in Pinar del Rio, the traditional conservative enclave. At the suggestion of Crowder —who had not open his mouth to support anyone— Menocal sent a congratulatory note to Machado. There was an air of optimism in the streets. Cuba had never had such peaceful elections before.

The best compliment the government of Zayas ever received was made by the *Diario de la Marina*:

«*It does not seem that for a long time we will have in Cuba a government that would be as effective as that of Zayas, even in the midst of a bankrupt treasury, the meddling of the US, the unfair public opinion, the opposition of Congress, the banking crisis and a formidable world economic depression.*»

Zayas proved that the **Cubans could govern themselves**; he strengthened the sovereignty of the republic, never mistreated his enemies, did not seek reelection and turned Cuba to his successor in better state that he had found it.

Photos from an Album recording the first quarter of a century of the Republic of Cuba.

Statue of Martí at the Central Park in Havana.

Relief at the base of the statue of Martí at the Central Park in Havana.

An old Church in Guanabacoa.

Area of the fort *La Chorrera* (1646) at the delta of Río Almendares.

The Almendares River.

An old fort In Guanabacoa.

Havana Carnival, 1922.

The SS Minneapolis in 1916, at Havana Harbor.

Country Club Park, 1921.

Car driving in Palatino, Havana, 1914.

A residence dining room, 1917.

A family in the living room of their residence, 1922.

VI

A Veteran Again in the Presidency
The Years 1925 to 1929

> «Republics endure until the day their leaders discover they can bribe the public with the public's money.»
> ALEXIS DE TOCQUEVILLE, French Political Scientist(1805-1859)

AS SOON AS MACHADO took over the presidency of Cuba there was a return to the *caudillismo* that had prevailed during the first years of the Republic. Voters, tired of the *laisez-faire* attitude of Zayas, welcomed the strong hand of Machado. They particularly supported the campaign of the Secretary of the Interior, Rogerio Zayas-Bazán, to eliminate graft in public service and reform the Judicial Branch of government.

Machado undertook a vigorous program of public works in areas of enormous need for the country:

The construction of the first central highway in Cuba in 1927, a two way single road starting in La Fé, Pinar del Río and ending in Maisí, Oriente. Total length: 1250 km or 777 miles.

Next was the construction of the National Capitol where the Train Station of Villanueva had been since 1839. The previous partially completed Capitol building was demolished and work began on a new building on April 1, 1926. 8,000 laborers worked 8 hour shifts, 24 hours a day for over three years until it was finished.

Not far were the monumental steps leading to the main entrance of the University of Havana, as well as the elegant *Avenida de las Misiones* linking the presidential palace with the *malecón*. It was a time of continuous visible progress. New industries began to flourish in Cuba, new investments flew into the island, offering employment and paying taxes. It all seemed too good to be true.

By 1927 people began to hear that a constitutional reform was been considered to allow for the re-election of the president. A system was in place at the time —the *Cooperativismo*— by which the *Conservadores* and the *Liberales* were sharing power in Cuba, taking turns according to the mandates of the electors. Such arrangement eliminated any political hopes for all except the two parties in the agreement. Machado, like Estrada Palma, was not immune to adulators. He also felt he was a providential and indispensible man. Enrique José Varona, Juan Gualberto Gómez, Cosme de la Torriente, Carlos Mendieta and Aurelio Hevia unsuccessfully tried to bring Machado back to earth. Machado and his followers, nevertheless, launched their project with self-defeating stubbornness. They asked for a new Constitutional Convention in 1928; this body called upon Machado to accept a new term in office. In the meantime the world was experiencing an uncontrolled economic depression and Cuban living standards plummeted to the primitive state they were 30 years earlier.

Machado was re-elected in 1928. The man who had been one of the youngest Cuban Generals in the War of Independence — only Calixto Enamorado (1874-1951) and Enrique Loynaz del Castillo (1871-1936) had been younger; who had suppressed the Estenoz-Ivonet rebellion; who had fought and lost with dignity against José Miguel Gómez in *La Chambelona* and had been the acclaimed leader of the Liberals; who had referred to Cuba as the Switzerland of the Americas, was now succumbing to his ego and placing the Republic in peril.

Photos above: Gerardo Machado during his presidential campaign in 1925 (with a hat on his hands); Machado on the cover of *Time Magazine*, which identified him as —*Cuba's Mussolini*; a caricature based on the characterization of Machado as *un asno con garras*, (an ass with claws) by Julio Antonio Mella.

Gerardo Machado, the three-fingered presidential candidate in 1924 (he had had an accident while working in a butcher shop as a young man), had been on and off in the service of President José Miguel Gómez and his Cabinets. In 1924 he was supported by the *Electric Bond and Share Company* —who practically had a monopoly of Cuban energy supply— at the tune of $0.5 million for his campaign expenses.

Machado was a likable rascal and an aggressive businessman. Most members of the Liberal party felt Colonel Carlos Mendieta was the best candidate but Machado, with the help of **Vázquez Bello** as his campaign manager (**Orestes Ferrara** was the manager of Mendieta's campaign and proved to be too complacent) outsmarted and outcampaigned Mendieta. At the July party convention, presided by General Pino Guerra —brother of Ramiro Guerra— after many squabbles, Machado was chosen.

Photos above: the succession Menocal, Zayas and Machado; Vázquez Bello, the campaign manager; Machado (not Menocal) on a horse

Carlos de la Rosa supported Machado in 1925 after he was offered to be his VP; **Zayas** supported him after he was offered three ministerial and several minor positions. There were rumors that **Menocal** was about to force a *coup-de-état* when he (Menocal) began to campaign riding on a huge white horse and his followers popularized the slogan «*a caballo*» (on horse). Machado's followers responded with the slogan «*a pie*» (on foot). The elections were peaceful and honest and Machado won.

Photos above: Machado campaigning in 1924; Machado and his campaign manager Orestes Ferrara; a bond of the *Havana Electric Railway Company*, Machado's largest political contributor.

Gerardo Machado y Morales (1861-1939) took possession as the 5th president of Cuba on May 20, 1925. With his *Coalición Liberal-Popular* he had defeated the team **Menocal-Méndez Capote** 200,000 votes to less than 136,000. Machado's father had fought in the *War of 1868-1978* and he fought in the *War of 1895* under José Miguel Gómez, reaching the rank of General. In fact, he was one of the youngest Cuban generals on that war.

He was never a cultivated man and until his death spoke like an unsophisticated *campesino*. Machado was a very popular president in his first term and his worse mistake was to push for his re- election to a second term. He was a very assertive person and used to tell his friends that his purpose in life was to «***vencer, no convencer***» (to prevail, not to persuade).

He was awarded a *Doctorate Honoris Causa* by the University of Havana, a politically charged decision that enraged the students and faculty of the University.

His government was the **best** (economic policy, anti-corruption campaign and public works) and the **worst** of his times (a dictator in his second term, in the worse Latin American tradition).

Photo left: Machado as seen by Massaguer. *At right:* Machado on the day of his election with his VP Carlos de la Rosa.

Four of the extraordinary public works projects of President Machado. *Left to right, top to bottom*:

The magnificent **Capitolio Nacional** de la Habana, at Prado, Dragones, Industria and San José streets, with its 92-meter high dome;

The **Cuban Central Highway**, a two-way road, extending 777 miles from La Fé, Pinar del Rio to Baracoa, Oriente;

The 50 meter wide, 88-step stone **Escalinata Universitaria** at the main entrance of the University of Havana at L and San Lázaro streets;

The **Hotel Nacional**, originally planned to face the lighthouse of el Morro at the entrance of Havana Bay but finally built at the ancient site of the *Canon Battery of Santa Clara* on 21 and O streets, Vedado, at a cost of $3 Million dollars.

Other important works were the extension of the **Malecón** to reach *El Vedado*; the remodeling of the **Maceo Park**, the **Torreón de San Lázaro** and the monument to the **Maine**; the construction of the **Parque de la Fraternidad** where the old *Campo de Marte* was; the Avenue and Park of **Las Misiones**, to mention only a few.

Photos above, top to bottom: the finished *Hotel Nacional*; the *National Capitol* under construction; the course of the *Carretera Central* built by Machado; the front side of the *University of Havana* before the magnificent steps were built; Carlos Miguel de Céspedes placing the first stone of the new building for the *Cuban National Bar* in Havana.

Several important **organizations**, some positive and others negative, were revitalized or created early in Machado's presidency. The *Confederación Nacional Obrera de Cuba CNOC* (1925), an umbrella workers organization of anarcho-syndicalist leanings; the *Asociación Unión Nacionalista* (1927), founded by Liberal Colonel Carlos Mendieta (a split-off of Machado's *Liberal Party*); the *Cuban Communist Party* (1925) led by Julio Antonio Mella; the *Directorio Estudiantil Universitario*, DEU (1927); and the *Partido Demócrata Sufragista* (1927) seeking women's suffrage legislation.

Except the last one, all were grounds for Machado's concerns. He considered the political attitude of students and workers as «*not very patriotic*,» and unleashed a relentless and merciless campaign against them. He began a program of intimidation, coercion, bribery, jailing and deportation.

Top left, **Julio Antonio Mella** founder of the Cuban Communist Party, a student of law at the University of Havana. Machado was accused of murdering him but he was more likely a victim of the Communists internal Stalin-Trotsky's vendettas in Mexico.

Center left, **Alfredo López Arencibia**, leader of the *CNOC*, anarchist, promoter of solidarity with the Russian workers, suppor- ter of *Mella's Universidad Popular José Martí*, allegedly murdered by Marxist extremists who resented his opposition to subordinate the Cuban workers' syndicates to Moscow's III International;

Top right, **Enrique Varona González**, leader of the railroads syndicate in Cuba in 1925, murdered in the town of Morón in 1925 for favoring such alliance to Moscow's III International.

The communists, without any solid evidence, accused Machado of having killed all three.

Julio Antonio Mella (1903-1929), the activist most responsible for creating a *Communist Party* in Cuba, was fundamentally a man in search of a cause that he could lead.

Initially, it was the world of sports; basketball, swimming and especially rowing, where he strived to be the lead crew member controlling all other rowers. Later in his youth, he founded a secret student society, "*los Manicatos*," with initiation rites that included meetings in the cemeteries, vociferous protests at —*high society* gatherings of academic or political associations, and violent encounters with members of exclusive sport clubs that he characterized as —*the pirates*.

These youthful fantasies were the prologue to a life of political protagonism. It led to the creation of the *Federación Estudiantil Universitaria (FEU)*, the protests and the occupation of schools and University buildings in Havana, countless debates during which he made hot and feverish speeches, statements and publications such as those leading to a radical student congress in 1923, and finally to a well orchestrated hunger strike in 1925.

The 1925 strike was Mella's response to an evident disenchantment of the *FEU* with his leadership. As the man looking for a cause he could lead, he expanded his efforts to the *Instituto de la Habana*, the most visible high school in Cuba. A few years later he would be trying his leadership with the Mexican Communists.

Photos above: Mella as a youngster and as man trying to be identified with the working classes. *On the right*, **Tina Modotti (1896-1942)**, his mistress and, most likely, an accomplice to his murder in 1929.

Without doubt, the hunger strike in late 1925 sharply expanded Mella's national dimension and made him an internationally celebrity. His expulsion from Cuba, favored by the *Communist Party* as it **resented his self-serving attitude during the hunger strike**, left him without followers and no leadership prospects. He settled in Mexico, where the *Communist Party* received him within its ranks.

Soon Mella became member of its Central Committee as **responsible for agitation and propaganda**; by 1928 he was Acting Secretary General, a position he held briefly.

Eventually the Mexican Communists —many of them proud veterans of the 1910 Mexican Revolution— were of two minds when it came to the role of Mella. On one hand they agreed with his emphasis on land reform issues, his preaching about social control in a Communist political system, the need for new institutions, the destruction of organized religion, the exaltation of Mexican ethnicity, the rupture of relations with the United States and the alliances he proposed with Latin America and the USSR. On the other hand they abhorred his **prepotency** and his dreams of international leadership, like his solidarity with Sandino in Nicaragua and his identification with the *Comintern* (the *Third International*, 1919–1943, the communist worldwide organization set up by Moscow).

When the opportunity came to get rid of Mella, after the mandate of the VI Congress of the *Comintern to Bolchevizate the Communist Parties* (return to strict dogmatism), the Mexican Communists, clearly **with the blessing of Moscow**, decided to take advantage of his weakness for women (Tina Modotti, his mistress made all the arrangements for his assassination) and had Mella killed. The *Communist Party* immediately blamed Machado for the death of Mella. This accusation was widely known to be false. *Above*: the Communist newspaper *El Machete*, Mexico.

Gerardo Machado ran one of the most efficient governments in Republican Cuba. In fact, even today many historians feel that, during his first presidential period, he was a president who really knew how to govern Cuba. After years of promised economic diversification and reforms, he was the first president to initiate programs to accomplish goals like these:

He fired the *botelleros*, fought against **gambling** and **prostitution**, insisted on **efficiency** and **honesty** in all government departments, instituted the **eight-hour work day** and gave a larger **budget** to Education than Defense. He cleaned the public administration and surrounded himself some of the **best minds of the times** like Antonio Sánchez de Bustamante, Ramiro Guerra, Carlos Manuel de Céspedes Quesada, Rogerio Zayas-Bazán, Orestes Ferrara, Enrique Hernandez Cartaya and Octavio Averhoff Plá.

Unfortunately he was not a man committed to individual rights. Even in his first term he acted like an autocrat; he never got used to lead without opposition. Márquez Sterling characterized him, from 1925 to 1933, as both «*dictatorial and constructive*».

Photos above: *top left:* Machado, Orestes Ferrara and Carlos Manuel de Céspedes Quesada; *center*, Antonio Sánchez de Bustamante on the *left* and Ramiro Guerra on the *right*.

Typical of the quality of men that Gerardo Machado was able to attract to his first Cabinet in 1925 was **Rogerio Zayas-Bazán (1876-1931)**. He had reached the rank of Major during the War of 1895. In 1917 he joined the liberals under José Miguel Gómez in the *Chambelona* uprising that opposed Menocal's re-election. He was elected **Governor of Camagüey** in 1922 and was appointed by Machado **Secretary of the Interior** in 1924. He was the man that created and supervised the construction of the **Presidio Modelo** in *Isla de Pinos*. In 1928 he resigned his post in the cabinet, firmly opposing the re-election of Machado. In 1930 he was elected **Senator** from Camagüey and was in line for a presidential candidacy. Challenged to a duel on July 14, 1931, he was murdered after a surprise attack by his opponent before he had time to defend himself.

During his tenure as Secretary of the Interior he struggled fiercely to **end gambling and prostitution in Havana**; pimps had their head shaven and hundreds of foreign prostitutes were deported in the strongest anti-corruption campaign since 1902.

Photos above: Machado's ministers and collaborators in 1925 (*Zayas-Bazán sixth from left*); the *Presidio Modelo* under construction and a portrait of Zayas-Bazán.

During Machado's presidency student leaders **Antonio Guiteras**, **Eduardo Chibás** and **Aureliano Sánchez Arango** (*photos, left to right*) were expelled from the *University of Havana* by the *Council of Teachers and Administrators* in April of 1928. *With their photos the Coat of Arms of the University*.

As soon as Machado made public his intention to be a candidate for a second term, Liberal Colonel **Carlos Mendieta Montefur (1873-1960)**, committed to oppose him. (*photo on the right*).

He was one of the central figures of the *Movimiento de Veteranos y Patriotas*, and had founded the *Asociación Unión Nacionalista* (1927) as a splinter of Machado's Liberal Party. He brought with him many of the old reformist politicians.

In spite of his promises to eliminate **botelleros** (sinecures) and create a climate of efficiency and honesty, Machado was soon submerged in the political benevolent and munificent traditions of past governments. The state payroll increased to 48,000, demanding $38.5 million in salaries a year. The old practice of creating public jobs to satisfy the **sargentos políticos** (political operatives) came back with a furor.

On February of 1927 Machado's followers started his re- election campaign. A request to extend his presidential period from four to seven years was presented on March 28 to the House of Representatives; it was approved in 24 hours. It included the possibility of a re-election although that was **explicitly prohibited in the 1901 Constitution**. On March 30 the university students demonstrated in the streets and on campus; the police evacuated the school; the students reassembled at **Enrique José Varona's** home. Varona had been with Julio Antonio Mella the day the FEU was founded in 1923. Machado was so secure of his power that left for a two week visit to Washington.

In the photos above, Varona seated at the center of a group of students and the last portrait of Enrique José Varona in 1933.

Machado was a complex leader and also an authoritarian and brutal man; he was very determined to promote Cuba's development. He was eager to secure American investments, but without turning into a mere puppet of foreign interests. In 1926 he appointed **Orestes Ferrara** as ambassador in the United States with a mission to seek the revision of the Treaty of Reciprocity between Cuba and the United States.

Under Machado — for the first time— Cuba had a customs tariff of its own, designed to defend its own interests. The production of poultry, eggs, meat, butter, cheese, beer and footwear increased significantly. Cuba also signed several trade agreements with Spain, Portugal, Japan and Chile. Finally, in 1927, to **ingratiate himself with the government of the US**, he renovated the beautiful monument to the victims of the *Maine*.

Photos above: A Pan American Fokker F-VIIa Tri-Motor plane inaugurated mail service from Key West to Havana in 1927. The plane was baptized *Gerardo Machado* to honor the Cuban president (see arrow); caricatures of General Machado by Arroyito and Massaguer; the renovated *Maine Monument* that Machado reopened in 1927 after the original eagle had fallen in the 1926 hurricane.

Times were tough in the international world in 1927. **Chiang Kai-shek** placed China under Sun Yat-Sen's *Kuomintang* control and unleashed a sudden and brutal slaughter against the communists. The Soviets broke off relations with China. **Trotsky**, who had been expelled from the PC early in 1927 and had gone into exile, criticized Stalin harshly for his attitude of alliance with the bourgeoisie and called him an opportunist. **Stalin**, at the VI Congress of the *Comintern* in 1928, proclaimed the Social Democrats as the "*main enemy*" of the working class. This position would lead Cuban Communists to **criticize Antonio Guiteras** relentlessly in 1933.

Photos above: Sun Yat-Sen, Chiang Kai-Shek, Stalin and Trotsky.

Machado went to Washington for the *Sixth International Conference of American States* in January and February 1928. He was at the peak of his popularity in Cuba. He discussed with Coolidge the **abrogation of the *Platt Amendment***. He was also disposing of as many communists as his people could handle. Just out of Havana, a shark appeared with the remains of a Spanish leftist agitator named *Claudio Bouzón* in its stomach. The story went that three youths accused of being Communists had been tied up and thrown to the sharks, Claudio Bouzón among them. Machado was irritated by the gruesome discovery; his solution was to **ban shark fishing in Cuban waters**.

Eager to secure his re-election Machado called for a *Constitutional Assembly* to meet on March 5, 1928. The spurious Assembly ordered elections to be held November 1, 1928, so that Machado could be re-elected for six years. The three existing parties nominated him and left the electorate without a voice of opposition. To make it double-sure, he signed a law banning the reorganization of political parties.

In 1929, in the United States, the collapse of the Stock Exchange and the onset of the Great Depression became inevitable. In Cuba, on September 30, a demonstration by university students was confronted by the police. In the fighting, **Rafael Trejo** was mortally wounded; it gave rise to mass demonstrations of popular grief. Machado suspended consti- tutional guarantees. The newspapers *Diario de la Marina* and *El País* were closed. The students began to organize themselves as political groups. All the leaders of the 1927 generation were there, led by Aureliano Sánchez Arango, Eduardo Chibás, Ramón Hermida, Edgardo Butari, and Antonio Guiteras. A revolution in Cuba seemed inevitable.

Photos Above: US President Coolidge visits Cuba and meets with Cuban President Machado.

Cuban born **Fernando Ortiz (1881-1969)**, one of the most distinguished essayists, ethnomusicologists and ethnic scholars in America, was for many years actively engaged in politics, first as a member of the House of Representatives (1916-1923) by the *Liberal Party* and later as a participant in several reform movements during the late 20's. He left politics in 1930, **repelled by the «*political cannibalism*» of 1928**, by the cult of personality of Gerardo Machado and the growing repression of its regime.

In his own words «*The serious danger in politics is not the multiple parties that aspire to the truth, or those who even tend to make mistakes; the problem is the protean political personalism in politics that we inherited from Spain, because this personalism in politics is almost always a lie.*»

Photos above: Fernando Ortiz in his younger years; two studies of ethnic parameters in the Cuban nation: the cult of Our Lady of Charity and the African musical roots.

After trying unsuccessfully to establish a new political party with such outstanding men as **Manuel Sanguily, Manuel Márquez Sterling, Enrique José Varona, Carlos Manuel de la Cruz, Cosme de la Torriente, Juan Jose de la Maza, Enrique Loynaz del Castillo**, and others, Fernando Ortiz in 1919 assisted Enoch Crowder, who would later be the first US ambassador to Cuba in 1923, to prepare a new electoral code; its essence was the reorganization of political parties in order to **weaken the rule of the *caudillos*** (sort of warlords). *Caudillismo*, however, grew to unusual dimensions around Machado, the fifth Cuban president (1925-1933). Machado received exalted honors that had nothing to do with his accomplishments such as *Doctor Honoris Causa*, *Cubano Egregio*, *Salvador de la Patria* and *Primer Obrero de Cuba*. In the late 1920s the party system broke down when liberals and conservatives banded together to create the *cooperativismo*, in order to support the reelection of Presidents.

Before the independence of Cuba many Spanish anthropologists had insisted that «*el ajiaco racial Cubano era un obstáculo insuperable para desarrollar una civilización independiente en Cuba.*» (the Cuban racial melting pot was an insurmountable obstacle to developing an independent civilization in Cuba). Cuban anthropologists, led by Fernando Ortiz, claimed that the Cuban nation could **conform and surpass** the nineteenth century separatist ideal, even with the obstacle of an incomplete independence.

Photos above: Fernando Ortiz in his older years; a study of one of the elements of the Cuban ethos: the sugar and tobacco economy.

Fernando Ortiz, on many occasions, reminded the Cubans that «*a good government was as valid a measure of a successful transition from colony to republic as national sovereignty without hindrance.*» or in the words of Manuel Márquez Sterling «*To the foreign interference, we need to oppose the domestic virtue.*»

Disappointed by Cuba's political life Fernando Ortiz dedicated his energies to **scholarly studies of Cuban ethnicity**. The loss of Fernando Ortiz to the political life of Cuba was regrettable, yet it allowed this wise and generous man to explore, record and understand all facets and roots of the Cuban cultural synthesis, as well as the implications of its converging cultures as they melted through the phenomenon of *transculturation*.

His last admonitions in the 1940s were «*Conflicts among the elites are the consequence of personal desires for hegemony that always impede reaching a strong and long lived consensus. The Republic still has to smooth out new roads that can turn into reality the ideals of independence. The hallmark of Cuba is the inability of political society to secure a stable institutional path.*»

Photos above: two studies of the basic elements of the Cuban identity: black music and black religion.

VII

Times of Revolution And Violence:
The Years 1929 to 1933

> «When dictatorship is a fact,
> revolution becomes a right.»
> VICTOR HUGO, French Poet and Dramatist(1802-1885)

ON MAY 20, 1929, Gerardo Machado y Morales was inaugurated as the re-elected president of the Republic of Cuba. The times were bad for the Cuban economy and he was forced to reduce the salaries of all public employees. The following year a general strike organized by the outlawed *Confederación Nacional Obrera de Cuba (CNOC)* and supported by 200,000 workers paralyzed the island. Many workers were killed in confrontations with state security forces. The *Unión Cívica Nacionalista* —not yet a political party in the formal sense— responded with the organization of a monstrous gathering in Havana's central park and another political rally in Artemisa, west of Havana. Before speakers had time to address the gathering in Artemisa, the army opened fire on the panic-stricken crowd. In September, at a student protest in front of the University of Havana, Rafael Trejo was shot and killed by the police in front of newspaper cameras. In November the government proclaimed a state of siege. A few days later Mario García Menocal and Miguel Mariano Gómez joined the opposition against Machado.

In December of 1930 Machado closed the University. Menocal and Mendieta —perhaps trying to revive the era of intervention— aroused the anger of the students by initiating suspicious conversations with the US embassy. Their actions were frustrated when they were captured by Machado forces in Rio Verde, Pinar del Rio. Cubans were disappointed and aggravated. Three quarters of a million youngsters —the Baby-Boomers of the Cuban Independence War— could not find jobs at the peak of their economic productivity.

The press began to publicize events that incited the people against Machado. Captain Arturo del Pino on August 9, 1931, had rebelled against Machado and single-handed fought the police in his house for several hours. After surrendering he was tortured and killed. Antonio Guiteras took to the mountains in Oriente, General Francisco Peraza in Pinar del Rio and Blas Hernández in Las Villas. The followers of Peraza were massacred. At the port of Gibara, Oriente, an expedition disembarked led by two well known politicians, Carlos Hevia and Sergio Carbó.

After some disillusioning failures to remove Machado, a new organization, with very different tactics, emerged for the first time in Cuba: the ABC. Its program included «*New men, new ideas, new strategies... political freedom, economic equality, social justice, recovery of the land*<»> In spite of its young middle-class professional leaders, the ABC began to spread fear in government circles with bombs and terrorist attacks. Machado responded to the ABC by declaring that he would be in the presidency until his term ended in May 20, 1935.

Most government works and public services were interrupted. Wages to public employees, the police, firefighters, bureaucrats, the judicial branch, and the army, began to be paid late. The US president, Franklyn Delano Roosevelt began to be apprehensive about the permanency of Machado in power. He sent Benjamin Sumner Wells to observe and mediate. The ABC and the University professors were pleased; Menocal, the CNOC, the communists and the *Directorio Estudiantil Universitario* were not.

The metastable situation finally exploded. Bombings, kidnappings, weapon seizures, street protests, marches, boycotts and fly-by assassinations began to be daily events. A general strike was called for early August 1933. Cuba was paralyzed. Workers, students, businessmen, banks, schools, clinics, stores, everything closed. Nobody supported Machado anymore, except the most loyal members of the Liberal, Conservative, and Popular parties. At the last minute, Welles tried to reach a peaceful agreement: he suggested that Machado appoint a VP agreeable to everyone and immediately resign, thus limiting his term to only three years. Machado could not believe Welles overbearing arrogance and went into a rage. He called for a special session of Congress to reject publicly the proposal, vowing to remain president of Cuba until his term expired.

Finally, on August 12, 1933, the general strike forced the hand of Machado. He and most of his main followers left Cuba. The country went into a state of anarchy; the strike that had helped to topple Machado continued. In Havana and other provincial capitals the populace was taking personal vengeance against the former *Machadistas*, lynching many of them in the streets in plain daylight. Most of their homes and many government offices were sacked and their contents burned on the streets. It was —until then— the most sordid episode in the three decades of Republican life.

Machado was always surrounded by *guatacas* (literally *hoes*, i.e., sycophants). In Cuban-Spanish a *guataca* is a flatterer, someone always ready to give insincere compliments to a person. The reason for calling them ―hoes‖ is because they were always reeady to «*smooth out the road in front of their bosses.*»

Gerardo Machado was led to believe by General Crowder (who was US Ambassador to Cuba until 1927) and many of his followers, that a majority of the Cuban people favored his continuation in office in spite of his promise in 1924 (during the campaign and after his inauguration) not to seek re-election.

Resistance was immediate and it came from the *Conservative* and *Popular* parties as well as from his own *Liberal* Party. Very cleverly Machado secured a joint nomination by all parties: the **Cooperativismo**. In 1927 he had secured congressional passage of an amendment to the Constitution extending his presidential term for two years. Congressmen were included in the amendment; their consecutive terms were extended from eight to twelve years for Senators and from four to eight for Representatives.

In addition an *Emergency Law* from Congress prohibited presidential nominations from parties other than the three nominating Machado. That left **Carlos Mendieta** out of the elections. In the US President **Calvin Coolidge** tacitly approved Machado's plan for a second term. Soon lottery *Colecturias* and *State Sinecures* were hastily distributed to compliant politicians. All promises of a better political fiber in Cuba were demolished. The sincerity of Machado's commitment to the Constitution was irrevocably discredited.

On November 1, 1928 he was re-elected, unopposed. It would mark the end of the participation in politics of all former generals of the independence War of 1895.

Photo above: President Machado presiding a 1926 meeting to auction off contracts for the construction of the *Carretera Central* in Cuba.

Charles A. Lindbergh, the pilot who first flew non-stop from the US to France in May of 1927, arrived in Havana from Haiti piloting the *Spirit of St. Louis* during the **Sixth Pan American Conference**. He was on his Goodwill Tour of the Caribbean and stopped in Cuba for five days in February. The 8th of February was proclaimed as *Lindbergh Day* and on the 12th of February, 1928, President Gerardo Machado y Morales flew over Havana, with Charles Lindbergh on the *Spirit of St. Louis.*

Following his Atlantic crossing, Lindbergh visited many countries in the same plane; he had the national flags of each country painted in the fuselage. The Cuban flag was the last one; following his trip to Cuba, Lindbergh donated "*The Spirit of St. Louis*" to the *Smithsonian Institution*; it is now part of an exhibit at the National Air and Space Museum in Washington, D.C.

Photo above: President Coolidge speaking at the Pan American Conference in 1928 during his visit to Havana. In his keynote address Coolidge mentioned Simón Bolívar on two occasions.

Bolivar had organized the first Pan American Conference in Panama City in 1826. Coolidge, however, forgot to mention José Martí, the heroes of their hosts, who had also worked incessantly for the advance of the en- tire continent.

Photo on the left: Machado presenting a medal to Lindberg.

From 1928 on, as the economy of Cuba deteriorated and Machado's power shrank, Cuba entered a prolonged period of **caudillismo** and incessant **revolts**. On March 30, 1930, a general strike was organized by the clandestine *CNOC* (the anarcho-syndicalists). Many workers were killed; other lucky ones were simply fired.

At the University of Havana, a few days later, on September 30, 1930, **Rafael Trejo**, a *Directorio* member, was fatally wounded in a confrontation with police. The photo at right shows the precise moment. *Photo at the left*, Rafael Trejo, aged 20.

In the US, the *Hawley-Smoot Tariff Act* reduced the Cuban share of the US sugar market, forcing salaries of all public employees to be reduced. On November 30 Machado proclaimed a **stage of siege** and closed not only the University but also many secondary schools. They remained closed for three years.

Two new characters began to be well-known in Cuba. *Photo on the left*, **Rubén Martínez Villena (1899-1934)**, leader of the *Protesta de los Trece*, founder of the first *Partido Comunista Cubano*. *Photo on the right*, **Ramón Grau San Martín (1877-1969)**, professor of physiology at the *University of Havana* and future Cuban President.

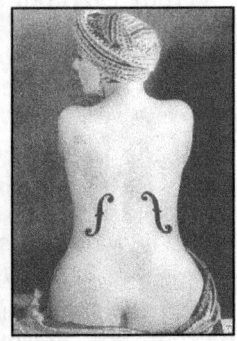

Julio Antonio Mella (1903-1929), founder of the *Federación Estudiantil Universitaria (FEU)*, the *Partido Comunista Cubano (PCC)* and the *Universidad Popular José Martí*, took refuge in Mexico after he was expelled from the *University of Havana*. There he got involved with the Mexican Communists. On January 10, 1929 he was assassinated in the streets of Mexico City.

Most probably, Mella was victim of an internal fight within the *Mexican Communist Party*. His murder was accomplished by **Vittorio Vivaldi**, an Italian born Stalinist sent by the *Comintern* to Mexico to discipline the Mexican Communists. There is little doubt that Mella's lover, **Tina Modotti** (*above right,* on a Man Ray photo very popular among book sellers along the Seine in Paris), was an accomplice.

The protagonists are shown in the Diego Rivera mural, —At the Arsenal,‖ where *Frida Kahlo* is at the center, distributing arms to the people. *Vivaldi* (with black hat), *Mella* (with light hat) and *Modotti* (leaning against wall), are shown at the right of the mural. *On the photo on top*, a newspaper giving account of the murder. The assassination of **Julio Antonio Mella** in Mexico was investigated by Mexican and US authorities and Machado was exonerated.

1930 marked the begining of three years of bloody confrontations and repression. Public gatherings were outlawed. Newspapers were threatened with censorship and closings. Police hunted down and jailed or killed members of the *Directorio Estudiantil*. Violent groups like the **ABC**, a middle class intellectual and activist organization, began to retaliate. A special police force, under the name of *Liga Patriótica (LP)*, also known as *La Porra,* repressed any public dissent and punished anyone opposing Machado.

Friends and foes of Machado were surprised when he unexpectedly turned into a dictator. He had been one of the youngest Cuban Generals of the 1895 War. Only **Calixto Enamorado (1874–1951)** and **Enrique Loynaz del Castillo (1871–1963)** had been younger. He had fought alongside **José Miguel Gómez (1858–1921)** and had been in the *Chambelona War* in 1917, fighting on the defeated liberal side. It was out of character that he would launch *La Porra* against his political ad- versaries in 1930.

On August 1931 Mendieta and Menocal (photos at left) attempted an uprising in Pinar del Rio, known as the *Rebelión de Río Verde*, and were made prisoners. The event had far reaching consequences since it became evidence of the **political bankruptcy** of the former generals of the War of 1895, now proven incapable of governing Cuba after trying for 30 years. When the opposition realized they could not oust Machado by political means they resorted to terrorism, sabotage, vandalism and political assassinations.

Photos above: Menocal and Mendieta insurgents at the *Rebelión de Río Verde* in Pinar del Rio. *Below,* friends with which Machado could count unconditionally in 1931: **Guas Inclán** (right of Machado, at left of picture) and **Vázquez Bello** (on his left) on the top left; **Carlos Manuel de Céspedes** on the top right and **Orestes Ferrara** on the bottom left photo.

The **ABC** was organized in December 1931. Some of its leaders were Harvard graduates and many of them, after years of violent activity —which included political assassinations— went on to prominent positions like **Joaquín Martínez Saenz**, future presi- dent of the *National Bank of Cuba*, and **Pastor González**, who af- ter the fall of Machado entered the priesthood and served for many years as a *Piarist Father* in the schools in Cuba. *Photos on top*: Martínez Sáenz (left) and Father Pastor González, SchP.

The founders of the ABC group were three young lawyers, **Joaquín Martínez Sáenz**, **Jorge Mañach** and **Carlos Saladrigas**. ABC really had no program except an illusion of radical idealism, goals which are «*not quite clear but full of beautiful promises*,» according to Mañach. In 1932 the president of the Senate and close friend of Machado, **Clemente Vázquez Bello**, was assassinated by the ABC.

The retaliation was swift: within hours four *anti-machadistas* were dead, including Leopoldo, Guillermo and Gonzalo Freyre de Andrade, lawyers for the revolutionary students. **The Terror** began to prevail in Cuba.

Photos at right: on top, **Clemente Vázquez Bello**, in the middle **Leopoldo** and **Gonzalo Freyre de Andrade**, at the bottom, Major **Arsenio Ortiz**, Machado's strong-man, chief of police of Havana, who allegedly «*found it easier to shoot and hang suspects rather than catch and try them*,» according to a reportage in *Time Magazine* June 5, 1933.

The *Directorio Estudiantil Revolucionario (DEU)* was founded in 1927 in opposition to Machado's re-election. In 1931 the organization split into two revolutionary groups: the **Ala Izquierda Estudiantil**, on the radical left, controlled by communists, and the **ABC**, mostly composed of middle class students with radical but *non-communist* activism. If fact, oftentimes they were accused of *fascism*.

The assassination of **Vázquez Bello** by the *ABC* was a failed attempt to gather around, during his funerals, the top members of Machado's government to liquidate all of them with a bomb in a broad sweep. The plan failed when Vázquez Bello's body was interred in a cemetery in Santa Clara and not in Havana, which had been loaded with explosives.

Photo on top: students of the *University of Havana* as they armed themselves in 1933 to fight the government on the streets of Havana. *Photo on bottom*: a demonstration against the Machado government in front of the presidential palace in 1933.

At the start of 1933 Cuba was immersed in an atmosphere of hate, blood, explosives and strikes.

Liberal **politicians** like Mendieta and Méndez Peñate and Conservatives like Menocal were out of the political life of the republic;

The **communists** were maneuvering (firm ideology but flexible tactics) to prevail regardless of who came on top at the end;

The **ABC**, *la esperanza de Cuba*, had a programmatic plan (nationalization of public service business and ultra nationalism), that was not compatible with the 1901 Constitution;

The University **students**, fighting to clean up the University, proved to be better conspirators than politicians since their sanitization was more political than academic;

The University **professors** favored autonomy but not student participation in the governance;

The **workers** were not organized except for communist cells;

Businessmen were looking after their profits with a disdain for politics;

A feminine branch of the *Porra* dissolved **women demonstrations** by stripping the protesters from their clothes.

On top: newspaper accounts about Cuba in the US in 1933.

There was a theory, not far from reality, that stated that what occurred in 1933 was a *coup d'ètat* by Ambassador **Benjamin Sumner Welles** to Cuban President Gerardo Machado. In fact, the theory went on to affirm that Sumner Wells designated General Alberto Herrera-Franchi (a sort of outsider in Cuba's military world) as temporary president simply to send a message to the high hierarchy of the Cuban Army that those that collaborated with Machado had no future in Cuba.

Two of Machado's collaborators were almost immediately out of the way with the fall of the regime:

In the corner of Prado and Virtues Streets, **José A. Jimenez**, veteran and chairman of the *Liga Patriótica* (Patriotic League, in Spanish it was shortened by people as *La Porra*), which supported Machado, was riddled with bullets; he was taken in front of the American embassy and his corpse left outside, in the street.

Two days before **Antonio Ainciart-Raggi**, the Chief of the *National Police*, set out with a machine gun squad, brandishing a big pistol under shopkeepers' noses while compelling them to break a national strike and open their shops for business. Havana had been paralyzed by a series of strikes among bus drivers, waterfront workers and railway employees; they were joined by slaughterhouse and market men, newspaper staffs, telegraphers, and the staffs of Havana's best hotels. Ainciart personally peppered the shutters of several shops with machine gun bullets. He was so intent on abusing shopkeepers that did not realize he was surrounded in front of the *National Capitol* by a mob that began to break the pavement and throw heavy cobblestones at him.

Totally encircled and without escape or possible defense, he killed himself with his own gun after his head had already been split in two.

Photos: Alberto Herrera, Gerardo Machado, Sumner Welles.

At 4:30 in the morning of March 17, 1896, the expeditionary ship —*Three Friends*— (see page 23), arrived at the beach in Varadero, Matanzas, with a large group of arms, munitions, two horses and about 70 Cuban patriots, under the command of **Enrique Collazo**. Their mission was to reinforce the troops of Antonio Maceo. There was a small Spanish army detachment close to the point where they landed. Collazo and his men found out their mistake and hurried to bury their weapons in the sand; by 9:30 am they were prisoners of Spain. Juan Valderrama, the Spanish highest officer of the region, told them that Maceo was not near Varadero but close to the town of Madruga.

Thirty five years later, in 1931, those arms were found during the construction of the **Hotel Kawama**, a pioneer establishment in what would be the most sought after beach in the world. Varadero was first visited by Sebastián de Ocampo in 1508. For many years it was a community living out of its *salinas* (saltworks). Its touristic value began in the 1880s, when a group of investors acquired several acres of beach land for $1,350 in Spanish gold. Its enormous popularity occurred after **Irenée Dupont de Nemours** built *Xanandú*, a fabulous mansion on the best part of the beach; he also formed a company to sell beach property in 1928. At the end of the republic, Varadero counted with 18 hotels, 20 guest houses and about 60 restaurants and nightclubs, as well as a small airport, a fast highway access and over 7,000 permanent residents.

Photo above: the Varadero mansions in the 1930s and *Xanandú*, the beach residence built by the Duponts.

Daily life scenes during the times of Gerardo Machado in the Presidency

Carriages in front of a private home in *El Vedado* in 1931.

A house at *Country Club Park* in 1929.

Traffic in front of the *Centro Gallego* in 1925.

The ferry across Havana Bay to the town of Regla in 1931.

A patriotic parade in May 20, 1926.

Cuban Navy ships *Máximo Gómez*, *Estrada Palma* and *José Martí*, anchored in Havana in 1928.

VIII

Failed Attempts to Reform:
The Years 1933 to 1940

> «In revolution there are only two sorts of men,
> those who cause them and those who profit by them.»
> NAPOLEON BONAPARTE, FRENCH EMPEROR(1769-1821)

CUBA WAS BRIMMING with joy after the fall of Machado. The streets were crowded with the citizenry and their great expectations. Politicians, however, were apprehensive because there was no easy solution to the power vacuum that Machado left behind. The man that had been elected in one of the most fairly conducted elections in Cuban history but had chosen to re-elect himself, left behind no one but General Alberto Herrera, his Chief of the Army. Herrera had been promoted a few days earlier to Secretary of State with the hope that this would guarantee a peaceful succession. But neither politicians, nor revolutionaries or the army accepted this solution and out of nowhere Carlos Manuel de Céspedes y Quesada, a diplomat and principled citizen, the son of Cuba's founding father, was chosen to lead the Republic. Sumner Welles himself had chosen the Cabinet and it included such important figures as Martinez Sáenz, Saladrigas, Zayas, Sanguily, Guillermo Belt, Horacio Ferrer, Cosme de la Torriente, Eduardo Chibás, Laredo Bru and even Raúl de Cárdenas.

      Céspedes, however, had neither executive experience nor a strong following that would make people trust his ability to bring order into chaos. The *Directorio Estudiantil Universita-*

rio, who had not been consulted about the appointment of Céspedes, did not support him. It began to contact the young enlisted men in the army to sanitize the armed forces and to take over the government. The lynchings and vandalism continued unabated. It was said that 1,000 people perished in three months. Fulgencio Batista began to prompt his military people for action (mostly all sub-officers and enlisted men): José Pedraza, Desiderio Sánchez, and lieutenants Tabernilla, Barquín and Benitez. The Batista group began to run Columbia like if they were the people in command and nobody objected. In the midst of this uncertainty a young intrepid student leader showed up in Columbia on September 4, 1933. He had been jailed for two years for his anti-Machado activities and was now leader of the Law students at the University of Havana.

Carlos Prío Socarrás became that day the president of the *Junta Revolucionaria de Columbia*, a new group that included leaders of the *Directorio Estudiantil Universitario* (Carrera Jústiz, Tony Varona, Eduardo Chibás, Carlos Hevia, Ramiro Valdés Daussá, Justo Carrillo and others) and the Batista conspirators. They appointed a collective government to run the destinies of Cuba, the celebrated *Pentarquía*: Sergio Carbó, Porfirio Franca, Ramón Grau-San Martín, José Irrisari y Guillermo Portela. The following day they visited Céspedes at the *Palacio Presidencial* and asked for his resignation. He had his bags already packed and did not object. Carbó apparently became the leader of the *pentarcas*. He left the palace that day driving Machado's bullet-proof limousine and in a few days, without consulting with any one, promoted Sergeant Batista to the rank of General.

When the high ranking officials of the Cuban Army resisted being removed or bypassed from Cuba's political life, they revolted against the soldiery and the non-commissioned officers. They took possession of the almost brand-new *Hotel Nacional* and on October 2 began to be fiercely bombarded by the government forces. Only the intervention of the Cuban Red Cross on November 8 stopped the carnage after they ran out of ammunition.

The *Pentarquía* lasted exactly five days, during which time unrest did not subside in Habana. Worse, no one —

particularly the US embassy— recognized its legitimacy. The *Junta Revolucionaria de Columbia* decided to appoint one of the *pentarcas* as president: Dr. Ramón Grau San Martín, who took possession on September 10, 1933.

Sergio Carbó, a very shrewd marketing man, created the motto *Paso a la Revolución Auténtica*, and under that slogan the new government went forward, including the *Auténtico* qualifier to the name of the party; from now on it was the *Par- tido Revolucionario Cubano (Auténtico)*. That did not alter the position of the US embassy. They did not recognize a Grau government either. The ABC, the deposed military chiefs during the September 4 events, and Sumner Welles began to fight Grau arguing he had become accustomed to the agitation, violence and anarchy prevailing in Cuba and was unable to stop it, particularly in Havana.

By then Batista had entrenched himself even though the students had tried to convince Grau to turn him over to them to be summarily executed in Columbia. Grau had also promulgated several revolutionary laws, some of which would stay in the books forever: *Ley del Cincuenta por Ciento* (50% of employees had to be Cuba-born in every business —it was later abolished); the *Law of University Autonomy* (the police could not enter the campus —it stayed in the books); creation of the Ministry of Labor (it stayed in the books); the Law of the 8 Hours Day (it stayed in the books). Other laws included the minimum payment of fifty cents for cutting one hundred pounds of cane in the fields, the lowering of electrical tariffs, a minimum wage for all workers, reform of workers' compensation law, the formation of the *Asociación de Colonos* (small owners or renters of sugar lands conjoined to a sugar mill), the control of loan interests to avoid usury and the ‚*right of first refusal*` for the state in real estate auctions, to prevent the sale of valuable property without paying taxes.

Batista nevertheless —not wanting to disappoint the US embassy— deposed Grau on January 15, 1934. He installed as President a very clean figure, Carlos Hevia. He lasted less than 24 hours as president. Once more a selection was made, this time Colonel Carlos Mendieta, also a very honorable man with the credentials of having opposed Machado.

Things more or less stabilized until the ABC party organized a gathering in Havana on June 17, 1934. Its purpose was to show-off their numbers and their unconditional loyalty to the government. They were surprised when a large and disorderly swarm of mobsters descended upon them causing a serious carnage. Alleging not having been defended by the public forces, the ABC decided to withdraw its support from the government.

The reign of terror took hold again in Cuba. A general strike was called for March 1935. Batista decided to show that he was the strong man in Cuba. The strike was stifled mercilessly. He went beyond this show of force. Knowing that Antonio Guiteras was about to embark clandestinely for Mexico to organize an expedition to overthrow Mendieta in Cuba, he had his people pursue the former Interior Minister until he was cap- tured and executed at *El Morrillo*, north and east of Matanzas.

To try to stabilize the political life in Cuba Mendieta promulgated a provisional Constitution and called for elections in December of 1935. The *ABC* and *Auténtico* parties refused to participate. The *Liberal* and *Nationalist* parties, together with *Acción Republicana*, presented Miguel Mariano Gómez, son of former president José Miguel Gómez, as a candidate. Menocal, once more, was the candidate for the *Conjunto Nacional Democrático*, the successor of the old *Partido Conservador*. Miguel Mariano, having Federico Laredo Bru as his VP and the support of *el hombre fuerte*, won and carried with him long tailcoats that insured that Congress was on the side of Batista.

After a disagreement over an approved law assigning one cent tax to every sugar bag, a tax destined to support Batista's pet project of rural schools similar to the ones Vasconcelos had established in Mexico in the 1920s, Batista decided to get the Congress to impeach Miguel Mariano. He made it happen with a favorable vote on Christmas Eve of 1936. Before the end of the year VP Federico Laredo Bru assumed the presidency.

Midway into the presidential period of Laredo Bru, Batista began to make approaches to the Cuban Communist Party. In

May of 1938 he authorized the publication of the communist newspaper *Hoy* and became good friends with Juan Marinello, Blas Roca and Joaquín Ordoqui, leaders of the communists. Skillfully playing all cards he visited Washington DC and met Roosevelt; visited Mexico City and met Lázaro Cárdenas; discussed politics with ABC's Martínez Sáenz and Jorge Mañach; received the Autentico's leader Grau San Martín at Columbia.

On January 5, 1939, Grau, Menocal, Gómez, and Martínez Saenz, representing all parties, met and declared publicly that the only way to solve Cuba's domestic problems was to hold a Constitutional Assembly and give a fresh start to the republic. A few days later all parties —having lost their accreditations— were reinstated by law: *Partido Unión Revolucionaria, Partido Agrario Nacional, Partido Laborista Cubano, Partido Nacional Revolucionario (Realistas), Partido Auténtico* and *Partido Comunista de Cuba*.

Batista, still the strong man, stunned everyone by agreeing to the founding of the *Confederación de Trabajadores Cubanos (CTC)*. Its first congress was held immediately with the attendance of 1500 delegates.

Under the slogan of *Constituyente Primero y Elecciones Después*, a slogan presumably created by José Francisco Martí, *Ismaelillo*, the only son of José Martí in 1938 (see page 341), Batista got all politicians in Cuba to agree to the 1940 Constitutional Assembly and the elections in which he would prevail and be elected as constitutional president of Cuba. He gained the support of one of Cuba's most prestigious men, José Manuel Cortina, who agreed to open the first meeting of the Constitutional Convention. Prior to 1940, Cuba had never been led by such a talented and masterful politician.

Uncle Sam complaining about Cubans asking him once more to intervene in Cuba

In the region of Sabanilla del Encomendador, in Matanzas, on a 12th day of July in 1854, a black house slave named Fermín Gómez, known as *Yeye*, gave 25 pesos in gold to his master on behalf of his future child; the child's mother was Serafina Ferrer, a slave-born woman who had bought her freedom a few months earlier. Thus came to the world as a free man **Juan Gualberto Gómez Ferrer (1854-1933)**. He died on March 5th, 1933, as Cuba was entering the saddest period of its history since 1902; times that were marked with the blood of many Cubans.

Juan Gualberto's parents took the baby as soon as he was born and moved to Havana; there they opened a small grocery store, where the father worked, and a small laundry where the mother toiled. They dedicated their lives to make sure that Juan Gualberto had a bright future. He was sent to **Paris** to for his university studies. After difficult times in Cuba his parents could no longer afford to pay for his education but he remained in Paris on his own, working at days and studying during nights. He became a follower of the *Comuneros* and this led him to independence ideals and to José Martí. In time José Martí came to love this man and trust him un- conditionally. Eventually they both got to work in the law offices of **Nicolás Azcárate** and the day when Martí was made prisoner to be deported to Spain, he trusted no one but Juan Gualberto with his personal papers.

Photos above: Young Juan Gualberto, at the time he worked with José Martí in the Law Offices of Azcárate in Havana in 1880; sitting in the Cabinet of President Alfredo Zayas in 1921 (fourth from left).

The honesty and great merits of **Juan Gualberto Gómez** were such that even his greatest adversaries, such as Rafael Montoro —an avowed *autonomist* and an important figure with whom Juan Gualberto debated many times about the benefits of independence above autonomy— praised Juan Gualberto calling him «*the man with the most valuable service to Cuba.*»

By one of those ironies and whims of destiny, Gerardo Machado was the first Cuban president that saw fit to **honor Juan Gualberto**. A few months before his death, when Juan Gualberto was still strong and vibrant, Gerardo Machado, honored him with the *Grand Cross of Carlos Manuel de Céspedes*, the greatest tribute the Republic could confer on a citizen. The words of Juan Gualberto on this occasion were «*I am Juan Gualberto, with or without this Medal.*»

Photos above: Juan Gualberto laid to rest in 1933, his last photo and a view of his mausoleum in Colon Cemetery, Havana.

The situation in Cuba in 1933 had no easy solution. The terror created by the Machado government could not defeat his adversaries. The terrorist actions of the opposition could not overthrow the government. The economic situation was getting unsustainable. The communists, behind the curtains, were ready to seize power in the middle of the chaos. The US, on the other hand, was **not willing to intervene** invoking the Platt Amendment.

The solution was to set in motion the process of *Mediación*. **Franklin Delano Roosevelt (1882-1945)** had assumed the presidency of the US and had inaugurated the policy of the *Buen Vecino* (Good Neigh- bor). He sent his friend **Benjamin Sumner Welles (1892-1961)** as Ambassador to Cuba «*to placate the opposition and work within the existing order.*» Photos at right, FDR and Sumner Welles.

The arrival of Sumner Welles in Cuba in 1933 was the last episode of a long chain of US interventions in the internal affairs of Cuba. They were mostly positive and were generally requested and accepted by the Cuban governments and the opposition parties. They reinforced, however, the notion that **Cubans could not govern themselves**.

The interventions started with Taft after the re-election of Estrada Palma in 1906; continued with the landing of marines after the *Estenoz* and *Ivonet* rebellion in 1911; they resumed with the 1917 liberal uprising by Gómez and supporters; then there was the strong hand of Crowder during the governments of Menocal and Zayas (1913 to 1925). It seemed that the US always had the solution to problems in Cuba. *On the left* **Sumner Welles** (with the cane) and **Cordell Hull**, US Secretary of State.

In April of 1933, at the suggestion of Sumner Wells, and with the concurrence of the opposition, all interested parties came together on a *Comité Conjunto de la Mediación*, also known as the *Mesa Redonda*.

The press, the University professors, the Liberals, the Conservatives and the Populars, the ABC, the OCRR, the Union Nacionalista and the Acción Republicana, all came together under the moderation of **Cosme de la Torriente (1872-1956)**. The only absences were the *Directorio Estudiantil*, the communists, the *Menocalistas* and the *Ala Izquierda Estudiantil*.

The *Mediación* failed: it stopped most acts of terrorism but could not dissuade the workers —heavily influenced by the Communists— to stop the strikes that paralyzed Havana.

On August 4, 1933 a radio station misleadingly announced Machado had resigned. People ran to the streets and were shot by the police. 20 people died. The Communists offered Machado to stop the strikes if the party and their CNOC were legalized. Machado agreed, believing the Communists were controlling the strikers, which was not the case.

At the military barracks in *Columbia* and at the fortress of *La Cabaña* in Havana, a group of officers revolted. **Machado decided to resign August 12 and flew to Bahamas**. A former Cuban Ambassador to the US assumed briefly the presidency, **Carlos Manuel de Céspedes Quesada (1871-1939)**, son of Carlos Manuel de Céspedes, the leader of the War of 1868-1878.

Photos: Cosme de la Torriente, Carlos Manuel de Céspedes and Machado the day he left Cuba.

By the time Machado was ready to resign, things had been happening in the streets of most Cuban cities that had never occurred before. *Bohemia* magazine reported the facts with lots of detail, and **to a certain extent exhorted the citizens to take the streets to assure the fall of Machado**. On its cover there were a soldier and a student, symbolic of the alliance being forged at the *Columbia Barracks*. Hundreds of Cubans began to riot and vandalize the homes and offices of former Machado followers, as shown in the pictures above. Cuba, for the first time in its history, was in total chaos; the police was gone and for many days nobody knew who was in charge.

Photos above: soldiers at the entrance to the *Hotel Nacional* in 1933; scenes from the riots and vandalism in the streets of Havana after the fall of Gerardo Machado on August 12, 1933.

Initially Machado had appointed **General Alberto Herrera** (*photo on top*) as his successor. He lasted less than 24 hours, as people began to congregate in front of the ABC headquarters (*photo at center*). **Carlos Manuel de Céspedes** was then appointed president after Herrera ceased in this function. He was sworn in by the Chief Justice of the Supreme Court (*photo at bottom*). He lasted 23 days in office before the *Pentarquía* was appointed.

A provisional government was established to bring order after the fall of Machado. After about four months of mediation by Dr. Carlos Manuel de Céspedes y Quesada, son of founding father Carlos Manuel de Céspedes, the provisional government took possession of the republic, **supported behind the scenes** by the U.S. Ambassador Benjamin Sumner Welles, as the personal representative of President Roosevelt. Many Cubans appreciated this covert intervention by the US government in the domestic affairs of Cuba. The provisional government included **Dr. Cosme de la Torriente** (State), **Dr. Joaquín Martínez Sáenz** (Finance); **Demetrio Castillo** (Public Works), **Dr. Federico Laredo Bru** (Interior), **Dr. Carlos Saladrigas** (Justice); **Nicasio Silverio** (Trade), **Rafael Santos Jiménez** (Foreign Relations) and **Emeterio Santovenia** (Secretary of the Presidency.) The Senate and House of Representatives were dissolved immediately.

Most groups and parties shared in the provisional government. The governing coalition was composed of the *Union Nacionalista,* the *ABC, Acción Republicana* and the *OCRR*. The opposition consisted of the *Partido Republicano,* the *ABC Radical* and the Left Wing Students.

The new government was **powerless** since a conspiracy by sergeants, soldiers and students began to be organized in the army by Fulgencio Batista, Pablo Rodriguez, Manuel López Migoya, Ignacio Galíndez, José Estevez Maymir, Mario Hernández, Jaime Marine, Belisario Hernandez, Cruz Vidal and other soldiers, joined by students Rubén de León, Carlos Prío, Eduardo Chibás, Antonio Varona, Rafael García Bárcena, Justo Carrillo, José Antonio Rubio Padilla and Sergio Carbó, editor of *La Semana* journal.

Photo at the top: riots continued in Havana during the short government of Carlos Manuel de Céspedes, several weeks after the fall of Machado; *At the bottom*, a photo of Machado after his arrival in the Bahamas, his first stop on his long escape from Cuba.

THE REVOLUTION IN CUBA
The Young Soldier Who Assassinated Antonio Jimines, Leader of President Machado's Secret Police, Raised to a Pedestal to Receive the Acclaim of the Public.

When on August 12, 1933 **Gerardo Machado** left Cuba, the Revolution of 1933 became *triumphant*. As many revolutions, it was a movement that succeeded because the doors were opened by those who eventually would be its victims. The intent of many Machado opponents was not only to replace the old politicians but also to bring about social, political and economic changes.

The photo above shows the front page of the *New York Times Magazine* on August 26, 1933. The crowds were acclaiming the soldier that killed **Col Antonio Jiménez**, the chief of La *Porra*, the political police of Machado. The photo appeared in hundreds of publications worldwide.

Knowing that Machado had finally left, the people of Havana invaded the streets with **extreme jubilation**. Some in the crowds were angry and continued to loot and vandalize. Others were vindictive and began to look for *machadistas* to take revenge. Soldiers and police, in solidarity with the citizens and trying to preserve the order, corralled the mobs to prevent that their frustrations and resentment would turn them violent.

Hounded like wild animals, the *machadistas* were running away from the angry mobs and trying —many very successfully— to hide. Some of them fell in the hands of their pursuers in Prado Avenue, on Belascoaín and Infanta streets, and in the neighborhood of the *ministerios*.

Those merrymakers who had cars took long rides along the Malecón, up Galiano Street, across to Reina and Prado Streets and back to Malecón, like in the days of Carnival, all the way sounding their claxons and flying Cuban flags.

The home of **Octavio Averhoff**, a collector of antiquities, was emptied and set on fire; his bookcases, cabinets, and Egyptian treasures were scattered over the wet sidewalk of the Malecón. The home of **Orestes Ferrara**, across from the University, was riddled with bullet impacts on its fabulous Florentine marble façade. **Carlos Miguel de Céspedes** had a yacht anchored at the *Almendares River* and it was made to slowly be consumed by flames.

The Star of David flag of the ABC's followers could be seen everywhere; so were their green streamers. The homes of the members of *La Porra* were identified with hand-written painted signs spelling in perfect latin *Sic Semper Tiranis*, as it well corresponded to the enlightened, cultivated and refined university throngs.

Aside from that, the prevailing mood was **elation and not vengeance**. The photo above shows a celebration around the statue of *Alma Mater* at the University.

No president in Cuba had received more mixed and conflicting reviews than Machado. His deeds went from a magnificent slogan —*Water, Roads and Schools*, to outstanding accomplishments building a progressive infrastructure with valuable public works, ending with an ambition for power and a tyrannical imposition over the same citizens that had supported and adored him.

His enemies were implacable. **Rubén Martínez Villena**, his most virulent communist opponent, characterized him as an «*asno con garras*» (a jackass with claws). **Julio Antonio Mella** went even further «*Cloistered in his stubbornness, unresponsive to popular demands, megalomaniacal and stupid, Machado is using his henchmen to perpetrate the most brutal repression of workers, students and intellectuals who are opposing his despotic government.*»

The photos show **Martinez Villena** addressing students from the *University of Havana*; vandalism after Machado's demise and an allegorical front page of *Bohemia* showing a suffering republic.

The 1933 revolution was not an event inspired by José Martí; in the 1930s his essays and articles were the subject of study by scholars and not by the students or the general population. No one in 1933 claimed to be an ideological descendant of José Martí, with the possible exception of **Julio Antonio Mella**. In 1933 the students were inspired by the liberal and nationalistic ideas of people like **Ramiro Guerra (1880-1970)**, director of the scholarly magazine *Cuba Pedagógica*, and above all by the writings of **José Ingenieros (1877-1925)**, the Argentinean author of *El Hombre Mediocre*, an outstanding *best seller* with the serious reading public in Cuba.

These ideas were presented in scholarly and popular Cuban magazines like *Revista de Avance*, *Social*, *Bohemia*, *Cuba Contemporánea*, and others. They inspired fundamentally liberal and democratic concepts such as civil liberties, the rights of the individuals, political pluralism, an independent judiciary, sovereignty of the people, honest elections and honesty in government.

At the time of the fall of Machado, the US ambassador to Cuba was **Harry Frank Guggenheim (1890-1971)**, a graduate of *Columbia Grammar* in Manhattan, *Yale* in New Jersey and *Cambridge* in England. He was also, of course, heir to a large fortune. He tried to convince Machado to moderate his despotic reactions to the opposition and not to seek re-election, both to no avail. Machado, according to Guggenheim, always felt he was facing a movement of subversive and fanatical revolutionary students with more than only grievances.

Photos above, from top to bottom: The last photo of Machado's full presidential staff at Cuba's presidential palace; a photo of the last strike, organized by the teachers of Santiago de las Vegas the day before he resigned; Machado's last official act, the presentation of medals for two US airmen trainers that were in Cuba for three years, to US ambassador **Harry Frank Guggenheim**, second from left. At the right of the ambassador is the Cuban Army Chief of Staff **General Alberto Herrera**.

The newspapers in Cuba could not keep up with the flow of news following August 12 of 1933. On the 13th **Carlos Manuel de Céspedes** took possession of the presidency and Roosevelt declared Céspedes was *de facto* recognized. On the 14th **Rafael Montoro** died and Welles informed Roosevelt that all members of the new government were reputable and capable people. On the 15th the *Directorio* prosecuted and executed **José Soler**, an anti-Machado spy. On the 17th **Manuel Marquez Sterling** was appointed ambassador to Washington and **Carlos García Velez** ambassador to Spain. On the 18th **Grau San Martín** returned from exile and an unknown sergeant called **Fulgencio Batista** acted as the main speaker at a funeral for man murdered by the Machado police. On the 20th **Menocal** returned from exile in Miami. On the 24th the **1901 Constitution** was declared back in force. On the 25th a group of sergeants began to meet in Columbia, under the leadership of **Fulgencio Batista** and **José Eleuterio Pedraza**.

Photos in August 1933: The mobs vandalizing the *Heraldo de Cuba* newspaper (property of **Orestes Ferrara**); Fulgencio Batista and José Eleuterio Pedraza.

Photos: public demonstrations against Machado in 1933. Former Machado followers held at a detention cell inside the fortress of *El Príncipe*, in Havana.

On September 3 a hurricane struck the northern coast of Cuba and President Céspedes visited the town of Sagua la Grande. The following day, taking advantage of his absence a group of non-commissioned military officers in Columbia, under the leadership of a stenographer-sergeant called **Fulgencio Batista (1901-1973)**, took over the Camp with the support of the *Directorio Estudiantil Universitario*.

They deposed the president in what was called the **Revolt of the Sergeants** and installed a *Consulting Commission* which people baptized as the *Pentarquía*, i.e., a committee of five to assume the presidency: professors **Ramón Grau San Martín (1887-1969)**, and **Guillermo Portela Möller (1886-1958)**, journalist **Sergio Carbó Morera (1891-1971)**, banker **Porfirio Franca Alvarez de la Campa (1878-1950)** and economist and attorney **José Miguel Irizarri Gamio (1895-1976)**.

FDR and his ambassador Sumner Welles were surprised since they though the Cuban problem was solved with the resignation and escape of Machado and the appointment of **Carlos Manuel de Céspedes Quesada (1871-1939)** as president of the Republic.

Photo above: from left to right, the five *Pentarcas*: (Irizarri, Franca, Portela, Grau, Carbó), plus Batista. *Below*: without Batista.

In spite of the nominal authority of the *Pentarquía,* it became evident that Batista **was in charge** in Cuba since he had been recognized explicitly by Sumner Welles. A good part of this support was due to the threat that the communists posed to **the very existence** of the *Directorio Estudiantil* and the belief that Batista was the man that could control them.

Photo at left, Batista and Sumner Welles in 1933.

A week later it was evident that the *Pentarquía* and Batista were not getting along. The students appointed **Grau San Martín** as president by acclamation. A cheering crowd gathered in front of the presidential palace for his inauguration (*photo above*); no diplomats attended. It soon became clear that Sumner Welles and the US government had **strong reservations about Grau San Martín**. By December Batista had joined ranks with Sumner Wells and was openly conspiring against Grau.

In 1933, as the Pentarquía came into power, Ambassador **Sumner Welles** moved to the *Hotel Nacional* and asked Washington to send marines to protect the American Embassy and the hotel. General Julio Sanguily and other officials of the Cuban army also took refuge in the hotel, since it looked like an impregnable defensive fortress. The new army, all non-commissioned soldiers loyal to Batista, began a day long siege on October 2. The hotel was bombarded with considerable damage to the installation and numerous deaths. The chiefs and officers were immediately imprisoned at *La Cabaña*.

Many historians have run over the *Hotel Nacional* incident as an inconsequential and curious event. The siege, however, shaped the discourse of political action in Cuba over the next decades. It legitimized revenge and violence and the practice of granting no mercy to vanquished opponents or dissidents. On the short term it made possible Batista's rise to power.

In the midst of all the turmoil after August 12, 1933, an improvised and indiscreet move was made by **Sergio Carbó**, the journalist who had been part of the *Pentarquía*. Without any consultation or justifiable reason he single-handedly promoted **Batista** to the rank of *Colonel*. Going a bit further, Batista took the opportunity to proclaim himself **Chief of the Army**. *Photo at left*: Carbó and Batista.

On November of 1933, an interesting episode took place that could have changed half a century of Cuban history.

The *Directorio Estudiantil* found out (actually it was Carlos Prío who did) that a conspiracy was in the works for a **coup d'état** by Batista, who had ambitions to be *President* and not just *Chief of the Army*. A meeting was agreed on Carbo's home at 17th between O and N streets in *El Vedado* to deal with Batista. Grau, Guiteras, the entire *Directorio* and the top military commanders were to be present. The strategy was that Grau would accuse Batista of trea- son and the soldiers would take him prisoner to *La Cabaña* fortress to be shot.

After a serious confrontation, Batista pleaded for forgiveness (kneeling according to some witnesses) and **Grau decided not to press his accusations**. The result was that Batista left the meeting alive and stronger than ever. No one ever knew why Grau did not finish the plan to get rid of Batista. Some thought he was trying to assert his **political independence** from the *Directorio*. Days later, frustrated by Grau's indecisiveness, the *Directorio* decided not to support him anymore, quit its militancy and dissolved itself.

Photo: on top, Grau and Batista on September 4; *on the bottom*, Batista, now in full control, pronouncing a speech on a balcony of the presidential palace, with Carlos Prío, Ramón Grau and Sergio Carbó by his side.

The meeting at Carbó's house had weakened the position of Grau as well as Batista's. **Grau lost the trust of the students** because his last minute indecision, which many interpreted as cowardice. Batista became aware that his **alliance with the students** was frail and unreliable and that his real strength was with his fellow soldiers.

On November 8, 1933, some units of the army and the air force were joined by members of the ABC in an open rebellion under the leadership of **Colonel Juan Blas Hernández (1879-1933)**. Batista, pressed by his officers, ordered the army to defend the government.

By midnight there were rebels only at the *Castillo de Atarés* at the end of Habana harbor. They surrendered the next day. **Blas Hernández was shot after surrendering**. In the eyes of the people the *ABC* had not only failed to retain its political clout but had also failed to recover it with arms. The party began to lose its popularity and finally disappeared in 1952.

Photo on top, left to right: Batista, Blas Hernández and Grau. *On the bottom*: the Castillo de Atarés in 1933.

In the 1930s, aside from the theater, one of the most popular forms of public entertainment, in the best borrowed French tradition, was the circus. Two of the pioneers of this traveling form of amusement were Pablo Santos and Jesús Artigas, both tobacco workers born in Havana.

Initially they had secured the representation of the French *Gaumont Films* and started in Cuba the enthusiasm for the movies. On a visit to Paris they discovered the *Cirque d'Hiver*, which for the first time was presenting a *flying trapeze*, soon to be the toast of Europe. Santos and Artigas dropped the business of movies, which they had cultivated to perfection, and decided to go into the world of circus.

Santos y Artigas became a regular institution in Cuba in a few short years. In fact it lasted from the early days of the Republic until the closing of democracy in Cuba, when it was confiscated by the government; horses, elephants, clowns, tents and railroad cars, the government impounded everything in the 1960s. During fifty years of republican Cuba *Santos y Artigas* had made famous many of their performers such as *Marga*, the lady midget with an ape-like face, *Valpomar*, the four legged girl, the *Hércules Brothers*, bodybuilders extraordinaire, *Adelfa*, the bearded lady, *Lalo and Lali*, the Korean midgets, *Ilona*, the Hungarian trapeze dancer and many others.

Photos: the *Santos y Artigas Circus* and a poster of the *Circo Publillones* in 1916.

For many years the main competitor of *Santos y Artigas* was the *Circo Pubillones*. It was in fact an earlier and just as successful circus spectacle. In 1909 its shows were presented at the *Campo de Marte* on days when there were not bullfights on schedule for that venue; it was sometimes featured at empty lots in San Rafael and Oquendo Streets or at 61 Aguila Street, along the block between Barcelona and Zanja Streets. The term *Pubillones* was so popular that it became a generic designation for *Circus*, to the point that when *Santos y Artigas* debuted in Havana it was called —the Pubillones Santos y Artigas.‖

One of the most emblematic and unforgettable acts of the *Santos y Artigas circus was* **Chacumbele**. His real name was José Ramón Chacón y Velez, born in Santa Cruz del Sur, Camagüey, in 1912. He left his town in 1932 when his entire family perished in the floods that wiped out that entire seaside town. He first worked in Havana as an ambulant florist in Central Park and joined *Santos y Artigas* in 1935, becoming an important trapeze attraction. Soon he partnered with *Ilona* (Ilona Szabó), a Hungarian trapecist, and fell in love her. Distracted by Ilona's flirting with a circus strong man, he fell from the trapeze and his multiple fractures ended his career. Returning to Central Park to sell more flowers, he became despondent and committed suicide. It gave rise to a song by the *Trío Servando Díaz* called **Chacumbele, el mismito se Mató**, (Chacumbele he indeed killed himself) a phrase that became part of the folkloric heritage of Cuba.

Photos: *Chacumbele* and a 1922 poster of Santos y Artigas showing the two owners at the bottom corners.

Photo above: some of the members of the Grau San Martín Cabinet in 1934. **Manuel Márquez Sterling** (Minister of State), **Manuel Despaigne** (Finance Minister), **Antonio Guiteras** (Interior Minister), **Carlos J. Finlay** (Health Minister), **Manuel Costales Latatú** (Minister of Public Education), **Carlos Hevia** (Minister of Agriculture), **Joaquin River Balmaseda** (Minister of Justice), **Gustavo Moreno** (Minister of Public Works), **Angel Alberto Giraudy** (Labor Minister), **M. Fernandez de Velasco** (Minister of Communications) and **Ramiro Capablanca** (Minister of the Presidency).

Photo below: the *Pentarquía*, with Fulgencio Batista, in a photograph in 1933 with the top military men in the Cuban Army. By this time all commanding officers had been deposed after the *Conspiración de los Sargentos* (the uprising of the sergeants).

In 1933-34 Grau **San Martín** lasted only four months in the presidency of Cuba. He had been overwhelmingly supported by the students but not by the US government. His programs included agrarian reform, minimum wage, nationalization of public services, industrialization, housing reform and control of monopolies.

His closest associate was **Antonio Guiteras (1906-1935)**, his *Interior Minister*, a non-communist former associate of Julio Antonio Mella. Guiteras founded a socialist organization called *Joven Cuba* in 1935, a few months before he was killed when he was intending to escape from an arrest warrant.

During their four months in the government of Cuba Grau and Guiteras **unilaterally abrogated the *Platt Amendment*** (it was no longer functional for all practical purposes), encouraged labor unions, gave the vote to women and restricted the power of American companies.

Photos above: *on the left*, Antonio Guiteras; *on the right*, Guiteras on his way to nationalize the *Havana Electric Company* in 1934. The company's main investor was **William Van Home**, a wealthy Canadian who also owned the *Cuban Railroad Company*.

During his short presidency, on September 14, 1933, Grau abrogated the **1901 Cuban Constitution** that had been restored by Céspedes a few days before, on August 24, after the fall of Machado. The constitution had already been repealed during the period called the *Cooperativismo* in April 1928. Originally the *1901 Constitution* had been approved on February 21, 1901. It had included the *Platt amendment* and had been strongly inspired by the American Constitution of 1789. *On top*, Grau at a staff meeting in 1933.

On December 18, 1933, a new US representative arrived in Havana to substitute Sumner Welles: **Jefferson Caffery (1886-1928)**. Being a staunch conservative, he was greeted with contempt by the revolutionaries in Cuba. He did not like the abrasive, undignified Batista either, but was duty-bound to make him an ally. On January 10, 1934, he reported to Roosevelt that «*the government here is inefficient, inept and unpopular, supported only by the army and ignorant masses that have been misled by utopian promises.*»

Photo, top: Carlos Hevia and some members of his staff, including Dr. Carlos Findlay (son), sitting on his left.

Photo, bottom: President Carlos Mendieta in 1934 at an official function, with ambassador Caffery at his right.

In the midst of the revolutionary chaos after the fall of Machado, the press in Cuba —unlike the newspapers in the US— neglected to give proper attention to the death of **Domingo Méndez Capote (1863-1934)**.

He was a member of an aristocratic family in Cárdenas and graduated from the Law School at the *University of Havana*, where he taught for several years. He joined the independence war in 1896 and reached the rank of *General de Brigada*. He presided the *Asamblea de la Yaya* in 1897 and the *Asamblea de Santa Cruz* in 1899, and was elected VP of the Republic in Arms. In 1901 he became president of the *Constitutional Assembly* while a member of the US temporary government. In 1902 he presided the *Cuban Senate* and was the VP candidate with Estrada Palma in 1906. In 1924 he was again a VP candidate. He presided the Revolutionary Junta that ruled Cuba after the fall of Machado.

Photos above: Méndez Capote as a young man in 1887 and in his last photo in 1934. *Photo below*: at a meeting in the home of the *Marqueses de Pinar del Rio* in 1897 (he is second from right; this picture was published in *La Ilustración Española y Americana,* Madrid.)

By January 1934 Batista had enough political power to force Grau to resign, particularly because of Caffery's position that there would not be US recognition for his government.

After considering Carlos Hevia and Manuel Márquez Sterling for the position, **Colonel Carlos Mendieta (1873-1960)** was proclaimed president; Grau and many student leaders went into exile. The ABC, all Cuban *politicos,* the businessmen and the US government supported the new president. A general strike proved ineffective. For the next six years Batista would be the **power behind the throne**.

Photo on the right: Mendieta honoring Batista in 1934.

The ascent of **Fulgencio Batista** to be the most powerful man in Cuba was a remarkable accomplishment.

He was a member of the poorest classes with no social ties to anyone remotely connected with money or power. He was looked down as a colored man. He did not have a political base within the civil population at a time when people were suspicious of the military. Initially his hold on the army was rather tenuous. He had to step over his superiors in the military knowing that they had fought the Spaniards during the war of independence. Finally, he knew how to find puppets among many old style *politicos* who longed for his support; he used them and ruthlessly discarded them if and when they became just a little too assertive.

During the brief government of General Carlos Mendieta (Jan 18, 1934 to Dec 11, 1935) the Secretary of the presidency was a fair and unblemished political man who would be chosen *Cuban National Poet* in 1955 by the Cuban Congress: **Agustín Acosta Bello (1886-1979)**.

Acosta, one of the cleanest men of the generation that came of age at the dawn of Cuba's twentieth century, had been born in Matanzas, at a modest home in 40 Calzada de Tirry, close to the railroad station. It was there that he found his first job as a telegraph operator. By 1901 he was writing poetry and in 1915 he published his first book, **Ala**, followed by **Hermanita**, dedicated to his loving wife María Isabel Schweyer. In 1918 he moved to Jagüey Grande after receiving his doctorate in law from the *University of Havana*.

As Domingo del Monte had done in his time, Acosta became the **center of the famous literary *tertulias*** (gatherings) at *Hotel Vista Alegre* in Jagüey Grande. In 1926 he published *La Zafra*, probably the most influential political and literary book in the first quarter century of the young Republic of Cuba. From 1933 to 1937 Acosta presided the *Partido Unión Nacionalista* and served in the Cuban Senate. He suffered political prison when he opposed the Machado dictatorship and for two years afterwards became governor of Matanzas province. In December 1972 he became an exile and died in Miami in 1979, after the Cuban Communist regime stripped him of his title as *Poeta Nacional de Cuba*.

Photos above: Acosta as a young man and as a senior; Acosta in exile, with poets Luis Mario and José Angel Buesa.

On February 8, 1934, Grau joined the leaders of the *Directorio Estudiantil* and founded the **Partido Revolucionario Cubano** (Auténtico), named after the party Martí had started in New York in 1892. A year later Guiteras set up a group more prone to engage in armed activity, the **Joven Cuba**. He decided to go to Mexico to organize an armed expedition to fight Batista's regime. As he was departing Cuba on May 8, 1935, he was captured by the army and shot to death at *el Morrillo* in Matanzas. With the death of Guiteras died all hopes of quickly reaching political goals through revolutionary violence.

On March 1935 the *Auténticos*, *Joven Cuba*, the *ABC* and the *Communists* joined forces in an anti-Batista strike that engulfed Cuba and sank it into a crisis. The reaction to the strike wiped out any evidence that there had been a constructive revolution in Cuba in 1933. The strike itself (200,000 participants) failed but the **repression** that it elicited from the military changed forever the extent to which men in power in Cuba respected lives and defended themselves with civility.

Photos: at left, firing squads as retaliation to the rebels; *at right*, Batista rewards the troops in front of a speechless Mendieta.

Photo above: the founders of the Partido Revolucionario Cubano *(Auténtico)* on February 8, 1934. *In the photo, left to right*:

Sitting: Edgardo Buttari, Joaquín del Río Balmaseda, Salvador Masipp, Carlos Hevia, Ramón Grau San Martín, Carlos J. Finlay, Ramiro Capablanca, Conchita Castanedo, Otilia André.

Standing, center row: Gustavo Moreno, Lincoln Rodón, Enrique Perozo, Rafael Suárez, Alberto Inocente Álvarez, María T. Freyre, Enrique C. Enríquez, Manuel Arán, José Fresneda, Manuel Antonio de Varona, Fidelio Durán, Carlos Prío Socarrás, Alfredo del Valle, Julio López Maza.

Standing, back row: Rubén de León, Josefina Pedrosa, Antonio del Valle, Luis Martínez Sáenz, Segundo Ceballos, Armando Roda, Félix Lancís, Alberto Cruz, Roberto Coloma, Laudelino Gonsa, Rafael Trejo, Segundo Curti.

Photos above: Havana carnivals in 1934; it was the first time in years without the presence of Machado; the *Topes de Collantes Hospital* on the Escambray Mountains, near Trinidad, (a favorite Batista project) under construction in 1935.

By the end of 1935 four political parties had emerged: Menocal's *Conjunto Nacional Democrático*; the Partido *Acción Republicana* and the *Partido Unión Nacionalista*; they joined forces under **Miguel Mariano Gómez (1889-1950)**, son of former President José Miguel Gómez; the *Liberal Party* embraced ex-President Céspedes' *Conjunción Centralista Nacional*.

The parties could not agree on new election rules and, facing no opponents, Mendieta resigned and his Secretary of State **José Agripino Barnet (1864-1945)** assumed the presidency. The five times postponed presidential elections were held in January 1936 and Miguel Mariano Gómez was elected. Grau, the communists and the ABC had refused to participate.

Photos on top: José A. Barnet (left) and Miguel Mariano (right); *Below:* Miguel Mariano with Batista in 1938.

On February 1934 the government of Mendieta approved a provisional constitution **extending the vote to women**. Until then voting rights were obtained via presidential decrees and *politicos* were using the notion of women's suffrage to get support for their policies.

It took one disingenuous pledge from Machado, a decree from Grau and a quick-fix by Mendieta to confirm that women could vote. The first attempt to give women the vote had been made by **Miguel Gener**, former mayor of Havana, during the *1901 Constitutional Convention*. It was defeated 17 to 9.

Other women issues had been dealt with before. In 1917 the *Ley de Patria Potestad* was approved, giving women the right to administer their wealth. In 1918 Congress approved the *Ley del Divorcio*. In 1920 Zayas introduced a Constitutional amendment that included the vote for women. *Photo below*, members of the *Feminist Club of Havana* in 1922.

Two extraordinary Cuban women, by their deeds, impacted the growth of the feminist movement in Cuba:

Mariana Grajales (1815 - 1893) (*top left*), was born in Santiago de Cuba. All of her children joined the Liberation Army; 11 of the 13 died in combat in the Cuban jungle, including Antonio Maceo, Major General and José, Lieutenant General in Cuba's Wars of Independence.

Mariblanca Salas Alomar (1901-1983) (*bottom left*), was born in Santiago de Cuba; she was a writer and journalist and the first woman to be in a Presidential Cabinet (under Grau first and later under Prío). She belonged to the *Grupo Minorista* and was elected to the Cuban *1940 Constitutional Convention*.

Mercedes García Tudurí (1904-1997) was a Cuban educator, poet and philosopher; one of brightest minds produced by Republican Cuba. At age 17 she obtained an Arts degree from the University of Havana, where she also obtained doctorates in Philosophy and Letters (1925), Education (1934), Political Science and Economics (1952), as well as a BA in Diplomatic Law (1949).

At 19 she was teaching at the Institute of Havana, of which years later she was the director. In 1946 she became Professor of Philosophy at the *University of Santo Tomas de Villanueva*; later she was Professor of Philosophy of its School of Education and became Dean of that school. She was president of the School of Philosophy at the *University of Havana*; president of the *National Board of Education*, the *Cuban Society of Philosophy* and the *National Council of Education* of Cuba.

She went into exile in 1960. In the US she was Regent of *Marygrove College* in Michigan and *Biscayne College* in Miami. The last class she taught was at age 90.

She received numerous international awards, including, on April 6 1997, the *Pro Eclessia et Pontifice* bestowed by Pope John Paul II, just weeks before May 25, when he died in Miami.

Photos: Mercedes García Tudurí, her *Pro Eclessia et Pontifice* and the abandoned campus of the *Catholic University of Villanueva* in Cuba.

On December of 1936 Batista sought a nine-cent tax on every bag of sugar to create rural schools under the army's control. Miguel Mariano was opposed. Batista maneuvered to impeach him; the House complied with a vote of 111 to 45 and the Senate 22 to 12. Within hours, on December 24, Vice President **Federico Laredo Bru (1875-1946)** took the oath of office as the new President. On December 30 the new law went into effect and every bag of sugar was taxed $0.09, nine cents, as Batista wished.

Photos below: Batista and Laredo Bru; Lazaro Peña González.

As **Laredo Bru stood by the side unobtrusively**, Batista sought to bring organized labor under his control; the Cuban communists were the best vehicles Batista could find. In 1937 they had founded the *Partido Unificado Revolucionario (PUR)* and started to organize the labor movement. In 1938 the **Confederación de Trabajadores de Cuba** —the *CTC*— was recognized. Sergio Carbó and Rubén de León joined Batista's forces at a serious cost to Grau's *PRC (Auténticos)*. Magnanimously, Batista legalized the *Communist Party* on September 15, 1938. On 23 January 1939, the *CTC* had its first National Assembly (*photo above*) where its new Secretary General, **Lazaro Peña González (1911-1974)**, was elected.

Photo above: President Laredo Brú (with a document in his hands) and his Cabinet at the end of 1936. During his administration, the *Sugar Coordination Law* was approved: it gave the farmers, settlers and workers a pro-rata share of the selling price of sugar.

Photo below: the newly constructed *Avenida de las Misiones*, running from the presidential palace to Havana's *malecón*.

Once Laredo Brú was in power and Batista in control, the interest of Cuban intellectuals, academics, politicians and people in general turned to the engaging subject of the **Spanish Civil War**.

Cuba provided one of the largest contingents of voluntary fighters on the side of the Republic when the Spanish Civil War (1936-1939) exploded in the Iberian Peninsula. Cuban volunteers were mostly from the opposition to Fulgencio Batista. They went to Spain to fight what they called the *nazi-fascismo* emerging in Spain (Francisco Franco's nationalists).

Three **pro-Republican groups** were organized in Cuba during the Spanish Civil War: a committee was formed to collect and display propaganda and to support acts of solidarity with Re- publican Spain. A second group was created as a clandestine committee to recruit volunteers. A third group consisted only of members of the *Communist Party of Cuba* who were heeding the call of the *Kominterm* to contribute men to the International Brigades fighting in Spain on the side of the Republicans.

Most Cuban combatants belonged to the detachment sent clandestinely from Havana by the *Communist Party*. A group mostly comprised of Cuban revolutionaries and communists who were in exile went directly from New York, organized by the Julio Antonio Mella and the Antonio Guiteras Clubs in that city; they traveled as part of the *Abraham Lincoln Battalion* of U.S. communists. An additional group of fighters consisted of Cubans living in Mexico, the Caribbean and Central America, as well as dozens who were already in Spain when Gen. Francisco Franco staged the uprising on July 18, 1936. There are **no records of Cubans fighting for Franco's Nationalists** during the war; many of the republicans, back in Cuba years later, had to admit «*Franco no lo hizo mal.*» (Franco, after the war, did not do it that bad).

Photos: **Pablo de la Torriente Brau** and two posters of Republican propaganda in Cuba during the Spanish Civil War.

The total number of Cuban volunteer combatants was variously estimated between 700 and 1000, most of them fighting on the 59th Battalion of the 15th International Brigade. Some had some celebrity in Cuba like **Pablo de la Torriente Brau**, a Communist journalist, **Jorge Agostini**, a professional military man, **Isidro Gener**, a well know boxer, **Julio Cuevas**, a popular musician, **Wilfredo Lam**, the painter and **Rolando Masferrer**, a notable gangster. Most of these groups reached Spain through France, pretending to be tourists for the *Paris World Exposition*. Once in France, the *French Communist Party* would take them near the Pyrenees, which they crossed on foot.

Cubans fought in Madrid under the well known Republican slogan «*No pasarán*» (they shall not pass), a reference to their resistance to the Nationalist troops that besieged Madrid for most of the war. The Cuban volunteers became known for their performance in the battles of *Brunete*, *Belchite* and *El Ebro*.

At the end of the war, when they found themselves on the losing side, they covered the backs of the defeated Republican troops as they escaped towards France. Close to 200 Cubans perished during the civil war. Those that survived were interned in French Concentration Camps and had a difficult time returning to Cuba, where they were not particularly received with acclamations.

Photos: Cuban fighters in Spain during the Civil War; Republican refugees escaping into France; the slogan of the Republicans as they defended Madrid: *No Pasarán*.

On May 10, 1938 Batista and Laredo Bru announced a Constitutional Convention where all parties could participate. The Communists worked feverishly to register 90,000 voters out of a total of 1.6 million citizens that qualified. Many political refugees, including Grau, returned from exile and on September 25, after 15 years underground, the **Communist Party** was legalized. Its posture had changed from moderate opposition to unconditional support for Batista, whose political fortunes had plunged. Its membership had evolved from agitators to rapacious gangsters. The **Auténticos**, however, had matured into a moderate left-of-center party that advocated democratic reforms rather than turmoil.

Elections to the *Constitutional Assembly* took place as scheduled on **November 15, 1939**. Two electoral coalitions emerged: the government and the opposition. When the results came in Grau's *Auténticos* led all the other parties; the *Liberals* came in second, Menocal's *Partido Demócrata Republicano* placed third; the pro-government *Nationalist party* was fourth; the *Communist party* was fifth. Miguel Mariano Gómez' *Acción Republicana* and Joaquín Martínez Sáenz' *ABC* party, both opposition parties, were sixth and seventh. The pro-government *Democrats* placed eight. About fifty to sixty percent of the electorate voted. The opposition bloc elected 41 delegates to the Constitutional Assembly; the government coalition elected 35. Several veterans from the 1930 generation were elected as delegates, **Carlos Prío Socarrás** and **Eduardo R. Chibás** among them. On 10 February 1940 the *Constitutional Assembly* met for the first time in the House chamber of the Capitol. The delegates elected **Ramón Grau San Martín** as president of the Assembly.

Photo: arrival in Havana of the *Campana de la Demajagua*, the bell that called Cubans to the war of independence in 1868; it would now preside the sessions of the 1940 Contitutional Assembly.

The drawing on the left shows a sketch of the first Cuban Constitutional Assembly held at Guáimaro on April 10, 1869. Céspedes presided its sessions.

ASAMBLEA CONSTITUYENTE DE 1940

Carlos Marquez Sterling
Emilio Nuñez Portuondo
Rafael Alvarez González
José R. Andreu Martínez
Manuel Benitez González
Fernando del Busto Martínez
Juan Cabrera Hernández
Ramiro Capablanca Graupera
César Casas Rodríguez
Ramón Corona García
José M. Cortina y García
Pelayo Cuervo Navarro
Francisco Dellunde
Arturo Don Rodríguez
Nicolás Duarte
José A. Fernández de Castro
Simeón Ferro
Adriano Galano Sánchez
Félix García Rodríguez
Ramón Granda Fernández
Rafael Guas e Inclán
Alfredo Hornedo Suárez
Felipe Jay Raoulx
Amaranto López Negrón
Juan Marinello Vidaurreta
Antonio Martínez Fraga
José A. Mendigutía
Joaquin Meso Quesada
Eusebio Mujal
Emilio Ochoa Ochoa
Manuel Parrado Rodes
Francisco J. Prieto Llera
Santiago Rey Perna
Mario Robau Cartaya
Primitivo Rodríguez Rodríguez
Esperanza Sánchez Mastrapa
Juan Antonio Vinent Griñan
Cesar Vilar Aguilar
Ramón Zaydín

Alberto Boada Miguel
Salvador Acosta Casares
Francisco Aloma y Alvarez de la Campa
Aurelio Alvarez de la Vega
Antonio Bravo Acosta
Antonio Bravo Correoso
Miguel Calvo Tarafa
José Manuel Casanova y Diviño
Romerico Cordero Garces
Felipe Correoso y del Risco
Miguel Coyula Llaguno
Eduardo R. Chibas
Mario E. Dihigo Llanos
Manuel Dorta Duque
Mariano Esteva Lora
Orestes Ferrara y Marino
Manuel Fueyo Suárez
Salvador García Agüero
Quintín George Vernol
Ramón Grau San Martin
Alicia Hernández de la Barca
Francisco Ichaso Macias
Emilio A. Laurent
Jorge Mañach Robato
José Maceo González
Joaquin Martínez
Manuel Mesa Medina
Gustavo Moreno Lastres
Delio Nuñez Mesa
Manuel A. Orizondo Caraballe
Juan B. Pons Jane
Carlos Prío Socarrás
Eugenio Rodríguez Cartas
Blas Roca Calderio
Miguel Suarez Fernandez
Alberto Silva Quiñones
Maria Esther Villoch Leyva
Fernando del Villar de los Rios

The mandate of the 1940 Constitutional Assembly was clear and simple: revise the 1901 Constitution and incorporate the novel ideas that had surfaced since the 1933 revolution. The members of the 1940 Assembly (listed above), collaborated with each other for the first time in the history of the republic, regardless of their past differences. They gave Cuba one of its most glorious and extraordinary political documents.

The 1940 Constitution, however, proved to have four basic flaws. The first was that many of its **mandates were above the political will** of most Cuban *politicos*, who had deep-rooted notions that the purpose of political discourse was to prevail at all costs. The second was that it included **provocative legislative ideas** that would eventually lead to confrontations, conflicts and unending discussions. The third was that too many idealistic and well-meant **dispositions were difficult to implement**. Finally, it left too many difficult decisions in the hands of **legislators that perhaps were not at the intellectual and patriotic levels** of the Constitutional Assembly members. It was, nevertheless, a formidable attempt to close the revolutionary cycle that started in the early 1930's and truly implement a social democracy in Cuba.

No party **supported Batista and praised him more** than the Communists during the years 1933 to 1944.

Juan Marinello and **Blas Roca**, in a pamphlet published in 1944 wrote: «*Since 1940, our party has been the most loyal and unswerving supporter of your government and the most energetic promoter of your inspired platform...*»

Joaquín Ordoqui, director of *Hoy*, the Communist newspaper, wrote «*People who are working to overthrow Batista are not acting in the best interests of the Cuban people.*»

Juan Marinello, Communist Party president said «*Batista is the first president of Cuba able to say that his electoral promises were drawn from the impulse of popular service.*»

Batista reciprocated. Juan Marinello entered his cabinet as Minister without Portfolio. The CTC was legalized. 31 year old Carlos Rafael Rodríguez, a Communist leader from Cienfuegos, also joined Batista's Cabinet.

Photo above, left to right: Logo of the *Partido Socialista Popular (PSP)*, the Communists; Blas Roca, Lazaro Peña and Juan Marinello.

Every civilized society creates an elite class that prevails over the general population. In capitalistic countries the elite class are the wealthy, those few who transfer across generations their social position and patrimony. In socialist countries or in dictatorships, there is an aristocracy too: those who are in power, usually supported by the coercive muscle of weapons and abuse.

In Republican Cuba, during the 1930s, the aristocracy of capital consisted of very few but well known families. Most of these descended from entrepreneurial and hard working founders who arrived in Cuba penniless and developed their capital after long years of toil and perseverance. Very few of the wealthy brought their capital from abroad when they immigrated into the island. They made their capital there, whether in land, sugar or commerce.

In the 1930s the powerful in Cuba met on Tuesday at the *Casino Nacional*, on Wednesday at the *Jockey Club*, on Saturdays at the *Havana Yacht Club* and on Sundays at elegant teas at the *Hotel Almendares*. They also gathered together at weddings, where families linked their lineage through intermarriage, or at *Fiestas de Quince Años* (Debutant Balls) organized by the mothers of the lucky girls.

 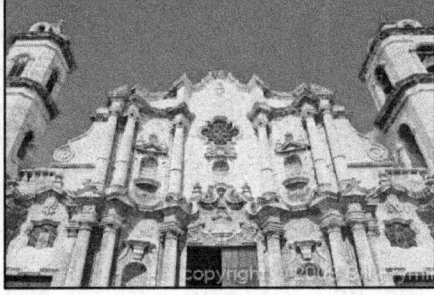

On June 27, 1932, at the *Colegio de Belén*, for instance, Conchita Urrutibeascoa married Miguel Lasa y Broch; On August 1, Encarnita Cruzet Bernal espoused Ignacio Morales Herrera at *La Iglesia de la Merced*; and on December 30, Chea Pedroso Mendoza wed Marcelino García Beltrán at the church in the Mendoza's property in *La Coronela*. That same year, on August 31, Rosita Rayneri, future wife of Raúl de Armas, Cuba's VP, celebrated her 15th birthday at her parent's estate at *Baracoa Beach*; Cristina Kindelán was feted on *Milagros*, her parent's property in *Wajay*.

Photos, clockwise from top left: the *Casino Nacional*, the *Havana Yacht Club*, the *Cathedral of Havana* and the *Hotel Almendares*.

So many such celebrations were organized during those years that a selection of the most significant ones is difficult: Micaela Freyre y Valdespita married a scion of the Argüeyes-Menocal; Vivian Conill e Hidalgo wed Pedro Romero y Ferrán, *marqués de Nuñez de Villavicencio*; Antonieta de Goicoechea wed Pedro Duquesne y Zaldo, joining the *marqueses de Valle-Siciliana* with the *marqueses de Duquesne*; Lillian Gómez-Mena Seiglie tied the knot with Alfonso Fanjul Estrada; Adelaida Gutiérrez Falla married Andrés Castillo y García-Mendoza; María Maciá Tremols wed Jorge Casteleiro Colmenares; Conchita Menocal y Nadal married Miguel Mendoza Kindelán; Cristina Gelats and Solis wed Alberto García Tuñón and Margarita Pedroso y Aróstegui married Raúl Valdés-Fauli y Juncadella, to name just a few of those happy nuptial ceremonies.

Among the most interesting parties, *Una Noche en España,* in *1937,* was the joint celebration of Lolita and Carolina Gutiérrez Falla and Alina and Helena Johnson at the residence of the Johnsons at B Street between 11th and 13th Streets.

On certain occasions the best families in Havana would also participate in aristocratic carnival celebrations: Chea Pedroso de García would dress like the *Countess of Merlín,* Alfie Fanjul and Lilian Gómez-Mena like *Anna Karenina's siblings* and Raúl Arango and Cristy Kindelán as *Othello* and *Desdemona* at an unforgetable *Baile Rojo* at the Country Club in Marianao.

The year 1948 was especially memorable because two royal visits invigorated Cuba's aristocracy: Juan and María de Borbón visited Havana, as well as Leopoldo and Rethy of Belgium; all four were feted by José Gómez-Mena and his wife Elizarda Sanpedro at their home.

Photos: The dinner party for the Count and the Countess of Barcelona at the home of the Marquise of Revilla Camargo; Margarita Pedroso; the wedding of Alfonso Fanjul and Lilian Gómez-Mena.

Once More on the Road to Democracy:
The Years 1941 to 1944

> «Sometimes the best argument
> against democracy is to have
> a five minute conversation with a voter.»
> WINSTON CHURCHILL, British Prime Minister(1874-1965)

BATISTA FELT MILITARILY and politically secure in 1939. He knew he had to enhance his image in the US and align himself with reform-minded democratic governments in Latin America. He accomplished that by allowing free and open elections for the new Constituent Assembly, a decision in which he overvalued his own strength. Sixty five percent of all eligible voters went to the polls on November 15, 1939. Of the 76 delegates for the Constitutional Assembly only 35 were loyal to him. The *Auténticos* elected 19, the *Liberales* 16 and the *Comunistas* 6. In all, delegates with progressive leanings composed the majority of the Constitutional Assembly, while radical activists made up the largest minority faction. Only two of the delegates were women. Before the end of 1939 Batista resigned his position as chief of the Armed Forces and formally accepted the presidential nomination of a newly formed *Socialist Democratic Coalition*. Seven years of authoritarian rule were about to end.

Things proceeded in a very orderly fashion from then on. The date for general elections was postponed from February 28, to July 14, and Laredo Bru, whose term expired on May 2, agreed to remain in office until the inauguration of the new president, scheduled for October 10. In the meantime Congress would continue to function and the incumbents —even if they were not re-elected— would stay until they had finished the terms for which they had been elected.

The work of the Constitutional Assembly was considered exceptional by all political parties. It represented the full spectrum of political alignments, from the old *Machadistas* to the *Auténticos* and the *Comunistas*. It was a true forum to debate all current and pending issues of Cuba's political life. It became one of the most liberal and progressive Constitutions ever written in the American hemisphere. It extended the right to vote to all citizens and limited the power of the presidency. The President was to be elected by universal suffrage and could not serve consecutive four year periods. There had to be an eight year lapse before a person previously elected to the presidency could run again. The *Tribunal Superior Electoral*, which would consist of three justices from the Supreme Court and two justices from the Havana Court of Appeals, all chosen by their respective members, was given ultimate responsibility in electoral disputes.

The elections were held in July 1940, following the completion of the work of the Constitutional Convention. The *Comunistas* supported the candidacy of Fulgencio Batista for president and Gustavo Cuervo Rubio for VP, forming part of his *Coalición Socialista Democrática*. The *Unión Revolucionaria Comunista*, the Communist party, won big by their association with Batista; they elected ten members to the Chamber of Deputies, and more than one hundred to city councils throughout the island. Batista won both houses of Congress, the provincial elections and many local races. Raúl Menocal, son of ex-President Menocal, defeated ex-President Gómez for mayor of Havana. The opposition claimed massive fraud, but impartial observers said there was evidence of little fraud.

Batista indeed had proven to be popular —within the army and among the population— and to have long coat tails.

Batista's first action was to appoint a very intelligent *político*, Carlos Saladrigas, as his Prime Minister. He became the key for good relations between the executive and the legislative branches of government.

Batista's accomplishments during 1940-1944 cannot be ignored: the creation of the *Comisión de Fomento Nacional*; the imposition of gold as support of the Cuban currency; serious advances in labor legislation; a welcomed reform of the *Retiro Azucarero*; the creation of the *Consejo Nacional de Educación y Cultura* and the founding of the *Escuela Profesional de Periodismo*; the transfer of the direction of the *Hospital Calixto García* and the *Central Limones* to the University of Havana; the construction of buildings for the *Archivo Nacional* and the *Sociedad Económica de Amigos del País*; the creation of the *Order of José María Heredia* to acknowledge distinguished writers, artists and scientists.

When WWII exploded Batista made an appeal for unity to prevent shortages and price increases. Joaquín Martínez Sáenz and Emeterio Santovenia, former *ABC* politicians, joined his government as Ministers of Agriculture and State. The *Auténticos* provided support in the legislature on many issued dealing with Cuba's national security. Carlos Hevia, a popular member of the *PRC (Auténtico)* became president of the ORPA, the *Oficina para Regulación de Precios y Abastecimientos*.

In accordance with the 1940 Constitution, on October 1940 new elections for president took place. The main candidates were Carlos Saladrigas for president and Ramón Zaydin for VP for the governmental coalition; from the opposition by the *Auténticos* Ramón Grau San Martín for president and Raúl de Cárdenas for VP.

In 1944 the *Auténticos* were at the pinnacle of their popularity. The elections proceeded cleanly and honestly. The *Partido Republicano*, under the leadership of Guillermo Alonso Pujol, had left the Batista coalition and joined Grau San Martín. One of the most hard-hitting public speakers of the *Auténticos*, Eduardo Chibás, with almost preaching devotion, became the loyal sermonizer for Grau, whom he called, "*el divino Galimatías*" (the divine gibberish man). Grau won five of the six provinces and Saladrigas congratulated him. Batista left for an extended vacation in Daytona Beach.

Grau ascended the presidential chair as the most popular man to sit there since the times of José Miguel Gómez.

Cuba was a loyal friend of the United States during World War II

As the election year 1940 was approaching, Batista resigned his post as Commander of the Armed Forces to run for the presidency under a new coalition; the *Unión Revolucionaria Comunista* (URC), —formed by a merger of the *Partido Comunista de Cuba* (PCC) and the *Partido Unión Revolucionaria* (PUR)— and four other parties plus the *Liberales*.

It was later renamed the *Coalición Socialista Democrática*. His VP partner was **Gustavo Cuervo Rubio (1890-1978)** —*photo above right*— a prestigious physician and politician who was a signatory of the 1940 Cuban Constitution. The partnership with Batista yielded generous benefits to the communists as they elected ten members to Congress in the 1940 national elections.

The alliance of Batista with former president **Mario García Menocal** was decisive in the 1940 elections. No other support was more crucial to Batista than Menocal's, a conservative out of the presidency for almost 20 years but still a powerful king-maker in Cuba.

Photo at left: Batista and Menocal at Menocal's home.

On October 10, 1940, Cubans gave themselves one of the most progressive and remarkable Constitutions in the American continent. It was the culmination of months of work by 76 delegates from 9 political parties during the presidency of Federico Laredo Brú. The new *Carta Constitucional* had been authorized by a Decree published in the *Gaceta Oficial de Cuba* on February 3, 1934, by then president Carlos Mendieta. After a long dispute of what should come first, the new presidential elections or the new Constitution, the later finally prevailed under the slogan «***Constitución primero, elecciones después.***» The members of the Constitutional Assembly were elected on November 15, 1939; on February 9, 1940 they met for the first time; upon conclusion of their works on June 8, 1940, the new Constitution was promulgated in Guáimaro, a historic town in southern Camagüey province; it was there that in 1869 a group of *mambises* had created the first Cuban Constitution challenging the colonial government of Spain.

Some of the difficult topics that the delegates faced were: **Invocation to God** in the preamble of the Constitution, the principles of **Equality before the Law**, **Retroactivity of the Civil Law**, **Death Penalty**, **Habeas Corpus**, **Free Speech**, **Freedom of Worship**, **Banning of Political Organizations**, **Equality in Marriage**, **State Secularism**, **Religious Education**, **Freedom of Unionization**, **Prohibition of Landlordism** and the establishment of a **Semi-Parliamentary** regime.

On the same day in October of 1940, while **Carlos Márquez Sterling**, as the president of the *1940 Constitutional Assembly* was signing the document in Guáimaro, Cubans were going to the polls; they elected **Fulgencio Batista** over his main rival Ramón Grau San Martín in what was the first democratic and free elections since 1925.

Photo at left: Carlos Marquez Sterling receives the gold pen with which he signed the 1940 Cuban Constitution. The pen had been acquired through a collection among Cuban school children.

The Delegates at the 1940 Cuban Constitutional Assembly:

Partido Liberal: Manuel Benítez González, César Casas, José Manuel Casanova, Miguel Calvo Tarafa, Felipe Correoso, Arturo Don, Rafael Guas Inclán, Orestes Ferrara, Quintín George, Alfredo Hornedo, José A. Mendigutía, Delio Núñez Mesa, Emilio Núñez Portuondo, Juan Antonio Vinent Griñan y Fernando del Villar.

Partido Nacionalista: Francisco Alomá, Fernando del Busto, Nicolás Duarte Cajides, Simeón Ferro Martínez, Ramón Granda, Felipe Jay Raoulx, Armando López Negrón, Juan B. Pons Jane y Francisco Prieto.

Partido Comunista: Romárico Cordero, Salvador García Agüero, Juan Marinello Vidaurreta, Blas Roca, Esperanza Sánchez Mastrapa y César Vilar.

Conjunto Nacional Democrático: Antonio Martínez Fraga, Eugenio Rodríguez Cartas y Alberto Silva Quiñones.

Partido Nacional Revolucionario (*Realista*): José Maceo González.

Partido Revolucionario Cubano (*Auténtico*): Salvador Acosta Casares, Aurelio Álvarez de la Vega, Ramiro Capablanca, Eduardo R. Chibás, Mario Dihigo, José Fernández de Castro, Ramón Grau San Martín, Alicia Hernández de la Barca, Emilio Laurent, Gustavo Moreno, Eusebio Mujal Barniol, Manuel Mesa Medina, Emilio Ochoa Ochoa, Manuel Parrado Rodés, Carlos Prío Socarrás, Primitivo Rodríguez, Miguel Suárez Fernández y María Esther Villoch.

Partido Demócrata Republicano: José R. Andreu, Rafael Álvarez González, Antonio Bravo Acosta, Antonio Bravo Correoso, Alberto Boada Miqueli, Juan Cabrera, Ramón Corona, Miguel Coyula, Pelayo Cuervo Navarro, Francisco Dellundé, Joaquín Meso, Manuel Orizondo, Mario Robau, Santiago Rey y Manuel Fueyo.

Partido Acción Republicana: Adriano Galano, Félix García Rodríguez, Carlos Márquez Sterling, Ramón Zaydín y Manuel Dorta Duque.

Partido ABC: Francisco Ichazo Macías, Joaquín Martínez Sáenz, Jorge Mañach Robato, Salvador Esteva Lora.‖

Batista's alliance, the ***Coalición Socialista Democrática*** swept the elections of June 14, 1940, wining 60% of the vote (more than 800,000), both houses of Congress, all provincial elections and a multitude of local races. Even Raúl Menocal, son of ex-President Mario Garcia Menocal, defeated ex-President José Miguel Gómez for mayor of Havana.

Most impartial observers attested to little evidence of fraud or irregularities.

In the photo at top, on the forefront, Grau congratulating Batista and Cuervo Rubio for their success. Behind Grau is Raúl Cárdenas, his future VP candidate in 1944.

Photo at bottom, official portrait of Batista as President of Cuba in 1940.

Photos above, from top to bottom: Batista swearing his position as president in 1940. Batista's family in 1940: **Elisa Godínez**, his first wife, and children **Mirta** and **Rubén** (*Papo*).

Bottom Left: **Dr. Raúl Menocal**, son of President Mario García Menocal, elected Mayor of Havana in 1940. Next to him his opponent, **Juan Marinello**, a true case of —*la izquierda de terciopelo*— (the velvet left.) Marinello was heir to a substantial family fortune that included his personal ownership of a sugar mill in Cuba yet it was a solid leader of the *Communist Party*.

Finally, Batista on the cover of *Newsweek* Magazine.

In 1940 Batista knew that his followers alone could not carry him to the presidency; they were a minority in the elections for the *1901 Constitutional Assembly*. That was the reason he sought the **support and an alliance** with former president Mario García Menocal and his *Partido Demócrata Republicano*. The *Communist Party* protested energically this Batista-Menocal alliance. They claimed it weakened their socialist-popular credo. The *menocalistas* also resented the Batista-Communist alliance since they believed the reds did not bring enough votes and/or prestige to the contest.

In the end Batista won the elections thanks to the seven parties in his coalition; at the time, Grau had only three parties on his side.

The true losers in 1940 were the Communists. They were able to elect only 10 members of the House and no Senators. In Havana they only elected **Salvador García Agüero** (7,000 votes), **Blas Roca** (5,900 votes), **Lázaro Peña** (3,100 votes) and **José M. Pérez** (1,750 votes). In Las Villas they elected two, **Joaquín Ordoqui** (2,100 votes) and **Jesús Menéndez** (1,700 votes) Only in Manzanillo they were successful electing a city mayor. In Havana their candidate, **Juan Marinello**, by far their strongest candidate nationwide, obtained only 2% of the popular vote.

Those elected Communists would try over and again for the next 20 years to gain popular support and were **repeatedly rejected by the voting population in Cuba.**

Photos above: The top leadership of the Communist Party (aka *Unión Revolucionaria Comunista* in 1939, aka *Partido Socialista Popular* in 1944) at the time of the 1940 national elections in Cuba. *Top row*: Salvador García Agüero, Blas Roca Calderío and Lázaro Peña. *Bottom row*: Juan Marinello, Joaquín Ordoqui and Jesús Menéndez, who died in 1948. In the 1960s they were all still lead- ers of the *Cuban Communist Party*; none of them was ever legally elected in any type of municipal, provincial or national elections.

Batista was favored by the economic boom of World War II. The war led to the collapse of sugar production in Asia and Europe. Cuba's crop increased from 2.7 million to 4.2 during the war and Cuba's sugar income from $110 million to $251. Facing that **unwonted bonanza** Cubans developed a positive mythical memory of the Batista government, a fatal attraction for which they would have to pay a serious price in 1952. *On the left*: a 1940 UN poster showing Cuba —second column, third row— as one of the allies in WWII.

Some of the politicos that collaborated with Batista during his presidency 1940-1944. *Top row*: **Carlos Saladrigas Zayas (1900-1956)**, Prime Minister and former ABC chief; **José Manuel Cortina (1880-1970)**, Secretary of the Presidency during Zayas and Cuba's foremost orator and diplomat; **Andrés Morales del Castillo (1890-1979)**, former Secretary of Justice under Mendieta, Secretary of Treasury for Batista in 1940;

Bottom Row: **Ramón Zaydin (1895-1968)**, Batista's VP candidate in 1944; **Col. Manuel Benitez**, Chief of Police; Col **José Eleuterio Pedraza**, Chief of the Armed Forces.

Since the early 1940s, **Ernest Hemingway (1899-1961)** had a romance with Cuba; it lasted to the day of his suicide in 1961. In the 1930s and 1940s he was a literary idol and role model for his spare prose and his life full of adventure, women, sports and daring acts of gallantry and courage in the face of danger. He was the epitome of manhood as well as, in the words of Gertrude Stein, «*the bard of the lost generation.*» The fame he acquired was also the source of his destruction. He ended up writing for money and drinking heavily. His public persona became a parody. He was accused of wife-beating and turning his friends into enemies.

In 1940 Hemingway, with his new bride Martha, bought a home in San Francisco de Paula, on the outskirts of Havana. He lived there until he left for Idaho in what was his funeral trip. Hemingway named the property **Finca La Vigía**, (the lookout farm). There, as well as in a property he acquired later in Key West, he shared his space with dozens of his beloved cats, the descendants of which still prowl the sands in the southernmost point of the US.

Soon after moving to Cuba he became a fixture of Havana's popular *Floridita's Bar*, and began to travel through Cuba. He fished daily aboard his 40 ft cabin cruiser, **Pilar**, and welcomed in his home many Cuban celebrities, artists, painters, show girls, literati, boxers, TV personalities, politicians and such.

At the outset of WWII Hemingway converted the *Pilar*, into a Q-Boat. Between 1942 and 1944, he **patrolled the coasts of Cuba** looking for German submarines. He carried radio equipment, machine guns, bazookas and barrels of high explosives. Lucky for him, no U-Boats ever came within his reach. Spruille Braden, then US ambassador to Cuba had provided the armament and once declared to the press «*I believe Ernest would have won the battle if he ever made contact with a Sub.*» He recommended Hemingway for a War Decoration, an advice the War Department decided to ignore.

Photos above: Hemingway, the *Pilar*, his fishing boat and his home at the *Finca La Vigía* in San Francisco de Paula.

Professional gangsters came to Cuba starting in 1940 to reap the spoils of out-of-control government corruption.

During the days of Batista, US gangster **Charlie Luciano** was issued a Cuban passport. He moved to 29 Thirty Street in Miramar. **Meyer Lansky** talked to a few corrupt Batista associates and got the control of the *Jockey Club* at the *Hotel Nacional Casino* and the *Oriental Park Horse Racetrack*.

The control of gambling, money laundering and prostitution continued unabated during the four year presidency of Grau San Martín. In 1947 the *Havana Post* showed a photo of **Frank Sinatra** at the *Hotel Nacional*, where a large US mafia meeting had taken place in December 1946. It included figures like **Frank Costello**, **Albert Anastasia**, **Joe Profaci**, **Tommy Lucchese**, **Vito Genovese**, **Joe Bonano** and **Santo Trafficanti**.

Photos: *top*, a bulletin board from the Miami FBI office; *center*, the *Oriental Park Horse Racetrack in* Marianao, Havana; *bottom,* a page from *Life Magazine* in 1946.

The Batista administration ran from 1940 to 1944. It carried out major social reforms, assisted by several members of the Communist Party, and established economic regulations and pro-union policies. Many errors of the past, however, were repeated: by decree Batista limited profits for wholesalers at 10% and for retailers at 25%; a commission was set up to control all products of need to the US, including sugar. On December 1940 **Cuba declared war** against Japan and on the 11th War was declared on Germany and Italy. Citizens of these countries were sent to camps in Torrens, near *Santiago de las Vegas*. Cuba allowed the stationing of US troops, aviation and training facilities in its soil. The entire 1940 sugar crop was sold to the US at $0.0265 dollars a pound, producing some resentment among *colonos* and sugar magnates.

Photos above: naval training at Guantanamo Bay in 1942; a drawing used by the opposition to criticize the giveaway of Cuban sugar at prices that barely covered costs.

The time for new elections in Cuba came with the end of the war. Six Political Parties were certified for 1944. Top two, left to right: **Partido Republicano** and **Partido Revolucionario Cubano** *(Auténtico)*, the coalition that supported **Grau San Martín**; bottom four, left to right, top to bottom: **Partido Demócrata, Partido Liberal, Partido Socialista Popular** *(Comunistas)* and **Partido ABC**, the coalition that supported **Fulgencio Batista.**

An article in *Time Magazine* (June 12th 1944) entitled *Cuba: Evolution of a Dictator*, pointed out the remarkable surprise Batista gave everyone when he turned the presidency of Cuba to the opposition party and not to his candidate. Carlos Saladrigas had the backing of Batista, the Cuban Army and most public job holders; he was backed by a substantial campaign fund. Yet Batista made a move that surprised everyone, including his candidate; **he turned over the keys of government**.

In the words of *Time*: «*He had set rules: compulsory, secret voting; hands off by the Army; no shooting or slugging at the polls.*» U.S. Ambassador Spruille Braden forbade U.S. business firms or individuals to contribute to the parties, later on adding:
«*Batista said he wanted democracy, and he has kept his word.*»

It was the first time in almost 30 years that a government candidate had lost at the polls. It would take 10 more years before a similar situation would happen in 1950, when Antonio Prío lost his bid for mayor of Havana while his brother was in the presidency. After the polls were closed 25,000 Cubans surrounded the Presidential Palace to ask Batista to say a few words. He came to the balcony, looked to the crowd and spoke slowly: «*Pueblo de Cuba. We have waited long for true democracy. At last we have come to see that day of freedom. Salud, Salud, Salud.*» The crowd went frantic and applauded frenetically. An old veteran of the War of 1895 exclaimed «*Now I have seen everything.*» **A remarkable conversion for a man that had deposed seven presidents in seven years**. His parting shot, however, was a warning: «*If the people ever needs me I will hear their cries.*»

Photos above: Batista in the cover of *Time Magazine* in 1937; Batista and FDR in 1942; a poster of Batista as a candidate of the *Communist Party* in 1940. The Communists had joined the *Unión Revolucionaria*, adopting the new name *Partido Unión Revolucionaria*. In January 1944 *Unión Revolucionaria* changed its name to ***Partido Socialista Popular,*** a term the Communists kept until 1965.

Cuba in the 1940s.

Photos above, top to bottom: crowded *tranvías* (tramcars) moved people across Havana; *Sears Roebuck and Co.* opened its first store outside the US at Reina and Galiano Streets, in Havana; the *Topes de Collantes Hospital* was inaugurated by Batista in 1944; the students from the *University of Havana* often paralyzed public transportation in Havana during a protest, causing huge traffic jams.

The Republic back on its Feet
The Years 1944 to 1948

> «*It is more difficult to organize a peace, than to win a war, but the fruits of victory will be lost if peace is not organized.*»
> ARISTOTLE, Ancient Greek Philosopher (384 BC-322 BC)

GRAU SAN MARTIN, now almost sixty years old, swept the free elections of June 1, 1944, bringing back to power the men of the 1933-1934 revolution. Batista —who had betrayed them— was surprised. The communists, knowing that the end of their PSP control of organized labor was imminent— cynically asked Batista to disown the election and retain power. Batista restrained himself and let things stood as they were.

Eduardo Chibás, still a loyal *auténtico*, called it the "*jornada gloriosa del 1 de Junio*." And the slogan stuck. Later that year, in October, a forceful hurricane castigated the island. It was an omen for the political trouncing that the *Auténtico* rivals were about to suffer. A stipulation of the 1940 Constitution had made vote-splitting possible, and Grau had mostly lost the municipal and provincial elections, but he was firmly in charge. One of his first actions was to retire all army officers that were loyal to Batista; the second was to place friendly followers in most sensitive government positions.

The economy of Cuba could not have been better as Grau assumed power. Sugar was at record highs at the end of WWII.

Grau agreed to pass the *Ley del Diferencial Azucarero*. It was promoted and had the support of Jesús Menéndez, the General Secretary of the *Federación Nacional Obrera Azucarera* (he was known as *General de las Cañas*) and was possible by the business creativity and support of José Manuel Casanova, President of the *Asociación de Hacendados de Cuba* (Cuba Landowners Association). The law stipulated that the price of Cuban sugar exported to the US would rise annually at the same percentage rate than the price increase of goods that Cuba imported from the US, and that increase would be paid to the sugar workers. In 1944 this amounted to 13.5% bonus to the *azucareros*. The law also assigned a participation to the *Colonos* (sugar land tenants) in the final molasses.

Among the valuable projects undertaken by Grau were a good number of public works; the professionalization of careers and trades through registration and the creation of several retirement plans for lawyers as well as tobacco and textile workers. He was intent in following his interrupted 1933 programs with 1944 projects, but this led unfortunately to excessive tolerance with a new generation of power-hungry and office-seeking individuals that supported this approach. Cuba went back to corruption and malfeasance in the hands of third or fourth level tiers of party leaders and thugs. The eagerness for reform was soon replaced by disillusion; the government — full of honest and hard-working first rate ethical figures — became incapable of controlling the embezzlement and graft of the low level hoodlums and gangsters.

In December 1945 the Communists retired their loyalty to Batista and joined the *auténticos* in a coalition that also included the remains of the ABC. In the 1946 elections the coalition won both houses of Congress as well as many provincial and municipal governments. Grau began to rule Cuba with reckless abandon. Corruption continued to be rampant. Party supporters were enjoying their *botellas* (sinecures). The public responded by stoning the Capitol several times.

Grau San Martín continued to be a man committed to civil liberties and freedom of expression. His popularity was being affected by the rampant chaos, particularly with the founding of a party of *Auténtico* dissidents led by Eduardo Chibás, the former student leader of the 1930s. They called themselves the *Ortodoxos*, implying that they were the real successors of José Martí's *Partido Revolucionario Cubano*. Some people criticized Chibás; they believed he had brought about a schism because he was being by-passed as the presidential candidate in favor of Carlos Prío Socarrás.

Grau broke with the Communists in May 1947 on occasion of the Fifth Congress of the *Confederación de Trabajadores de Cuba*. The party went underground until 1959.

The *pistolero* violence abated during the electoral period leading to June 1, 1948. The specter of uncontrolled mob competition disappeared briefly. Four coalitions went to the polls. The *Auténticos* presented Carlos Prío for president and the Republican Guillermo Alonso Pujol for VP; the *Coalición Socialista Democrática* presented Ricardo Nuñez Portuondo for president and Gustavo Cuervo Rubio for VP; The *Partido del Pueblo Cubano* presented Eduardo Chibás for president and Emilio (Millo) Ochoa as his VP; the *Partido Socialista Popular* made Juan Marinello his presidential candidate. Carlos Prío won handily but not overwhelmingly (36% of the vote). 22% of the voters abstained. The communists won 5.6% of the votes. The Liberals obtained 30%. The *Auténticos* elected 65% of the House and 50% of the Senate in Congress. Batista was elected Senator, remained for a while in Daytona, Florida, and returned to Cuba in November 1948. He seldom showed up in the Senate; never criticized the Prío government leaving that important initiative to Eduardo Chibás. Quietly he began to reestablish his links to the military apparatus.

Cubans made **sacrifices in Cuba** during World War II. Gasoline was expensive and scarce. Unemployment in the tobacco industry was at an old time high since leaf tobacco was exported in bulk to the US. Tourism did not show up for five years. Fruits and vegetables rotted in port for lack of shipping space. People rarely got to see beef in the stores. No machinery or supplies could be imported. Inflation reached 100% between 1940 and 1945. The building industry was paralyzed for lack of steel. Brigands exploited the black market.

Photo on the left: an *anti-agio* demonstration in Havana (a protest for abuses in the exchange of US and Cuban currencies).

Once his four year term came to an end, **Fulgencio Batista** surprised everyone with an out of character decision. He was going to conduct a fair election and transfer his powers to a new president even if it was not his favorite. He was hoping that **Carlos Saladrigas (1900-1956)**, his prime minister and a former top man of the *ABC* would win the 1944 election. It was a move without precedent in Latin America: a strong man ready to leave his power in the hands of his lifetime adversary. **Grau San Martín** swept the country. His first task: to move against the Communist Party and liberate the Communist dominated CTC from its radical left leaning leadeship.

Photo on the right: President Grau and his VP Raúl de Cárdenas congratulate each other on the day of the «*jornada gloriosa del primero de junio*,» (June 1, 1944), in the words of **Eduardo R. Chibás**, the *Auténtico* leader that would soon turn against the party.

No period in the history of Cuba has been more thoroughly studied and documented than the time between 1933, the bloody termination of Machado's second term, and the bitter end of the republic in 1959. A long series of very notable scholars, many of whom participated in the actions in one form or another, have scrutinized these events in search for an explanation of the republic's relatively easy collapse in 1959. Such was the case for **Fernando Ortiz (1881-1969)** and **Emeterio Santovenia (1889-1968)**

Most of these learned studies were the result of the creation of the *Cuban Academy of History* in 1910. This institution, modeled after the *French* Academy, was a center which nurtured such intellects as **Enrique José Varona (1849-1933)**, and **Raimundo Cabrera (1852-1923)**. These men directed their work towards illustrating and understanding the events they witnessed directly or indirectly. Their work was in the best tradition of those methodical historians that inquire into facts and reasons without prejudice or personal perspectives. They were witness to and left behind a treasure of historical, sociological, anthropological and even folklorical information. Their motivation was always a strong believe that by knowing the errors of the past the republic could be safer in the future.

Photos, left to right top to bottom: Fernando Ortiz, Enrique José Varona, Raimundo Cabrera and Emeterio Santovenia.

The **cabinet of Grau San Martín** in 1944 included prestigious men like Carlos Prío Socarrás, Raúl López, Sergio Clark, Cossío del Pino, Carlos Azcarate, Alberni, Casuso, Cuervo-Rubio, and Andréu. After the initial flirting he had had with the Communists, Grau in 1944 moved decidedly to the right.

The move triggered great resentment within the lines of the *Auténticos,* causing one of his most loyal followers, **Eduardo R. Chibás (1907-1951)** to set camp apart and launch the *Partido del Pueblo Cubano (Ortodoxos)*. He had coined the frase «*la jornada gloriosa del primero de junio*» to characterize the 1944 electoral triumph of the *Auténticos*.

When it was announced that Grau had won the presidency in June 1944, an outburst of delight and expectations was felt throughout Cuba. The man who had captivated the best hopes of the generation of 1933 had reached the top position in Cuba in ways that no one could challenge.

Cubans anticipated the implementation of the best ideas of the revolution, including public honesty and democracy.

On the photo at left: Grau with Eduardo Chibas, a solid anticommunist whose political goal was to end government corruption and restore the respect for the *1940 Cuban constitution*.

At the time of his election Ramón Grau was close to sixty years old. He was already a rich man, having inherited a sizable fortune from his father, a tobacco farmer from Pinar del Rio. His campaign promised a socially active government free of the sleaze and fraud that was attributed to Batista.

He was to rule Cuba during an era of world progress and expansion after World War II. The US sugar quota for Cuba had been set at close to 30% of US needs. Everyone was predicting a new era of *vacas gordas*. (literally fat cows, i.e., prosperity for everyone.)

Grau, however, **turned the popular hopes and optimism into a great disappointment**; a binge of theft, larceny and public pilfering trashed illusions in Cuba. Government contracts had to include heavy commissions for the public officials in charge. Bogus positions consumed the budgets. Buildings were rented to the government at outrageous prices. Pardons for even the most serious offenses could be bought. Spurious checks were issued and changed for non-existing purchases and services. All along Grau kept his distance from the misappropriations and crimes. The felonies, according to rumors, came most times through **Paulina Alsina** (*photo at the top*), Grau's widowed sister-in-law.

All told, the government of **Ramón Grau San Martín**, from 1944 to 1948, brought Cubans an appalling and broad disillusion. In addition to white collar felonies and transgressions, mobsters and crooks became a plague as they tried to enrich themselves and obtain political power through terrorism. Batista had allowed an open raid on the Treasury in his final days and Grau's heavy duty cohorts went beyond embezzlement, looting, larceny and fraud into gangsterism, racketeering and crime when they found empty bank accounts in most government departments.

The greatest disappointment of Grau's presidency, however, was the wasted opportunity to advance the great cause of the Republic. Once more, Cubans failed to use the skills of a distinguished group of its citizens that were willingly committed to public service.

The 1944 *Auténtico* Cabinet included:

Félix Lancís Sánchez, Prime Minister, son of Ricardo Lancís, member of Crowder's *Cabinet of Honestry* in 1922-23;

Gustavo Cuervo Rubio, Foreign Minister, professor at the *University of Havana*;

Carlos Azcárate Rosell, Minister of Labor, scholar of the philosophy of law;

Manuel Fernández Supervielle, Minister of Finance, former Dean of the *Havana* Bar Association;

José Antonio Presno, Minister of Health, former Chancellor of the *University of Havana*;

Carlos Eduardo de la Cruz, Minister of Justice; **Gustavo Moreno Lastres**, Secretary of Public Works;

Salvador Menéndez Villoch, Minister of Defense;

Germán Alvarez Fuentes, Minister of Agriculture;

Sergio Clark Díaz, Minister of Communications; **Julian Solorzano**, Minister of the Presidency; **Segundo Curti**, Minister of the Interior;

Alberto Inocente Alvarez, Minister of Commerce;

Luis Pérez Espinos, Minister of Education;

Photo above: a multitude was present at the *Zayas Park*, in 1944, across from the Presidential Palace, to witness Grau's swearing in.

Photo above: A group of notable Cuban poets meeting in Cojimar, Havana, in January 1944. It included **1**-Agustín Acosta; **2**-José Angel Buesa; **3**-Nicolás Guillén and **4**-Regino Pedroso.

Photos above, on the left: Grau San Martín, on a train stop, campaigning for the presidency in 1943. *On the right*: Grau San Martín and Paulina Alsina on June 17, 1945, at the wedding of Carlos Prío and Mary Tarrero on the Cuban Presidential Palace.

On October 22, 1945, after several years of a chronic pulmonary disease, **José Francisco Marti y Zayas-Bazán** (*Ismaelillo*), the only son of José Martí and Carmen Zayas-Bazán, died in Havana. His funeral took place at the *Salón de los Pasos Perdidos* of the National Capitol.

Before the death of José Martí, his son *Ismaelillo* lived with his mother in Camagüey until in 1894; that year they moved to a house on 3 Zulueta Street, in Havana, when he began to study law at the University of Havana.

After the death of Martí he and his mother went to the US and from Brooklyn he took an expedition with **Carlos Roloff** and **Enrique Nuñez** to participate in the Cuban War of Independence. He lost his hearing at the many encounters where he served as an artillery leader.

Among his first responsibilities after the inauguration of the Republic was to be **head of procurement for the Army of Cuba**, which took him to *Saint Cyr* and *Creusut* in France. He later became **Chairman of the Joint Chiefs of Staff** of the Cuban Army. In 1916, at 37, he married María Teresa Bances; they moved to a comfortable house at 103 Calzada Avenue in *El Vedado*, where he died in 1945.

In life he was a very good friend of **Jorge Mañach, Joaquín Martínez Sáenz, Juan Gualberto Gómez, Carlos Mendieta** and **Cosme de la Torriente.** In spite of his frail health he never missed a meeting or political rally where he could contribute to Cuba's good government.

Photos above: Ismaelillo as a military man (1925); as a diplomat (1935) and his last photo (1945) with his wife María Teresa.

Grau's solution to violence, which had been less prevalent before him thanks to Batista's strong hand, was to provide public jobs for the leaders and redouble the *botellas* (sinecures) for members of the fighting gangs. The most important of these groups were the **Movimiento Socialista Revolucionario (MSR)** under the control of Rolando Masferrer, Manolo Castro, Fabio Ruiz and Mario Salabarría, the **Unión Insurreccional Revolucionaria (UIR)**, led by Emilio Tró, and the **Acción Revolucionaria Guiteras (ARG)** de Eufemio Fernández y Jesús González Cartas, alias *El Extraño*.

In 1946 Grau made *Fabio Ruiz* Chief of Police of Havana; *Manolo Castro* became the Sports Director; *Mario Salabarría* the Director of the Bureau of Investigations; *Emilio Tro* Director of the Police Academy.

All four hid their criminal activities by speaking in revolutionary language. They alleged a higher political-revolutionary motive for their felonious behavior. With Grau they worked out in the open; they even tried to gain popularity and admiration from the general citizenry. They proudly subscribed to a new profession: **gangsterismo** and had no objection when the papers referred to them as **pistoleros**.

At a meeting of the *Ortodoxo Party* in Holguín on September 21, 1947, **Eduardo R. Chibás**, its president, ended his presentation with these words:

«*Cubans have found the actions of Grau's government more inhumane, more monstrous and more vicious than the actions of Machado. Their cruelty can be seen in the photographs published on the central pages of the magazine Bohemia. The Apostle of Cuba has now become the Apostle of the Gangs. No matter. The Cuban people in the entire Republic, tired of so much crime and theft in a government of mud and blood, have stood to tell the gang YOU SHALL NOT PASS! The people of Cuba now has the last word.*»

Photo at the top: Eduardo Chibás at a meeting of the *Partido del Pueblo Cubano (Ortodoxo)* in 1950.

Photo at the bottom: Eduardo Chibás at a meeting with executives of the *Partido del Pueblo Cubano (Ortodoxo)* in 1951.

Photo on top, Supervielle's bust at Teniente Rey and Bernaza Streets in Havana.

Not all was corruption when Grau came to power in Cuba. There were public servants in high positions with a well deserved prestige of honesty and integrity. His appointed *Minister of the Treasury*, **Manuel Fernández Supervielle (1894-1947)**, for instance, had impeccable credentials. His *Minister of Public Works*, **José A. San Martín** immediately initiated an ambitious plan to create a better infrastructure and repair damaged streets in Cuba.

Grau regulated the eviction of renters and increased salaries regularly, in spite of which Cuba had an increase of strikes and slowdowns during his presidency.

Supervielle was later, in 1946, the *Mayor of Havana* and committed suicide on May 5, 1947 when he could not fulfill his campaign promise of building a new aqueduct for the citizens of the capital. The *auténticos* were blamed for his death; most people believed that this man of honor was victimized by the venality of the *políticos*.

During the mid-term elections in 1946 Grau and the *Auténtico* party joined forces with the Communists and the smaller ABC to form a coalition they hoped would obtain a majority in both houses of Congress. They won a sweeping victory. Grau then broke with the Communists and moved to take control of the labor movement, which he did. From then on the *Auténticos* ruled Cuba with reckless abandon.

In the photo at bottom: Grau at a political meeting with Communist leader **Lázaro Peña**.

 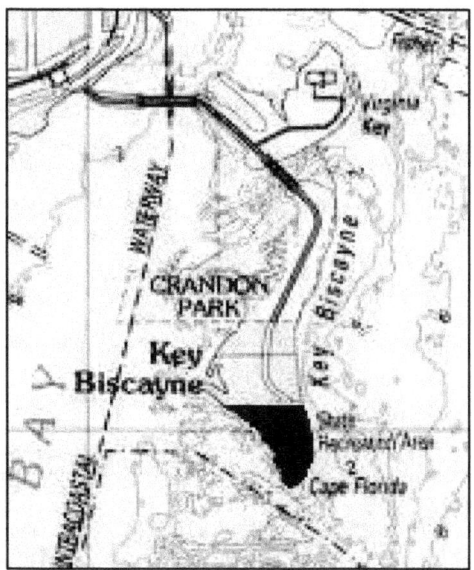

Corruption in Cuba during the Grau period grew to unimaginable levels. Mayors, ministers, top officials, all felt that part of their salaries was to secure themselves either bribes, sales commissions or even outright physical carry-home of funds from the Treasury.

At lower levels the inspectors who visited factories were taking cash for favorable reports or for not even making the inspections. Policemen were eating and drinking free at the *bodegas* in their routes. Graft had no social stigma. Some Judges sold their decisions for a few dollars.

One celebrated case involved **José Manuel Alemán (1902-1949)**, photo above left, Grau's favorite minister, in charge of the *Department of Education*. On the afternoon of October 10, 1948, while people were celebrating the *Grito de Yara*, Alemán and four of his henchmen drove four *Ministry of Education* trucks into the *Treasury* building. All five entered the premises carrying suitcases, where they loaded francs, lires, pounds sterling and $19 million in US dollars. The loaded trucks went directly to a DC-3 waiting for them at Havana airport. Once in Miami they went straight to the *Du Pont building* and left the bills at Aleman's office.

When a curious employee asked him «*How did you manage to take all those bills from the Treasury building?*» he answered «*We used suitcases!*»

In 1948, with those monies, José Manuel Alemán bought from the James Deering estate the southernmost tip of Key Biscayne with its 1825 lighthouse, (shaded area shown above at right). His widow, Elena Santeiro, sold it in 1966 to the State of Florida to pay for uncollected taxes. The land is now the *Bill Baggs Cape Florida State Park*; it opened in 1967.

The Orfila Events.

Two groups of gangsters became well-known in Cuba in the last years of Grau's government. One of them was the *Movimiento Socialista Revolucionario*, led by 34 year old **Mario Salabarría**, chief of the Intelligence Service of the Cuban Army; it included Rolando Masferrer and Orlando León Lemus (*el Colorado*). The second group was the *Union Insurreccional Revolucionaria*, led by 29 years old **Emilio Tro**, a former US Army veteran, director of the Cuban Police Academy and a bitter enemy of Salabarría. Among others, it included Antonio Morín Dopico, chief of Police of the city of Marianao.

Both of these groups had its origins in **Joven Cuba**, the movement founded by Antonio Guiteras before he was killed at *El Morillo* in Matanzas trying to escape to México.

Continued...

Continuation...

At 3 pm on Monday September 15, 1947, two high speed cars (Masferrer's?) fired on the Morín Dopico home at 8 and D Streets in the neighborhood of **Orfila**, in Marianao. Within two hours there were over 200 of Salabarría's men firing into the home.

The chief of the Army gave orders to stop the fighting and sent several tanks from nearby *Camp Columbia*. Morín Dopico's wife was shot when she tried to leave the house in the company of Emilio Tró, who was seriously wounded.

A legendary photo of the event (*previous page, at the top*) shows one of Salabarría's men, José Fallat, aka *el Turquito*, finishing off Emilio Tró, who was laying on the ground at the entrance of Dopico's house. The *lower photo on the same page* shows Emilio Tró trying to bring back to the house the body of Aurora Soler, Morín Dopico's wife, who was pregnant and already mortally wounded. The *photo above, on top,* shows Morín Dopico entering a car to take his daughter to the hospital. The *photo on the bottom* shows the general aspect of the street the day of the event.

The photo at left shows General **Genovevo Pérez Dámera (1910-1978)**, head of the Cuban Army at the time of the **Orfila** events with President Ramón Grau. Genovevo, from his hotel in Washington, DC, where he was on an official duty, ordered the army to intervene and later had Salabarría charged with murder. There were rumors, never confirmed, that he was in Havana at the time but wanted the gangster groups to do away with each other.

While the events of **Orfila** were taking place, in *Cayo Confites*, a Cuban key located in the coast of Camagüey, several revolutionaries from Santo Domingo were conspiring to overthrow the government of **Rafael Leonidas Trujillo (1891-1961)**, President of the Dominican Republic. They were led by **Juan Bosch (1909-2001)**, later to be himself President of the Dominican Republic; other leaders were **Manolo Castro (1926-1948)**, a Cuban student of the University of Havana, member of the MSR, (allegedly murdered by Fidel Castro on February 22, 1948) and **Rolando Masferrer (1918-1975)**, former member of *Joven Cuba*, a professional gangster and revolutionary. Their contact with the Grau government was **José Manuel Alemán**, the Education Minister with property in Key Biscayne. Their operation failed when **General Genovevo Pérez**, Cuba's Army Chief, at the suggestion of Washington, decided to confiscate all the military supplies of the group.

Photo on the left: Juan Bosch; *on the right*: Rafael Leónidas Trujillo; his enemies called him *Chapita* (for his ever present medals).

In spite of the freedom and democratic atmosphere during Grau's presidency, it was during those years that Cuba began to experience a devastating moral crisis.

The generation that had fought the 1895 War of Independence (Estrada, Gómez, Menocal, Zayas, Machado, Mendieta and others) was discredited for having resorted so often to the **protection of the US**; far too many times they requested the intervention of the US in the affairs of Cuba, in spite of their many claims that they were in opposition to the *Platt Amendment*.

The generation of the revolution that germinated from 1927 to 1944 (Grau, Batista, Carbó, Mella, Guiteras, Prío, Chibás, Hevia and others) was miserably throwing away the **opportunity to build their country**; they openly tolerated corruption, self-interest, depredation and banditry.

It was also true that discrediting Grau became a popular sport in Cuba before and during his presidency.

In 1926, from his position as Professor of Physiology at the *University of Havana*, he was one of the few teachers who spoke about the **deprived labor conditions** of the Cuban workers. In 1930 he supported the students and refused to teach with a University under a **military occupation**. As the result of these actions he **landed in the prisons** of *Principe* and *Isla de Pinos*. He refused to accept the *1901 Constitution* because it was **stained with the *Platt Amendment***. He could not stop the times of the *gatillo ale- gre* but made sure **all sentences to *pistoleros*** were carried to the end.

Grau survived all efforts to accuse him of stealing public funds. On October 7, 1944 he declared his capital: $70,642 in cash and $180,000 in mortgages, 7 houses in Habana, a house in Miami and a farm in Consolación del Sur. Grau in fact died in 1969 **almost without means**. His followers argued correctly that the $174 millions of the famous **Causa 82** were proven to be a myth; no one ever presented enough evidence to merit a judicial process.

Drawing and photo on top: Batista sweating out the difficult decision to leave government; a portrait of Ramón Grau in 1944.

On Monday March 25, 1946, a 25 carat diamond under the dome of Cuba's National Capitol mysteriously **vanished**. It had been placed there to mark the kilometer zero from which to measure all distances across the island of Cuba. The diamond had a striking yellow glow and had been embedded in agate and platinum before inserting it into a block of *andesite*, the strongest granite in the world; this in turn was covered by a cut glass so thick and strong it was believed unbreakable by any means. The glass cover was then implanted in concrete so that it could never be removed. The diamond was one of five that **had been in one of the crowns of Russia's last Tsar**. In 1927 it had been offered to María Jaén, wife of former president Alfredo Zayas, for $17,000. She found it too expensive and a **source of bad luck** since the Tsar and his family had been overthrown and murdered. In addition, several people that had handled the diamond, according to legend, had mysteriously died, were assassinated or went blind.

Carlos Miguel de Céspedes, former Minister of Public Works under Machado, immediately began a public collection to purchase the jewel. Many school children, workers, technicians and teachers contributed. After several months the total reached $9,000. The jeweler agreed to reduce the price but only to $12,000, and Carlos Miguel graciously completed the rest with a personal donation of $3,000. By May 20, 1929, when the Capitol was inaugurated, the diamond was already in place.

The only clue left behind by the robbers were the lining of a blood-stained hat, a child's left hand glove, a box of matches and a pencil writing on the floor saying simply: «3:15 am - 24 carats.»

Months passed and on June 2, 1947, President Grau called to his office Carlos Prío, Senate President; Guillermo Alonso Pujol, Senator and Chairman of the Republican Party, and Alejandro Cossio del Pino, Minister of Justice. Grau told them that some **unknown person** had deposited on his desk the missing jewel. He did not know who it was, and that was the end of the story.

Years later, Segundo Curti, a high government official during the presidency of Carlos Prío, affirmed to a newsman from *Bohemia Magazine* that the recen- tly deceased Abelardo Fernández, aka **El Manquito**, a common *ratero* (pickpocket) had been the man who perpetrated the most celebrated theft in the history of Republican Cuba.

In the midst of all the corruption and insecurity that Grau allowed, it is fair to agree on some important successes of his government:

Knowing that Batista had sold the 1945 sugar crop for $2.65 a pound, Grau worked out with the recently appointed US Ambassador **Spruille Braden (1894-1978)** a re-negotiation of the contract, which raised the price to $3.10; it brought to Cuba an additional $30 million, which Grau used partly for a permanent 20% raise in wages, not only for the sugar workers but for every salaried person in the island. This action inspired his best presidential line: «*hay dulce para todos.*» The photo above shows Grau negotiating with Braden (center) in the presence of **Guillermo Belt (1906-1989)**, the prestigious Cuban Ambassador to the US. As a delegate to the UN he was the person who signed on behalf of Cuba the **Charter of the United Nations** in 1945.

For the first time in Cuba Grau established the principle of *Obras Públicas sin Empréstitos* (No loans for Public Works). His plan included building roads, schools and hospitals with surplus funds and funds from the lottery; the later was under carefully continuous inspection and produced yearly more than three times the entire combined earnings of 45 years of lottery since 1902.

Grau produced a sizable increase in the number of teachers and schools. In 1944 there were 8,000 teachers and 15,000 school rooms; when he left the presidency in 1948 there were 40,000 teachers and 15,000 additional rooms. His motto was «*Más Maestros que Soldados.*» (More teachers than soldiers.)

But most of all, on balance, for the average Cuban resident, Grau provided a civil and democratic atmosphere of liberty, opportunity, social justice, full sovereignty and good humor.

As the 1948 elections approached, the Communists were losing their stronghold on the labor movement. They decided to formally be in opposition to Grau. On March 2, 1948 they attempted to form an alliance with Chibas' *Partido del Pueblo Cubano (Ortodoxos)*, but Chibás refused. In early May Grau took over the Communist radio station *Mil Diez (1010 AM)* on the spurious ground that it had deviated from its assigned frequency. The Democratic and Liberal parties also rejected any pact with the Communists.

For the first time in ten years they had no friends. *Photo below at right*: Chibas with his loyal follower **José Pardo Llada (1923-2009)**, an extraordinary radio commentator that years later, in exile, became a legislator in Colombia. *On the left*: Grau embracing Carlos Prío Socarrás.

During the 1948 presidential campaign the *pistoleros* packed their guns and remained quiet. The violence that had become endemic and had not been repressed during the early 1940s ceased briefly.

June 1st was the day of the national election; **Carlos Prío Socarrás (1903-1977)** (*Alianza Auténtico-Republicana*) won handily but not decisively. He received 36% of the vote. His rivals were **Ricardo Nuñez Portuondo (1898-1978)** (*Coalición Liberal-Democrática*) with 24%, **Eduardo Chibas (1907-1951)** (*Partido del Pueblo Cubano (Ortodoxo)* with 13% and **Juan Marinello (1898-1977)** (*Partido Socialista Popular (Comunista)*) with less than 6%.

Batista was elected in absentia as Senator from Las Villas. He would stay quiet when he returned from Daytona Beach to Cuba, leaving to Chibás the work of belligerently opposing the *Auténticos*.

An important episode was barely reported in the Cuban press due to the absorbing theme of the national election political campaigns. A few weeks before June 1, on April 9, in Bogotá, Colombia, delegates from all Latin American nations met for the *IX Pan-American Conference* to create the OAS, the *Organization of American States*. On the table there was a motion to declare **Communism** a «*vicious doctrine incompatible with the political philosophy of the Latin American countries.*»

On that day an assassin took the life of **Jorge Eliécer Gaitán Ayala (1903-1948)**; as a former mayor of Bogotá and former Minister of Education, he was an admired liberal leader in Colombia. He was a thoughtful and electrifying speaker, a populist, a vibrant denouncer of social and political evils. He was vilified equally by Liberals (his party), Conservatives and Communists.

A popular riot followed; shoe shiners, craftmen, newpaper vendors took the streets in anger. Stores were sacked, public buildings were set on fire; the bloodshed (later known as *la violencia*) covered the entire nation, eventually, after many years, at the cost of nearly 300,000 deaths. Among the rioters was a young Cuban leftwinger hothead called **Fidel Castro**.

On the photos above: Eliécer Gaitán (right); Castro in the midst of the **Bogotazo** mayhem at left, in the company of Alfredo Guevara and Enrique Ovares from the Cuban *Federación de Estudiantes Universitarios (FEU)*.

The Consolidation of Democracy:
Events and Memories on the Years 1948 to 1952

> «Mistakes are the foundation of truth.
> If a person does not know what something is,
> it is at least an increase in knowledge
> to know what it is not.»
> CARL GUSTAV JUNG, Swiss Psychiatrist (1875-1961)

CARLOS PRIO SOCARRAS BECAME in 1948 Cuba's *Presidente Cordial*. From his first days in office he tried to make that slogan come true. He almost broke with Grau San Martín when Grau felt he could push around his former Minister of Labor and be the power behind the throne. Prío quickly implemented his *política de nuevos rumbos* — the policy of new bearings— meaning rectifications, course corrections and reparations.

As a jurist he knew he had to create laws and regulations that would complement the unfinished 1940 Constitution and bring about the institutions that would allow the country to advance and take good care of the public patrimony. He had an obsession to create a government that would be not only compliant with civil liberties but also strictly constitutional and fully institutionalized.

His first actions were to create the *Banco Nacional de Cuba*, the *Banco de Fomento Agrícola e Industrial*, the *Tribunal de Garantías Constitucionales* and the *Tribunal de Cuentas*. Historians still wonder how Cuba could have functioned for half a century without the protections and guidance of these institutions. Investors did not overlook the promise and favorable climate in Cuba in the early years of Carlos Prío. The nation had reached a fairly sophisticated level of urbanization; the labor movement was active but fair; almost the entire rural population had jobs in the sugar industry and other export crops, at least during most of the year. Americans felt secure with the investments policies of Prío and the government eagerly supported the progress they would bring to Cuba. On a per-capita basis, no other country in the world had more US capital invested than Cuba, with perhaps the exception of the oil producing countries in the Middle East.

Prío's energy and vision also undertook an Agrarian Reform, supported the free trade in the *bateyes* of the sugar mills (services and commerce areas, where the practice had been to redeem merchandise for company-controlled vouchers and tokens and not for cash), wrote legislation for gender civil rights equality and created several Judicial Districts.

There were three very decisive and persistent problems, however, which Prío could not solve during his government:

The first was to put a stop to the growth of political racketeering and gangsterism. Alejo Cossío del Pino, proprietor of Radio Cadena Habana, for instance, was murdered in plain daylight at a centric restaurant in Havana.

He could not prevent either the excessive growth of public employees; it reached 11% of the population during his presidency. Fully 80% of the 1949-1950 budget went into civil servant and retirees' salaries.

But more than anything else he could not prevent the growth of the *Ortodoxos* and the demagogy of its president Senator Eduardo Chibás. He had become the advocate of a group of frustrated oldies that had not reached the high spheres of government, seeking desperately to be leaders of a new generation that would bring morality and honesty to Cuban public life. It was Chibás, and practically nobody else, who lined the road for public discontent and a *coup-de-état* with his constant and cantankerous admonitions, irritating calls for change, and a contentious onslaught on Cuba's political leadership. The military conspirators were sure —listening to Chibás— that Prío had lost its popularity and was leading a weak government with very small public support. Although it was not true, the perception became an eventual opportunity for the military.

By 1950 VP Alonso Pujol had chosen Grau's side on the Grau-Prío friendly antagonism. It began to be known as the *Coincidencia*. The Communists had lost their shine and no party wanted to enter an alliance with them. Prío conducted such an honest election that his brother Antonio lost the race for mayor of Havana (52 to 37%) to Nicolás Castellanos, a handsome but colorless candidate backed by both Batista and Grau. By 1951 the strikes, manifestations and violence continued unabated. Within the last 10 months of the year the government of Prío had to deal with 120 strikes, 160 public protests asking for higher wages, 13 attempts on the life of gang rivals and numerous boycotts and graffiti crews papering the cities in Cuba.

As the 1952 elections approached, the general impression of the voters was that Prío was leading a party ruined by corruption and impotence; a party that could not even maintain the public order. There were rumors of massive changes in the Cabinet; the Communists were still legal but had lost a majority of its followers and political gurus estimated they numbered less than 50,000 all across the island. The *Ortodoxos* were predicted to win; Batista was considered to have the least chance of winning the elections even though he had concocted a constellation of old politicians who still believed that "*Batista es el hombre.*"

Nobody was paying any attention to a conversation that Batista had with Guillermo Alonso Pujol in 1951. He had told Prío's VP that «*There is a movement of young officers in the Army who are heading for the impeachment or a coup of President*

Prío and his replacement by the Vice President. I have been chosen by them to give a historical perspective to the movement. If we do not pay attention we run the risk that they would do it on their own. This is very dangerous considering that the military have no sense of political direction.» No one was paying attention either, to the many times General Quirino Uría, head officer of the *Columbia* military base in Havana, had warned President Prío that there was «*un golpe de estado en ciernes.*» (a *coup d'état* in the making).

A cartoon dated 1949 by David, **Juan David (1911-1981)**, the most popular caricaturist in Republican Cuba. It shows Carlos Prío on the right (holding a bottle) and his VP Alonso Pujol in mid air, with many other Cabinet members and friendly supporters holding their hats to receive part of the sovereign loan the government of Prío had received in 1949.

If anybody in 1948 deserved to be elected as President of Cuba it was **Carlos Prío Socarrás (1903-1977)**. He had been the leader of the 1930 generation that fought against the Machado dictatorship, had been in prison for two years, suffered years of exile and was a founding member of the *Partido Revolucionario Cubano (Auténtico)*.

During the Grau administration he had served as Minister of Public Works, Minister of Labor and Prime Minister. He proclaimed himself to be *el Presidente Cordial* and committed his party to rule in a civil and honest fashion, under constitutional order and political freedom.

Unfortunately his presidential period would be marked by an increase in corruption —by now an irrepressible national trait— and a raise in the violence that characterized the Cuban political life since Machado.

Photo below: President Prío, after the election, at his country home in *La Chata*, in Arrollo Naranjo, Habana. He was one of the most popular *politicos* in the history of Cuba.

Carlos Prío, a liberal democrat and an uncompromising defender of civil liberties, allowed **Fulgencio Batista** to return to Cuba in November 1948. For a while Batista kept quiet, not even attending the Senate sessions. His friends knew he was patiently developing a new political strategy that would get him back in power.

Photo at right: **Batista** and his second wife **Marta Fernández Miranda** in 1948.

On October 10, 1948, Carlos Prío Socarrás took charge of the presidency of Cuba. He got to the top job in Cuba with relatively few commitments, although he had hundreds of political debts to pay. His close friends were the old members of the *1930 Generation*. People thought they had to be better, more idealistic and high minded than the 1902 *Generation*, but time showed that was not the case.

His cabinet was, once more, a group of honorable, hard working and honest men:

Manuel (Tony) de Varona, Prime minister;
Carlos Hevia, Minister of State;
Ramón Corona, Minister of Justice;
Rubén de León, Minister of the Interior;
Ramón Nodal, Minister of Defense;
Antonio Prío Socarrás, Minister of the Treasury;
José R. Andreu, Minister of Commerce;
Aureliano Sánchez Arango, Minister of Education;
Francisco Grau Alsina, Minister of Agriculture;
Virgilio Pérez, Minister of Communications; **Manuel Febles**, Minister of Public Works;
Alberto Oteiza, Minister of Health;
Edgardo Buttari, Minister of Labor;
Orlando Puentes, Secretary of the Presidency.
Ramón Vasconcelos, **Primitivo Rodríguez** and **Mari Blanca Sabas Alomá** were Ministers at large.

Photo above: Prío during his presidential campaign in 1948. On the forefront his wife Mary Tarrero.

Immediately after occupying the presidency Prío put in motion the fulfillment of several promises from his 1948 campaign.

The creation of a *Central Bank*, for which he brought from the *International Monetary Fund* the best economist Cuba had ever produced, **Felipe Pazos (1912-2001)**, a former friend from his student days.

The institution of a new *Land Law* that, as mandated by the *1940 Constitution*, prevented idle lands to be used for speculation.

The creation of a *Tribunal de Cuentas*, to inspect and control all government expenses.

But most of all, Prío broke with Grau and began to review the public finances during 1944-1948, particularly a misappropriation of $174 million during Grau's government.

Right photo: Felipe Pazos.

On January 16, 1949 an investigation launched by Prío found that indeed there was a large shortage of funds in the Treasure due to apparent thefts during the government of Grau.

Immediately, **Eduardo Chibás** made this the obsessive topic of his CMQ Sunday night radio program. The case became known as ***la Causa 82*** and eventually it threatened to implicate also Batista and Prío. Years passed with no action taken until July 4, 1950 when all pertaining documents (more than 3,000 folders) were stolen from the *Víbora Correctional Court* where they were stored.

The man in charge of the investigation, Senator **Pelayo Cuervo Navarro (1892-1957)**, *photo on the left*, would be murdered by a hired political assassin in 1957.

There is no doubt that the one unmanageable challenge for Cuban presidents, practically since the inauguration of the repub- lic, was the recurrent and irrepressible political violence. At the smallest political misfortune, Cuban *políticos* were either taking arms against the legitimate power or requesting the intervention of the US government to restore —*their rights*.‖

Eventually this led to the formation of —*action groups*,‖ within which **politics coexisted with gangsterism**. The three most prominent urban groups operating in Cuba during the governments of Grau (1940-1944) and Prío (1948-1952), for example, were **Jesús Gonzalez Cartas's** (aka *El Extraño*) *Acción Revolucionaria Guiteras* (ARG), **Rolando Masferrer's** *Movimiento Socialista Revolucionario* (MSR), and **Emilio Tró's** *Unión Insurreccional Revolucionaria (UIR)*.

Prior to those, during the 1930s, there were **Pablo de la Torriente Brau's** *Organización Revolucionaria Cubana Antiimperialista (ORCA)*, and **Ramiro Valdés Daussá's** *Izquierda Revolucionaria (IR)*, among others.

Political gangsterism and violence in Cuba originated in 1934 under President Carlos Mendieta, with the killing of a group of ABC followers on June of that year, followed by the attack on president Mendieta himself. The gangs grew and crime was rife during the administrations of Grau San Martin and Carlos Prío, from the theft of the Capitol's diamond in March of 1946, to the theft of about 40 million dollars that should have been incinerated and were not at the Ministry of Finance in 1949.

Photos above, left to right: **Pablo de la Torriente Brau** (extreme left, during the Spanish civil war) of *Organización Revolucionaria Cubana Antiimperialista*; **Ramiro Valdés Daussá**, of *Izquierda Revolucionaria;* **Sergio González López**, aka *El Curita*, of *Acción Revolucionaria Guiteras.*

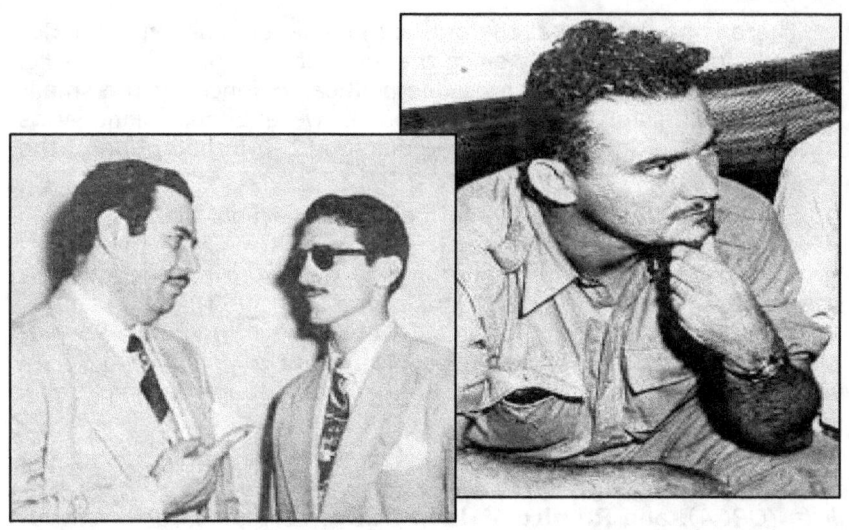

Gangs and organized crime groups evaded Prío's laws against *gansterismo* by seeking a political presence in Cuban life. Prío was not able to control this; the most he could do was to find them positions outside the island in order to keep them isolated. Even then he could not make a dent on their illicit activities.

Rolando Masferrer, a former leader of the *Lincoln Brigade* during the Spanish Civil War and a participant in *Cayo Confites*, (see page 348) and in 1948 was elected Senator from Prío's party;

Manolo Castro, leader and president of the *Federación, de Estudiantes Universitarios (FEU)* (see page 342) was assassinated; two prominent communists, **Jesús Menéndez** and **Aracelio Iglesias**, both labor leaders, were also felled by the gangsters.

The death of Manolo Castro was avenged by **Orlando León Lemus**, *el Colorado* (see pages 346 and 379), by killing **Justo Fuentes**, the VP of the University Student Union.

The students protested and went on strike, even though they were part of the problem; they had a genuine arsenal within the Agricultural building on campus.

By 1951 the group of *vigilantes-terroristas* called **Acción Revolucionaria Guiteras (ARG)** counted with more than two to three thousand thugs, most of them living off the sinecures provided by Prío to attenuate or discontinue their *actividades gangsteriles*.

Gangsters even began to seek election to the House of Representatives, as was the case of **Policarpo Soler**, a man wanted by police for charges ranging from murder to shoplifting.

Photo at left, **Policarpo Soler** (left) and **Orlando León Lemus** in 1949. *Photo at right*: **Rolando Masferrer**.

Political violence in Cuba could be partly explained as a legacy of Spain, a feudal colonial power that imposed a slavery-based economy in the island. **Spain continued to be feudal** after many nations in Europe had established *bourgeois* political systems. The Spanish feudal system prevailed in Cuba for 388 years, and was a greedy, barbaric and cruel scheme with only one ambition: to plunder and get rich quick. When the Cuban criollos reached matu- rity they had access to wealth and culture **but could not satisfy their political ambitions**. In search of their complete freedom, Cubans fought for 30 years until they could finally form a republic.

What did the Independence-Generals-turned-*políticos* do once Cuba became fully independent in 1902? They repeated what they had seen in years of submission to Spain. They enriched themselves; opened opportunities to their friends; thought nothing of misappropriating public funds. They knew that all their pillage could be funded by recurrent loans from US and European banks.

The people ultimately **lost respect and trust in the politicians**. Few of them cared to fulfill their promises and commitments. Extreme corruption in the midst of abject poverty became Cuba's reality. Eventually, as it happened in Mexico in the 1910 and in the US during the out-of-control mafias of the 1930s and 1940s, those who had not achieved power through political participation formed —*action groups*‖ to take from society and from each other what they knew the politicians were taking for themselves.

Photos above: **Orlando León Lemus**, aka *El Colorado,* died on a fight with the Batista police in February of 1955; **Rolando Masferrer**, was blown to bits in Miami by a car bomb on October of 1975; **Policarpo Soler** who, after a life of political crime in Cuba and gangsterism for the *Gotti* family in New York, escaped to Spain and the Dominican Republic after Batista's March 10, 1952 *coup d'ètat.* He was shot to death by Trujillo's men in early 1960.

On March of 1951, the best Finance Minister Cuba ever had —according to the March 19th *TIME Magazine*— resigned from the Carlos Prío cabinet. He was **José (Pepín) Bosch (1897-1992)**, Lehigh-educated millionaire businessman, former top executive and large stockholder of *Bacardí Corporation*. He had joined the Prío government as an old friend from the revolutionary days of the 1930s. When he took over *Hacienda* (the Treasury), Cuba had a deficit of $18 million. When he left, 18 months later, it had its largest surplus since President Estrada Palma's days: $15 million.

Bosch increased **income-tax collections** from $6 to $25 million, and **business profit taxes** from $20 to $45 million. He knew every rich person and industrialist in Cuba and accomplished these feats through persuasion and appeals to national pride. He **eliminated corruption** in customs overnight and had every business complying with **registration** regulations. Old *politicos* hated him; many congressmen threatened him with investigations; he would be called to testify at midnight and many times he refused to attend alleging those were his sleeping hours. He told Prío that his reasons to resign were the upcoming elections in 1952; he knew they would be financed with public money and he was not ready to tolerate it.

Bosch **ran the Bacardi rum empire for 32 years** and retired in 1976 at age 79. He had been born in Santiago de Cuba, the son of a Spanish banker and sugar mill owner. He married Enriqueta Schueg Bacardi in the 1940s and turned the 1862 Corporation into the world's larger hard liquor distiller and distributor. After retirement he lived in Nassau and Miami, dying when he was 95.

Photos above: Carlos Prío, Pepín Bosch and Luis Casero, Mayor of Santiago de Cuba, in 1951.

While these things were happening in the realm of politics, Cubans were becoming **obsessed with the radio** as a popular form of entertainment. There was nothing like the power of the *soap operas* in those golden days of radio.

In 1942, **Caridad Bravo Adams (1908-1990)** launched in Cuba *La Novela del Aire*, the first soap opera that impacted thousands of listeners. She was compared to Margaret Mitchell for her explorations of innermost human feelings and hidden ambitions.

In 1948 she was displaced by **Felix B. Caignet (1892-1976)** as the master of audiences in the radio in Cuba with his soap opera *El Derecho de Nacer*, transmitted in its entirety (314 episodes) by CMQ radio. Don Rafael del Junco, one of the main characters in the novel, tried to reveal to María Elena the name of her long lost son, which happens to be Alberto Limonta, a friend of the family. The audience became almost desperate when Don Rafael, unable to speak fluidly after a stroke, was at the point of revealing his secret for 274 consecutive episodes, (numbers 199 to 273); each episode always ending with «*María Elena... Albertico es ...(mutis).*»

Caignet never went to school because the low income level of his Santiago de Cuba family. His father was French and his mother a Cuban *mulata*; they had nine children.

Inspired by his accidental friendship with **Juan Ramón Jiménez**, Caignet was the first to write for children in the radio in Cuba, as well as the first to write in episodes to grab the continuous attention of his listeners. Inspired by his friend **Miguel Matamoros**, he wrote a popular children's song, *El Ratoncito Miguel*. Machado thought it was a sneer against him and Caignet spent several days in jail at the Moncada barracks. Caignet also wrote *Chan-Li-Po* in 1937, a popular detective series in suspense format.

Due to his success, not only in Cuba but in Madrid, Mexico, Buenos Aires, Rio de Janeiro and the rest of Latin America, **Caignet ended up a multimillionaire**, with a farm estate near Havana and a mansion in Varadero. After 1959 he was ostracized because his novels «*exalted the bourgeoisie.*» He died poor and forgotten in Cuba at age 84.

Photos: Carlos Badías as Albertico Limonta. Caridad Bravo Adams and Felix B. Caignet.

In June 1951, **Aureliano Sánchez Arango (1907-1976)**, Prior's Minister of Education, attacked **Eduardo Chibás** accusing him of speculating illegally in coffee futures. Chibás, in spite of his left-leaning anti-communist principles, was a rich man.

Chibás retaliated by accusing Aureliano of stealing children's breakfast funds and investing them in Central America.

For weeks these two *politicos*, who had befriended each other in 1927, denounced each other. When finally challenged, Chibás could not prove his accusations (presumably, documents in his briefcase).

On his next radio program (August 5, 1951) he shot himself after he went off the air roaring «*People of Cuba arise... this is my last aldabonazo (knock) at your door.*»

Pictures above: *top left,* Chibás carries the celebrated portfolio with the —*proofs. Top right:* one of his last radio transmissions at the CMQ radio station. *Bottom left*: Aureliano Sánchez Arango. *Bottom right:* the clash as seen by the press in Havana.

The unexpected death of Chibás shocked the country. Prío tried to recover his composure by mounting a strong anti-Communist campaign.

Gangsters like **Policarpo Soler** announced their candidacies for the Senate and the House. **Anibal Escalante**, director of *Hoy*, the Communist paper, almost died in a machine gun mayhem.

Corruption continued. Two well known politicians, **Alejo Cossio del Pino** and **Segundo Prendes**, were killed on the streets.

The papers reported that $3 million (Batista insisted it had been $47 million) worth of old currency were not burned but distributed among the president's friends.

The political parties were getting ready for the 1952 elections. The *Auténticos* presented **Carlos Hevia** as candidate; the *Ortodoxos* presented **Roberto Agramonte**, Chibás cousin; the Communists had no candidate; **Batista** was the candidate of the *Partido Acción Unitaria*, expected to come in third place.

Photos at the top: Chibás funeral on August 27, 1951. *Below, left to right*: the 1952 presidential candidates. Carlos Hevia, Roberto Agramonte and Fulgencio Batista.

By the time the elections were very close, in February 1952, all sort of rumors began to circulate in Havana:

Rumors were that the *Auténticos* had offered Batista $10 million to retire his candidacy to make it easier for Hevia to win; that the old military officers would not allow to be excluded from power by a victory of the *Auténticos* or the *Ortodoxos;* that Batista was conspiring with some officers to effect a *coup d'état* while pretending that he was been pressured by the young in the military to restore order; that Prío was about to make a *pronunciamiento*, a self inflicted *coup d'état*.

Unknown to everyone in the military, **General Quirino Uría López**, *Inspector General of the Cuban Army* and former *Chief of the National Police* had warned President Carlos Prío that Fulgencio Batista was seriously conspiring to depose him. Uría had resigned as *Chief of the National Police* in April 1951 after receiving orders from the highest levels of government to free some gangsters he had just apprehended and was in the process of booking.

President Prío ignored Uría's warnings and was taken by surprise, completely unprepared, on March 10, 1952, a day that would forever live in infamy in the history of Cuba.

On the photos: left, General Uría in Columbia; *right*, General Uría confronting Fidel Castro, a social dissolution agent, at one of the disturbances created by him in 1950 in front of the *University of Havana*; on the bottom right two portraits.

On the night of March 10, 1952, **Mary Tarrero de Prío (1924-2010)**, the first lady of Republican Cuba, went into exile, in Mexico, after the *coup de état* of Fulgencio Batista. Her plans for that night had been to attend a concert by the *Orquesta Filarmónica de La Habana*, at the *Auditorium Theater*.

The concert, part of the XXVII season, featured Sergei Rachmaninoff and Richard Strauss in what would have been the 590th appearance of the *Filarmónica* in Havana. Mary Tarrero was Honorary President of the Board of the Philharmonic. The patrons of the season were, aside from the **Cuban government**, the **Widow of Humara y Lastra, Enrique Godoy y Sayán, Teté Bengochea de Pedraza** and **Frank Bartés**.

By 1952 classical music in Cuba had acquired an important role in the cultural live of the nation. As the Republic came into being in 1902, **Ignacio Cervantes (1847-1905)** was in his fifties, at the zenith of his craft, and had just published his *Danzas Cubanas para Piano*. **Hubert de Blanck (1856-1932)**, the patriarch of musical teaching in Cuba, had founded the first musical conservatory in Cuba's history. **José White (1836-1918)**, Cuba's outstanding violinist, had already written *Bella Cubana* and was leading the effort to make Beethoven a household name in the island. **Eduardo Sánchez de Fuentes (1874-1944)**, an extraordinary romantic composer committed to the survival of the songs of the *siboneyes*, was getting ready to inaugurate the *Auditorium Theater* with his *Anacaona*, a delightful symphonic choir; his *Habanera Tú* would soon be played all around the globe.

Photos above: Mary Tarrero de Prío, Cuba's first lady from 1948 to 1952. The program of the Havana Philharmonic for March 10, 1952, a concert that was cancelled by the unforeseen *coup-de-état* of Batista.

Classical music was very important in Republican Cuba. Almost with the inauguration of the Republic came the birth of **Amadeo Roldán (1900-1939)**, a director of the *Philharmonic*, a scholar of afro-Cuban rhythms and one of the top symphonic composers in Latin America. He was followed by **Alejandro García Caturla (1906-1940)**, self-taught, rivaled in Latin America only by Villalobos and Silvestre Revueltas. Musical critics at the time thought of Roldán as the civilized composer and Caturla as the exotic *fauve* of vivid colors and sharp contrasts.

Musical societies began to sprout in Cuba with this proliferation of musical geniuses. **Pro Arte Musical**, the **Sociedad de Conciertos**, the **Lyceum**, the **Ateneo**, the **Sociedad Universitaria de Bellas Artes**, the **Casa Cultural de Católicas**, the **Juventudes Musicales**, and others. In a blessed act of reciprocity, the many musical societies brought about the organization of new orchestras. In 1924 the ***Orquesta Filarmónica de La Habana*** was born. Agustín Batista, the great Cuban *Maecenas* was its support for many years, turning a precarious effort into a powerful organization.

In the days close to the ending of the Republic, Cuba had the fortune to count with two extraordinary musical figures: **Gonzalo Roig (1890-1970)**, the author of *Quiéreme Mucho* and *Cecilia Valdés*, and **Ernesto Lecuona (1896-1963)**, the author of *Siboney* and *Danza Lucumí*. As Manuel de Falla, the great Spanish composer, once said «*Cuba's classical music is unique in the continent for its inimitable musical rhythms linked to the ancient roots of the natives of its soil.*»

Photo above top row: Ignacio Cervantes, Hubert de Blanck, José Blanck and Ernesto Sánchez de Fuentes. *Bottom row*: Amadeo Roldán, Alejandro García Caturla, Gonzalo Roig and Ernesto Lecuona.

Popular music, in the years before the end of the Republic, was also at the peak of its popularity. It had become a self-sustaining business with the advent of recording studios based in Havana. Among the first Cuban artists getting their songs recorded for posterity were **Celina y Reutilio**, interpreters of *A la Caridad del Cobre*, *El Hijo de Elegguá* and *Oye mi Olelolei*. Soon other artists were recording their works: **Olga Guillot, Abelardo Barroso, Manolo Alvarez Mera, René Cabell, Rita Montaner, María Luisa Chorens, Orlando Vallejo**, as well as the orchestras **Riverside, Sensación, Conjunto Casino** and many others. Most of these artists were made famous by the recording studios of *Puchito Records* on San Miguel Street.

Competing with *Puchito Records* was *Panart Records*. It began in 1954 with the production of music from the Hermanas Martí and the Spanish group *Los Chavales de España*. They followed with the **Trio Servando Díaz** and the guitarist **Francisco Repilado**, later known as Compay Segundo. *Panart* eventually acquired the exclusive representation of *Decca*, from New York. One of its best sellers at that time was **Ramoncito Veloz**, with several of his very successful *Guajiras de Salón*. *Panart* was soon surpassed by *Humara y Lastra*, representatives of *RCA Victor*. At the time *Panart* was paying its artists $5 for each side of a disc, RCA began to pay $25, thus absorbing almost the exclusivity of record production in Cuba. Panart records almost declared bankruptcy in 1953.

An extraordinary phenomenon occurred in the world of recording when the **Orquesta América** recorded for *Panart* the most successful disk ever in the history of musical Cuba: *La Engañadora* on one side and *Silver Spring* on the other, by **Enrique Jorrín**, a violinist-composer with limited visibility in Cuba until then. The record sold 23,000 copies in six months, saving the life of *Panart Records*, now bringing in close to $2 million a year. The success of *Orquesta América* was followed by **Orquesta Fajardo y sus Estrellas, Miguel Failde** with his nostalgic *danzón Alturas de Simpson*, the **Sonora Matancera, Fernando Albuerne, Alberto Beltrán**, and others. Cuba had secured by 1958 its position in the world of popular music.

Photos: Popular records during the late years of the Republic.

Since **Carlos Prío** was the last Constitutional President of Cuba, historians have analyzed his presidency more than any other prime magistrate in Republican Cuba.

At 45 years of age, Prío became the first president born in the 20th century. He was also **a product of the 1930 Revolution** and was an intelligent charismatic natural leader with strong democratic convictions and ample experience in the political arena.

On the national sphere his accomplishments were many and solid, including the following laws: *Against Gangsterism*; creating the *National Bank*; creating the *Court of Constitutional and Social Guarantees*; creating the *Agricultural and Industrial Development Bank (BANFAIC)*; creating the *Tribunal de Cuentas* (Court of Auditors); implementation of an *Agrarian Reform*; the creation of the *Universities of Las Villas* and *Santiago* and the accreditation of the University *of Villanueva*; establishing *Equality of Rights* for married women; decree paying pending payments to *War Veterans*; creation of the *National Economic Board*.

On the international sphere he was equally committed and active: Cuba signed the *International Declaration of Human Rights*; assumed the presidency of the *UN Security Council* and became a powerful supporter of democracy across the world.

In spite of Cuba's tradition of sinecures and favoritism, when Dr. Pelayo Cuervo filed with the Supreme Court an accusation against President Grau for embezzlement of public funds, Prío did not interfere and **allowed the Cause 82 to proceed**. Prío, however, was violently attacked with allegations and unproven insinuations, among them that his brothers were stealing public funds, that time-worn currency was not burned but pocketed by dishonest friends; that drugs were been consumed in the Presidential Palace; that the president had been bought by the mobsters.

The truth was that the gangs of criminals continued the same level of nefarious and reprehensible activities they had conducted during Grau's presidency, in spite of the creation of a *Grupo Represivo de Actividades Subversivas (GRAS)* **intended to stop gangsterism** in Cuba. It will be difficult for historians to establish if Carlos Prío did everything he could to stop this or if he did not do enough. He certainly had nothing for which to be thankful to them, on the contrary.

Photos above: Prío visisting Truman. *Bohemia* Magazine, to its great regret later on, joined forces with Batista against Prío in 1952.

When **Carlos Prío** was deposed by Batista's *coup de état* in March of 1952, he joined a selected group of presidents named –**Carlos**, none of whom ever got to finish their presidential terms; they were all ousted or by-passed.

Carlos Manuel de Céspedes y del Castillo, Cuba's first president of the Republic in arms was deposed at a meeting held at *Bijagual*, on October 27, 1873. He died a few weeks later.

Carlos Manuel de Céspedes y Quesada, appointed president after the fall of Machado in 1933, was deposed by the army and students when they selected the five members of the *Pentarquía* to rule in Cuba.

Carlos Hevia replaced Grau San Martín on January 14th 1934 but his appointment was objected by the US; he kept that position until the 18th day of January, when Batista replaced him with Mendieta.

Carlos Mendieta succeeded Carlos Hevia on January 18th of 1934 and lasted until the 12th of December of 1936 when he was replaced, again by Batista, by José Agripino Barnet.

Carlos M. Piedra, the oldest magistrate in the Supreme Court of Cuba on January 1st 1959, nominally became President of Cuba after Batista, his VP Rafael Guas Inclán and Anselmo Aliegro, President of the Senate, had all left the country. Piedra became the president with the shortest presidential period, if you count as such his wasted time in *Columbia* waiting in vain to be sworn.

Photos top row: Carlos Manuel de Céspedes Castillo, Carlos Manuel de Céspedes Quesada, Carlos Hevia; *Bottom row*: Carlos Mendieta. Carlos Prío, Carlos M. Piedra.

A Relapse into Illegitimacy
The Years 1952 to 1958

> «The only power a government should have is the power to crack down on criminals. But if government asks too many things to be done, it will be impossible to live without breaking the law.» AYN RAND, Russian born American Philosopher (1905-1982)

BY THE END OF 1952, political parties were finished in Cuba for all practical purposes. On Monday, March 10, Batista had broken the democratic and constitutional rhythm of the Republic. He had given the widely expected coup and his *de facto* government had been recognized by the US and every civilized nation on earth. Prío, who had initially attempted but failed to mount a resistance, had safely flown to Mexico with his family. Most of his ministers and confidants stayed at home listening to the news. One by one the army, navy and air force Generals pledged support for the conspirators at the Columbia Barracks. Banks remained opened; so were restaurants, stores and even night clubs. Some schools took precautions and sent the students home. The University of Havana was sizzling with rumors but no one descended the front steps in protest. A large group of Batista supporters began to enter Columbia to congratulate the general after his bloodless coup. The only entity that had ostensibly suffered a fatal blow to its existence was the young Republic of Cuba. With this successful coup Batista showed Cubans that his instincts and reflexes were as good   in

1952 as they had been in 1933, when he had masterminded a similar uprising. He had been plotting for months his return to power in Cuba. He had waited until the morning after a jubilant carnival night to surprise his adversaries.

His co-conspirators met with him at 2:40 AM at his country estate of *Kukine* on the outskirts of Havana. He had only trusted his full plans to General Francisco Tabernilla, his most loyal comrade and Roberto Fernández Miranda his brother-in-law. He could count with faithful followers at the Columbia Barracks —seat of the command of the Cuban Armed Forces, where the coup was to be perpetrated— as well as every military camp and armory in Cuba, with the exception of the *Cuartel Goicuría*, a military garrison in the city of Matanzas. All ranks of the police, the army, air force and navy had been infiltrated and every radio and police station had a reliable inside man pledged to the Batista cause. Batista would later brag «*by the time we entered and took possession of Columbia we had already taken possession of the hearts of its military men*». Every one of his accomplices was timing their moves listening to *Radio Reloj*, a 24-hour AM radio station broadcasting the time minute by minute. The station had been seized at 1:00 in the morning. Not even his wife knew of the intentions of Batista; she was placidly sleeping at *Kukine* while the coup was occurring. By the time she woke up she was first lady of the Republic.

Batista knew he had to win the consent of many Cubans that were crushed by his desecration and disruption of fifty years of hope for a life of democratic rule. He immediately began to dispose of the credit institutions that Prío had created and began an accelerated program of very visible public works. In addition he dedicated $350 million to an intrepid plan of economic and social development. Yet he retained the military dictum of always placing more reliance in coercive power than in seeking consensus. He suspended the civil liberties, controlled the press and limited dissent and active political participation by the former members of political parties and the students.

He tried to mutate from military strong man to popular president but the formula that he had so easily found in 1940 was now a mystery to him. Also, at his age, he reasoned he would rather be a comfortable gentleman president —as Zayas had been— than a confrontational ideological *caudillo*. His followers and co-conspirators, however, were thirsty for an autocratic governing mandate, lavish life-styles and plenty of enrichment opportunities. The students, on the other hand, were outraged by the coup and the pretensions of these new and old *Batistianos*. They were never ready to forgive and for- get. In their minds, March 10, regardless of Batista's arguments to the contrary, was simply an ordinary barracks revolt. They decided that Batista and his minions would never again have a night of tranquil sleep. Under the leadership of José Antonio Echeverría the University of Havana students began to give him a run for his money.

Not able to gain the trust and loyalty of the Cubans, Batista decided to woo and flatter the Americans. He became an entrenched anti-communist; broke relations with the Soviet Union; asked and obtained military assistance grants from the US; opened Cuba to investments from Americans with very favorable terms; turned Cuba into a Mecca for American tourists looking for gambling, night club fun and well managed prostitution, like they had in Las Vegas.

The *Auténticos* and the *Ortodoxos* continued to languish, not knowing how to get rid of Batista without bringing a lot of bloodshed to Cuba. They met in Montreal and produced a good looking but toothless document that, more than anything else, demonstrated that they distrusted each other.

On July 26, 1953, Castro attacked the Moncada Barracks in Santiago de Cuba with a bunch of youngsters from Artemisa, Pinar del Río. Most people knew that he kept himself out of the range of the defender's weapons in spite of the ruthless defense mounted by the soldiers at the *Moncada*. Unhurt, Castro escaped the scene, reached and ran through the mountains for a few days, surrendered and hid behind the cassock of Manuel Pérez Serantes, Santiago de Cuba's Archbishop. In the eyes of *Batistianos* he had become public enemy number one. In the eyes of his followers he became a promising redeemer.

Thirty months after the 1952 coup, Batista called for national elections; as in the classical biblical banquet, nobody came. Batista nevertheless developed a strong campaign and claimed to be the legitimately elected president, arguing that half the qualified electors had participated. No one bothered to object. In May 1955 Batista released Castro from prison. Weeks later Castro fled to Mexico. By then politicians, lawyers, priests and nuns, lay Catholics, University and High School students, some businessmen, most foreign investors, bankers, diplomats, sugar barons, all in Cuba began to sympathize with Batista's opponents. Don Cosme de la Torriente organized the *Sociedad de Amigos de la República (SAR)*, the Society of Friends of the Republic, trying to bring together the government and the opposition. Its *diálogo cívico* never got anywhere. Batista even mocked Torriente publicly as an old arteriosclerotic man.

By 1956, the encounters between students and the sympathizers of Batista —including the political police—were so frequent and bloody, that the University of Havana decided to close its doors. A systematic policy of unmitigated brutality was assumed by the official powers. By the end of the year Castro and a group of his followers, after training in Mexico, disembarked in Oriente province.

During 1957 the University of Havana students, under the leadership of Echeverría (for the FEU) and Menelao Mora (for the *Auténticos*) attempted to take the life of Batista with an intrepid assault to the presidential palace and Radio Reloj in broad daylight. Both leaders and many of their followers were killed. Castro, hoping not to be upstaged, breathed more secure and denounced the attempted magnicide as a worthless loss of combatants. The following month Carlos Prío sent and supported an expedition from Miami; all 16 members were captured and executed.

All through the years between 1952 and 1958 the communists sided with Batista in the hopes of a new coalition that would make it easier to increase the rolls of the party. In mid 1958 the FEU —recovered after the fiasco of the attack to the presidential palace— opened a guerrilla operation in the *Escambray* Mountains, in Las Villas, roughly similar to what the Castro brothers had mounted in Oriente province.

In urban areas, growing resistance complemented the expanding struggle of the mountain fighters; many frightening but innocuous terrorist actions took place; mostly banging noises and threatening blusters rather than criminal blasts. Batista, in the meantime, was launching all out offensives into the mountains knowing that the US government was reaching the limit of its patience and needed to see peace and tranquility in an island 90 miles from their coasts and full of American investments.

By the end of the summer of 1958 Batista's offensive collapsed. The Cuban armed forces were disintegrating. The only men fighting —aside from well protected high officers in the rearguard— were *casquitos*, young recruits with hardly any military experience, who were paid $33.33 a month and were easy prey for the *guerrilleros*.

The last Batista-held elections took place on November 3, 1958. Voters were so frightened by the threats and so easily persuaded by the Castro operatives to stay away from the polls that they mostly abstained from voting. In Oriente and Las Villas provinces less than 5% of qualified voters went to the polls. The elections were unmistakably fraudulent; instead of strengthening the government they undermined it. Cuba had no place to go and any solution was better than the *status quo*.

At an end-of-the-year party in 1958 Batista announced to his surprised guests his intention to depart from Cuba. His family was already on its way to Columbia were an airplane was waiting to take them to the Dominican Republic. A fellow dictator, the Generalissimo Rafael Leonidas Trujillo, had offered a full floor of the *Juragua Hotel* in Santo Domingo for the moderate rent of $1 million a year or fraction, paid in advance. Marta, Batista's wife, felt the asking sum was a little steep. Batista though that he had the money< and it was an offer he could not refuse.

The news in the days preceding the elections to be held on June 1 1952 were typical of the entire presidential era of Carlos Prío:

In September of 1951 the composer **Ernestina Lecuona** and the painter **Leopoldo Romañach** both died.

William L. Beaulac was appointed new US ambassador to Cuba.

The printing press of the communist newspaper **Hoy** was vandalized and burned.

President Prío inaugurated the offices of the **BANFAIC** (Banco de Fomento Agrícola e Industrial) at the *Lonja del Comercio* (Havana's Mercantile Exchange)

Rolando Masferrer and his mob fired against police in Havana.

A large **school** and a **hospital** were inaugurated in Pinar del Rio (Prío's birthplace)

Number one mob leader **Policarpo Soler** was arrested. He escaped with the help of **Orlando León Lemus** (el Colorado)

The ex Chief of the Army **Genovevo Pérez Dámera** was hurt in an attempt on his life.

Cuban composer and band director **Dámaso Pérez Prado** launched a new rhythm, the mambo

Prío opened for business the **Tribunal de Cuentas**.

A bomb exploded at the home of **Maria Luisa Gómez Mena**, *Countess of Revilla de Camargo*, who was the wife of Cuban painter Mario Carreño.

Alejo Cossio del Pino, former Minister of the Interior, was assassinated inside a café in Havana.

Rolando Masferrer survived another attempt on his life.

A bomb exploded at the law offices of **Pelayo Cuervo Navarro**, the accuser in the famous *Causa 82*.

The *Auténticos* were almost finished as a winning political party for their failure to provide a decent environment in Cuba during the last two presidential terms. Their Candidate, who had almost no chance, was **Carlos Hevia Reyes (1900-1964)**, who had been Cuba's president for 40 hours in 1934.

The *Ortodoxos*, thanks in part to Eduardo Chibas' conspicuous sacrifice —who had erased the notion that he was a warmonger and a demagogue— were posed for a landslide victory. Their candidate was **Roberto Agramonte (1904-1995)**, former ambassador of Cuba to Mexico.

Fulgencio Batista (1901-1973), the candidate of the *Partido Acción Unitaria*, was supported by a mixed bag of political oldies (*camajanes* in the Cuban argot) and was given cero chance of making a decent run at the presidency.

HOW REVOLUTIONS OCCUR IN CUBA: A *COUP D'ETAT*—AND BUSINESS AS USUAL.

BEFORE THE *COUP D'ETAT* BY WHICH HE WAS DEPOSED: DR. CARLOS PRIO SOCARRAS (LEFT), ELECTED CUBA'S PRESIDENT IN 1948, IN THE PALACE WITH UNIVERSITY STUDENTS.

SURROUNDED BY SUPPORTERS: DR. CARLOS PRIO SOCARRAS (CENTRE, FACING CAMERA) BEFORE HE FLED FROM THE PRESIDENTIAL PALACE.

AT A RALLY OF HIS SUPPORTERS NEAR CAMP COLUMBIA: GENERAL FULGENCIO BATISTA (SEATED AT THE TABLE, CENTRE, BETWEEN TWO WOMEN), THE EX-PRESIDENT WHO SEIZED POWER ON MARCH 10.

CUBA'S EX-DICTATOR, WHO SEIZED POWER BY A SUCCESSFUL *COUP D'ETAT* AT THE REQUEST OF A MILITARY JUNTA: GENERAL FULGENCIO BATISTA WITH A GROUP OF CUBAN SOLDIERS.

THE REVOLUTION IN PROGRESS ON MARCH 10: A TANK AND A LORRY WHICH CONTAINED ARMED TROOPS, OUTSIDE THE PRESIDENTIAL PALACE, HAVANA.

RELEASED AFTER ARREST DURING THE REVOLT: DR. RAMON GRAU SAN MARTIN, PRESIDENT FROM SEPT. 1933 TO JAN. 1934, AND FROM OCT. 1944 TO JUNE 1948.

The revolution in Cuba by which General Fulgencio Batista, a former dictator, and President from 1940 to 1944, seized power on March 10, was carried out at lightning speed, with the loss of only two lives; and is reported only to have interrupted business in the island for one day. General Batista, supported by the Army, seized command at Camp Columbia, Army Headquarters, early on March 10, and broadcast to the nation. One of his supporters took over Police H.Q., and tanks and lorry-loads of armed troops converged on the Presidential Palace, in Havana. Dr. Prio Socarras, President since 1948, took refuge in the Mexican Embassy, and on March 13 flew to Mexico. On arrival there he stated that he has not resigned, but has left Cuba "under pressure." On March 10, General Batista selected the members of his new Cabinet and they were sworn in on March 11. No provisional President was appointed and General Batista is directing the Government as Prime Minister. He states that his Government is to remain in power "so long as was necessary to establish normal conditions and to arrange for honest general elections." The reason for the revolt is stated to have been "because people could not put up with the existing state of affairs."

On March 10, at 1:00 AM, **Carlos Prío** was at *Finca La Chata*, in Arroyo Naranjo, 20 Km from Havana. His lieutenant Segundo Curti and several of Prío's ministers were having after-dinner cocktails at *Rio Mar Restaurant and Hotel*, at First and O streets in Miramar.

Havana residents had already retired from a night of Carnival. At this precise moment three large black Buick cars left *Finca Kukine*, **Batista's** villa in Arrollo Arenas, near Havana. Batista, wearing a leather jacket and packing a .45 caliber pistol, was in the third car of the procession.

They drove around Havana to verify that there was no military activity anywhere. After several tense moments they headed for **post four at Camp Columbia**. At this back gate they were allowed in by an officer who was waiting for them. Also waiting were several young soldiers who were party to the plot. They proceeded to arrest the top generals: **Ruperto Cabrera**, chief of staff and **Quirino Uría**, the army's inspector general. Cuban democracy was doomed at that moment.

Photos: Batista speaks to the *soldadesca* on March 10; a closer picture, with his famous jacket. Post four entrance at Columbia Camp.

Batista (shown here with many groups of friends who ran to support him after his *coup d'état*) was militarily well prepared to take over the presidency without spilling blood in 1952.

At 1:00 pm, *Radio Havana* was already giving the list of new ministers in his cabinet; they were all trusted friends that were now echoing the slogan «*Batista es el hombre.*»

They would forever disallow the notion that they had undone a dozen years of constitutional government in a day of opprobrium. Every one of them ended in exile in 1959 when Batista was thrown out of power after the violent communist revolution that they unwillingly had made possible.

The new Cabinet Ministers were: **Miguel Angel Campa** (Foreign Secretary); **Miguel A. de Céspedes** (Justice); **Ramón Hermida** (Interior); **José A. Mendigutía** (Public Works); **Alfredo Jacomino** (Agriculture); **Marino López Blanco** (Finance); **Andrés Rivero Aguero** (Education); **Oscar de la Torre** (Commerce); **Pablo Carrera Justiz** (Communications); **Andrés Domingo Morales del Castillo** (Presidency); **Nicolás Pérez** (Defense); **Ernesto de la Fe** (Information); **Enrique Saladrigas** (Health); **Jesús Portocarrero** (Labor).

Batista took full advantage of the unpreparedness of Prío on March 10, 1952. **General Cabrera's** wife, knowing her husband was under arrest in *Camp Columbia*, called the presidential palace. They in turn called La *Chata* to let President Prío know there was a *coup d'état* in the making. Very soon Prío found out that he could only count with the loyalty of **Colonel Martín Elena**, the leading military man in Matanzas province, 100 Km east of Havana.

Prío had led a party that for years had been sunk in corruption; although everybody knew the coming elections would be fair and honest, the A*uténticos* had failed to present themselves as a viable alternative to dictatorship.

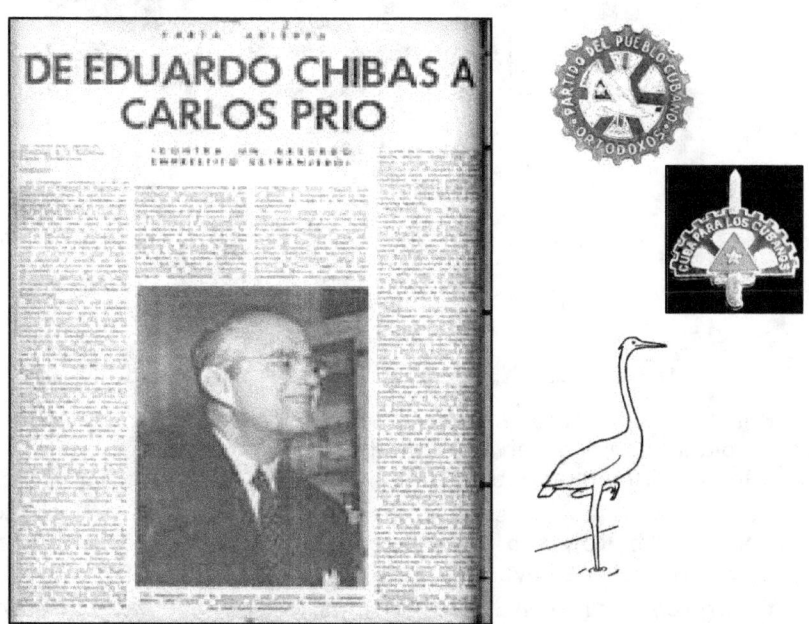

Eduardo Chibás, former president of the **Ortodoxos**, with his interminable diatribes about corruption in government (over the CMQ radio every Sunday night) had so much softened the commitment of Cubans to democratic government that there was little resistance to the colossal damage that Batista was doing to Cuba with his *coup d'état*.

People, on the other hand, were expecting a rally or a call for support by Prío, which never came. The CTC called for a general strike and waited in vain. Nobody showed up at banks, schools, most businesses and all government offices. Newspapers were not circulated. Only the University was packed with protesters, waiting for weapons that Prío had promised but never arrived.

By 1:00 pm Prío had already made his way to the Mexican embassy, where he found most of his cabinet.

Photos: One of the many denunciations orchestrated by Chibás against Prío in *Bohemia Magazine*; the emblems of the *Ortodoxos,* the *Auténticos* and Batista's *Grulla* (the crane).

Batista's *coup d'état* had been so sudden and his initial moves so ambiguous and deceiving that the popular resistance to it was slow in gathering momentum.

Some of the gangsters like **Policarpo Soler** were sent into exile. Others like **Rolando Masferrer** were incorporated in the repressive arms of the government.

Organized crime ceased to exist as such in the face of *state gangsterism*. Even the prostitutes of *Pajarito* Street began to complain about the insecurity of the *red zone*.

The *CTC Union* came under government control as its leader, **Eusebio Mujal**, moved in great haste to Batista's side.

Cardenal Arteaga, the highest Catholic Church authority in Cuba, first congratulated Batista but later was physically attacked by one of Batista's fanatical followers.

Botellas (sinecures) increased, since they were now given mostly (for government positions) through corrupt labor leaders. The **Auténticos** began to lure the **Ortodoxos** to form a common front against Batista but the latter were so split that no one could ascertain who would sanction such participation. In the meantime Batista's men were disgruntled since the boss was the only one taking credit for the *coup*.

Photos above, left to right: *Batista* on the cover of *TIME*, Batista inside *Bohemia Magazine*; *Eusebio Mujal* with Batista's Minister of Labor, *Suárez Rivas* (behind him), at a CTC gathering in 1952.

At the time of Batista's *coup d'ètat* the *Auténticos* were Cuba's largest and best organized political party. Its president was **Antonio (Tony) Varona,** a man untouched by scandal, president of the Cuban Senate, who remained in Cuba when Prío fled to México. When on March 17 he obtained from the legislature a statement denouncing the end of constitutional order, Batista dissolved all political parties, replaced the 1940 constitution with his own 1952 Statutes and announced elections for November of 1953.

Varona responded with a manifesto on April 2 describing the achievements of the *Auténticos* and the integrity of **Carlos Hevia** and **Luis Casero**, the President and VP candidates for his party, two men renowned for their ability and respected for their uprightness. The same could have been said of the *Ortodoxos*, who presented as candidates for the 1952 elections two men of similar reputation: **Roberto Agramonte and Emilio (Millo) Ochoa**.

To compound things, Varona refused to participate in the 1953 elections organized by Batista; Agramonte broke with him announcing that the *Ortodoxos* would probably participate; Grau proclaimed himself the *Auténtico* candidate and registered the par- ty behind Varona's back. The *Liberal Party*, in the meantime, began to be too friendly to Batista and several of its members; with oth- ers from the *Republican Party*, they began to join the *Auténticos*. An organized opposition became a fact when on June 2, 1953, the *Auténticos* and the *Ortodoxos* signed the **Montreal Charter**, signaling their joint resistance to Batista's regime. A few weeks later, July 26, Castro attacked the *Moncada Barracks* in Santiago de Cuba. Batista's triumphal response was to issue **Decree 997**, establishing all sorts of limitations to personal rights for Cubans and rescheduling elections for 1954. At that point Varona went into exile.

Photos above: Four of the signers of the 1953 *Montreal Charter*: Carlos Prío, Antonio Varona, Emilio Ochoa and José Pardo Llada, on top, in or around 1953; on the bottom in exile, 50 years later but still active trying to rescue the republic and its 1940 Constitution.

In the meantime, in 1953, Batista was harassed not only from outside but also from inside his inner circle.

His Chief of Staff, **Francisco Tabernilla Dolz** would not talk to **Nicolás (Colacho) Hernández**, Batista's Minister of Defense;

Rafael Salas Cañizares, the Chief of Police, refused to take orders from **Ramón Hermida**, the Minister of Interior.

What they all enjoyed was taking members of the opposition into custody. At any given time, when any Cuban family knew that a member had been made prisoner, the first order of the day was to find out who was the arresting official and where did he keep his prisoners.

Resistance to Batista's government soon began to develop among university students and gradually spread to include practically all sectors of Cuban society.

Batista had no real political base. He ruled with the Cuban army as his party. He was never able to reassure the political and the business classes that he was one of them. As with most Cuban presidents, he had difficulties walking the fine line between pleasing Washington and protecting Cuban interests. In the end his *karma* was to lose both supports. By 1958 most Cuban believed that «*Mejor que Batista Cualquiera.*» (Anyone but Batista).

On the photos above, left to right, top to bottom: some of the earliest opponents of Batista: **Pelayo Cuervo**, **Rafael García Bárcena**, **Roberto Agramonte**, **José Pardo Llada**, **Carlos *Hevia***, **Aureliano Sánchez Arango**, **Manuel Márquez Sterling** and **Ramón Barquín.**

During the early months of 1953 a series of important events took place.

In January a student called **Rubén Batista** (no kin) was shot and killed during a demonstration in memory of Julio Antonio Mella in Havana.

Batista postponed the elections first until June 1954 and later to November 1954, presumably because of too many **conspiratorial activities**.

In April **Rafael García Bárcena** and a group of students marched to *Camp Columbia*. The students were arrested; García Bárcena was mercilessly tortured.

In May **Pelayo Cuervo** wrote an article in *Bohemia Magazine* accusing the military of swindling the lottery. He was arrested and battered.

In June the **Auténtico** and **Ortodoxo** parties met in Montreal and signed the declaration condemning attacks, gangsterism and terrorism and asking for the return of the *1940 Constitution*.

A series of **bombs** began to go off in Havana breaking the silence of the night but not producing any victims.

Most news were normally not reported in **Bohemia** Magazine due to censorship. Every now and then Batista felt stronger and allowed several issues of **Bohemia *Sin Censura*** to run the news that had been previously suppressed in the censored editions.

There were numerous newspapers in Cuba during most of its republican history: *Información, El Mundo, El País, El Crisol, Alerta, El Excelsior, Prensa Libre* and *Avance,* to mention only the most popular. The dean of the Cuban press was the *Diario de la Marina*, where journalists with great talent were writing regularly: **Jorge Mañach, Ramiro Guerra, Francisco Ichaso, Gastón Baquero, Emeterio Santovenia, José María Chacón y Calvo**, and many others.

The **Diario de la Marina (1844-1960)** was one of the exceptional newspapers read by most Cubans for over a century. It started as a paper that presented to Cubans the colonial perspective; after the independence it became a conservative newspaper that soon acquired a great reputation for honesty and independence. Since before World War I, without rest, the *Diario* always opposed «*the ascending tide of communism,*» according to its Editor in Chief **Gastón Baquero (1914-1997)**. From 1944 to 1960 José Ignacio Rivero, son of Pepín Rivero, grandson of the founder Don Nicolas Rivero, was the head of the paper; he also owned **Alerta**, an evening daily paper of smaller circulation.

On the photos above: Jose Ignacio Rivero, Gastón Baquero and the *Diario de la Marina* building at Prado, corner of Teniente Rey Street, in Havana.

EL VOTO DEL PUEBLO

Regardless of political realities, Cubans have always enjoyed cartoons that in humoristic fashion analyze, elevate or destroy political figures, reflecting the feelings of the people. Over the years, three characters have become popular icons that have transcended time and became indelible in the memory of the citizens: *Liborio, El Bobo* and the *Loquito*.

Liborio was created in the 1920s by **Ricardo de la Torriente (1867-1934)**, inspired by the apathetic and cynical *Guajiro* that had been created by Landaluce during colonial times. According to Juan David (1911-1981), another masterful caricaturist and lampooner, Liborio was «*the vivid picture of the national frustration and impotence.*»

Victor Patricio Landaluce (1828-1889) was a Spanish illustrator and writer living in Cuba. He received a careful education, including learning of several languages, and for a time lived in Paris. He moved to Cuba in the early 1850s. His first work was *Cubans painted by themselves*. On the right, a rare self-portrait.

El Bobo de Abela

-Aquí entre nosotros, Apóstol, ¿qué fue lo que usted quería?

Sharper, smarter, and just as critical and rebellious was *El Bobo*, created in 1925 by the painter and caricaturist **Eduardo Abela, (1889-1965).** *El Bobo* first appeared in the magazine *El Zorro Viejo* (San Antonio de los Baños) in a drawing that was to announce a brand of shoes. The enigma of *El Bobo*, a man a little weird, with a chubby face and a wide-brimmed hat, was that his face was the back of a woman's torso. *El Bobo* was a mischievous, sly character that always pretended to silly but respectfully transmitted serious messages. It appeared in the newspapers *Diario de la Marina, El País* and *Information*, always with a concern for political and social issues, including the anti-Machado struggle.

Also born in San Antonio de los Baños was **René de la Nuez (1937-)**, the creator of *El Loquito*, a cross-eyed man with a cone nose, and with a newsprint cap on his head, who first appeared in the early 1950s.

The first drawing showed him leaving *Mazorra*, a clinic for the mentally insane. It was published in the weekly newspaper *Zig Zag*. The **Loquito** knew, in the hands of Nuez, to circumvent censorship and synthesize national rebellion during the dictatorship of Batista.

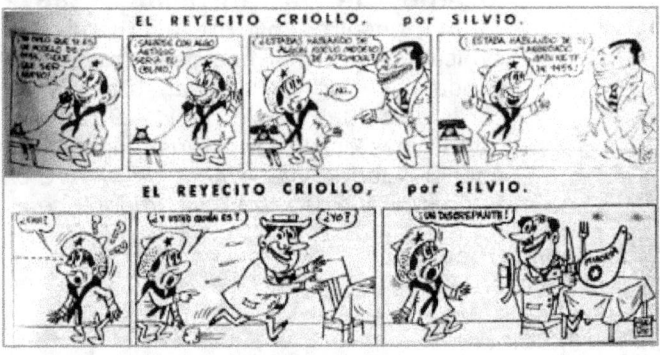

On December 5, 1954, the magazine Bohemia showed for the first time a satirical strip made by **Silvio Fontanillas Quiroga (1913-2000)** under the title *El Reyecito Criollo* (The little Criollo King); it was dedicated to strike at the evils of domestic politics. Its favorite target was Fulgencio Batista, a man who had crowned himself as the *King of the Cubans* on March 10, 1952.

Antonio Prohías (1921-1998). His satirical drawings, which mostly poked fun at Castro, appeared in many Cuban political magazines during the 1950s. On May 1, 1960 Prohías fled the country to avoid arrest. He arrived in the US virtually penniless. In 1961 he began to draw for MAD Magazine and the 500 episodes of "*Spy vs Spy*" were born.

Among the most celebrated cartoonists in Cuba, one of the best was **Conrado Walter Massaguer (1889-1965)**. He was born in Matanzas, and was a shareholder of the company that published *Social* and *Carteles,* as well as a great draftsman and caricaturist. Most of the *Social* covers were drawn by him before he became a political cartoonist.

On July 26, 1953, a Carnival night, Fidel Castro and 135 of his friends and supporters, one third of them from the town of *Artemisa* in Pinar del Rio province, attacked the **Moncada Army Barracks** in Santiago de Cuba.

They claimed to be followers of **Eduardo Chibás, Rafael García Bárcena, Julio Antonio Mella, Manolo Castro** and **Rolando Masferrer**.

None were or had ever been members of the *Communist Party* or *Juventud Socialista*, with the exception of Raúl Castro, Fidel's brother, who had not shared with the party his intentions to join the attack to the *Moncada*.

Fidel, nominally an *Ortodoxo*, had not cleared his plans with the leadership of the party. The attack failed, many of the attackers were killed and Fidel Castro escaped to the mountains around Santiago de Cuba, from where he was rescued days later by **Mons. Pérez Serantes**, archbishop of Santiago de Cuba.

Photos: Moncada Barracks before and after the July 26 attack and an aerial view. It has been said that, in order to make the assault look more heroic, many bullet marks were added years later, after 1959, by partisans of the attackers.

Over the years **the Moncada attack has been the subject of many myths**. Some of them are false yet have never been repudiated.

Castro, for instance, never entered the garrison. A paraffin test after the encounter showed that brother Raúl never fired a shot. Fidel Castro refused the paraffin test; therefore it will never be known if he fired a single round. He insisted that the report should show that he had fired his pistol and that he stipulated to that fact.

Contrary to what followers of Castro have insisted over the years, the rebel prisoners were not tortured, their eyes were not removed from their sockets, no one was castrated or mutilated, nobody had to suffer burns with a cattle branding tool.

On the other hand it has been proven that 30 of the rebels were executed by the military after they surrendered. It is interesting that of the 99 surviving attackers, 27 eventually turned against Castro once he declared himself a *Marxist-Leninist*.

Photos: *above left*, the prisoners of the *Moncada*, with Castro on the right; *top right* the interrogation of Castro after his surrender and before being sent to the *Prisión de Boniato* in Oriente. *Below*: the Bishops of Cuba in the early 1950s: **Evelio Díaz**, Pinar del Río; **Pérez Serantes**, Camagüey; **Zubizarreta**, Santiago de Cuba; **Cardenal Arteaga**, La Habana; **Martínez Dalmau**, Cienfuegos and **Martín Villaverde**, Matanzas. Perez Serantes (with an arrow), was in the late 1950s Archbishop of Santiago de Cuba; he saved the life of Fidel Castro after the attack to the *Moncada* garrison.

An interesting anecdote was related by *The New York Times* on January 17, 1992, and by *The Chicago Tribune* on January 19, on occasion of the death of Cuban historian **Herminio Portell Vilá (1902-1992)**.

Portell Vilá had been a teacher at the *University of Havana* when Fidel Castro was one of his students. The NY Times reported that «*in the early summer of 1953, historian Portell Vilá was sitting in a bar in Havana when a young ex-pupil of his at the university, passing by, told him that he was planning an attack on a military installation of the Batista Government.*» According to British historian Hugh Thomas in his 1971 book **Cuba: The Pursuit of Freedom**, «*Portell Vilá tried to dissuade the conspirator, but he was adamant, explaining how the attack would be a great moral blow against the regime.*»

Herminio Portell Vilá was a very independent historical writer and journalist, one of the most thorough students of the history of Cuba. In 1930 he published a three volume definitive study of *Narciso López*, the *filibuster* who tried to obtain independence for Cuba in the 1850s; it gained for him a *Guggenheim Fellowship*. He used the funds for research and wrote a thorough study that ended in another seminal book: *History of Cuba in its Relations with the US*.

Portell Vilá was a fearless scholar, writer and speaker, although on several occasions it meant prison, threats of execution and exile for him. He never hesitated in his search for historical truths and perspectives, regardless whether or not they were favorable or displeasing to anyone in Cuba or in the US.

Photos above: Portell Vilá and two of his books.

Batista scheduled elections for the first day in November 1954, launched his own party (*Partido Acción Progresista, PAP*) and nominated himself as its candidate.

At the last minute the *Ortodoxos* and the *Auténticos* refused to participate. Only 40% of the eligible voters took part and Batista won. To improve the national political climate Batista declared an amnesty for political exiles but not for any Moncada participant.

On the photos below, the electoral activity in Havana in 1954.

In May 1955 Batista, against the advice of several of his Ministers, repealed the severe measures that had given him martial-law powers, declared a general amnesty and released Fidel Castro (prisoner 4914), his brother Raúl and eighteen other Moncada prisoners.

The *Ortodoxos* offered Castro an important role in the party but he opted to leave for Mexico.

Photo above: the brothers Castro and other *Moncada* prisoners leaving the *Isla de Pinos* prison in 1955.

Two important events took place in Cuba in 1955.

In February **Jorge Mañach (1898-1961)**, a member of the 1933 generation, ex-Foreign Minister and professor of *Columbia University,* joined **Rufo López Fresquet, Luis Botifoll, Justo Carrillo** and **José Pardo Llada** to launch the **Movimiento de la Nación (MN)**, with the purpose of resolving the Cuban institutional crisis.

A few months later, in November, Don **Cosme de la Torriente (1872-1956)**, a veteran of the War of Independence formed, with the help of *Auténtico* leaders, university students and *Ortodoxos*, the ***Sociedad de Amigos de la República (SAR)***, trying to find a solution to the political impasse created by the mock elections of 1954.

A popular rally called by **SAR** on 19 November 1955 was attended by all political parties except the Communists and the followers of Castro, who encouraged *Ortodoxos* to boycott the meeting.

Batista ignored the efforts of the SAR and the MN and the exploratory meetings of the so called *Diálogo Cívico* collapsed.

A few days later Cuba read the news that **Orlando León Lemus**, aka *el Colorado*, a notable gangster, was captured and killed by the police.

In the photo left, Jorge Mañach. *At right*: Don Cosme de la Torriente in the process of negotiating a solution with Batista. They had two meetings, 29 December 1955 and 10 January 1956. No agreement was ever reached. Batista believed he was the savior of the Republic and had to protect her against the unruly.

A negotiated solution of the Cuban impasse seemed possible when Batista agreed to meet with the members of the *Sociedad de Amigos de la República*. The talks were baptized as the **Diálogo Cívico** by the *Diario de la Marina*. Soon, however, a dissagreement came up. **SAR** was resolutely opposed to the participation of **Carlos Márquez Sterling**, whom they judged not sufficiently impartial because of his presidential ambitions. Márquez Sterling agreed to his exclusion from the talks so as not to be an obstacle. Just as important was the feeling by Batista that **SAR's** strategy was to make him look intolerant. His feeling was that to entice the opposition to accept the resulting formula, **SAR** was informing the public that it had been difficult to extract concessions from Batista.

Batista's pride was hurt and on March 11, 1956 he made a speech over radio and TV **rejecting the demands of SAR** and stating that the elections would be held no earlier than the announced date: June of 1958. The following day Cosme de la Torriente and the members of **SAR** and the **Movimiento de la Nación** declared their work had ended in failure. It was a cat and mouse game that would be very expensive for the Republic in a matter of a few years. The only parties that boycotted the **SAR** efforts were the **Communists** and the **26 of July Movement** (Castro's), who even organized a counter-meeting in Miami.

Photos above: leaders of the organizations that participated in the *Diálogo Cívico* in 1955 trying to provide an honorable and acceptable solution to the unconstitutional nature of Batista's government. *Top row*: Rufo López Fresquet, Luis Botifoll, José Pardo Llada and José Miró Cardona. *Bottom row*: Cosme de la Torriente, Jorge Mañach, Justo Carillo and Amalio Fiallo.

Jorge Mañach (1898-1961), launched the *Movimiento de la Nación (MN)* in 1955; he was one of the most important Cuban intellectuals of the 20th century as well as a man **committed to improving the cultural and political life of Cuba**. He graduated *Cum Laude* at *Harvard University* in 1920 and studied Law at the *Sorbonne* in Paris. Upon returning to Cuba he was a member of the *Grupo Minorista* and participated in the *Protesta de los Trece* against the corruption of the Zayas government. He edited the *Revista de Avance*, 1927-1930, the arbiter of the literary media in Cuba. During the Machado dictatorship he joined the ABC.

In 1932 **Mañach** founded the *Universidad del Aire*, an innovative and pioneering use of radio to expand the reach of culture among the citizenry. He broke with the *ABC* and went into exile in 1933, when he was appointed professor at *Columbia University* in NY. He came back to Cuba in 1939 and became a member of the *1940 Constitutional Assembly*. He joined the *Ortodox Party* in 1947, and **started the TV program *Ante la Prensa* in 1953**. After founding the *Movimiento de la Nación* he went again into exile, this time in Spain. Upon returning to Cuba in 1959, **he was fired from his tenured position** at the *University of Havana* and went to teach at the *University of Puerto Rico* where he died in 1961.

Photos: Mañach at the typewriter and at the *Universidad del Aire* radio program, Sundays at CMQ in the 1950s.

Don **Cosme de la Torriente (1872-1956)**, the man who founded the *Sociedad de Amigos de la República (SAR)* in 1955, had been a Colonel in the *Hispano-Cuban-American War of Independence,* fighting under Calixto García. He was a member of the *1897 Asamblea Constituyente de La Yaya*; was president of the *League of Nations* from 1923 to 1924 and was conferred the *French Legion of Honor* after World War I.

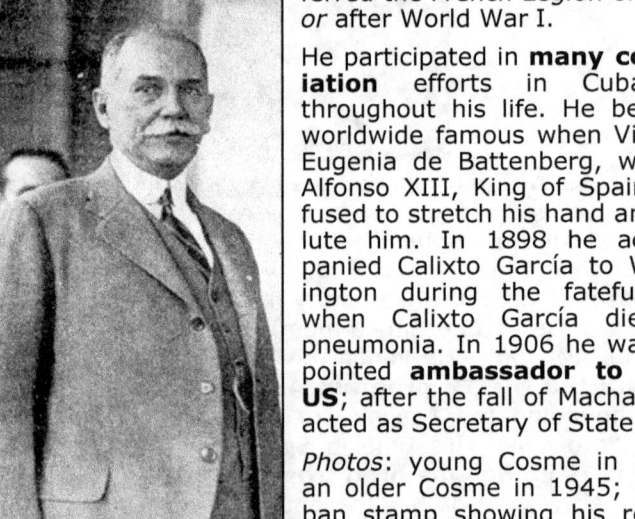

He participated in **many conciliation** efforts in Cuba all throughout his life. He became worldwide famous when Victoria Eugenia de Battenberg, wife of Alfonso XIII, King of Spain, refused to stretch his hand and salute him. In 1898 he accompanied Calixto García to Washington during the fateful trip when Calixto García died of pneumonia. In 1906 he was appointed **ambassador to the US**; after the fall of Machado he acted as Secretary of State.

Photos: young Cosme in 1902; an older Cosme in 1945; a Cuban stamp showing his resting place at the Colon Cemetery in Havana and Cosme as seen by Massaguer.

The skirmishes between the *Directorio Estudiantil* of José Antonio Echeverría and the police were so persistent and bloody that **Don Clemente Inclán (1879-1965)**, Chancellor of the *University of Havana,* closed the institution.

Working out of empty university buildings the *Directorio* continued its campaign of **subversion** and **urban violence**, dismissing the guerilla option of the Castro brothers in the mountains of Oriente province as ineffective.

For months on end, Havana and most country towns had an atmosphere of alarm, fear and insecurity. Batista responded by announcing he would not be a candidate in any future election. It never became a reassuring promise.

The news got to Cuba that Fidel Castro had founded in Mexico, where he was exiled, the *Movimiento 26 de Julio*, named after the day of the Moncada attack. José Antonio Echeverría, on behalf of the *Federación Estudiantil Universitaria (FEU)* signed a compact with Castro to join forces for the armed struggle.

The students of the FEU attempted against the lives of **Antonio Blanco Rico**, Chief of Batista's Military Intelligence Service (SIM) and **Marcelo Tabernilla**, son of the Chief of the Armed Forces. **Juan Pedro Carbó Serviá** and **Rolando Cubela** lead the attack, which took place at *Montmartre Night Club* in Havana. **Blanco Rico** died; **Tabernilla** survived.

Photo: *left*, José Antonio Echeverría. *Right*, a bomb explodes in the Paseo del Prado. *Below*, Echeverría elected president of the FEU in 1954.

Photo above: students at the University of Havana exercising their right to protest. *Photos below*: Havana continued to progress in spite of the charged political atmosphere. Two views of the *Havana Hilton* under construction. It was owned by the *Cuban Gastronomical Syndicate* but was confiscated by the Communists in 1960 as they expropriated everything.

Brutal, savage and barbaric acts occurred in Cuba from 1953 to 1959, but particularly after October 28 1956. On that day **Colonel Antonio Blanco Rico** was gunned down by an elite squad of students led by Pedro Carbó Serviá as he was leaving the *Cabaret Montmartre* in Havana. The son of **General Tabernilla**, Chief of Staff of the Army, and his wife were wounded when the gunmen mistakenly killed Blanco Rico, one of the men in Batista's army that was opposed to torture and violence.

The following day **General Rafael Salas Cañizares**, the Chief of Police, led a raid at the *Haitian Embassy* in Miramar; at the time it was full of students seeking sanctuary, most of them members of *Organización Auténtica*. Salas died in the action, as well as 10 civilians. Salas had been previously accused of killing **Orlando León Lemus**, a well know terrorist during the presidencies of the Auténticos, 1944 to 1952.

It was said that Batista kept for himself the $750,000 gambling protection monthly income that Salas was receiving at the time from several hotels in Havana.

Photos above: *on the left*, FEU leaders **Fructuoso Rodríguez**, **José Antonio Echeverría** in the foreground, **Pedro Carbó Serviá** behind Fructuoso. *On the botom*, Salas Cañizares (*left*) examining a wall at the *Montmartre*. *On the right*: Rafael Salas Cañizares.

José Antonio Echeverría Bianchi (1932-1957) was the last great leader of the *Federación Estudiantil Universitaria (FEU)* in Cuba. He was an architecture student at the *University of Havana*, elected to the presidency of the *FEU* in September 1954.

He was a pacific, idealistic and amenable person, an intelligent and dedicated student leader, member of the *Juventud Católica*; after having been detained, beaten and jailed on several occasions by Batista's forces he founded with others the *Directorio Revolucionario*, which became the armed wing of the *FEU*. He never stopped fighting Batista after that.

On March 13, 1957, as part of the plan to assault the *Presidential Palace*, he burst in *Radio Reloj* in Havana, took its microphones and announced that the tyrant had been executed. As he was speeding back to the University, he died in a shootout with police.

Photos: Echeverría's graduation photo from the *Maristas High School* in Cárdenas, Cuba; giving a speech in front of the bust of **Mella** in front of the campus and defiantly descending the *escalinata* of the *University of Havana*.

One of the most brutal reactions of Batista's followers (often without the knowledge or direct orders from Batista) was the assault on the Goicuría Barracs in Matanzas (see next page).

Photos: *top*, the **Domingo Goicuría** garrison in Matanzas, under the command of General Pilar García, after the attack by men from *Organización Auténtica* on April 29, 1956. *Center*: Batista **responding** to the attack to the Goicuría and Batista troops **deploying** strategically in Nicaro, Oriente, in December 1957; *Bottom*: a 1957 **rally** in Santiago de Cuba in support of Batista.

The attack on the **Domingo Goicuría** garrison in Matanzas culminated a record of crimes committed by a sinister couple of father and son, **Pilar García García** and **Irenaldo García** Báez. Pilar García had been a captain, chief of Regiment 3 of Santa Clara in the 1940s. He had already retired when Batista produced the *coup-d'état* in March of 1952. His son Irenaldo was one of the conspirators in the *coup* and on March 11, the day after the events in Columbia, he was promoted to the rank of Commandant. He convinced Batista to issue **Decree 94** —the first released by Batista— recalling his father to the army with the rank of Colonel.

Once Batista realized the serious discontent of the citizens in Cuba due to his breach of the constitution, he began to place his strong men in important places in the country. Pilar García was transferred in 1955 to the province of Matanzas, as Chief of the Regiment No. 4 of the *Guardia Rural*. He was accompanied by his inseparable son.

When on April 29, 1956 the Goicuría garrison was attacked, both father and son perpetrated one of the most horrible massacres in the history of the Republic. But that was not enough.

Two years later, in 1958, the revolutionary fervor reached a climax with the strike called for the 9th of April. Pilar Garcia was summoned to Havana to throw his gang on the trail of the strikers. Early in the morning the police radio began broadcasting his fierce instructions and warning his minions: «*We do not need wounded or prisoners; get rid of all of them.*» That's how young Cubans like **Ciro Hidalgo Pérez**, **Luis Morales Mustelier** and **Juan Fernández Duque** perished. (see page 413)

Photos above: Pilar García and his son Irenaldo; the dead at the Goicuría Barracs with Pilar García looking them over.

On December 2, 1956, **Fidel Castro** left the port of Tuxpán, in Mexico and landed in Cuba, at the *Playa de los Colorados,* a swamp land full of insects and small crabs, in Oriente province. He was accompanied by 82 other rebels among which were his brother Raúl.

Carlos Prío had purchased for them a leisure 58-foot yacht, the **Granma**, for $15,000. They had landed close to *Central Niquero*, property of **Julio Lobo**, one of the richest men in Cuba.

The Castro brothers and a dozen survivors took refuge in the *Sierra Maestra* as Batista's air force tried unsuccessfully to corral and shot them.

Photo at top left, the *Granma*.

The turning point for Castro and his men, who could not increase their power by more than a few recruits and weapons every month, occurred on February 24, 1957, when **Herbert Matthews** published in *The New York Times* an interview in the *Sierra Maestra*, proving that Castro was not dead as Batista had alleged.

The interview became famous when Castro hoodwinked Mathews into believing he had hundred of followers in his troops when in reality he had eighteen. Unknownby Mathews the men were walking in circles around the table where Castro and Mathews were sitting.

After the publication of the interview Castro had plenty of recruits and never again lacked funds.

Photo at right: Castro and Matthews in the *Sierra Maestra*.

The story of Matthews interview with Fidel Castro in the Sierra Maestra dazzled and astounded most journalists across the world.

In January 1957, Castro had sent a message to Havana inviting journalists to climb up the Sierra to interview him. Not even **Sergio Carbó**, director of *Prensa Libre*, or **Miguel Angel Quevedo**, owner of *Bohemia magazine*, agreed to it. Castro then sought a foreign journalist. The economist **Felipe Pazos** knew the *New York Times* correspondent in Havana and through his son **Javier**, member of the *July 26 Movement*, asked someone from the NYTimes to go up the Sierra. The correspondent, Rubi Hart Phillips, telephoned **Herbert Matthews**, chief of the NYTimes editorial page. Matthews had been a war correspondent in Ethiopia and Spain and decided to personally do the interview.

On Saturday February 16 he was next to Castro in *Los Chorros*, near Jibacoa. On Sunday February 24 the **NY Times** published the interview. On Monday February 25 a group of inspectors with scissors showed up at the NYTimes distribution warehouse in Havana and cut out the photo of Castro with Matthews from the front page of every copy of the Sunday edition, in the most idiotic **act of censure** in the history of the republic. On Wednesday, February 27, Batista himself called the newspaper **Prensa Libre** in Havana to claim the photos were a *fake*; Prensa Libre published Batista's allegations on the 28th of February.

Photos above: The *NYTimes* in New York and *Prensa Libre* in Havana publishing the true and the false news. For many years Herbert Matthews became known as «T*he man that got Fidel Castro his job through the New York Times.*»

During February of 1957 a plan more daring and intrepid than the assault to the *Moncada* or the landing by Castro in Oriente province was brewed by the *Directorio Estudiantil* and several of Carlos Prío's followers: a **magnicide** that would do away with Batista, in his own residence, the *Palacio Presidencial*.

The brains were **José Antonio Echeverría (1932-1957)**, president of the FEU and **Menelao Mora Morales (1905-1957)**, a former member of the ABC during the fight against Machado, member of the *Auténticos*, member of the Cuban House of Representatives and president of the *Cooperativa de Omnibus Aliados (COA)*.

The plan consisted of a commando attack on the presidential palace (carried out by Menelao Mora and his men, mostly *Auténticos*) followed by a nationwide announcement through *Radio Reloj*, one of the most powerful radio stations in Cuba (carried out by Echeverría and his men, mostly from the *Directorio Estudiantil*).

They almost succeeding in killing Batista but the attack failed and Echeverría and Mora were both killed. Batista's repression practically decimated the entire roster of the *Directorio Revolucionario*.

Photos above: The day's paper; portraits of Echeverría and Mora.

On July 12, 1957 **Raúl Chibás (1916-2002)**, brother of Eduardo Chibás, the former *Ortodoxo* leader, and **Felipe Pazos (1912-2001)**, former President of the *Banco Nacional de Cuba* under Prío, met Castro at his outpost in *Sierra Maestra*.

Pazos had been the man who got *The New York Times* to visit and interview Castro a few months earlier. Chibás, Castro and Pazos signed a pact called *Manifiesto de la Sierra Maestra* by which they would join forces to end the Batista regime.

Before the ink had a chance to dry the pact was suspended by Pazos and Chibás, who were already suspicious of Castro's motives. Days later the Communists denounced Castro as a «*blind and injudicious proponent of the strategy of armed struggle.*»

In February of 1958 the rebels opened up *Radio Rebelde*, a short wave radio station in the Sierra Maestra under the leadership of **Carlos Franqui (1921-2010)**, a journalist from the Communist newspaper *HOY* who, after breaking ranks with the party, became a master at psychological warfare.

Photos above on the left, Raúl Chibas, Felipe Pazos and Castro in the *Sierra Maestra* mountains. *On the right*, Carlos Franqui during a transmission of *Radio Rebelde* to the entire territory of Cuba. *Bottom*: Carlos Franqui as an exile in Puerto Rico in 2005.

Felipe Pazos (1912-2001) was an economist and a world renowned expert in managing economic policy. He had attended the *Breton Woods Conference* when the *World Bank* was founded and the *International Monetary Fund* was established; there he met John Maynard Keynes, with whom he corresponded frequently. He was the founder and president of the *National Bank of Cuba* in 1950.

In 1942 he was the Commercial Attaché of the Cuban Embassy in Washington, and in 1959 Cuba's Ambassador-at-Large for economic affairs in Europe. From 1952 to 1953 he was Senior Economist of the *World Bank*; from 1961 to 1966 member of the *Committee of Nine* that ran Kennedy's *Alliance for Progress*. His scholarly works on inflation from 1963 to his death in 2001 are to this day classical theoretical sources to understand the mechanics of inflation.

Pazos fidelity to democratic ideals put him at peril many times in his life, beginning as a student in 1930, and notably in 1959 when he denounced Communism and accused Castro of unjustly deposing and jailing General Hubert Matos in Cuba. As he resigned all his positions in Cuba, Raúl Castro —Fidel's brother— asked for the execution of Pazos; only his international prestige saved his life.

Photos: Felipe Pazos, the logo of the IMF and Keynes addressing the *Breton Woods Conference* in 1944.

Journalists are constantly faced with the dilemma of reporting facts or expressing opinions. They delight in the power to select which stories are reported and how they are covered. Often the media (newspapers, radio, TV, magazines) support or attack political parties, candidates, or ideologies or, just as bad, bask in the glare of sensationalism with news that could bring fame and prestige simply because they are rare, controversial, morbid or likely to result in a game-change.

Cubans had to suffer the consequences of two such media biases during the 1950s: the **sensational interview** of Castro by Matthews and the **unbalanced support** of *Bohemia* magazine to the events in *Sierra Maestra* at the end of the decade.

Herbert Matthews' report in the *NYTimes* became a true epoch-making journalistic event in the US. He wrote of Castro «*He has strong ideas of liberty, democracy, social justice, the need to restore the Constitution, to hold elections... he is anti-Communist... hundreds of highly respected citizens are helping him.*» He never publicly corrected those false first impressions.

A few months later *Bohemia Magazine* in Havana, in one of the occasional censorship lapses offered by Batista, published an open letter from Fidel Castro asking Cubans to support his revolution. *Bohemia's* director, **Miguel Angel Quevedo,** a fierce enemy of Carlos Prío, the Cuban constitutional president deposed by Fulgencio Batista, became the most consisting propagandist of Castro's attempts to overthrow Batista in Cuba.

In 1969, after the loss of the Republic to the Communists, Quevedo repented of his militant support of Castro and wrote a political testament to journalist Ernesto Montaner in which he expressed: «*I am not the only one guilty for the misfortune of Cuba... I die disgusted, outlawed, banished, betrayed and abandoned by all my friends... This is my last goodbye. Tell my countrymen that I forgive all with my arms crossed over my chest... that I hope they forgive all the wrong I've done.*» Days later he committed suicide.

In the photos: the two journalists that preferred to be part of the news and not simply to report it. *Herbert Matthews* of the *NYTimes* and *Miguel Angel Quevedo* of Havana's *Bohemia Magazine*

On September 5, 1957, the *Auténticos*, under the leadership of **Antonio (Tony) Varona (1908-1992)** and Second Lieutenant **Dionisio San Román Toledo (1930-1957)**, organized a coordinated air-naval-land attack on the *Cayo Loco* naval station in Cienfuegos; their purpose was to establish a land base from which to attack the military installations in Havana and do away with the military dictatorship of Fulgencio Batista.

For reasons not yet well understood, the plotters inside the base acted prematurely and declared an insurgency. They initially succeeded: they placed non-participant offices under arrest and moved into town in jeeps, carrying arms from the post arsenal. A 60-man troop of maritime police were waiting to join them. The rebels swept into Marti Park in the center of town, surrounded the pro-Batista national police headquarters and demanded surrender. The police refused. After a vicious fight that littered the street with corpses, the building fell, but the rebels decided to retreat to the security of *Cayo Loco*. It was the first time that some of Batista's military forces had taken arms against him.

Batista responded decisively. A squadron of B-26s and F-47s Thunderbolt fighter bombers was sent from Havana to bomb *Cayo Loco* to crush the revolt. The F-47 squadron chief, however, declared his sympathies to the rebels, disobeyed his orders and dropped the bombs in the open sea.

Moments later, land forces loyal to Batista, invaded *Cayo Loco* and, with the help of a formidable tank detachment, overcame the rebellion. Close to 300 men perished in the effort. Surviving rebels were court-marshaled an found guilty; several were sentenced to execution by firing squad but Batista, in a calculated act of benevolence, commuted their death sentences for life imprisonment.

Photos above: Dionisio San Román and Antonio (Tony) Varona.

Tony Varona, charged as a conspirator, was protected by the *Auténticos* in Havana until he could reach the Chilean embassy to request political asylum. Batista, in another calculated act of benevolence, granted him a safe conduct to leave the island.

Two practical impacts resulted from the attempt to establish a beach head at Cayo Loco. The first one was the reaction of the US government. It imposed an **arms embargo** to Batista's government. The second was the malaise it created in the Cuban military, particularly the Air Force. The failed revolt brought about a **military purge** that led to imprisonments, dishonorable discharges and early forced retirements. Batista never again trusted the Air Force, which led to insurmountable logistic problems when he had to deal with the *Sierra Maestra* rebellion.

Time Magazine reported that «*By proving they could subvert Batista's well-fed, well-trained military, the subversive anti-Batista groups have punched a worrisome hole in the dictator's armor.*»

The *New York Times* added «*The effect on the life of the nation has been serious. Merchants all over the republic complain that sales are steadily declining. The motion picture theatres are empty and many in the interior towns have closed. Other places of diversion have also suffered heavily. In Havana the tourist trade has fallen off sharply. The big casinos and night clubs in Havana are losing money. Two of them were said to be desirous of closing, but have not been permitted to do so by the Government... Commerce, industry and capital are growing impatient with the continued violence in the island.*»

The harsh repressive measures of the police and the armed forces of Cuba began to be the prime factor in **turning many Cubans against the Batista Government.**

Photo above: the Cayo Loco Naval Base in Cienfuegos, Cuba.

From the early hours of April 9, 1958, militant groups across Cuba were preparing to go on a **general uprising**, intended to defeat the Batista tyranny. Several radio stations simultaneously transmitted a call to battle: «*Attention, Cubans, attention. A general strike has been organized for today. From this moment on Cuba enters in the final struggle to overthrow the dictatorship of Fulgencio Batista. ¡Everyone to the streets! The strike has begun.*»

Hundreds of young Cubans **took to the streets**, fought, and died in the effort. There was significant action in Havana, Santa Clara, Ciego de Avila, Camaguey and Santiago de Cuba. In Havana the strikers had absolute control of Guanabacoa for several hours, but at noon the strike began to recede. Poor coordination and lack of weapons caused that many youngsters were massacred by Batista's police.

It was said that April 9, 1958 was **not an urban rebellion** but simply a day when many workers did not show up for work. Most people in the cities were suspicious of Castro because of his brother Raúl and his lieutenant Ernesto Guevara, both well known Communists. This caused people not join the events of the day. Neither the CTC nor the Communists participated; some buses were overturned; several shops were attacked; some fires were started in the streets; most schools closed their doors but few businesses did. The strike was a total failure. About eighty revolutionaries and ten common citizens lost their lives. It was rumored that Rolando Masferrer, the notorious gangster, took advantage of the confusion to eliminate his political enemies.

Among the many killed on that day were **Ciro Hidalgo Pérez**, President of the JEC in Manzanillo, not yet 23 years old, **Luis Morales Mustelier**, President of the JEC in Oriente and **Juan Fernández Duque**, member of the National Secretariat of the *Juventud Católica*. They were taken from the offices of the *Juventud Estudiantil Católica (JEC)* at 461 L Street, in Havana, and brutally tortured and murdered.

Photos above, left to right: Ciro Hidalgo Pérez, Luis Morales Mustelier and Juan Fernández Duque.

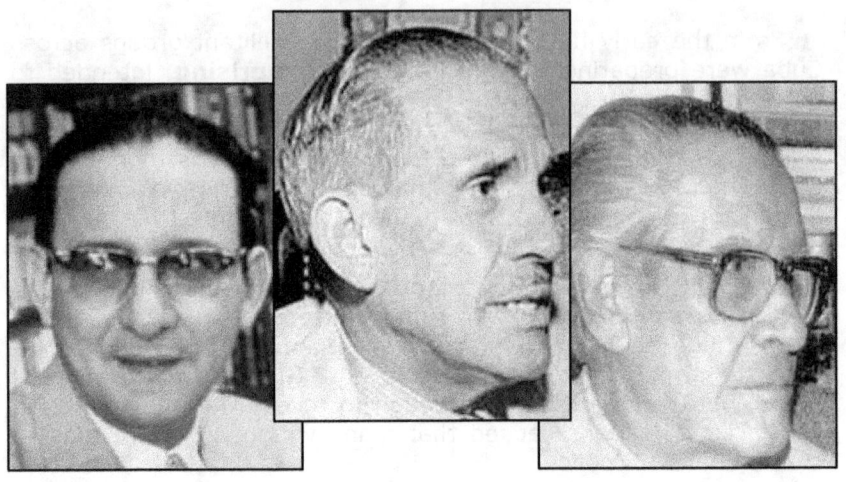

By 1958 the strength of Batista's position had deteriorated and the US began to seriously consider an alternative.

The summer offensive against the rebels, now in *Sierra Maestra* (southern Oriente), *Sierra del Cristal* (northern Oriente) and *Sierra del Escambray* (southern Las Villas) seemed doomed towards an inevitable collapse (*see map above*).

It was the right time for the Communist party to join the rebels and so they did. The national elections called for November 3 were the most dishonest and deceptive in the history of Cuba. **Andrés Rivero Agüero (1905-1997)**, Batista's prime minister and presidential candidate from the *Partido Acción Progresista (PAP)*, won over Grau San Martín, the *Auténtico* candidate and **Carlos Márquez Sterling (1898-1991)**, the *Ortodoxo*. The US rejected outright the results of the elections and announced there would be no recognition of Rivero Agüero's presidency.

Photo above: Andrés Rivero Agüero, Ramón Grau San Martín and Carlos Márquez Sterling.

Carlos Márquez Sterling (1902-1991), was the nephew and adoptive son of former Cuban President Dr. Manuel Márquez Sterling (his mother's brother). He was a man of great intuitive intelligence, eloquence and integrity, a professor at the *University of Havana* and the second President of the 1940 *Constitutional Assembly*.

On two occasions he presided the House of Representatives and served as both Minister of Education and Minister of Labor during the constitutional government of Batista in 1940. He was arrested years later when he opposed Batista's dictatorship.

In 1958 he founded the *Partido del Pueblo Libre* and joined forces with another great patriot, Nestor Carbonell, trying to find an electoral solution to the serious crisis originated by the *coup d'état* of Batista. In the early 1970s, in exile, he taught Political Theory at Columbia University in NY.

Photos: *Above*, Marquez Sterling as a young boy and in exile in Miami; *below*, before his death in 1991.

On 26 March 1958, responding to the requests of all political parties, Cuba's Supreme Electoral Court postponed the June elections until November because of the **continued violence and threats against election candidates**. Prime Minister **Gonzalo Güell** had a conversation with US Ambassador Earl Smith, who in turn sent a confidential telegram to the US State Department. Güell believed the constitutional guarantees had been restored too fast and the radical elements were taking advantage of it.

In the photos, top row: Earl Smith, US Ambassador; Batista conferring with his Prime Minister Gonzalo Güell.

Bottom rows: Political posters for the 1958 Elections.

Photos above, top to bottom: the political propaganda for the **1958 elections**, the last opportunity Cubans had to contain what later became a Communist takeover; the frightening results of **bombs in Havana** during the last days of Batista; General Tabernilla receiving the **last batch of US weapons** to fight the rebels in the Sierra Maestra: 7 Sherman tanks. The next time the army in Cuba obtained tanks it would *be Soviet T-34-85's in 1960.*

Photos of the last days of Batista as President. *Top*: a caricature. *Middle top*: **Bahía de Nipe**, Oriente, where a *Cubana Airlines* Viscount hijacked by rebels plunged into the bay on 1 November 1958. The Cuban captain, **Ruskin Medrano**, and all passengers perished. It was the first of many airline highjacks to follow. *Bottom right*: the **office of Batista** at the Presidential Palace the day of his escape. *Bottom left*: aerial view of **Columbia**

Finally, it all came down to a **final battle in Santa Clara**, in December 1958. The Cuban army was demoralized, not wanting to die for a regime that was about to collapse.

Batista had dispatched east an armored train full of materials and 340 officers and engineers. They were sent not to fight (for which there were 3,000 men in Santa Clara's garrison) but **to repair bridges and roads in the area**, in order to facilitate movement of troops eastward.

All accounts by the participants in this operation agree that a *Colonel Rosell,* a Batista close friend and confidant in charge of the train, **sold the armored train to Ernesto Guevara** after the rebels had immobilized the train by destroying the tracks in front and back.

The men in the train did not fight. Not a *casquito* (the disparaging name given to the army's young recruits) died that day.

Photo on top: a **Cuban stamp** presents a mythical and false image of the assault of the train by the forces of Ché Guevara. The *photo at right* shows the **derailed train** and at left the **historical reality**: the rebel army entered Santa Clara without firing a shot.

Most of the attention that **Fulgencio Batista** has generated since 1959 describes him as —*the US backed dictator*‖ or —*the brutal assassin of 20,000 Cubans.*‖ Such simplistic characterizations do little justice to the history of the half century of the Cuban republic. The **real Batista** was a complex man, at times a skillful politician, charming and righteous; at other times a despotic, reprehensible and conceited dictator.

Batista was born in 1901, inside a dirt floor *bohío*, in Banes, Oriente; the Republic was then about to be born in the midst of the destruction and chaos left by the war of independence. His first job was as a *railroad ground man*. By the time he was 20 he had become an avid reader and had joined the Cuban army. The army at that time was controlled by numerous independence war veterans that felt entitled to a lifetime of privileges and prerogatives. Batista soon became the leader of the non-commissioned officers and earned their trust with his push for breaking the glass ceiling that affected all non-veteran rank and file men.

By the late 1930s he became the Cuban *king-maker* after leading the soldiery fight against the Machado tyrannical regime. Instead of becoming a perpetual dictator in the best Latin American tradition, he chose to restore peace, democracy and constitutional life, retiring in 1944 to Daytona Beach, in Florida, after having been elected President in 1940.

Unfortunately in 1952 he **destroyed a fairly good and patriotic personal record** by overthrowing the constitutionally elected President Carlos Prío Socarrás; instantly —even for his most decided followers— he became a blemished hero that had surrendered to his ambition and thirst for power. He tried to appeal to his former supporters but only the most fanatic agreed to legitimize his betrayal. He was abandoned to his fate, poorly serviced by unscrupulous and criminal men that remained by his side. Finally he was given the boot by the US. He will forever be remembered as the man who precipitated the collapse of the best dreams of a century of Cuban patriots.

Photos, left to right: young Batista, the hero of 1933; Batista the loving family man; *Bohemia*, after his downfall, January 11, 1959.

Photos above: January 1st, 1959 news in the Cuban press about the ending of Batista's unconstitutional 1952-1959 government.

Photos below, on the left: young Batista, as a 19 year old railroad worker. *On the right*: last known photo of Batista, on a day of mourning for the death of one of his sons..

Barely two years after his escape from the island, Batista began to sustain a **serious correspondence** with some of his political adversaries. The tone of his letters was polite and somewhat condescending, even when responding to negative comments. What follows are some of the comments he made to some of his correspondents.

«*The infamy of the slander and lies have conjured up a distorted image of Republican Cuba as a subnation, without development and illiterate; a tribe dominated by brutes, with no sanitation and no culture.*» Letter to **Gastón Baquero** in July of 1961.

«*For Cuba and the unity of all Cubans, I have decided not to appear in groups or to encourage anyone to fight. It is already quite hard to see how the rivalries and conflicts have divide people; those who believe they deserve immediate benefits con- tribute to decimate the best impulses of the others.*» Letter to **Carlos Márquez Sterling** in March 1964.

«*So far I do not see the threshold of a mass action or the dawn of the claimed sovereignty. I think that the Cuban drama seems to have no immediate outcome; Cuba is just a chip in the inter- national arena, subject to the will of others and the mercy of imponderables.*» Letter to **Carlos Már- quez Sterling** in October 1965.

«*Sometimes there are groups which are symbolic as tools of two or three people interested, anxious and desperate to take advantage of the exile condition, and simply add to the factors that produce dispersion,*» Letter to **Eusebio Mujal** in April 1967.

« [The historical reexamination of Batista] *is not a mass phenomenon; we are only two or three individuals, no more. I think it's been a long time, and that the figure of Batista has begun to grow; compared to Castro, he was not the dictator that people thought; he did much for his country on the one hand, and lived a decent exile until his death.*» commentary by **Zoé Valdés**.

In 1971, Directors of the *Brigade 2506* wrote to Batista from Miami to thank him for his "*valuable economic donation*," which made possible the construction of the memorial to the members of the 2506 Brigade who died in the 1961 invasion of *Playa Girón*.

The End of the Republic:
The Fateful Year 1959

> «*It is necessary to have witnessed death in order to know how good it is to live.*» ALEXANDER DUMAS PÈRE, French Writer (1802-1870)

WHEN THE INDEPENDENT republican way of life crumbled with Batista leaving Castro taking over in Cuba, it became a political and sociological phenomenon that no one anticipated. Most Cubans were taken by surprise and began to consider it a dream come true. Very few showed the slightest signs of skepticism about Cuba's future. Some of the classical Cuban politicos felt they were victims of an unimaginable nightmare. The US Department of State was also apprehensive and had grave doubts about Castro and his followers yet, because of its pragmatic tradition, decided to assume a wait and see attitude. The US government, nevertheless, was visibly concerned; no other Latin-American country —except Venezuela— had more US investments than Cuba. At the time the US supplied 80% of Cuban imports and was taking 70% of its exports.

Castro, however, had come down the mountains with rosaries on his neck, squarely swearing his allegiance to the 1940 Constitution and promising free elections within a reasonable time. There was no reason to fear that anything could possibly go wrong: the dictator had left...

As he traveled from Oriente province to Havana, Castro knew he had to deal with three revolutionary movements in Cuba instead of half a dozen political parties: his *Movimiento 26 de Julio* (loyal followers of his that had lived in the underground in the cities and in the mountains for two years); the *Directorio Revolucionario* (students from the University of Havana and some High Schools across the island, to a certain extent his rivals); and the old Communist party elements, the rather thin collective of the outcast PSP (at the moment thought to be non-players by most people). Altogether they probably totaled no more than 10 thousand followers, many of them with rather different political ideals and positions.

To solve any potential in-fights or any illusions of shared power, Castro took a big chance ordering a general strike throughout Cuba. The strike had no specific target or reason but everyone complied; taken that as evidence of a unanimous consent Castro established his absolute leadership over the entire island of Cuba. The students, the non-affiliated revolutionaries and the Communists began to retire from public light and be quiet. The road was open for Castro and his followers to take over what until then had been a very rebellious group of citizens.

During a short period of time the honeymoon was in full force, particularly in Havana and the provincial capitals. There were no army, no police, no serious work, and not even petty crimes worth reporting. People were enjoying *their* popular victory hoping that the indispensible instruments of their social contracts (cops, bills, fines, inspections, traffic tickets, car payments and the like) would not be needed for a while.

The first objections —very mildly— appeared when Castro began to conduct a series of public trials (and re-trials) leading to the execution of hundreds of military men and civilians charged with collaboration and crimes under Batista, particularly the pilots that had bombed and strafed Castro's guerilla territories in the mountains of the *Sierra Maestra*. Most people forgave those excesses (about 500 executions) as inevitable in a revolution. The lessons of Paris in 1789, Moscow in 1917 or Mexico City in 1911 —executions as a show of force and a deterrent to potential rivals— never came to the minds of most Cubans. It was surprising since the only issue that had brought the population in tune with the revolutionaries was not ideological but a common opposition to the dictatorship of Batista.

By mid 1959 it became evident that the Cuban right, the Churches, the US embassy, the former *Auténtico* and *Ortodoxo* party loyals, most professionals and businessmen opposed the government intentions to start radical social reforms. Castro responded by moving even closer with the left.

Still Castro was able to assemble a liberal cabinet: some *Ortodoxos*, some former members of the *Diálogo Cívico*, some veterans of the 1930 struggles, even some leaders from the *Juventud Católica* and several *University of Havana* professors lent their hand.

In the following months an inescapable wave of autocratic reforms began to consume the strength of the republic one decree at a time. Many old politicos were forever excluded from elective positions; many proprietors were victimized and their properties stolen by the *Ministerio de Recuperación de Bienes Malversados* (Ministry of Recovery of Misappropriated Assets); all political parties were outlawed; the titles and credits earned by students of private universities were invalidated; the 1940 Constitution was abrogated in favor of a new *Ley Fundamental de la República*; the legislative function was transferred to the Cabinet; rents were reduced to 50% to gain the loyalty of renters and provide the first salvo against the bourgeoisie; an agrarian reform was set in motion, limiting the size of all rural properties to 1000 acres; the promised elections were postponed for four years instead of 15 months; militias were organized as a supplement to the military might of the *Fuerzas Armadas Revolucionarias*; the student and labor movements were forced to have rigged elections that placed Castro supporters in top leadership positions; to mention only the most significant revolutionary actions.

In 1959 the Catholic Church had 72 schools, each with an average of 600 students; 128 centers for orphans, the aged and youth and adult rehabilitation; 33 hospitals each with an average of 230 beds; 700 priests and brothers; 1350 sisters and nuns, mostly dedicated to social or educational work. Protestant Churches had also a large contingency of pastors, social workers, teachers and institutions. Within a few months they all lost their establishments whether schools, psychiatric hospitals, asylums, nursing or rest homes, institutes, colleges and medical facilities and clinics.

The independence of the Cuban Republic was in its death throes after the injection of the East-West struggle into the Cuban political life. Castro began to make overtures to the Soviet empire and to make Cuba a pawn in the US-USSR conflicts. Not even the presence of one million Catholics in Havana in November of 1959 could stop the sovietization of the island. Many middle-class Cubans began to choose the path to exile, in New York, Madrid, Mexico but mostly in Miami. They were the backbone of the republic, the men and women with the know-how, the commitment and the dedication to bring progress to the republic; they were also the only internal opposition to the Communists. Their loss to Cuba, for many years to come, would be irreplaceable.

Cubans by the thousands began to leave the island once it was clear it had been taken over by the Communists. Eventually more than 1,000,000 would leave between 1959 and 1980.

The Cuba that Batista was leaving behind in 1958 was a prosperous nation on its way to resolve its half a century of growing pains. Here are shown some examples of the industries that **Cubans had forged** by themselves or with their trustworthy respect for the laws and regard for the rights of foreign investors.

Photos above: *La Estrella* food processing facilities in Havana; *Texaco* oil refinery in Santiago de Cuba; *Ron Arechabala* distillery in Matanzas; *Freeport Sulfur Company* nickel extraction plant in Moa, Oriente.

After the surrender of the Santa Clara train (see page 419) in December 1958, **the government of Cuba crumbled rapidly**.

Washington discarded outright the manipulated presidential election; **US Ambassador Smith** (until then a Batista supporter) declared that the elections were «*the most perfectly perpetrated fraud he had ever seen.*»

The CIA reported late in 1958 that the US should actively prevent a Castro victory. It was too late. By then **all civic groups in Cuba were opposed to Batista**: the Church, the intellectuals, the public employees, the unions, the artists, the media, the businessmen, the low ranks of the Armed Forces, the students, the women, the foreign investors and the diplomatic corps. Cuba's democracy had not been **destroyed**; it had **disintegrated** from within.

Photos above: the press on January 1, 1959. *On the bottom*, the apotheosizing reception to Castro and his rebels in Havana a few days later.

Batista could never understand why he could not persuade to collaborate with him the same politicos he was able to push around from 1933 to 1944. The press resented him after the 1952 *coup d'état* since had destroyed whatever hope there was to stabilize the republic. When his defeat was confirmed, the press took revenge. **Bohemia Magazine** attributed 20,000 deaths to his determination to stay in power; every newspaper in Cuba denounced him with solid and deep-seated *gusto*.

After the fall of Batista, for a few days, Cubans became wrapped in **an intoxicating national carnival**. No army, no police, everyone dedicated to the enjoyment of the moment. People believed Castro could do no wrong. Anyone from the old parties was automatically discredited.

The elite, businessmen, the clergy, all believed the revolution was theirs to mold and shape and Castro was simply its plain hero-leader. Only the strongest supporters of Batista moved abroad.

In reality there were three revolutionary groups in Cuba: Castro's **July 26th Movement**; Faure Chomón, Pedro Luis Boytel and others with the **Directorio Revolucionario;** and Blas Roca, Juan Marinello and Lazaro Peña with the **Partido Socialista Popular** (Communists).

Together these three groups had a combined membership of perhaps a few thousand. However, people were so anxious to have Batista out of the way that they accepted the notion of a revolution, an unexpected and unnecessary overkill for most Cubans and a far cry from a simple wish for peace, honesty and a principled government; people enthusiastically acquiesced to the desires of the revolutionaries.

At a speech in Columbia Camp, Castro's followers released dozens of pigeons with their maws full of lead pellets so that they could not fly far and would perch on the Commandant's shoulders. It was interpreted by feverish fans as a signal that the *máximo leader* had been invested by nature as a man of peace.

Photo at left: the pigeons and the leader. Behind Castro is his right hand man Camilo Cienfuegos, whose charisma defied Castro; he would soon be dead. *At right,* **Pedro Luis Boytel**, a martyred student leader at the *University of Havana*; he was denied his elected presidency of the FEU, was condemned to 30 years and died in prison from neglect by the authorities.

Photos from the first few days after the revolution success.

Top: hundred of **parking meters** were destroyed in Havana for the simple reason that the government of Batista had installed them. *Middle*: the start of **revolutionary trials** was unexpected and scandalous. It was a warning on the cruelty that would follow. *Middle bottom*: the students at the *Catholic University of Villanueva* were told **their grades were null** and had to repeat the last two years. *Bottom*: the presses of the *Diario de la Marina* were **vandalized and destroyed** while the police watched in silence.

Once the Batista regime collapsed, the US Department of State had nothing to do but to **observe and hope**. Cuba was strangely and for the first time out of its control. Castro promised to respect the *1940 Constitution*, promised not to confiscate any US property and was refraining from producing diatribes against the US. The US decided to recognize the revolutionary government.

Abnormal things began to occur, however, such as a series of **outrageous speedy trials** leading to the execution or incarceration of people charged with crimes under Batista.

In practice, no civil organizations existed anymore. Only the Communist party had survived (it had been banned by Batista in the 1950s and legitimized again by him in 1959). The other parties had succumbed with the old regime; their leaders were self-compelled to do like the US State Department: observe and hope.

Photo on the left: *El Crisol* newspaper reports the unprecedented second trial of army Pilots accused of bombing the rebels in Oriente. Castro objected to the jury's decision on the first trial that had exonerated them. *On the right*: a public trial at the Havana sports arena. Most of these trials resulted in death penalties. *Bottom*: Firing squad at La Cabaña fortress.

Very soon in January of 1959 a revolutionary government was formed in Cuba. Its president was appointed by Castro: **Manuel Urrutia Lleó (1901-1981)**, the man who had absolved the raiders of the *Moncada Barracks* on July 26, 1953.

The ministers were professionals with an impeccable reputation, all with solid democratic credentials:

    José Miró Cardona, Prime Minister;
    Manuel Ray Rivero, Minister of Public Works;
    Elena Mederos, Minister of Social Welfare;
    Rufo López Fresquet, Minister of the Treasury;
    Angel Fernández, Minister of Justice;
    Luis Orlando Rodríguez, Minister of Justice; **Roberto Agramonte**, Minister of Foreign Relations;
    Humberto Sori Marín, Minister of Agriculture;
    Armando Hart, Minister of Education;
    Felipe Pazos, President of the National Bank;
    Justo Carrillo, Director of the BANFAIC.

Over the course of perhaps a year, Castro overrode, discredited and defamed one by one all these men, with the exception of Armando Hart. The *1940 Constitution* was abrogated; the promised elections postponed indefinitely; a popular militia was created and grew to about half a million men; all weapons were requisitioned under the slogan —*Armas, ¿Para Qué?*

Photos above: two views of the initial cabinet of the revolutionary government.

The revolution of 1959 in Cuba had started as a protest against Batista and his illegitimate government; he had seized the institutions of power and intended to perpetuate himself indefinitely by means of spurious elections.

As the master of this illegal kidnapping of an entire nation Batista had committed a deadly and unforgivable transgression by interrupting the normal democratic process that seemed to be taking hold in Cuba.

Without consent or participation of most citizens, a group of former gangsters and professional subversives responded to the seizure of their country with a cruel and unforgiving revolution that went much further than just restoring the institutions of power to their rightful owners. They created two new instruments to secure themselves in power and expand their new national model: the *Militias* and the *Committees for the Defense of the Revolution*.

They changed the laws and the mores. Private education was eliminated. God was made to disappear from the lives of everyone. So was freedom of religion, freedom of the press and freedom of assembly. Property was seized. Private property was eliminated. The labor movement was turned over to the communists. Revolutionary tribunals rendered life, liberty and the pursuit of freedom as exclusively dependent of the whim and fancy of the government. From there on the opponents to the government would never be granted a fair trial.

Photos above: Castro with *Nikita Khrushev* at right; Castro with *Anastas Mikoyan* at left, signing an economic pact on Feb 13, 1960.

Anastas Ivanovich Mikoyan (1895-1978), a strong supporter of Stalin during the immediate post-Lenin years, was the man who compiled Stalin's death-lists and passed them on to the NKVD; he was also one of Khrushchev's closest allies during the cold war. He was the first Soviet official to visit Cuba after the revolution in 1959 and became a Castro sympathizer, as well as his master and facilitator of soviet goods. During one of his visits to Cuba he was informed his wife had died in Moscow; he decided he was too busy to return there for her funeral and sent an aide in his place. One of his colleagues characterized him as follows: «*The rascal was able to walk through Red Square on a rainy day without an umbrella [and] without getting wet. He could dodge the raindrops.*»

From 1960 to 1962, **14,048 children and adolescents** were sent by their parents to the US, fearful that the Communists would take the future of their children in their hands as they did in Spain during the Civil War. This unprecedented clandestine exodus was known as **Operación Pedro Pan**; it was made possible with the support and approval of the US federal government. It became the largest mass escape of unaccompanied minors in the history of the Americas.

Photos on top right: Hundreds of priests and nuns were expelled from Cuba in 1961. *Below*: some of the children sent by their parents to the US during *Operation Peter Pan*.

The main killing field during the first years of the Communist Revolution of 1959 was the fortress of *San Carlos de la Cabaña*, situated on the eastern side of Havana Harbor, on the south side of the fortress *El Morro*. Castro had placed Ernesto Guevara in charge of the fortress in January of 1959; in a manner unequivocally evocative of Lavrenti Beria in Russia, Guevara presided over one of the darkest periods in the history of Cuba. He became a «*one-man cold-blooded killing machine*,» according to many Cuban historians. Guevara's men were in charge of getting things ready for the night time quick trials that almost always resulted in death penalties at La Cabaña.

Guevara was known for his bloodthirsty style of justice. In his Message to the *Tricontinental Conference*, a 1966 gathering of Third World revolutionaries from Africa, Asia, and Latin America, he had said:

«Hatred is *an element of the struggle; unbending hatred for the enemy, which pushes a human being beyond his natural limitations, making him into an effective, violent, selective, and cold-blooded killing machine.*»

In one of his *-motorcycle* diaries he had written:

« *I felt my nostrils dilate savoring the acrid smell of gunpowder and the blood of the enemy.*»

In a 1954 letter to his mother, written while he witnessed the overthrow of Jacobo Arbenz in Guatemala, he wrote:

« *It was all a lot of fun, what with the bombs, speeches, and other distractions to break the monotony I was living in.*»

In January of 1957 he killed a suspected spy in the *Sierra Maestra* point-blank and declared:

«*I ended the doubt with a .32 caliber pistol, in the right side of his brain.*»

Guevara's instructions to the military court judges in La Cabaña was: «*If in doubt, kill them.*» Executions took place from Monday to Friday, in the middle of the night, just after the sentence was given and automatically confirmed by the appellate body, whose president was Guevara himself. A sentence was never overturned.

On a typical night, seven to ten men would be judged, appeals would be heard, and execution squads would shoot the men within minutes. The accused were former soldiers and officers of the *Cuban Republican Army,* not all of whom had been unconditional to Batista. There were also police officers, journalists, students, Catholic activists, business men and merchants.

By some estimates, four hundred people at least were executed between January and June of 1959. The American embassy estimated there were 500. When Guevara was confronted before his death in Bolivia he estimated «*more than two thousand,*» adding «*they were all CIA agents. I never cared for them or the number we killed.*»

Photos above: the wall used by the firing squads; a priest hearing the last confession of a condemned and two men dying.

Eight years later, on October 8 1967, after a tip-off from a farmer, **Ernesto (Ché) Guevara** and 50 of his fighters were trapped in a small town in Bolivia. **Félix Rodríguez** leading a small military unit had surrounded the group of *guerrilleros* led by Guevara; they heard him shouting «***Don't shoot. I'm Ché Guevara - I'm worth more to you alive than dead.***» The man who wrote that he was thirsty for blood, who had assassinated thousands of people without any regard for legal processes, who had murdered several hundred youngsters in the *Cabaña* fortress in Havana, was in Bolivia in a bid to spread the revolution when he was captured. He was **ready to s**urrender without conditions in the morning of October 8, although he was still well armed; he was trembling, scared for his future, willing to make any accommodations to continue living. «*Don't shoot. I'm Ché Guevara - I'm worth more to you alive than dead,*» was the only thing he ventured to say.

The **CIA wanted Guevara alive for interrogation**; they were overruled by Bolivian authorities. The President of Bolivia wanted him shot within the next 24 hours. They asked Rodríguez to let Guevara know what his future was. Guevara was kept under lock at the only strong building in the village where he was captured. Felix Rodríguez requested that René Barrientos, Bolivia's President, would confirm the orders that Guevara had to be shot without the benefit of a trial. The President confirmed the order saying «***Guevara has never believed in trials. He has no reason to expect one at this time.***» The exact time was to be indicated in a coded message that the president would send once he had consulted with other governments in the region. A message would be sent from the presidential palace. The number 500 indicated the name Guevara; 400 meant stand-by; 600 meant death; 700 meant sent to La Paz for trial.

Photo above: Guevara in the hands of Félix Rodríguez.

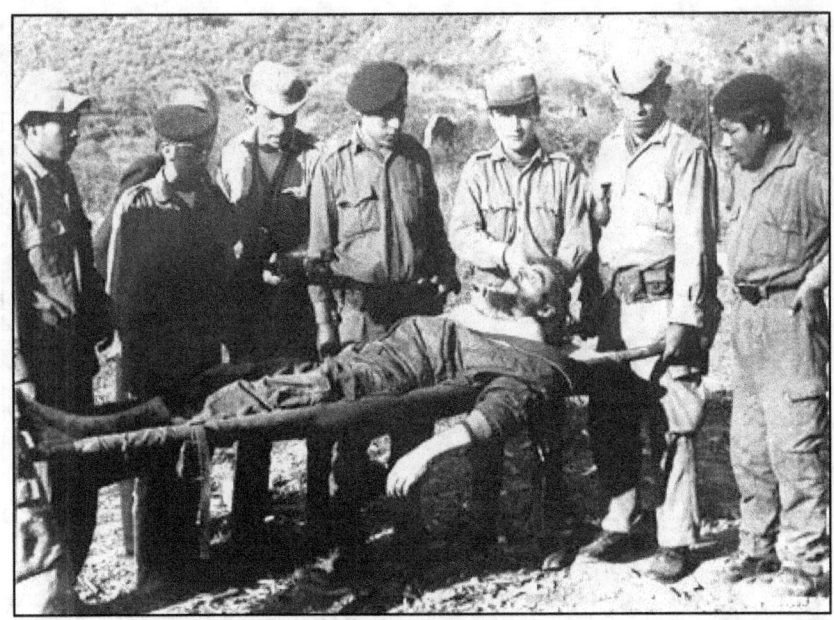

At the time of his capture, Ernesto Guevara looked nothing like the uniformed revolutionary the world had seen being feted by Soviet and Chinese leaders. The man that had studied dentistry in Argentina and who, according to his diary, had commanded the attention of beautiful woman across South America and Mexico was no more. He had been wounded in his right leg and was limping. He was also coughing non-stop due to his chronic asthma condition. He was unkempt, not having bathed for several weeks. His uniform was in rags and made him look like a beggar. He had found **no support whatsoever from the peasants** in the plains of Bolivia.

On the morning of October 10th a phone call came through the only telephone in town. A quiet voice simply said: «*500 and 600.*» Guevara was taken outdoors to a nearby field. Félix Rodríguez was waiting there with three men armed with machine guns. Guevara — whose face was white with fear, recognized Rodríguez and told him «*I am sorry I have to die this way. I should have died in combat.*» The squad was asked not to shoot at his face so that the cadaver would be easy to identify and Castro could not deny he was dead. A burst of machine-gun fire hit Guevara on his upper torso. At the last minute he had tried to look away from his executioners and most bullets hit him on the left side of his trunk. After he fell to the ground his body went into convulsions for two or three minutes and then it remained still. His face was buried into the ground, his arms grotesquely to his side with the palms opened in a protective gesture. His legs were bent at the knees and the knees were close to his chest. The man who had killed so many innocent and decent lives **looked now like a wild animal** ready to be tied to a stake and carried to a taxidermist.

Photo above: Guevara on a stretcher after his execution.

At the time of the end of the Republic of Cuba the nation placed 22 in the group of 122 largest nations in the world. Its *per capita* income (US $44) was larger than Italy, Spain and Portugal; its infant mortality rate (32 per 1000 live births) was the 9th lowest in the world, better than Austria, Italy, France and most other European countries. On a *per capita* basis there were more physicians in Cuba than in England. Cuba had an 80% literacy rate (compared with 35% at the founding of the Republic). It was all the result of the resourcefulness of the numerous Cubans that participated in the development of the young Republic and it attests to the strength of Cuba's civil society and character of its venture seekers and risk-takers.

Cuban entrepreneurs then and now have been recognized as among the most successful in the world:

In the world of **sugar** —5 million tons per year, which was 35% of the world sugar exports— there were **Laureano** and **Miguel Angel Falla** and **Eutimio Falla Bonet** (*Cía. Azucarera Atlántica del Golfo, Sucesión L. Falla Gutiérrez*), **Julio Lobo** (*Hersey Group, Galbán Lobo Trading Company*), **Francisco Blanco Calás**, the **Rodríguez de Mendoza** family, **Manuel Rionda** (*Cuban Trading Company*), **Leandro Vázquez, Higinio, Alfonso** and **Pepe Fanjul**, **Pepe Gómez Mena** and **Jose Manuel Casanova**, to mention a few. Together they possessed an irreplaceable amount of know-how about how to conduct businesses, provide jobs and develop an economy. Their loss to Cuba, through confiscation of their properties, was a serious blow to the Republic perpetrated by what in American history was once called a bunch of **know-nothings**.

In the photos, top row: Julio Lobo, Alfonso Fanjul Gómez Mena, Manuel Rionda y Polledo, José Manuel Casanova; *on the bottom row*: Carlos Fuentes (hijo), Amado Trinidad, Eutimio Falla Bonet and José M. Cubas, Hijo.

Among the successful entrepreneurs in the business of **tobacco** products —11 Billion cigarettes and 0.5 Million cigars per year— there were **Fernando Palicio** and **José Gener** (*Hoyo de Monterrey*), **José L. Piedra, Alonzo, Alonzo Jr.** and **Benjamín Menéndez** and **Pepe García** (*H. Upmann, Montecristo*), **Jaime Partagás, Ramón Cifuentes** (*Partagas Cigars*), **Pepe Méndez** (*Regalías El Cuño*) and **Amado Trinidad** (*Trinidad y Hermanos*).

In **other businesses** —chemicals, toiletries, textiles, services and others, **Facundo** and **Emilio Bacardí, Enrique Schueg** and **Pepín Bosch** (*Bacardí and Company*), **Ramón Arrechabala** (*Havana Club*), **Benjamín** and **Eduardo Camp, Evaristo** and **Claudio Alvarez** (*Ron Matusalem*), **Juan** and **José Crusellas** (*Jabón Candado, Colgate-Palmolive*), **José M. Cubas, Padre** (*Laboratorios Gravi, S.A.*), **Juan Sabatés** (*Sabatés, S.A.*), **Dayton, Burke** and **Jimmy Hedges** (*Rayonera, Textilera Ariguanabo*), **Antonio Fernández, José López Rodríguez** (Pote) and **Oscar Echevarría** (*P. Fernández and La Cultural*), **Benito Langueruela** (*Editorial Omega, printers*), **José Solís** and **Aquilino Entrialgo** (*El Encanto*), **Segundo Casteleiro** (*Papelera Nacional*), **Domingo Moreira** (*El Caporal*), **Gaspar Pumarejo** and **Goar Mestre** (*radio and television*), **Amador Odio** and **Agapito Amaro** (transports and deliveries), **Mariano Guastela** and **José M. Cubas, Hijo** (*marketing and advertising*), **Agustín Batista, Narciso Gelats** and **Carlos Nuñez** (*banking*).

All of them and/or their descendants left Cuba and committed their skills and knowledge to more stable and fair lands.

In the photos, top row: Facundo Bacardí, Ignacio López Trelles, José López Rodríguez (Pote) and Domingo R. Moreira; *bottom row*, Segundo Casteleiro y Pedrera, Goar Mestre, Amador Odio and Jorge Mas Canosa.

One of the first actions of the revolutionary government was to eliminate the freedom of the press in Cuba. It started on May 12, 1960, with the **closing of the *Diario de la Marina***, a newspaper that had been published continuously since 1832. The man who provoked Castro to eliminate the fee press was José Ignacio Rivero Hernández, who constantly denounced the atrocities in Cuba and the aggressions against freedom by the Castro regime. After the newspaper ***Prensa Libre*** protested for the closing and vandalization of the Diario, it was also seized by the government.

José Ignacio Rivero Hernández (1920-) was the last director of the *Diario de la Marina*, the dean of the Cuban press. He is the third of three generations of Riveros that directed the *Diario*: his grandfather *Nicolás Rivero Muñiz (1895-1919)*, his father *José Ignacio Rivero Alonso (1919-1944)* and himself, *director from 1944 to 1960*. Throughout his life he has been awarded many honors: the *Gran Cruz de Carlos Manuel de Céspedes* from the Cuban Republic; the *Great Cross of Isabel the Catholic*, the highest honor conferred by the Spanish nation; the *Knight Order of the Holy Sepulcher* and *Pro ecclesia et Pontiff*, both Vatican honorary distinctions; a *Doctorate Honoris Causa* from the *Universidad de Villanueva* in Havana.

Upon his arrival in exile in 1960, the *Inter-American Press Association (IAPA)* presented him the *Hero Award for Press Freedom* and the *Mergenthaler Award*; an additional title of *Doctor Honoris Causa* from *Marquette University* in Milwaukee, Wisconsin.

Photos above: the —burialll of the *Diario* on May of 1960 and José Ignacio Rivero after he went into exile in 1960,

In 1960 Cubans, once more, took the familiar road to exile. On June 22, in Mexico City, a pact was signed by **Antonio Varona**, **Aureliano Sánchez Arango**, **Manuel Artime Buesa**, **José Ignacio Rasco** and **Justo Carrillo**; they created the *Frente Revolucionario Democrático*, an organization that would eventually lead to the unsuccessful attempt to invade Cuba at the **Bay of Pigs**. It would be one of the many patriotic organizations that tried to recover the Republic from the abduction committed by the Communists in 1959.

Photo on top, from left to right: the founding members of the *Frente Revolucionario Democrático,* Manuel Artime, Antonio de Varona, José Ignacio Rivero, Aureliano Sánchez Arango and Justo Carillo. *Photo below, from left to right:* On the training camps of the Brigada 2506, Manuel Artime, José Pérez San Román and Antonio de Varona.

The photo above, taken in 1960 in Miami, shows a group of leaders of the *Frente Revolucionario Democrático* as they prepared the strategies leading to the failed invasion of Cuba in April of 1961. From left to right, Antonio de Varona, Justo Carrillo, Enrique Ros and Manuel Artime.

In spite of the lack of success and the obstacles due to international political imperatives, the leaders that fought Communism in Cuba in the 1960s have continued their commitment to a free Cuba for over almost half a century. Some of them –shown here in their senior years— are **Enrique Ros**, **Tony Varona** (†1992), **Aureliano Sánchez Arango** (†1976), **Manuel Artime** (†1977), **Justo Carrillo** (†1983), **José Pérez San Román** (†1989) and **José Ignacio Rasco**.

«Can real Cubans, with the heroic sacrifices of three wars of independence still fresh in their minds, accept the calm assertion as to an end of the Republic of Cuba?»

Tomás Estrada Palma, 1906

Epilogue

> «Nations never die a natural death. They die
> because their leaders did not know
> how to fulfill their promises and
> replenish their strengths.»
> VOLTAIRE, French Philosopher and Writer (1694-1778)

ONE HAS TO WONDER, fifty years after the end of the Republic of Cuba, if this experiment in Marxist social engineering has benefited anyone except the Castro family and a very few of their intimate friends and supporters. Cuba is today one of the most backward countries in the Americas. Its government has wasted the national patrimony in unproductive and senseless experiments, an absolute prohibition of free enterprise and personal property, a life style of luxury and indulgence for its leaders and unconditional supporters, irrational international ventures and a policy of allowing corruption as a means to secure loyalty among those who endorse the government.

There were no rational gounds for the disaster that befell on Cuba after its first half century of republican life. Cuba had its share of dictators, military coups, corrupt officials, unescrupulous judges, unprincipled politicians, fraudulent elections. Gangs and mobs terrorized its citizens, land owners abused its peasants; business owners underpaid its workers, vagrants, floaters and tramps abused the public payrolls, you name it. That was not exclusive to Cuba. In that sense Cuba was no different that almost any other nation in the world, including the most developed and civilized.

Cuba also had men and women of great character and condition, military heroes that gave their lives for their country, honest politicians that never took advantage of their access to priviledge, teachers that sacrificed their best years to educate the young, hard working men and women that never aspired to more than live their lives in peace and helping others, courageous civil servants and government officials that never stole public funds, inspiring writers, poets, and scientists that were always ready to make Cuba a larger-than life country.

In fact, Cubans as a whole were studious, fast learners, quick, enterprising, and very hard working. They had a passion for beautiful buildings, cleanliness and education, and a strong sense of pride in their accomplishments. They were also unrestrainedly gregarious, from neighborhood associations, to alumni societies, beach clubs, trade societies, sports consortiums, and the like.

Why is it that the spotless streets are now full of garbage, the buildings are rotting and crumbling, the roofs collapsing, the empty lots are full of rubbish, the patios are overcome by trash, the faces of people look unkempt, the population consists mostly of lethargic men, women and children sitting in crumbling and dilapidated furniture at their doorsteps, ill-dressed, sporting underwear for lack of humble shirts, with their children sitting around with bare torsos, idle, with sad and unemotional faces? What has happened to the Cuban ethos? What has happened to the former successful Cuba?

What happened was that a brutal communist dictatorship took over Cuba. It eliminated civil rights, private education, newspapers, private property and businesses of all sizes. This prompted one of the largest political migrations in the history of the American continent: an exodus of more than a million Cubans, largely middle class, to the United States and the rest of the world, particularly Miami. The description of the pre-Castro Cubans of 1959 applies perfectly to Cuban-born Americans that have left Cuba, particularly their children in contemporary Miami, Madrid, Paris, New York, California or New Jersey. Curiously, when new Cubans arrive, 8 out of 10 become industrious, hardworking and achievement oriented; they buy houses with great effort and they keep them immaculately clean. They send their kids to the best possible schools and demand excellence. In a few years, the former children of Castro's revolution, if they are able to escape the inferno, are graduating from Cornell, Yale, Johns Hopkins, and the University of Miami with honors. One must conclude that Cubans know how to succeed and surge to the surface when they live in freedom and in a competitive and challenging society.

It has never been worthwhile to live in a society where life is limited to days and days of doing nothing but sit in the thresholds of crumbling edifices; where people rarely have nothing to do but attend a rally to get free beer; where they don't have to pay for practically anything, hence they get nothing worthwhile; where it is immaterial if the streets are clean or not; where the best facilities are reserved for tourists or for the minions of the dictatorship; where common citizens have to live in *apartheid* and in dirt surroundings. It is almost universally so in Cuba; by now the people are immune to dreaming —and they couldn't care less.

The Castro regime pretended to be ideological, Marxist and Socialist in the manner of the Soviet Union of the '50s and '60s. Now they only pretend to be aging revolutionaries, knowing full well they are not. They have systematically destroyed every institution of republican Cuba, mounted a Stalinist repressive apparatus that exists to our days, all to give power to a new feudal dynasty of truly boring dictators, the brothers Castro. Their unconditional servants have access to money, traveling, houses, privileges. The children and grandchildren of the Castros and their cohorts live like young affluent heirs of some mythical crown—houses in Avenue Foch in Paris, thousands of acres in Chile, half of Sicily, whatever they desire in Cuba, Bentleys, Mercedeses, Rolexes, a superior education, use of stolen goods. The former ideologues have turned into dramatic and shameless *Mafiosos* that no longer need to fake their devotion to Marx or Socialism. Their actions speak louder than their voices.

We conclude this epilogue with a few views of Cuba in the 21stcentury. These are the scenes that Cubans in the island see everyday, although they are carefully concealed from visitors, former American presidents and American and European tourists. We invite you to see for yourself.

Cuba after half a century of Communism.

Entrance to an apartment building

A line at a former super-market

Balconies at an old apartment building

Inventory at a plumbing store

Taxies and drivers in downtown Havana

At an open-air butcher shop

Street corner in the center of Havana

A former department store in Havana

Façade of a condemned apartment building

Appendices

I   A Chronology of the Hispano-Cuban-American War of 1898

II A Quick Chronology of USA-Cuba Relations (1898-1959)

III Presidents of Cuba during its Colonial and Republican times.

IV Main Characters of the Republic of Cuba

V   Alphabetical Index

I - A Chronology of the *Hispano-Cuban-American* War of 1898

(The **Hispano-Cuban War** had been raging since the *Grito de Baire* or *Grito de Bayate*, February 24, 1895).

Jan 15	Hostile demonstrations in Havana against the US.
Jan 25	Battleship *Maine* arrives in Havana.
Feb 8	The letter from *De Lome* is published in Havana.
Feb 15	The Battleship *Maine* blows up in Havana.
March 5	Spain asks for recall of US Consul Lee. The US refuses.
March 11	US Army begins mobilization.
March 12	Spain offers armistice to insurgents.
April 2	The Spanish Fleet arrives at *Cabo Verde*.
April 9	All US diplomats leave Havana.
April 19	*Joint Resolution* approved by US Congress.
April 22	Blockade of Cuban ports starts.
April 23	McKinley asks for 125,000 volunteers.
April 24	Spain formally declares war on the US.
April 25	US declare that a state of war has existed since April 21.
April 27	US bombs batteries in *Matanzas*.
April 30	Cervera's fleet leaves *Cabo Verde* for Cuba.
May 1	Com. Dewey destroys the Spanish fleet in *Manila*.
May 5	Riots in Spain against the US.
May 11	US attack *Cienfuegos* and *Cárdenas*.
May 12	The US attacks *San Juan*, PR.
May 19	Adm. Cervera arrives in *Santiago de Cuba*.
May 25	McKinley asks for an additional 75,000 Volunteers.

May 30	The US fleet arrives at *Santiago* and fires against the forts at the entrance of the harbor.
June 3	The *US Merrimack* is sunk at the entrance of the channel in Santiago.
June 6	The *Reina Mercedes* is sunk by the US fleet.
June 11	US marines land at *Guantánamo*.
June 20	First US army troops land at *Daiquirí*.
June 24	US troops defeated at *Las Guásimas*.
July 1	The Rough Riders take *El Caney* and *San Juan*.
July 3	The Spanish fleet is destroyed as it attempts to leave the bay of *Santiago*. Adm. Cervera is taken prisoner.
July 10	The US resumes bombardment of the city of *Santiago*.
July 17	*Santiago de Cuba* surrenders. Gen. Wood appointed military governor of the city.
Aug 7	The *Rough Riders* leave Santiago.
Aug 12	US-Spain armistice is proclaimed.
Aug 20	The victorious US ships parade up the *Hudson River* in NY City.
Oct 1	Peace talks begin in Paris.
Oct 27	The US delegates force Spain to accept that Cuba does not owe reparations to Spain.
Nov 7	Gen. Domingo Méndez Capote elected president of the *Cuban Assembly of Santa Cruz del Sur*.
Dec. 10	The *Treaty of Paris* is signed at 8:45 PM.

⅄ It has been now widely accepted that the last War of Independence in Cuba was started in the town of **Bayate** by General **Bartolomé Maso Márquez**, who went on to win the encounters at *Demajagua, Bayazo, Yara, Pedralagón, la Bermeja, Baguanos, Punta Gorda, Naranjo, Ojo del Agua* and *las Guasitas*. On February 24, 1895, there were simultaneous uprisings at *Ibarra, Bayate, Guantánamo, Baire*, and *Jagüey Grande*. In 1936, however, the *Cuban Academy of History* concluded that the start of the 1895 war should be designated as **The Grito de Bayate** and not *The Grito de Baire*.

II - A Quick Chronology of USA-Cuba Relations (1898-1959)

April 1898   After the sinking of the *Maine*, the US Congress declares that Cuba has the right to be free and independent.

The US declares war on Spain. The *Hispano-Cuban-American* war starts. Spain surrenders on July 17.

Jan 1899   The US begins a rebuilding program in Cuba which includes construction of hospitals, paving of streets, education of teachers, founding of schools, sanitation and road construction.

Nov 1901   Cuba enacts its *1901 Constitution*. It includes the *Platt Amendment*, added by the US Congress on March 2.

May 1902   The U.S. military occupation ends as Tomás Estrada Palma becomes President.

March 1903   Cuba and the US ratify a treaty on commercial reciprocity.

July 1903   Cuba leases *Guantánamo* to the US permanently for $2000 a year in gold.

The US relinquishes its claim for the *Isle of Pines* but a date is not set for final ratification.

Aug 1906   Estrada Palma requests US intervention to put down an insurrection. The US intervenes for the second time. Future US President Taft is appointed as mediator.

Oct 1906   Charles Magoon begins a two year period as head of the government in Cuba.

Jan 1909   Magoon turns the Cuban government to President José Miguel Gómez.

1912   The *Agrupación Independiente de Color* rebels against the government of Gómez. US marines land in Cuba and

	two US warships anchor in Havana to prevent chaos. Gómez prevails and close to 3000 rebels perish.
Feb 1917	President Woodrow Wilson lands US marines in Cuba to shore up the government of President Mario García Menocal, leader of the Liberal Party.
April 1917	Cuba enters WWI the day after the US declares war. Menocal offers training facilities for US Marines, who stay until 1922.
1919-1933	Cuba becomes a destination to Americans distressed under the prohibition laws. Sugar prices plummet. US investors buy properties in Cuba at bargain rates.
1921	US President Wilson sends General Enoch Crowder to Cuba to supervise the elections. President Alfredo Zayas is elected. Crowder exchanges financial control for approval of loans to Cuba, as the IMF would do to other countries many years later.
Jan 1923	Zayas gets a loan for $50 million from J.P.Morgan. The US opens an embassy in Havana. General Crowder is appointed first US Ambassador to Cuba.
June 1923	Cuba opens an embassy in Washington.
1924	The *Veterans and Patriots Association* leads a rebellion in Cuba. President Calvin Coolidge sets up an embargo of shipments of arms to Cuba except to the Zayas government. Zayas quells the rebellion.
March 1925	The US Senate ratifies the 1904 treaty relinquishing US claims to the *Isle of Pines*. Hundreds of US citizens move back to the US mainland.
May 1925	General Gerardo Machado elected President of Cuba, to the delight of the US business community.
Aug 1925	Julio Antonio Mella founds the first *Cuban Communist Party*.

1928	President Machado gets himself re-elected for a six year term. There are uprisings, rebellions and acts of protest in Cuba.
1933	US President Franklin Delano Roosevelt considers there is a state of revolution in Cuba and dispatches Assistant Secretary of State Sumner Welles as Ambassador Extraordinary to Cuba.
Aug 1933	Machado resigns and flees to the US. Welles approves the selection of Carlos Manuel de Céspedes as provisional president of Cuba. The students and the military in Cuba oppose him.
Sept 1933	Sergeant Fulgencio Batista overthrows Céspedes and establishes a *Pentarquía*. 29 US warships move to Cuban waters.
	Ramón Grau San Martín is appointed president by the students and military. The US does not recognize him.
Jan 1934	Batista, now Colonel, overthrows Grau and tries several alternatives: Carlos Hevia, Manuel Márquez Sterling, and Carlos Mendieta. Mendieta is the only one recognized by the US government.
May 1934	The US agrees to abrogate the 1903 *Permanent Treaty* and to declare null the *Platt Amendment*, but keeps the naval base at Guantánamo.
1935-1936	Colonel Batista keeps trying other individuals for the presidency: José A. Barnet, Miguel Mariano Gómez, Federico Laredo Bru. None sticks.
Nov 1939	Cubans enact a new Constitution, to be effective in 1940.
June 1940	General Batista is elected fairly and becomes President of Cuba.
Dec 1941	Cuba enters WWII and provides air and naval bases to the US.

1943	President Batista legalizes the *Cuban Communist Party* and resumes relations with the USSR.
June 1944	Ramón Grau San Martí is elected President and Batista's candidate, Carlos Saladrigas, is defeated. Batista moves to Daytona Beach in Florida. World War II ends and Cuba joins the UN. Grau cannot control the US organized crime families or the Cuban gangster groups. Both reign almost freely in Cuba.
June 1948	Carlos Prío Socarrás, from the Grau's *Auténtico Party*, is elected president of Cuba. Batista is elected Senator *in Absentia*.
1948-1952	Prío establishes cordial relations to the US and visits US President Truman. He becomes one of the best presidents of Cuba but corruption in everywhere, including the top political leaders. The US stays on the sidelines.
Mar 1952	New elections in June. Batista runs for president with evident little change to succeed. On March 10 he stages a bloodless coup, sends Prío into exile, suspends the 1940 Constitution, cancels the elections and becomes a dictator. The Truman administration immediately recognizes him.
1952-1956	The US sends military and economic aid to the Batista government, while organized resistance begins in Cuba.
Dec 1956	A group of 79 revolutionaries under the leadership of Fidel Castro — former organizer of an attack on a military garrison in Santiago de Cuba—lands in Oriente province and establishes a rebel base at the *Sierra Maestra* mountains.
Feb 1957	The *New York Times* sends journalist Herbert Matthews to interview Castro

	at the *Sierra Maestra*. Arthur Gardner, the US Ambassador to Cuba, suggests that the CIA do away with Castro.
Mar 1957	Cuban students attack the Presidential Palace in a desperate magnizide action. It fails but contributes to turn US public opinion against Batista.
June 1957	Earl E. Smith is appointed by President Eisenhower as the new Ambassador to Cuba. On a visit to Santiago de Cuba he observes the excess of violence used by the police beating up women in a demonstration during the funeral of Frank País. He criticizes Batista for tolerating this cruelty.
March 1958	The US Eisenhower administration announces an arms embargo to the Batista regime. Ambassador Smith, who does not trust the rebels, complains to the State Department.
Nov 1958	Ambassador Smith expresses in a *Washington Post* interview that a free election will bring about an alternative to Batista and Castro.
	Batista's candidate for president, Andrés Rivero Aguero, is declared the winner in an election that even Ambassador Smith concedes has been rigged.
Dec 1958	William D. Pawley, secret envoy of President Eisenhower, tells Batista the time has come to return to Daytona Beach. Batista ignores the suggestion.
Jan 1 1959	General Fulgencio Batista flees to the Dominican Republic in the early hours of the morning. Five thousand Cuban soldiers surrender in Oriente province to the ragtag army of Castro.
Jan 7 1959	The US Eisenhower administration recognizes the new Castro government in Cuba. Philip W. Bonsal, a Castro sympathizer, replaces Smith as Ambassador.
	The Cuban Republican era comes to an end.

«There can be no task more civic or of greater importance than to deeply enhance the culture of Cuba, which has in the force of its civilization the only firm ground of their nationality.

Only active culture and not just talk can completely establish the dreams of Martí and of all those noble patricians who throughout the nineteenth century gave soul and dignity to this nation.

Only a culture deeper and wider in Cuba can restore our roots and foliage and make our spirit to bloom with the beauty and durability of their spirit, despite the historic hurricanes that have often disrupt the enjoyment of our inclement tropical endowments.»

Fernando Ortiz

III — Presidents of Cuba from Colonial and Republican times.

Cuban Presidents during the Ten Year War (1868-1878)

1. **Carlos Manuel de Céspedes y Castillo**
   (April 12 1869 - October 27 1873)
2. **Salvador Cisneros Betancourt**
   (October 27 1873 - June 28 1875)
3. **Juan Bautista Spotorno**
   (July 1 1875 - March 29 1876)
4. **Tomás Estrada Palma**
   (March 29 1876 - October 19 1877)
5. **Francisco Javier de Jesús**
   (October 19 - December 13 1877)
6. **Vicente Garcia y Gonzalez**
   (December 13 1877 - February 10 1878)

Cuban Presidents during the War for Independence (1895-1898)

1. **José Martí y Pérez**
   (May 5 1895 - May 19 1895)
2. **Salvador Cisneros Betancourt**
   (September 16 1895 - October 30 1897)
3. **Bartolomé Masó Márquez**
   (October 30 1897 - November 7 1898)

American Governors During the Military Occupations of 1898 & 1906

1. **John Rutter Brooke**
   (January 1 - December 23 1899)
2. **Leonard Wood**
   (December 23 1899 - May 20 1902)
3. **William Howard Taft**
   (September 29 - October 13 1906
4. **Charles Edward Magoon**
   (October 13, 1906 - January 28 1909)

Cuban Presidents during the Republic (1902-1958)

Tomás Estrada Palma
(May 20 1902 - September 28 1906)

Native of Oriente. Graduate in Philosophy. Teacher. Took office at age 70. One of two presidents who married a foreigner: Genoveva Guardiola, daughter of a former Honduras president. The first president re-elected. Was forced to resign. It is said that Genoveva Guardiola used to sit in the patio of the old presidential palace darning Don Tomas' socks. It was also said that Don Tomás had only three dress suits during his entire presidency.

José Miguel Gómez
(January 28 1909 - May 20 1913)

Native of Las Villas. Did not finish College. Took office at age 51. Father of Miguel Mariano (only father-son pair of presidents.) Family was in good position. Nicknamed *Tiburón* (Shark.) In the *1901 Constitutional Convention* voted to agree to the Platt Amendment since he found it better than no Constitution at all. Leading Liberal politician. Close friend of Machado.

Aurelio Mario García Menocal
(May 20 1913 - May 20 1921)

Native of Matanzas. Alumnus of the *Chappaqua Mountain Institute*. Engineer from *Cornell*. Leading conservative politician. Took office at age 47. The second president re-elected. His re-election resulted in the revolt of *La Chambelona*. Nicknamed *El Mayoral* (the foreman.) Went into exile in Miami in 1931 after attempting to start a revolution in Cuba.

Alfredo Zayas Alfonso
(May 20 1921 - May 20 1925)

Native of Havana. Lawyer. Took office at age 60. Nicknamed *El Pesetero* and *El Chino* (stingy and the chinaman.) Brother of Juan Bruno Zayas, a Cuban Independence War patriot. Only Cuban president who wrote poetry and essays. Deported to Spain in 1896, where he wrote *Al Caer la Nieve*, a notable poem. A leading Liberal politician. Participated in the *Chambelona* uprising and had to surrender in Guanabacoa after Menocal won the war.

Gerardo Machado y Morales
(May 20 1925 - August 12 1933)

Native of Las Villas. Only attended elementary school. Took office at age 54. Family was of humble origins. The third and last president re-elected. Nicknamed *Mocho* (Chopped Finger in Spanish.) First president thrown out of office by a revolution. After living in the Bahamas, Canada and Paris he died and is buried in Miami. Congress had passed a law that prohibited to ever bring his remains to Cuba.

General Alberto Herrera Franchi
(August 11 to August 12 1933)

Native of Las Villas. Served for 24 hours. Professional Army man. Army Chief of Staff during Machado's presidency.

Carlos Manuel de Céspedes Quesada
(August 12 - September 4 1933)

23 days in office. Born in New York during the exile of Ana de Quesada, wife of Carlos Manuel de Céspedes Sr. Lawyer. Took office at age 62. One of two presidents who married a foreigner: Laura Bertini, an Italian. Graduate of the *Instituto Stanislas* in Paris. Member of Cuba's diplomatic corps. Commander of the French Legion of Honor among many other distinctions.

Ramón Grau San Martín
(September 4 1933 - January 15 1934)

Native of Pinar del Rio. Physician. Professor at the *University of Havana*. Took office at age 51 the first time and 62 the second time. Family was in good position. Nicknamed *El Viejo* and *El Divino Galimatías* (the Old Man and the Divine Gibberish.) The only bachelor president. First time around (1933) served for only 100 days. Grau had his capital audited at the start and at the end of his second presidency. He was worth $22,000 less after 4 years and the state agreed to allow him a $500 monthly pension for him to survive. Grau died in Havana in 1969.

Carlos Hevia y de los Reyes
(January 15 - January 18 1934)

Native of Havana. Engineer, first Cuban to graduate from the *US Naval Academy in Annapolis*, Class of 1919. Took office at age 34. Served for 4 days and resigned. Was very unpopular with the military. Went into exile in 1959 and founded a *Private Naval Academy* in Miami. Died of a heart attack in 1964.

Manuel Márquez Sterling
(January 18 - January 18 1934)

Born in Lima, Perú, while his father was in a diplomatic position for the Independence Army. Friend of José Martí. Journalist at age 15. In 1903 was chosen as the best young Cuban writer. Sworn for office at the *Hotel Nacional* at 6 am January 18, 1934; deposed at noon the same day. Author of the famous phrase «*Contra la Ingerencia Extraña, la Virtud Doméstica.*»He died in Washington in 1934 during a diplomatic mission. He was the uncle of Carlos Márquez Sterling, president of Cuba's *1940 Constitutional Assembly*.

Carlos Mendieta y Montefur
(January 18 1934 - December 11 1935)

Native of Las Villas. Physician. Served for almost 2 years, with the support of Batista. Took office at age 62. Family was in good position. Nicknamed *El Solitario de Cunagua* (Cunagua's loner.) Mendieta died in Havana in 1960. During his presidency the *Platt Amendment* was rescinded. His only daughter married Calixto Garcia's son.

José Agripino Barnet y Vinajeras
(December 11 1935 - May 20 1936)

Born in Barcelona, while parents were in exile. Most of his life he was in diplomatic positions. Took office at age 71. Served for almost 5 months. He was the only ex-president to go back to work at the end of his presidency; he took employment as an officer in the Ministry of State, where he had been the Minister before assuming the presidency.

Miguel Mariano Gómez Arias
(May 20 1936 - December 23 1936)

Native of Las Villas. Dismissed by Congress after seven months because he opposed some policies of Batista. Lawyer. Took office at age 47. Son of José Miguel Gómez (only father-son pair of presidents.) Family was in good position. Died in Havana in 1950 after a long illness.

Federico Laredo Brú
(December 23 1936 - October 10 1940)

Native of Las Villas. As VP, replaced Miguel Mariano to the end of Mariano's term after he was impeached. Lawyer. Took office at age 61. Organized the *1940 Constitutional Assembly*. Unfortunatelly it was him who denied access to Cuba to the jewish people on the *San Luis* ship trying to escape Nazy Germany.

Fulgencio Batista y Zaldivar
(October 10 1940 - October 10 1944)

Native of Oriente. Only attended elementary school. Took office at age 39 the first time and at age 51 the second time. Family was of humble origins. Nicknamed *El Indio* and *El Mulato* (the Indian and the Mulatto.) In 1969 the Spanish press reported that Batista —a refugee in Portugal— was the richest man in the Iberian Peninsula. Batista died in Spain in 1973.

Ramón Grau San Martin
(October 10 1944 - October 10 1948)

See information above, during his first presidency.

Carlos Prío Socarrás
(October 10 1948 - March 10 1952)

Native of Pinar del Rio. Lawyer. Took office at age 45. Family was of humble origins. Was the most recognized student leader in 1927, for which he spent two years in political prison. Died of an apparent self-inflicted gunshot in 1977. At the time rumors abounded that he had been killed by the CIA.

Fulgencio Batista y Zaldivar
(March 10 1952 – December 31 1958)

See information above, during his first presidency.

IV – Main Characters of the Republic of Cuba

> «Los poetas no son bienvenidos en las repúblicas cuando dicen cosas incómodas sobre los tiranos.»
> PLATÓN (C.428 BC)

Eduardo Abela (1891-1965)

Cuban painter and caricaturist. Revived the famous popular character *The Bobo*, which had originated during the colonial period. He made it an instrument of struggle against the dictatorship of Gerardo Machado. Graduated from the Academy of Fine Arts San Alejandro After the fall of the dictator in 1933 Abela finished his caricature work and devotes the rest of his life to painting. Served diplomatic posts in Mexico between 1942 and 1945 and then in Guatemala, until 1951. He died in Havana at 74 years of age.

Agustín Acosta (1886-1979)

Cuban writer from the group of postmodernist poets of the 1920s, which anticipated the social and artistic upheavals of the decade that followed. He graduated Doctor of Civil Law at the University of Havana in 1918. Along with Regino Boti and José Manuel Poveda Acosta was one of the representatives of the Renaissance lyric in Matanzas before the 1920's. Precursor of social poetry in Cuba, where he expressed his love for Cuba. Translated from the original French many poems by Baudelaire, Verlaine, Lamartine. He was appointed National Poet by the Cuban Congress in 1955. During the dictatorship of Gerardo Machado suffered political imprisonment. After the fall of Machado was governor of Matanzas (1933-1934). During the Government of Mendieta was Secretary of the Presidency. Presided over the Nationalist Union Party (1936-1937); was elected senator and served as such from 1936 to 1944.

Roberto Agramonte (1904-1995)

Dean of the School of Philosophy and Letters of the University of Havana; Ambassador to México, Vice-Presidential Candidate with Eduardo Chibás as President in 1948; Presidential candidate for President in 1952; taught at the University of Puerto Rico after 1960; died in exile in Miami in 1995 at age 91.

José Braulio Alemán (1864-1930)

Former Brigadier General during the War of Independence in 1895. He was a lawyer and newspaper owner. In 1896 he was the leading author of the Constitution of La Yara and was a firm opponent to the Platt Amendment during the 1901 Constitutional Assembly. During the Republic he served as Senator, Minister of Education and Ambassador to Mexico and was very involved in the modernization of the University of Havana.

Anselmo Aliegro (1899-1961)

Mayor of the town of Baracoa; Member of the Cuban Congress in 1925, 1940 and 1945; Prime Minister in 1944; President of the Cuban Senate in 1954-1959;several times member of the Cabinet; Served as President of Cuba for one day after Batista left the country on January 1, 1959; died in exile in Miami at age 61.

José Arce (1881-1968)

Argentinean physician, politician, journalist, professor, and diplomat; Chancellor of the University of Buenos Aires; wrote more than 200 technical articles, performed more than 50,000 surgeries and developed numerous surgical techniques; former President of the UN General Assembly; received the French Legion of Honor in 1922 as well as many other awards. Died in 1968 at age 87.

Carlos Baliño (1848-1926)

Cuban lifelong communist leader. Founder of the *Liceo Cubano* in Key West and presumed friend of José Martí in New York. Supported the Russian Revolution in 1905 and 1917. Founder of the Cuban Communist Party with Julio Antonio Mella and Fabio Grobart in 1925. Died in Havana in 1926 at age 78.

José Agripino Barnet y Vinajeras (1864-1945)

Provisional President of Cuba in 1935-1936, when he replaced his former boss President Mendieta. He called for elections in 1936 when Miguel Mariano López was elected. Member of the Liberal Party. Died in Barcelona at an age of 101.

Fulgencio Batista y Zaldivar (1901-1973)

Rose to power in the rebellion of the Sergeants; elected President for four years in 1940; returned to the presidency after a *coup d'état* in 1952. Took refuge in the Dominican Republic in 1959 after been overthrown by Castro's revolution. Found political asylum in Portugal; he died of a heart attack in 1973 while visiting Marbella in Spain at age 72.

Pedro Betancourt Dávalos (1858-1933)

Born in Ceiba Mocha, Matanzas; studied Medicine in Philadelphia and Madrid; In 1895 he joined the war and was taken prisoner, serving in the Castle of San Severino. Fought under Generals Calixto García and Lacret, and finally went into exile in Paris. Served as Governor of Matanzas and as a member of the 1901 Constituent Assembly. Died in Havana in 1933. His name was given to the town of Corral Falso de Macuriges in the province of Matanzas.

Manuel Bisbé Alberni (1906-1961)

Founder of the University Reform movement and of the first Federation of University Students (FEU). Graduated as doctor in Public Law, Civil Law and Philosophy; served as professor at the Escuela Normal de Matanzas and the Secondary School in Havana. Member of the opposition movement to the dictatorship of Gerardo Machado; was expelled from Cuba in late 1930. Elected member of the House of Representatives in 1944 by the Cuban Revolutionary Party (*Auténticos*). In May 1947 participated in the founding of the Party of the Cuban People (*Ortodoxos*). Bisbé was a candidate for the Senate in the 1952 elections, frustrated by the *coup* of Fulgencio Batista. He died in New York in 1961 while serving as ambassador to the UN.

Lydia Cabrera (1899-1992)

Notable scholar of the linguistic and anthropological aspects of the Afro-Cuban culture. Daughter of Cuban historian Raimundo Cabrera and sister of Ramiro Cabrera. Her mentor in Afro-Cuban folklore was Fernando Ortiz, the most important Cuban ethnologist and anthropologist. In 1927 she went to reside in Paris, where she published her *Nègres Contes de Cuba*

(Paris, Gallimard, 1936), translated into French by Francis Miomandre. Her works were published in French magazine *Cahiers du Sud*, *Revue de Paris* and *Les Nouvelles littéraires*, and the Cuban magazines *Origins* (1945-1954), *Cuban Bimonthly Magazine* (1947) and *Lyceum* (1949). At the triumph of the Revolution left the country. She died in Miami in 1992.

Raimundo Cabrera Bosch (1852-1923)

Cabrera was a Cuban essayist, journalist, lawyer and patriot. He was born in Güines, Havana. At age 17 he tried to join the Cuban War of 1868-1878 but was made prisoner and sent to jail in the Isle of Pines. After the *Pacto del Zanjón* he became an autonomist and advocated for necessary reforms in the social, economic and political life of the island, without resorting to violence. The War of 1895 found him in New York where he was the publisher of *Cuba and America*, a patriotic newspaper. He was the father of Lydia Cabrera. After independence he became a member of the Liberal Party and presided the *Sociedad Económica de Amigos del País*. He died in Havana at age 71.

Esteban Cacicedo Torriente (1849-1932)

One of the richest and most powerful men in Cienfuegos at the start of the Republic. Founder of Sugar Mills, Trading Companies, Banks, Cattle and Rice Companies. Born in Santander, Spain. Immigrated to Cienfuegos in 1865. In 1922 opened *Cacicedo & Company*. Married Ramona de la Torriente, his cousin. Owner of the *Central Santa María* since 1909, as well as the *Central Carolina*. President of the *Casino Español*; founder of the *Asilo de Ancianos* de Cienfuegos. Died at age 81. His children Isidoro, Luís, Ramón, Rosalía, José María y Esteban inherited his fortune. All the family properties were confiscated in Cuba in 1959.

Sergio Carbó Morera (1892-1971)

Journalist at the newspapers El Fígaro, La Discusión, La Prensa, El Día, Prensa Libre. Was a member of the Pentarquía; In 1933 he was instrumental in appointing Fulgencio Batista as General. Was awarded the Justo de Lara Prize in Cuba (to the top journalists). His son was a member of the 2506 Brigade against Castro in 1961.

Luis Casero Guillén (1902-1978)

Former Mayor of Santiago de Cuba ; he was arrested during the attack to the Moncada Barracks. Minister of Public Works in the government of Carlos Prío; became notable for his plan of 60 public works completed in 60 days, a promise he carried to the end. Casero was one of the most outstanding public servants in Cuba during Republican times. Was a member of the Organización Auténtica and left Cuba after the triumph of the revolution.

Nicolás Castellanos

Former president of the City Council of Havana. A handsome truck driver that became mayor in 1950 opposing Antonio Prío, the president's brother and odd-on favorite to win. Castellanos was supported by Fulgencio Batista, Grau San Martín and the Communist Party, one of the most strange political alliances in the history of Cuba. His campaign was based almost exclusively in providing plenty of water for the capital. Time Magazine called the *Bathtub Election*.

Salvador Cisneros Betancourt (1828-1914)

Politician, land owner and engineer. Marqués de Santa Lucía, president of the *Republic of Cuba in Arms* (1873-1875) after the deposition of his emesis, Carlos Manuel de Céspedes and in (1895-1897) after the death of José Martí. Founder of the *Tínima* Masonic lodge in Camagüey. Member of the 1901 Constitutional Assembly. Died in Havana at the age of 86.

José María Chacón y Calvo (1892-1969)

Notable Cuban lawyer, writer and teacher. Graduate of Doctor of Law and Philosophy at the University of Havana. Professor of the Catholic University of Villanueva, between 1946 and 1961. Maintained working relationships with Ramón Menéndez Pidal in Spain. Elected VP of the Latin American Section, and academic of the Academy of History of Spain. Director of Culture at the Cuban Ministry of Interior, where he served between 1934 and 1944. VP of the Cuban National Academy of Arts and Letters and member of the Academy of History; president of the Cuban Academy of Language. He died in Havana, Cuba, November 8, 1969

Eduardo René Chibás (1907-1951)

Politician, radio personality and founder of the *Ortodoxo Party* in Cuba in 1947 as a splinter of the Grau and Prío *Partido Auténtico*. Denouncer of corruption and gangsterism. Anti-Communist. Senator. Warned his followers of Batista intentions of producing a *coup d'état* in 1952. Shot himself during his weekly radio program and after 11 days of intensive care died in a hospital. His funeral was attended by thousands.

Carlos Manuel de Céspedes Quesada (1871-1939)

Cuban Politician, diplomatic and intellectual, son of Carlos Manuel de Céspedes del Castillo, the man who started the 1868 Ten Years War. Was president of Cuba for a few days in 1933. Was born in New York when Ana de Quesada Loynaz, his mother, second wife of his widower father, was in exile. Never knew his father, who died in 1874 in Cuba.

Carlos Miguel de Céspedes Ortiz (1881-1955)

A descendant of a cousin of Carlos Manuel de Céspedes del Castillo, the father of the Cuban Nation. Lawyer and politician, born in Matanzas, a law graduate from the *University of Havana*. Secretary of Public Works (1925-1929), Justice (1929-1930), Education (1930-1932), and Senator from Camaguey and Matanzas. Nicknamed *The Dynamic* because of the many works that he inspired and supervised during the Machado government. His residence was destroyed at the fall of Machado and in its place was built the *Church of Corpus Christi* in Miramar. He died of sadness at age 74, shortly after the death of his wife Margaret.

José Manuel Cortina y García (1880-1970)

Cuban politician, lawyer and journalist; one of Cuba's most outstanding orators and diplomats. He graduated from the *University of Havana* as a lawyer in 1903 and for more than half a century wrote for several important cultural magazines in Cuba. Member of the Cuban House of Representatives and the Senate since 1906. He acted as President Alfredo Zayas' Secretary of the Presidency and President Miguel Mariano's Foreign Minister; was a delegate to the *League of Nations* in 1927. Cortina was instrumental in the elimination of the *Platt Amendment* in the early 1930s. Died in exile in Miami at age 90.

Alejo Cossio del Pino (1906-1952)

Member of the House of Representatives and Minister of the Interior in Cuba in 1947. Proprietor of *Radio Cadena Habana* and *Topeka*, a popular rural restaurant. During the events at *Orfila* (see page 346) the followers of Emilio Tró accused him to be a sympathizer of Mario Salabarría. His name was scrawled in the tombstone of Emilio Tró, indicating he was marked for death. On February 11, 1952, while having dinner with friends at the Café-Restaurant *Strand* in Belascoaín and San José Streets, he was murdered at age 48. He tried to eliminate gangsterism; his slogan was —*se acabaron las pistolas*.

Miguel Coyula Laguno (1878-1948)

Cuban self-taught journalist, commander of the Cuban Army of Independence in 1895, member and President of the House of Representatives in 1917, member of the Menocal administration, founder of the *Sociedad Interamericana de Prensa (SIP)*. In 1940 participated in the *Asamblea Constituyente* and often presided it. Fought to include the name of God in the Constitution of Cuba; his main rival was Blas Roca, a member of the Communist party. Was a very honest man throughout his life and was always recognized as such. Died without ever owning a house, paying rent in his house in *Reparto La Sierra* near Habana at age 70.

Gustavo Cuervo Rubio (1890-1978)

Cuban physician and politician. VP from 1940 to 1944 under Batista after he was unsuccessful in 1936 as a VP candidate under Grau San Martín. Was elected to the 1940 Constitutional Assembly. In 1959 went into exile and died in Miami at age 88.

Segundo Curti Messina (1910-2000)

Student leader against Machado. Minister of Interior in the government of Grau San Martín, a former student in the College of Architecture of the University of Havana. Founding member of the PRC (A). He was Minister of Defense in the government of Carlos Prío after having served in the House of Representatives for two periods. Went into exile in 1952 after the coup de état of Batista. Returned to Cuba in 1959 where he died at age 90.

Rafael Díaz-Balart (1926-2005)

Cuban politician that served as majority leader, Minister of the Interior and Senator during the second presidency of Fulgencio Batista. In 1955 he opposed the amnesty granted by Batista to Castro (his former brother-in-law) after the attack on the Moncada Barracks. He was the son of a representative of the same name elected to the House in Cuba in 1936. After his exile in 1959 he lived and prospered in Spain and served as a diplomat for several Latin American countries. He died at age 79 in Miami after a prolonged battle with leukemia.

José Antonio Echeverría Bianchi (1932-1957)

Elected President of the *Federación de Estudiantes Universitarios* in 1954 while studying in the School of Architecture at the University of Havana. Born in Cárdenas, Matanzas. Founder of the *Directorio Revolucionario* in Cuba in 1955. Was killed after an attempt to attack the Presidential Palace in Cuba to eliminate President Batista.

Evaristo Estenoz (1871-1912)

Founder of the *Partido de los Independientes de Color* in Cuba with Pedro Ivonet in 1908. At the time José Miguel Gómez was Cuba's president.

Most of the party members were veterans of the 1895 War of Independence. Estenoz Led a revolt to claim the rights of the black men in Cuba; it was suffocated by the government at the cost of 6,000 party sympathizers.

Tomás Estrada Palma (1832-1906)

General in the Cuban Independence War of 1868, during which he was taken prisoner and deported to Spain. Worked with José Martí in New York. Opened a famous school in Central Valley, NY, near West Point in between wars. Was instrumental in obtaining the *Joint Resolution* (recognizing the right of Cuba to be independent) from the US Congress. Was elected first president in Cuba in 1902 and re-elected in 1906. After a violent opposition he appealed to the US to intervene in Cuba. Estrada died poor in Bayamo that same year.

Eutimio Falla Bonet (1905-1965)

Falla Bonet was born in the *Central Andreita* in Cienfuegos. He was a descendant of Tomas Rodríguez de Alcinega, founder of Santa Clara; he was also son of Laureano Falla Gutiérrez, a humble Spaniard that left a fortune estimated in $35,000,000 to his children in 1929. His children formed the *Sucesión Laureano Falla*, a company that controlled the family fortune, including the Centrales *Adelaida, Manuelita* and *Patria*. Eutimio increased the capital of the Company to $75,000,000 through the acquisition of 13 Sugar Mills, 2 Bancs, the *Payret Theater* and many other businesses. His beneficiaries (through marriage into the family) were, among others, Viriato Gutierrez and Agustín Batista. He died at age 60, in Madrid, from a heart attack, after lifetime contributions to charitable causes.

José Fernández de Castro (1858-1916)

Brigadier General during the 1895 War of Independence. Fought under Calixto García. Elected to the *Yaya Constitutional Assembly* in 1897. Mayor of Bayamo during the Republic and member of the *1901 Constitutional Assembly*. Died in Havana at age 58.

Manuel Fernández Supervielle (1894-1947)

Cuban Lawyer and politician, a graduate of the University of Havana. Member of Congress from the *Partido Demócrata Republicano* in 1940. Joined the Auténticos and was Minister of the Treasury. Mayor of Havana in 1946. Died in Havana in 1947 of a self-inflicted gunshot when he could not fulfill his promise to bring water to the city.

Orestes Ferrara Marino (1876-1972)

Naturalized Cuban Military, political, diplomatic, university lecturer, writer and journalist of Italian origin. Cuban Liberation Army colonel (under Calixto García and Máximo Gómez) and one of the leaders of so-called historical liberalism. House Representative for various periods, diplomat, Secretary of State in the government of Gerardo Machado, a member of the *Constituent Assembly of 1940* and Cuba's ambassador to UNESCO in 1955. Author of numerous papers and studies on history and international relations. Ferrara was fired from all his positions in 1959, moved to Rome and died there at age 94.

Fernando Figueredo Socarrás (1846-1929)

Writer, public servant, politician. Born in Bayamo, Cuba. Student of Rensselaer Polytechnic Institute in Troy, NY. Friend of Teddy Roosevelt. Fought in the first and last combat of the Cuban Independence War of 1868. Was with Maceo at the *Protesta de Baraguá*. Friend and confidant of José

Martí. Mayor of West Tampa in 1895. Secretary of State in the Wood government. Died in Havana at the age of 83.

Carlos J. Finlay (1833-1915)

Cuban medical epidemiologist. A graduate of Jefferson Medical College (Philadelphia, USA) in 1855. Between 1859 and 1861 he studied in France. Since 1868 conducted extensive studies on the spread of cholera in Havana. Their studies showed that the spread of cholera was carried by water from the ditch called Real. Finlay's main contribution to world science was his explanation of the mode of transmission of yellow fever. In 1893, he made a series of studies and reported that the prevention of epidemics of yellow fever depended on the destruction of mosquito larvae breeding in the cities. In 1902, once proclaimed the independence of Cuba, Carlos J. Finlay named Superintendent of Health, and structured the country's health system on new bases. In this capacity he had to deal with the last epidemic of yellow fever recorded in Havana in 1905; it was eliminated in three months. He died in Havana Cuba, August 19, 1915.

Porfirio Franca Alvarez de la Campa (1878-1950)

Banker and financier. Member of the government of the *Pentarquía* after the fall of Machado in 1933, where it assumed the role of Secretary of the Treasury. Former participant in the *Movimiento de Veteranos y Patriotas* against President Zayas and took to the mountains under Laredo Bru. Died in Havana at age 72.

Aurelio Mario García Menocal (1866-1941)

Graduate of *Chappaqua Mountain Institute* in NY and the *Cornell University* School of Engineering. Major General of the Cuban Army during the Independence War in 1895. Fought under Máximo Gómez, Antonio Maceo and Calixto García. Havana Chief of Police and administrator of *Central Chaparra* for the *Cuban American Company*. Third president of Cuba, during WWI, with Enrique José Varona as his VP. Re-elected for a second term. Attempted a revolution in 1931 and had to go into exile in Miami. Ran for president once more in 1936 and lost. Member of the Constituent Assembly in 1940. Died in Havana at age 75.

Calixto García Iñiguez (1839-1898)

General in the three Cuban uprisings for Independence. A descendant of Iñigo Arista, a Basque King. A large, strong, well educated man with a short fuse. Had a total of 13 children. Captured and imprisoned by the Spaniards until the Pact of Zanjón in 1878, after attempting against his own life to prevent been detained. Produced —with the authority of the Cuban Government in Arms— the strategy for the participation of the US in the War of 1895. Died of pneumonia in Washington, DC, in the middle of a diplomatic mission, at age 59. See page 41.

Ramiro Guerra Sánchez (1880-1970)

Historian, economist and teacher. Graduated from Colegio La Luz in Batabanó in 1898 and participated in the Summer School for teachers at Harvard University sponsored by the US intervention government. Doctorate in Pedagogy in 1912; director of Havana's Normal School for Teachers in 1915. General Superintendent of Schools in Cuba in 1926. Founder with Arturo Montori of the magazine *Cuba Pedagógica*. Director of Diario de la Marina from 1943 to 1946. Died in Havana at age 90.

Rafael García Bárcena (1907-1961)

Poet, philosopher and Cuban revolutionary. Graduated in Philosophy and Letters from the University of Havana in 1938. Maintained an active opposition to Gerardo Machado; was a member of the first University Student Directory in 1927, and in 1930, directed his press agency *Cuba Libre* writing proclamations against Machado. One entitled "To arms" called to rebel against injustices of Machado; as a result ha was taken prisoner and imprisoned in the *Castillo del Príncipe* in Havana. On September 4, 1933 signed with others, including Sergeant Batista, the proclamation establishing the *Pentarquía*. He was involved in the founding of the Partido Revolucio- nario Cubano (PRC) in 1936. He was also one of the founders of the Cuban Society of Philosophy. On April 5, 1953 he was arrested along with other young students and was accused of organizing and leading an attempt to take by assault the fortress of *Columbia*; he was tortured and sentenced to two years in prison on the Isle of Pines. Seriously ill in 1961, he died of a stroke on June 13, 1961, at age 54.

Antonio Guiteras Holmes (1906-1935)

An important politician in Cuba during the 1930s. Participated in the overthrow of Machado in 1933 and founded *Joven Cuba*, a left-leaning political organization. He was a good friend of communist revolutionary Julio Antonio Mella and Minister of the Interior during the 100 days presidency of Grau San Martín in 1933. He worked hard to establish minimum wages, minimum labor regulations, academic freedom, and nationalization of important sectors of the economy. As he was trying to escape to Mexico in the midst of Batista's hegemony in Cuba, he was assassinated east of Matanzas bay, near the ruins of a fort called *El Morrillo*, at age 29.

Juan Gualberto Gómez Ferrer (1854-1933)

Cuban Journalist, poet, lawyer and politician. Personal friend and confidant of Francisco Vicente Aguilera and José Martí. Son of slaves; was sent by his parents and their owner to Europe to study. Became the main representative of Martí in Cuba in the 1895 war. After the *Protest of Baraguá* founded the newspaper *La Fraternidad*. Was sent into exile and made prisoner by the Spanish government and sent to the dark prison of Ceuta. Member of the *1901 Constitutional Assembly* and Senator of the Republic from the Liberal Party. He was a notable speaker. Died in Havana at age 79.

José Miguel Gómez y Gómez (1858-1921)

Cuban lawyer, military man (retired with the rank of Mayor General during the 1895 war) and politician. Member of the Liberal Party, second President of Cuba, from 1909 to 1913. Former governor of Las Villas. Received the nickname of *Tiburón* (the shark) because the presumed corruption incidents during his administration. On balance he was a very good president. A large monument on his honor was erected in Havana in 1936. Died in New York City at age 63.

Máximo Gómez (1836-1905)

Born in the Dominican Republic; a general in the Cuban Independence wars, both in 1868 and in 1895. Retired in 1898 as the highest ranking military figure in Cuba and a true hero for his strategic expertise. Good friend of Carlos Manuel de Céspedes, Antonio Maceo, José Martí and Tomás Estrada Palma. As the end of the American occupation in 1901 he emerged as the most popular figure in Cuba. He refused to be a candidate in the presidential election of 1901, claiming that «*I would much rather liberate men than govern them.*» See page 136. Died in Havana in 1905, at age 69.

Miguel Mariano Gómez (1889-1950)

Cuban lawyer, politician, son of José Miguel Gómez. Served as mayor of Havana in 1926. He was elected and served as President of the Republic for seven months in 1936 when he was impeached by Congress at the insistence of Fulgencio Batista, with whom he had an inconsequential disagreement. Left Cuba in 1936 and returned in 1939; in 1940 he ran for mayor of Havana again but lost to Raúl Menocal. Died in Havana in 1950 after a long illness at age 61.

Antonio Govín (1849-1914)

Born in Matanzas, a celebrated jurist, publicist, orator and patriot of distinction since the 1880s. Professor of Administrative Law at the University of Havana; author of a number of volumes on law and on Colonial history. He was one of the founders and strong advocates of the Autonomist party and a member of the Autonomist cabinet under Spanish Captain General Blanco.

Ramón Grau San Martín (1887-1969)

Cuban physician, professor of physiology at the University of Havana and author of several books in his specialty. He was appointed provisional president in 1933 and elected to the presidency in 1944. Son of a prosperous tobacco grower from Pinar del Rio; travelled extensively through Europe for several years until 1921. Because his support of the university students he was imprisoned in 1931 and upon release went into exile. Ex- cept for accusations of allowing corruption, nepotism and violence he has been considered a good president of Cuba. He died in 1969, at age 82, poor, desolate and feeble after the dissolution of the Cuban Republic in 1959.

Fabio Grobart, aka Antonio Blanco, aka Abraham Simjovitch (1905-1994)

Poland born communist of many aliases that, as a tailors' assistant, became a founding member of the Cuban Communist Party in 1925 with Julio Antonio Mella and Rubén Martínez Villena. For decades he served as a party ideologue and was the man who introduced both Fidel and Raúl Castro at party meetings. He was deported from Cuba in 1930 by Machado and in 1948 by the Prío government; recruited by Ernesto (Ché) Guevara, he returned in 1960 as top party planner. His role in Cuba after 1960 has never been fully documented. It is known, however, that he was the highest ranking representative of the *Third International* in Cuba. He died in Cuba in 1994 at the age of 89.

Rafael Guas Inclán (1896-1975)

Cuban politician, lawyer, graduated from the University of Havana; a lifelong member of the *Liberal Party*. In 1925 was the youngest member of the *Cámara de Representantes*; he presided it until 1933, when Machado was overthrown. Member of the *1940 Constitutional Convention*. Senator, governor of Havana, Minister of Communications, elected VP in the dubious elections of 1954 when Batista was declared elected. A street mob vandalized and burned his office on January 1st 1959 as he left for exile in Miami. His son died in combat at the Bay of Pigs in 1971.

Gonzalo Güell Morales (1895-1985)

Cuban lawyer and career diplomat. Cuban Ambassador to Mexico, Colombia, Brasil, Norway and the UN. Appointed by Batista as Foreign Minister of Cuba from 1956 to 1959 and Prime Minister until the fall of the

Republic (1958-1959). Güell left Cuba with Batista and 40 other people in 1959 and died in Coral Gables, FL, in 1985 at age 90.

Ramiro Guerra (1880-1970)

Cuban historian, economist and educator. He joined the Cuban special course for teachers sponsored by Harvard University in the United States in 1901. Obtained a doctorate in education at the University of Havana in 1912. In 1915 he was appointed director of the *Escuela Normal de La Habana*. He was director of the newspaper *Heraldo de* Cuba between 1930 and 1932, and secretary of the presidency of the republic in 1932 during the dictatorship of Gerardo Machado; this never meant prejudice to its integrity and his love for Cuba and its history. In 1933, after the fall of Machado, he moved to New York and then to Gainesville, Florida, where he completed his work on Cuban history. He represented Cuba at major international events. Between 1943 and 1946 he was editor of the newspaper *Diario de la Marina*. He joined the Cuban Academy of History in 1949. Between 1955 and 1960 supervised the publication of the Lex School Library a collection of books intended as primary textbooks. Died on October 29, 1970, in Havana at age 90.

Antonio Guiteras Holmes (1906-1935)

Cuban revolutionary leader, a strong participant of the 1930 revolution. He was born in Philadelphia, Pennsylvania. Nephew of José Ramón Guiteras, a *mambí* from the first Cuban war of independence in 1868. From the Institute of Pinar del Rio sympathize with Mella and in 1927, as a member of the University Student Directorate (DEU), made its first appearance in the Cuban political scene. In 1932 he broke with the old nationalist leaders and founded the Revolutionary Union (RU). He became part of Grau's cabinet as Minister of the Interior. In June of 1934 he founded *Joven Cuba*. His tactical plan was to organize an expedition from Mexico to launch the armed struggle against Batista. He was denounced by Carmelo Gonzalez, a childhood friend and member of the organization. Guiteras was caught in the *Morrillo*, Matanzas by Lt. Rafael Diaz Joglar, from the Batista Armed Forces, while trying to leave the country. In an unequal battle, he died on 8 May 1935 at age 29. It has always been debated whether or not he was a secret member or even a sympathizer of the Communists.

Juan Blas Hernández (1879-1933)

Colonel Juan Blas Hernández achieved an important role in the 1933 revolution against Gerardo Machado. He was known as *el Sandino de Cuba*, and, from the right, was a political and ideological enemy of Antonio Guiteras. He revolted against Batista and occupied the *Atarés Castle* in 1933 with the help of fellow revolutionaries from the *ABC Party*. Batista employed the weaponry from *Patria*, a Cuban Naval ship, and forced him to surrender; the heavy artillery almost destroyed the 1767 fortress. Upon surrendering Blas Hernández was right away assassinated by the soldiery.

Alberto Herrera Franchi (1874-1954)

Career military man. Chief of the armed forces during the presidency of Gerardo Machado. Member of the Liberal Party. Was assigned by Sumner Welles to be in charge of the government for a day after the fall of Machado in 1933; at the time Colonel José Antonio Jiménez, the head of *La Porra*, was lynched and Ainciart-Raggi, head of the National Police, committed suicide. Herrera died of mysterious causes in Havana at the age of 79, after he publicly rejected the government of Batista in 1954.

Carlos Hevia y de los Reyes (1900-1964)

Cuban surgeon, a graduate from the US Naval Academy at Annapolis in 1919. President of Cuba for three days (January 15 to January 18, 1934) after Fulgencio Batista removed Grau San Martín from the Presidency at the request of the military after the fall of Machado. He had been Minister of Agriculture under Grau. After lots of protocol, including a 21 gun salute during his inauguration, and after been sworn in by his father-in-law (Chief Justice Juan Federico Edelman) Hevia resigned in favor of Carlos Mendieta. During the administration of Carlos Prío Hevia served as Foreign Minister and was the 1952 candidate for president from the *Auténtico* Party. Died in Florida of a heart attack at age 64.

Francisco Ichaso Macías (1900-1962)

Lawyer, political analyst, journalist and former Cuban ambassador to the UN. Member of the 1940 Cuban Constitutional Assembly. His father, León Ichaso, had been Assistant Director of the *Diario de la Marina* newspaper. Paco Ichaso was a member of the *Grupo Minorista* with Martínez Villena, Marinello, Carpentier, Mañach and Fernando Ortiz. He was also a founding member of the *ABC Party*. On the radio he led the *Universidad del Aire* and *Ante la Prensa* programs on the CMQ radio station. In 1960 he went into exile and died in Mexico of a heart attack at age 62.

José Miguel Irizarry Gamio (1895-1968)

Cuban attorney and public man, attorney for the Royal Bank of Canada in the 1920s. He suffered imprisonment during the Machado regime and was member of the ten-day *Pentarquía* Cuban government in 1933. With Porfirio Franca Alvarez, Irizarry resigned from the *Pentarquía*, provoking its demise and the initiation of a new presidential system in Cuba. He had studied law in Spain and Cuba and was an expert in monetary issues and occupied important positions in the post-Machado period in Cuba. Irizarri was always a member of the Conservative party and died in Miami at age 73.

Pedro Ivonet (1880-1912)

Founder, with Evaristo Estenoz, of the first independent black political party in the Americas on August 7, 1908. The *Independientes* were made up of many veterans of African descent in the *Mambí* Army. Ivonet was of Haitian descent and one of the principal leaders of the party. When the 1908 elections were held, none of the black candidates for councilors and directors nominated by either the Liberal or Conservative parties were elected. In 1912 it led to an uprising during the José Miguel Gómez government in which both Estenoz and Ivonet were probably assassinated by government troops.

Alberto Lamar Schweyer (1902-1942)

Journalist and important political activist born in Matanzas with the Republic. In 1918 he began to write for the *Heraldo de Cuba* and the magazines *Social, Cuba Contemporánea, El Mundo, Smart, El Sol* and El Fígaro. His books elicited praise from Enrique José Varona, Max Enriquez Ureña and Rafael Montoro. Lamar was a member of the *Grupo Minoritario*. At the time of his premature death he was director of the afternoon edition of the *El País* newspaper.

Félix Lancís Sánchez (1900-1976)

Cuban physician, writer and politician, three times Senator, Minister of Education and twice Prime Minister from 1944 to 1945 and 1950 to 1951. Founder of the *Partido Auténtico* in 1934. During the government of Carlos Prío he was his right hand supporter in Congress. He was jailed after the interruption of the Republic in 1959 but never left Cuba. Died in Havana, childless, soon after the death of his wife Carmelina Barba de Lancís at the age of 76.

Federico Laredo Bru (1875-1946)

Cuban attorney, VP for Miguel Mariano Gómez; he served as president after Gómez was impeached in 1936. He searched for a reconciliation of the Cuban people and granted amnesties to Machado and all his ministers. His legislation included regulations and laws about pensions, insurance, farming coops and minimum wages. Unfortunately he was falsely accused as the man who turned back the refugees from Hitler aboard the ocean liner *SS St. Louis* in 1939; in reality the man who was trying to profit from their vulnerable situation was a high level government executive who was charging $150 to each refugee for landing permits available only to tourists. Only 29 persons were allowed to disembark.

Alfredo López Arencibia (1894-1926)

Top leader of the workers movement in Cuba in the 1920s. He was born in Sagua la Grande. His father was an Asturian anarchist. From early age he became a typographic worker; his first job was with the *La Mercantil* shop in Havana. He was among the founders of the *Confederación Nacional Obrera de Cuba* (CNOC). In 1925 he shared a jail call with Julio Antonio Mella. In July of 1926, at age 32, he was detained again, tortured and murdered; his corpse was thrown on the moats of the fortress of the Atarés Castle.

Raúl López del Castillo (1893-1963)

Cuban lawyer, writer and politician, Prime Minister of Cuba from 1946 to 1948 during the presidency of Ramón Grau. Member of the *Auténtico* Party. He was preceded by Carlos Prío and succeeded by Antonio de Varona in that position. After the disappearance of the Republic he went into exile in Miami and died in 1963 at age 72.

Enrique Loynaz del Castillo (1871-1963)

Cuban patriot, father of Cuban notable poetess Dulce María Loynaz Muñoz. Brigadier General during the War 95. Author of the lyrics of the Cuban *Himno Invador* (Invader's Anthem). Was Marti's friend and assistant, as well as adjutant of General Antonio Maceo; fought with him in the battle of *Mal Tiempo*. Marti assigned Loynaz to Costa Rica, where he was secretary of Major General Antonio Maceo, and saved his life in the attempt against his life on November 10, 1894, outside a theater in the city of San Jose. In January 1895 he participated in the organization of José Martí's Fernandina Plan. He was representative to the Constituent Assembly Jimaguayú. After the independence of Cuba he was minister plenipotentiary to Mexico, Portugal, Panama, Central America, Santo Domingo, Haiti and Venezuela. He fought the dictatorship of Gerardo Machado and retired from active life in 1947. Loynaz died on February 10, 1963, in Havana

Gerardo Machado y Morales (1871-1939)

One of the youngest of Generals of the Cuban War of Independence in 1895. Fought under José Miguel Gómez and during the Republic became affiliated with the Liberal Party. Became the fifth president of Cuba in 1925. He built many public works in Cuba, sought and secured re-election and was finally thrown out of power by a movement of intellectuals, students, businessmen, revolutionaries, and the American ambassador Sumner Welles, who could not stand his stubbornness in prolonging his presidential term. Machado went into exile in Canada, Europe and finally Miami Beach, where he died at age 68.

Jorge Mañach y Robato (1898-1961)

Cuban attorney, political analyst and writer, educated in Cuba, Spain and France. Harvard graduate in 1920 with a degree in Philosophy. Taught at Columbia University. Member of the *Grupo Minorista*; participated in the *Protesta de los Trece* and in the 1933 revolution. Mañach was one of the founders of the *Revista de Avance* and was Cuban Foreign Minister in 1944. His most important essays and books were *La Crisis de la Alta Cultura* (1925) and *Indagación del Choteo* (1928) and Martí el Apóstol (1933). Mañach was forced by Castro into exile and died in Puerto Rico in 1960 at the age of 62. See page 397.

Juan Marinello Vidaurreta (1898-1977)

Marinello was a lawyer and a leading Cuban communist intellectual and politician. In 1923 founded the *Falange de Acción Cubana*, a Marxist organization, with Rubén Martínez Villena. Later the same year he participated in the *Protesta de los Trece*. With Julio Antonio Mella he joined the *Movimiento de Veteranos y Patriotas* in 1923 during the government of Alfredo Zayas. Machado sent him to exile in Mexico. He was a propagandist for the Republican cause in the Spanish Civil War of 1936. He died in Havana at the age of 79.

Carlos Márquez Sterling Guiral (1898-1991)

Cuban attorney, diplomat, writer, politician and professor of law and economics at the University of Havana where he founded the School of Journalism that bears his uncle's name. Member of the Cuban House of Representatives; Minister of Education and Labor; president of the 1940 *Constitutional Assembly*. He was detained many times by the Batista government before he ran for President in 1958. Al the closing of the Republic he went into exile and died in Miami at age 93. See page 415.

Manuel Márquez Sterling Loret de Mola (1872-1934)

Cuban lawyer, writer and diplomat; ambassador to Mexico and the US. President of Cuba for a few hours on January 18, 1934. Exceptional chess player; tied for 16th in the Paris 1900 Chess Tournament won by Emanuel Lasker. Uncle of Carlos Márquez Sterling. Friend of José Martí; secretary of Gonzalo de Quesada. In 1913, as Cuban ambassador to Mexico, tried unsuccessfully to save the life of President Francisco Madero, who was executed by revolutionary partisans under the leadership of Victoriano Huerta. Márquez Sterling died in Washington at age 62, after participating in the abrogation of the Platt Amendment. See page 174.

Joaquín Martínez Sáenz (1902-1974)

Cuban lawyer, economist and politician. He served as Senator, Minister of the Treasury, Minister of Agriculture and President of the *Banco Nacional* in 1952. In September 1931 he had founded the ABC, a right-leaning movement that contributed to the fall of the Machado government. He became famous in the US for a .38 caliber pistols duel with his nemesis Oscar de la Torre where both men ended up firing into the air. Martínez Saenz was a member of the 1940 Cuban Constituent Assembly. He died in exile at age 72.

Rubén Martínez Villena (1899-1934)

Cuban lawyer, poet, writer and revolutionary leader; led the *Protesta de los Trece* in 1923 during the government of Zayas and was a founding member of the *Grupo Minorista*. Founder of the Cuban Communist Party with Julio Antonio Mella. After contracting tuberculosis in the late 1920s he traveled to the Soviet Union and in 1932 returned to Cuba seriously ill. He participated in the organization of the general strike that ended the government of Gerardo Machado in 1933. On June 16, 1934, he died of his illness in Havana at age 35.

Rolando Masferrer Rojas (1918-1975)

Cuban politician, congressman, newspaper editor of *El Tiempo* and *bona fide* gangster; he was an early member of *Joven Cuba*, the far-left organization founded by Antonio Guiteras in 1934. Masferrer participated in the Lincoln Brigades during the Spanish Civil War in 1936 and was a member of the Cuban Communist Party. In 1975 he wrote an editorial in his Miami newspaper *Libertad* condoning terrorism. He died at age 57 in Miami, victim of a bomb placed in his car.

Salvador Massip Valdés (1891-1978)

Eminent geographer; Doctor of Pedagogy and Philosophy at the University of Havana and Master of Arts from the Faculty of Pure Sciences of Columbia University; Professor Emeritus at the University of Havana. In 1912 he began his teaching activities as an assistant professor of anthropology at the Faculty of Sciences of the University of Havana and later as Professor of Geography at the Institute of Matanzas and the Faculty of Arts at the University of Havana and at Smith College in Puerto Rico. For his part in the strike of March 1935 he was arrested and deported to Mexico, where he served as Professor at the National Autonomous University. At the fall of the Gerardo Machado government he was appointed Ambassador of Cuba in Mexico. He died in Havana at age 87.

Bartolomé Masó Márquez (1830-1907)

General en Jefe of the Cuban Independence Army in 1895; an occasional writer and politician. In 1851 became an enemy of the Spanish authorities for his vigorous protest for the execution of Narciso López. As a result he spent time in the Santiago de Cuba jail. Masó was of the first who joined Céspedes and Aguilera at *La Demajagua* and *Yara*. In 1895 he proclaimed the independence of Cuba at *Bayate*, following the leadership of José Martí. Elected President in Arms of the Republic of Cuba at the *Jimaguayú Assembly*. He withdrew his candidature for the presidency of Cuba after the island became independent. Died in Manzanillo at age 77. See page 131.

Julio Antonio Mella (1903-1929)

Born Nicanor McPartland —after his mother— in 1903. Studied at *Chandler College* in Havana and the *Colegio de los Escolapios* in Guanabacoa, finally graduating from the *Instituto de la Habana* in 1921. After starting at the University of Havana was expelled accused of terrorism in 1925. In the 1920s founded the Cuban Communist Party —with Mella, Marinello, Baliño, Peña, Roca, Martínez Villena, Escalante, Roig and Grobart— during the presidency of Machado. The party later changed its name to *Partido Socialista Popular (PSP)*. Exiled in Mexico he became friends with Diego Rivera and the lover of Tina Modotti, a Russian infiltrate. He was killed in Mexico by Vittorio Vidale, a Trotskyist and earlier Modotti lover.

Domingo Méndez Capote (1863-1934)

Cuban lawyer, politician, intellectual and military man; fought in the war under Máximo Gómez, reaching the rank of Brigade General and his Chief of Staff in 1897. VP of the Cuban Republic at Arms in 1898, President of the 1901 Cuban Constitutional Convention. VP of the Republic of Cuba from 1904 to 1906 and president of the revolutionary junta that oversaw the fall of Machado in 1933. Died in Havana at age 91.

Renée Méndez Capote (1901-1989)

Daughter of Domingo Méndez Capote. She received general education classes in her paternal home with Swiss and English governesses and also French, Italian and English. She traveled to Paris in the *Morro Castle* to take a position at the Consulate and during the voyage the ship caught fire. She was accused of being the cause of it because her career as a Communist agitator. In Cuba she was imprisoned after the failed March 1935 strike organized by Guiteras' *Joven Cuba*, the *ABC* and the Communists to topple Batista. Took part in the underground resistance movement against the Batista tyranny in 1957 and was probably the best example in Cuba of the *Velvet Left*, those multimillionaires that spouse leftist and Marxists ideals. Died in Havana at age 88 after multiple services to the Communist regime.

Carlos Mendieta y Montefur (1873-1960)

Colonel in the War of Independence of 1895, provisional President of the Republic from 1934 to 1935, after Batista forced Grau San Martín to resign. Elected to the House in Cuba for 22 consecutive years starting in 1902. He was president of Cuba during the abrogation of the Platt Amendment. He was criticized strongly for his repression to strikes during his presidency. Resigned in 1935 and was replaced by José A. Barnet Vinajeras. Died in Havana at age 87.

Jesús Menéndez Larrondo (1911-1948)

Cuban sugar labor leader, General Secretary of the *Federación Nacional Obrera Azucarera*, known as the *General de las Cañas*. The man most responsible for the so called *ley del diferencial azucarero* (see pages 325 and 362). In 1940 became alternate delegate for the Constitutional Convention. Communist and member of the PSP. Member of the House of Representatives. In January 1948 he was murdered in Manzanillo as he resisted arrest on the basis of his parliamentary immunity. He was 37 years old.

Rafael Montoro Valdés (1852-1933)

Cuban lawyer, historian and literary critic. Studied at the Colegio El Salvador in Havana and at the school system of the city of New York. In Cuba was a disciple of Henry Piñeyro, Juan Clemente Zenea and Antonio Zambrana in Havana and Don Juan Valera in Madrid. In 1878 he founded the *Liberal Party* (Autonomist), for which he became its main ideologue for nearly twenty years. At the inauguration of the Republic, he served as Minister Plenipotentiary of Cuba in England and Germany during the presidency of Tomás Estrada Palma. In 1908 he was a candidate for VP with the *Conservative Party* and three years later served as Secretary of the Presidency under President Mario Garcia Menocal. He served as Secretary of State during the presidency of Alfredo Zayas y Alfonso. He died in Havana on August 14, 1933, at age 81.

Menelao Mora Morales (1905-1957)

Cuban lawyer and politician. Fought against Machado and became a militant of the ABC. Participated in the 1935 strike; he was detained, accused of terrorism and sent into exile in the US. In Cuba was secretary and chief executive of the *Cooperativa de Omnibus Aliados* (Havana public transportation buses). Became a member of the PRC (A) and served several periods as Representative. Was killed in Havana during the attempted magnicide against Batista on March 13, 1957.

Andrés Domingo Morales del Castillo (1892-1979)

Cuban lawyer, judge and politician; Senator from 1944 to 1952, Minister of the Presidency, Justice, Housing, Defense and Foreign Relations, and temporary President in 1954, when Batista wanted to run for President under very questionable circumstances. He was to be the last candidate for President in Cuba under even more problematic elections in 1959, when the insurgents were coming down from the *Sierra Maestra*. Morales never married and died in exile in Miami at age 87.

Martín Morúa Delgado (1856-1910)

Black Cuban writer, literary critic, translator and publisher, son of slaves and the first black president of the Cuban Senate in 1909. Morúa was self-taught, a prolific reader and fluent in several languages, including English, French, Italian and Spanish. He was elected to the 1901 Cuban Constitutional Assembly and served as Minister of Agriculture. He was the author of the celebrated *Morúa Law* that prohibited organizing political parties based on ethnicity. He died while serving as Minister, in Havana, at age 54.

José Miró Cardona (1902-1974)

Cuban lawyer, professor of the Universities of Havana and Puerto Rico, civic leader of the opposition against Batista in the late 1950s, Prime Minister briefly in 1959 and Ambassador to Spain in 1960. After breaking with Castro, he sought refuge in the Argentine embassy in Havana and went into exile in early 1961. He was a liaison between Cuban rebels and the US during the Kennedy administration and the Bay of Pigs invasion. As the invasion failed to achieve its objectives, Miró —whose son had disembarked in Cuba— denounced the CIA and John F. Kennedy for their failure to provide the promised support. He died in San Juan, PR, at age 72.

Emilio Nuñez (1855-1922)

Cuban soldier, military strategist, dentist and politician, a graduate of the University of Pennsylvania. He participated in the Cuban War of Independence of 1868 and attained the rank of Colonel. Nuñez became a good friend of José Martí and, during the War of 1895, became the chief of artillery and weapons as well as an organizer of expeditions. Member of the 1901 Constitutional Assembly, governor of Havana and the man who first raised the Cuban flag at *El Morro*, at noon, on May 20, 1902. He served as

Minister of Agriculture, Commerce and Labor in 1913 and VP of Cuba during the Menocal days, 1917 to 1921. Died in Havana at age 79.

Emilio Nuñez Portuondo (1898-1978)

Son of General Emilio Nuñez. Lawyer, politician and diplomat. Prime Minister of Cuba in 1958. Graduate of the University of Havana. Member of the House and the Senate for Las Villas province. Brother of Ricardo Nuñez Portuondo, Cuban presidential candidate in 1948. Ambassador to Panama, Perú, Holland, Belgium and Luxembourg. Member and secretary of the 1940 Cuban Constitutional Convention. Ambassador to the UN and president of the UN Security Council in 1956, during the Soviet invasion of Hungary, which he vigorously condemned. Died in exile in Panamá at age 80.

Emilio Ochoa y Ochoa (1907-2007)

Cuban politician, dentist and college professor. Member of the *1940 Cuban Constitutional Convention* —and its longest surviving signatory. Founder of the *Partido Auténtico* in 1934 and the *Partido Ortodoxo* in 1947. Served as Senator of the Republic from 1940 to 1948. Was arrested 32 times because of his political opposition —first to Batista and later to Castro. Went into exile in 1960; practiced dentistry until 1965; taught in Nebraska and Chicago until 1971 and retired to Miami to live his last days with rather modest means. Probably one of the most scrupulously honest politicians from Cuba. Died in Miami of cardiac arrest at age 99.

Arsenio Ortiz (1872-193?)

Officer of the Cuban Army, veteran lieutenant of the 1895 War, a presumed assassin of Pedro Ivonet in 1912 who became the right hand man of Gerardo Machado in the 1930s. His nickname was the *Chacal de Oriente* (the jackal from Oriente). At one point in time Congress pardoned him for 44 murders committed while Chief of Police in Oriente province. Presumably he was the assassin that took the life of Senator Clemente Vázquez Bello There are conflicting reports about Arsenio Ortiz' final days. Some say he fled the island in 1933 in the same airplane that was used by Machado. Other that he had been sent by Machado to Germany to learn from the Nazis. A third that he was lynched in Cuba in 1933 by an uncontrolled mob.

Fernando Ortiz Fernández (1881-1969)

Cuban Anthropologist, lawyer, archeologist, journalist, diplomat, criminologist, ethnologist, linguist, economist, historian and geographer. He has been called the third discoverer of Cuba after Colon and Humboldt. Studied in Havana, Barcelona, Rome and Madrid. Member of Congress in 1919; exiled in Washington from 1931 to 1933. Founder of several magazines: *El Eco de la Cátedra, Revista Bimestre Cubana, Revista del Folklore Cubano, Surcos, Ultra* and others. Coined the term *transculturation* in social studies. Died in Havana at age 90. See page 249.

José Pardo Llada (1923-2009)

Cuban journalist, politician, diplomat and radio personality. Attended the *University of Havana* but never graduated. In 1944 became famous while informing the public through CMQ radio of an impending hurricane during three consecutive days. Was a consummate critic of the government of Ramón Grau, at 1:00 pm through Union Radio, at the time the program with the largest audience in Cuba. His most famous slogan was «*que desparpajo señores.*» (gentlemen, what an imprudence!). He was elected several times for public positions in Colombia after leaving Cuba and died in Bogotá as an exile from Castro at age 86.

Genovevo Pérez Dámera (1910-1983)

Chief of the Cuban army from 1945 to 1949 during the government of Ramón Grau San Martín. He never got along with Carlos Prío and was replaced as Chief of the Army at the request of a group of officers, by General Ruperto Cabrera. He later became Senator for Pinar del Rio and finally left Cuba and died very poor in exile.

Carlos Manuel Piedra y Piedra (1895-1988)

The person occupying the presidency in Cuba for the shortest time, a few hours, during the transition Batista-Castro. He was at the time the oldest judge in the Cuban Supreme Court; the provisional Junta formed after Batista fled, presided by General Eulogio Cantillo, tried to appoint him was was met with the opposition from Castro. He died in exile at age 93.

Guillermo Portela Möller (1886-1958)

Lawyer and faculty member at the Law School of the *University of Havana*. In 1933, he was a member of the Executive Commission of the Provisional Government of Cuba, also known as *La Pentarquía*. He was in charge of supervising the functions of the Department of State and the Department of Justice during the short period of life of the *Pentarquía*. Died in Havana at age 72.

Antonio Prío Socarrás (1905-1990)

Cuban banker and Minister of Housing during the government of his brother Carlos Prío. In 1950 ran for mayor of Havana and, in one of the cleanest elections in Cuba, lost to Nicolás Castellanos, who had been Vice Mayor during the time of Manuel Supervielle as Mayor. Died in exile in Miami at age 85.

Carlos Prío Socarrás (1903-1977)

Lawyer, student leader, elected Senator for Pinar del Rio in 1940 and elected president of Cuba in 1948. Served as Minister of Public Works, Minister of Labor and Prime Minister in the Grau government. Lifetime member and founder of the Partido Auténtico in Cuba. Presided over a time of constitutional order and political freedom in Cuba. He was called *el Presidente Cordial* for his civility, accessibility and friendliness. He was credited by Arthur M. Schlesinger to say «*They say I was a terrible president of Cuba but I certainly was the best president Cuba ever had.*» He died in Miami, apparently of a self-inflicted gunshot at age 74.

Guillermo Alonso Pujol (1896-1968)

Cuban Politician, Senator and Senate President of the Republic in 1940, founder of the *Republican Party* in 1944; he united his forces to those of the *Auténticos* to elect Grau San Martin in 1944 with the *Authentic- Republican Coalition* against Carlos Saladrigas, Batista's candidate. He succeded as VP candidate with Carlos Prío in 1948 and broke with him almost immediately after becoming Vice-President of Cuba. They defeated Nuñez Portuondo, *the Liberal-Democra*tic candidate and Zoilo Marinello, the *Communist candidate* who, with his brother Juan, were the wealthy owners of a small fortune in Cuba.

Gonzalo de Quesada (1868-1915)

Lawyer, diplomat, writer, activist and key architect of Cuban Independence. Friend of José Martí; born in Havana, educated at *City College of New York* and *Columbia University*. An indispensable representative of the Cuban revolutionaries in the US during the War of Independence of 1895. In 1900 became Special Commissioner of Cuba to the US; in 1901 became a member of the *Cuban Constitutional Assembly*, in 1915 became ambassador to Germany. Died in Berlin of a heart attack at age 47.

Miguel Angel Quevedo (1896-1969)

Editor and proprietor of the popular weekly magazine *Bohemia*, widely read in Cuba and all Latin America. The magazine had been founded by his father in 1908; Miguel Angel (son) took over in 1927 a year before the death of Quevedo Sr. During the government of Carlos Prío (1948-1952) the magazine became his inexhaustible opponent. Quevedo later joined the cause of Fidel Castro and supported his movement to unseat Batista. Frustrated by the communist fervor of Castro, who confiscated his magazine in 1960, he went into exile and took his life at age 73.

Erasmo Regueiferos Boudet (1890-1958)

Lawyer and politician, former member of the Advisory Law Commission appointed by Governor Maroon during the provisional American government in Cuba in 1906; an eminent man of letters. Member of the *Liberal Party* of Alfredo Zayas. Later member of his Cabinet as Minister of Justice. He was the target of the dissenters in the *Protesta de los Trece* in 1923. After that event *The New York Times* came in his defense by saying «unaware of the serious harm caused by his gesture, he signed a decree that inadvertently concealed illicit, repellent and awkward business, not worthy of this moral condition.» Regueiferos died in Havana at age 68.

Juan Rius Rivera (1848-1924)

General of the Cuban Independence Army after the death of Antonio Maceo. Born in Mayagüez, PR., from a wealthy coffee-farming family. Studied in Barcelona and Madrid. Friend of Ramón Emeterio Betances. Participated in the War of 1868 and fought under Máximo Gómez. Married Estrada Palma's sister. Was made prisoner by the Spaniards and deported to a prison in Monjuich, Barcelona. He was secretary of the Presidency, Governor of Havana and Secretary of Agriculture. Died of a heart attack in Honduras on an official mission at the age of 76.

Andrés Rivero Agüero (1905-1996)

Cuban lawyer, writer and politician, elected president two months before the dissolution of the Republic in 1958. Never took possession. Graduated from the *University of Havana*, member of the *Liberal Party*. In 1940 was Minister of Agriculture; after 1952 Minister of Education, Senator and Prime Minister. After January 1, 1959 he went into exile and died in Miami at age 91.

Horacio Rubens (1870-1935)

American Lawyer friend of José Martí; participated in the Independence War of 1895 from Washington and New York, where he became Martí's lawyer and fund-raiser for the War; received the rank of Colonel. Very good friend of Gonzalo de Quesada. Both were graduates from *Columbia University*. In 1905 built a palace in Mariel, Pinar del Rio, to be the home of a Casino that was never authorized. The palace became the main building of the Cuban Naval Academy. After the independence of Cuba Rubens was involved in several businesses in Cuba. Died in New York at age 65.

Carlos Saladrigas Zayas (1900-1956)

Cuban lawyer, politician and diplomat. Served as Senator in 1936, Minister of Justice in 1934, Foreign Minister in 1933 and 1956, Prime Minister from 1940 to 1942 and Ambassador to Great Britain. After serving as Batista's Prime Minister he became the presidential candidate for Batista's party in 1944; he lost to Ramón Grau San Martín and the *Auténticos*. Died at his home in Havana at age 55.

Aureliano Sánchez Arango (1907-1976)

Cuban lawyer, university professor and politician. Active during the fights against Machado. Founding member of the Partido Auténtico. Minister of Education and Foreign Minister during the government of Carlos Prío. Took the road to exile in Mexico in 1952 and later participated in several underground movements against Batista. In 1958 financed the movement against Batista by Castro and later had to seek asylum in the US. Died of a heart attack in Miami at age 69.

Manuel Sanguily Garritt (1848-1925)

A student of José de la Luz y Caballero in the *Colegio El Salvador*; brother of Major General Julio Sanguily. Participated briefly in the war of 1895 and was a member of the *Asamblea de Santa Cruz*; went to the US in 1899 with Calixto García Commission to secure retirement payments to the *Mambises*. In 1901 began his public career as member of the *Constitutional Convention*. President of the Senate and was a Senator for Matanzas, Director of the *Instituto de la Habana*, Secretary of State in the government of Gómez. Died in Havana at age 77.

Emeterio Santovenia Echaide (1889-1968)

Cuban historian, journalist, politician and writer. In 1907 he wrote his first article in the *Diario de la Marina*, gaining fame under the pseudonym M.Terio. In 1914 he became a member of the Liberal Party and in 1916 was elected member of the Academy of History of Cuba. In 1920 he graduated in law at the University of Havana. In 1930 during the dictatorship of Gerardo Machado joined the secret organization ABC, which would help him to be elected senator in 1940. He was designated as chairman of the Political Law Committee. In 1934 he was secretary of the Presidency of Carlos Mendieta, traveling in Europe through Spain, Italy, Switzerland, France and Belgium. In 1943 he held the post of Minister of Foreign Affairs during the government of Fulgencio Batista. In 1952 working with Ramiro Guerra, José M. Pérez Cabrera, and Juan J Remos, he co-authored the monumental ten-volume work *History of the Cuban Nation*. In 1959 he went into exile, and died in Miami, at age 79.

Manuel Fernández Supervielle (1894-1947)

See Manuel Fernández Supervielle.

Policarpo Soler (1908-1961)

Gansgter *aka* Domingo Herrera. He dressed as a police lieutenant throughout the Batista presidency and in 1944 went into exile in Mexico where he met Orlando León Lemus (el Colorado), another Cuban gangster, also exiled in Mexico because the events in *Orfila* on September 1947 (see page 346). Returning to Cuba in 1948 he participated in numerous attacks as part of the *—muchachos del gatillo alegre.* (the trigger-happy boys). After he was taken into custody he escaped the *El Principe* prison, traveled to Spain and the Dominican Republic where he was shot in 1961 by Trujillo bodyguards at age 53.

Diego Vicente Tejera (1848-1903)

Cuban patriot, poet, journalist, essayist and literary critic. He studied at the *Seminary of St. Basil the Great*, in Santiago de Cuba, leaving before becoming a priest. In February of 1868 he participated in the independence movement in Puerto Rico under the leadership of Ramón Emeterio Betances. After the failure of the *Grito de Lares*, he moved to Venezuela with Betances, returning to Cuba after the *Zanjón Pact*. At age 37 he met José Martí and traveled to Cuba to inaugurate the Tomás Terry Theatre in Cienfuegos. He participated in efforts to create the first *Cuban Socialist Party*, which was founded May 22, 1899 but was dissolved after six months of existence. In 1900, after a further attempt to establish this party failed, he announced his final separation from political activities. At age 55, he died of an incurable disease.

Cosme de la Torriente Peraza (1872-1956)

Veteran of the War of 1995, under the command of Major General Calixto Garcia. He was elected representative to the *Constitutional Assembly of La Yaya*, where he was very active in drafting the constitution which was approved on October 29, 1897. Participated in the siege of Santiago de Cuba. On August 18, 1898 was promoted to Colonel and fought again with Calixto Garcia. He accompanied García on his trip to Washington to manage the recognition of the House of Representatives of the Cuban Revolution by the U.S. government, as well as to procure a loan to pay the members of the Independence Army. In 1901 he was a judge in the province of Matanzas and in July 25, 1903, was appointed first secretary of the legation of Cuba in Spain. From May 20, 1913 to January 10, 1914 he served as Cuban Secretary of State. In 1934 he was president of the *National Association of Independence Army Veterans* . He held several political offices during the first years of the Republic. In the 1950's, during the dictatorship of Fulgencio Batista, he chaired the *Association of Friends of the Republic*, an organization founded to seek a mediation between the dictator and the traditional political opposition. He died in Havana in 1956.

Pablo de la Torriente Brau (1901-1936)

Born in Puerto Rico of Spanish parents. After traveling to Cuba he began to collaborate in the *New World Journal* and the magazine *El Veterano* with a new style of journalism that many years later was called *literary journalism*; he was one of its precursors in Cuba. In 1923 he began working as a typist and he met Don Fernando Ortiz and a young law student named Rubén Martínez Villena, among other extraordinary men. His story *The Hero* was published in 1928 in the *Diario de la Marina* with the help of Martínez Villena and José Antonio Fernández de Castro. In 1931 he was taken prisoner to the *El Principe* Castle prison for his opposition to Machado, and later to the *Presidio Modelo* in *Isla de Pinos*, where he remained two years. In 1933 he went into exile in New York. On July 18, 1936 the Spanish Civil War broke out and he became obsessed with the idea of going to Spain. On November 29, 1936, he fell mortally wounded in *Majadahonda*, while serving as a member of staff of the 109th battalion of the seventh division of the Republican forces.

Quirino Uría, M.M.N.P., (1907-1984)

Chief of the *Columbia Military Camp* during the governments of Grau San Martín and Carlos Prío. In 1949 he was promoted to four stars Brigadier General and appointed *Chief of the National Police* substituting José M. Caramés. Uría became famous for his war against gangsterism. Within days of his appointment to the police he arrested members of the *Movimiento Socialista Revolucionario (MSR)* and the *Unión Insurreccional Revolucionaria (UIR)*, led by Policarpo Soler and Orlando León Lemus (El Colorado), as well as others in the —*most wanted*‖ lists. Uría was asked by Batista to be part of the March 10, 1952 coup and lead the Cuban Army afterwards. He firmly declined. On the day of the *coup* he was detained, removed from the base and sent into exile. He died in the US at age 77.

Enrique José Varona (1849-1933)

Cuban writer, philosopher, teacher and lecturer. Participated in the War of 1868; after the Pact of Zanjón became an autonomist and was elected to the Cortes in Spain. Wrote in numerous publications: *El Libre Pensamiento, La Habana Elegante, La Ilustración Cubana* and *La Revista Cubana*. Good friend of Martí and editor of the newspaper *Patria*. During the US occupation was Secretary of the Treasury and Secretary of Education and the Arts. Founder of the *Conservative Party*; VP during the term of Menocal. Founder of the *FEU* at the *University of Havana* in 1923. Died at his home in Havana at age 84.

Manuel Antonio de Varona y Loredo (1908-1992)

Cuban lawyer and politician. Served as Senator and Prime Minister during the Carlos Prío government. Member of *Organización Auténtica*. Was director of the *Brigade 2506* who attempted to overthrow Castro in 1961. In 1961 the *New York Times* called him «*Cuba's perennial rebel.*» He had been arrested at 16 for the first time, for taking part in anti-government activities during the presidency of Alfredo Zayas. In 1938 he became a lawyer upon graduation from the *University of Havana*. Varona spent time in jail during the governments of Machado and Batista. He was one of the first Castro opponents in 1959. Varona died in exile in Miami at age 84.

Clemente Vázquez Bello (1886-1932)

Cuban lawyer and politician, president of the Senate in Cuba during the presidency of his good friend Gerardo Machado. Vázquez Bello was murdered by a passing car in front of his home in Country Club, Havana. Within hours it is said that Machado followers made an attempt on the lives of Doctors Ricardo Dolz and Miguel Angel Aguilar, anti-Machado leaders, and murdered brothers Gonzalo, Guillermo and Leopoldo Freyre de Andrade, in their own home. The cemetery mausoleum where Vázquez Bello was to be interred had been loaded with enough dynamite to blow up the entire neighborhood; it was said that the dynamite load was in expectation of a large contingent of government officials in attendance at the funeral.

José Ramón Villalón (1864-1938)

Lieutenant Colonel in the 1895 War of Independence. Disembarked in Cuba with one of the expeditions of *The Three Friends*. Engineer by profession, a graduate from *Lehigh University*. Brought with him in 1896 a *Simms-Dudley pneumatic cannon*, the first used anywhere in the world, having participated in its design. Member of the *Santa Cruz Asssembly*; traveled with Calixto García to the US in 1899; member of the *1901 Constitutional Assembly*. He was appointed Secretary of Public Works in 1899 and was elected Representative from Pinar del Rio in 1900. He was also Secretary of Public Works during the Republic, from 1903 to 1917, and was a Senator from 1921 to 1929. Died at age 74.

Enrique Villuendas de la Torre (1874-1905)

Cuban lawyer, politician and member of the Armed Forces, reaching the position of *Chief of Staff* for José Miguel Gómez. Reached the war in Cuba in one of the expeditions of the *Labrada*. Was one of the members of the Commission from the *Asamblea de Santa Cruz* to Washington DC presided by Calixto García. Delegate from Las Villas to the *1901 Constitutional Assembly*; member of the House of Representatives from 1902 to 1904. Died in the hands of a policeman while at a Hotel in Cienfuegos at age 31 during the presidency of Tomás Estrada Palma.

Alfredo Zayas Alfonso (1861-1934)

Cuban lawyer, poet and politician. Brother of Juan Bruno Zayas, a revolutionary hero. Co-Editor of the journal *Cuba Literaria*; served a prison term in Ceuta during the 1895 war. He was mayor of Havana, Secretary of the *1901 Constitutional Convention*, Senator, President of the Senate, VP and President of Cuba from 1921 to 1925. During his term he started the process of granting the right to vote to women. Long time leader of the Liberal Party. He was known by the nickname —el Chino,‖ for his patience and careful analysis of issues. He died in Havana at age 73.

Rogerio Zayas-Bazán y Ramírez (1876-1931)

A veteran of the 1895-1898 War of Independence, born in exile in the Dominican Republic at the end of the Ten Year War (1868-1878). During the war he was wounded in the *Ceja de la Larga* combat. He was a descendant of one of the oldest Cuban families; was elected from Camagüey to the Senate and the Governorship. Served as Secretary of the Interior during the first Machado period and became widely known for his serious efforts to eradicate gambling and prostitution in Cuba. On July 14, 1931, he was murdered by a former friend turned political enemy.

Ramón Zaydín y Márquez-Sterling (1895-1968)

Cuban lawyer and politician. A very lucid and charismatic professor at the *University of Havana*, cousin of Carlos Márquez Sterling; Prime Minister of Cuba between 1942 and 1944; Member of the *1940 Constitutional Convention*; Senator for Camagüey; member of the Cuban delegation to the UN; VP candidate when Carlos Saladrigas was the presidential candidate in 1944. Lost to the *Auténticos'* Grau San Martín and Raúl de Cárdenas. Died in Madrid at age 73.

V —Alphabetical Index

1
1901 Constitutional Assembly, 209, 470, 482
1940 Constitution, 318, 332, 354, 423, 425, 459
1940 Constitutional Assembly, 272, 470, 479

8
8 Hours Day, 270

A
ABC 253, 270, 271, 272, 318, 333, 476, 479, 481
Academy of Arts and Sciences, 157
Academy of History, 157
Acción Republicana, 271
Agrarian Reform, 355
Aguilera, 19, 473, 480
Alberto Herrera, 268, 476
Alberto Lamar Schweyer, 477
Aldama, 15, 19
Alejo Cossío del Pino, 355
Alfredo López, 477
Alfredo Zayas, 104, 157, 159, 160, 457, 463, 478, 484, 487, 488
Partido Comunista de Cuba, 272
Antonio Guiteras 253, 271, 473, 476, 479
Antonio Maceo, 103, 473, 474, 484
Archivo Nacional, 318
Arturo del Pino, 253
Asociación de Hacendados de Cuba, 333

B
Banco Nacional de Cuba, 354
Baraguá, 16, 20
Bartolomé Masó, 101, 462, 480
Blas Roca, 272, 470
Botellas, 211, 333

C
Calixto García, 14, 158, 160, 318, 468, 473, 485, 488
Capitol, 20, 231, 333
Carlos Baliño, 468
Carlos Hevia, 253, 269, 270, 318, 464, 476
Carlos Manuel de Céspedes, 268, 462, 464, 469, 470, 474
Carlos Mendieta, 232, 271, 465, 476, 480
Carlos Prío Socarrás, 269, 334, 459, 466, 483
Carrera Jústiz, 269
casquitos, 378
Catholic Church, 71, 425
Caudillismo, 156, 231
Caudillos, 72
Chambelona, 158, 232
Charles E. Magoon, 103
Colonos, 270, 333
Columbia, 269, 270, 272, 357, 374, 375, 378, 478, 484, 485, 487
Comisión Consultiva, 103, 209
Comisión de Fomento Nacional, 318
Comunistas, 316, 317
Confederación de Trabajadores Cubanos (CTC), 272
Conservadores, 232
Convento Santa Clara, 210
Cosme de la Torriente, 158, 232, 268, 377
Cuartel Goicuría, 375
Cuba Ports Company, 157
Cuban Army, 15, 269, 470, 472, 482

D
Dance of the Millions, 159
Diálogo cívico, 377
Diálogo Cívico, 425
Diego Vicente Tejera, 15
Directorio Estudiantil Universitario, 253, 269
Directorio Revolucionario, 424, 471
Domingo del Monte, 19

E
Eduardo Chibás, 268, 269, 318, 332, 334, 355, 467
El Morrillo, 271
Emeterio Santovenia, 318
Emilio (Millo) Ochoa, 334
Emilio Nuñez, 482
Emilio Nuñez Portuondo, 482
Encomiendas, 72
Enoch Crowder, 103, 209, 210

Enrique Hernández Miyares, 209
Enrique José Varona, 158, 210, 232, 473, 477, 487
Enrique Loynaz del Castillo, 159, 232
Enrique Villuendas, 103, 488
Erasmo Regueiferos, 210, 484
Escuela Profesional de Periodismo, 318
Estenoz-Ivonet, 232

F

Fabio Grobart, 468, 475
Faustino (Pino) Guerra, 103
Federación de Estudiantes Universitarios (FEU), 211
Federico Laredo Bru, 211, 271, 458, 466, 477
Félix Lancís, 477
Fernando Ortiz, 482
Francisco Ichaso, 476
Francisco Peraza, 253
Francisco Tabernilla, 375
Franklin, 494

G

Galimatías, 319
Genovevo Pérez, 483
Gerardo Machado, 212, 252, 266, 267, 457, 464, 476, 478, 479, 482, 487
Gonzalo de Quesada, 14, 15, 479, 484, 485
Guantánamo Naval Base, 159
Guardia Rural, 103
Guas Inclán, 474, 475
Guillermo Alonso Pujol, 318, 334, 356
Guillermo Belt, 268
Guillermo Portela, 269, 483
Gustavo Cuervo Rubio, 317, 334, 470

H

Hay-Quesada Treaty, 211
Hispano-Cuban-American War, 20, 454
Horacio Rubens, 485
Hotel Nacional, 269

J

J.P. Morgan, 210
Jesús Menéndez, 333, 481
Jimaguayú, 16
Joaquín Ordoqui, 272
Jorge Mañach, 272, 478
jornada gloriosa del 1 de Junio, 332
José A. Barnet, 458, 465, 481
José Antonio Echeverría, 376, 471
José Arce, 468
José Irrizari, 269
José Manuel Casanova, 333
José Martí, 19, 209, 334, 462, 468, 470, 471, 472, 473, 474, 479, 480, 482, 484
José Miguel Gómez, 103, 104, 156, 157, 158, 232, 271, 319, 456, 463, 471, 474, 477, 478, 488
Juan Bruno Zayas, 209, 488
Juan Gualberto Gómez, 232, 473
Juan Marinello, 272, 334, 478
Juan Ríus Rivera, 101
Julio Antonio Mella, 457, 468, 473, 475, 478, 479, 480
Justo Carrillo, 269

K

Kukine, 375

L

Laredo Bru, 268, 271, 317, 472
Lázaro Cárdenas, 272
Leopoldo Cancio, 158
Ley del Cincuenta por Ciento, 270
Ley Tarafa, 211
Liberales, 232, 316
Library of Congress, 20
Lottery, 102, 211
Luis Estévez Romero, 102
Luz y Caballero, 19, 209, 485

M

Machadistas, 254, 317
Magoon, 156, 456, 462
Maine, 158, 454, 456
Mambí, 101
Mambises, 20, 485
Manuel Pérez Serantes, 376
Manuel Sanguily, 210, 485
Mario García Menocal, 156, 157, 252, 457, 463, 472
Márquez Sterling, 479, 488
Martín Morúa, 481
Martinez Sáenz, 268
Martínez Sáenz, 272, 318
Marxist, 447, 449, 478
Matanzas, 271, 375, 454, 468, 471, 473, 477, 485
Máximo Gómez, 14, 15, 103, 472, 474, 480, 484
Méndez Capote, 103, 212, 455, 480
Menelao Mora, 377, 481
Miami, 377, 426, 448, 467, 470, 473, 474, 475, 477, 478, 479, 481, 482, 483, 484, 485, 487

Miguel Mariano Gómez, 252, 271, 458, 465, 474, 477
Miró Cardona, 481
Movimiento 26 de Julio, 424

N
Nacionalista, 101
New York Times, 157, 460, 484, 487
New York Tribune, 494
Nicolas Castellanos, 356
Nuñez Portuondo, 482

P
Padres Escolapios, 160
Pardo Llada, 483
Partido Independiente de Color, 157
Partido Moderado, 103
Partido Revolucionario Cubano, 209, 270, 334
Pentarquía, 269, 458, 469, 472, 477, 483
Pistolero, 334
Policarpo Soler, 486, 487
Porfirio Franca, 269, 472, 477
Presidente Cordial, 354, 483
Protesta de los Trece, 210, 478, 479, 484

Q
Quirino Uría, 357, 487

R
Radio Reloj, 375, 377
Rafael María de Mendive, 19
Rafael Trejo, 252
Ramiro Valdés Daussá, 269
Ramón Zaydin, 318, 488
Raúl de Cárdenas, 268, 318, 488
Republicano, 101, 318, 472
Retiro Azucarero, 318
Rivero Agüero, 484
Roberto Agramonte, 467
Roberto Fernández Miranda, 375
Rolando Masferrer, 479
Roosevelt, 102, 103, 253, 272, 458, 472
Rubén Martínez Villena, 210, 475, 478, 479

S
Saco, 19, 102
Saladrigas, 210, 268, 318, 319, 459, 485, 488
Sánchez Arango, 485
Sergio Carbó, 253, 269, 270, 469
Socialism, 449
Socialist Democratic Coalition, 316
Sociedad de Amigos de la República, 377
Sociedad Económica de Amigos del País, 20, 318
Speyer and Company, 102
Sumner Welles, 268, 270, 458, 476, 478
Supervielle, 472, 483, 486

T
US Ambassador, 210
Tomás Estrada Palma, 101, 456, 462, 463, 471, 488
Tony Varona, 269
Tribunal de Cuentas, 355
Tribunal Superior Electoral, 317

U
Unión Revolucionaria Comunista, 317
University Autonomy, 270
University of Havana, 232, 252, 269, 318, 374, 376, 377, 424, 425, 467, 471, 472, 474, 475, 479, 480, 482, 483, 485, 487, 488

V
Vasconcelos, 271
Vázquez Bello, 482, 487
Vedado, 211
Villanueva, 231
Voluntarios, 20

W
WWII, 318, 332, 459, 487

Z
Zayas-Bazán, 231
Zayistas, 104, 157

This book was printed in the United States.

The font used throughout the text has been **Palatino Linotype**, one of the classic old style serif typefaces inspired by designs of the 16th century Italian calligrapher **Giambattista Palatino**. The font was reissued in 1948 by **Hermann Zapf** for the Linotype Foundy, the company created by Ottmar Mergenthaler, a German immigrant to the U.S. who invented the revolutionary line typesetting machine that was first used in 1890 by the **New York Tribune**.

The font used in the covers, title pages, headings and ornaments is **P22 Franklin Caslon**, a faithful interpretation of the type used by Benjamin Franklin in the 1750's in his printing shop and particularly in his **Poor Richard's Almanac**. This font was developed in 2006 by the International House of Fonts for the Philadelphia Museum of Art to commemorate the 300th birthday of our most remarkable Founding Father.

The font accompanying the photos and illustrations is **Verdana**; a humanist sans-serif typeface designed by **Matthew Carter** for *Microsoft Corporation*, with hand-hinting done by **Tom Rickner**, then at *Monotype*. Demand for such a clear and easy to read typeface was recognized by **Virginia Howlett** of *Microsoft's* typography group. The name "**Verdana**" is based on a mix of *verdant* (something green, as in the Seattle area and the Evergreen state of Washington), and *Ana* (the name of Howlett's eldest daughter

Raúl Eduardo Chao *received his PhD from Johns Hopkins University and after a brief stint in industry spent 18 years in academe, as full professor and Department Chairman at the* **Universities of Puerto Rico** *and* **De- troit**. *In 1986 he founded a very success- ful management consultancy, assisting companies and government agencies to develop positive work environments and process improvement techniques as the means to secure improvements in productivity and quality.*

The Systema Group *had as clients many Fortune 100 companies and Federal and State organizations, both in the US and abroad. As its Chairman, Chao has written seventeen books and numerous articles in newspapers and reviewed journals. He and his wife Olga live in Coral Gables, Florida and spend long periods of time in Paris.*

Sobre el Autor:

Raúl Eduardo Chao recibió su PhD en Johns Hopkins University, Baltimore, y después de una breve estancia en la industria norteamericana sirvió durante 18 años en el mundo académico, durante los cuales fue Director de Departamento en las **Universidades de Puerto Rico y Detroit**. *Ha sido consultor de la NASA y árbitro científico de las publicaciones de la National Science Foundation, así como Chairman de The Systema Group, una empresa internacional de consultoría. Ha escrito otros diecisiete libros y numerosos artículos en revistas técnicas y periódicos. Vive con su esposa Olga en Coral Gables, Florida, con frecuentes estadías en París.*

www.ingramcontent.com/pod-product-compliance
Lightning Source LLC
Chambersburg PA
CBHW070042080526
44586CB00013B/880